"Man of many sorrows, Abraham Lincoln seemed to have belonged more to the world of the occult than of politics."
Jan Bryant Bartell

ONE NIGHT in WASHINGTON

The True Story of America's Most Haunted President

TROY TAYLOR

A Book from American Hauntings Ink

© **Copyright 2020 by Troy Taylor**
and American Hauntings Ink
All Rights Reserved, including the right to copy or reproduce this book, or portions thereof, in any form, without express permission from the author and publisher.

Original Cover Artwork Designed by
© Copyright 2020 by April Slaughter & Troy Taylor

This Book is Published By:
American Hauntings Ink
Jacksonville, Illinois | 217.791.7859
Visit us on the Internet at http://www.americanhauntingsink.com

First Edition - December 2020
ISBN: 978-1-7352706-4-7

Printed in the United States of America

INTRODUCTION

"Who is dead in the White House?" I asked one of the soldiers. "The President," was the answer, "he was killed by an assassin."
President Abraham Lincoln recalling a dream that he had a few days before he was assassinated

More than a century and a half after his death, Abraham Lincoln continues to be an almost daily part of our lives - especially for those of us who live in Illinois. This is where he spent most of his life. He lived, worked, married, and first served in politics here. It was in Illinois where he was nominated to the presidency and was living here when he won the election. Lincoln didn't die here, but he was buried here after a long, tumultuous journey back home from Washington.

It can't be a surprise to know that we have towns, streets, highways, businesses, theaters, and even taverns that bear Lincoln's name.

For most of us who grew up in Illinois, Lincoln was part of our childhood. We visited his former home and his tomb on school trips, and we read about him in our books until he became an iconic symbol of another time. Lincoln was a legend. It was easy for us to forget that he had once been an ordinary man, likely unaware of the destiny that awaited him. As an ordinary man, he had all the same flaws that we all have. He was fallible, sometimes frightened, mournful, and prone to depression. He knew love, sadness, terror, and death and his life was never easy. He had great faith in man, in a higher power, and like many of his era - faith in the supernatural.

Lincoln grew up in a time of omens and portents. It was a period of superstition and strange beliefs, and those beliefs left an impression on the small-town young man who became president. He became a believer in the spirit world and would later take part in seances held at the White House.

Lincoln was connected to the spirit world and the supernatural throughout his life. There are many accounts of his prophetic dreams and of the hauntings that are connected to places where he lived, but none of those accounts tell the whole story of why he believed so fervently in the spirits - or why the occult had such an impact on him.

The melancholy from which Lincoln suffered made him especially open to the influence of the supernatural. The death of his mother when he was a child, the hard work that marked his life as a young man, his struggle for an education, and the profound personal losses that he experienced combined to make him a serious man, even when he was telling a joke. The Civil War caused him tremendous sorrow and the heavy losses on both sides plagued his thoughts, by day and night. Lincoln paid obsessive detail to everything about the war - and it showed on his face. By 1864, portraits of Lincoln showed a face etched with lines that hadn't been there a few years before. He slept little. He roamed the corridors and stared out the windows, his mind filled with worry. His only escape came from trips to the theater, from books, or from late night buggy rides on the streets of Washington.

Lincoln always used to say that all he longed for from life was peace and contentment, but he seemed to know he would never have those things - even after his presidency came to an end. All that he could hope for was peace and contentment after death, but even that seems to have eluded him. Abraham Lincoln's spirit is one of the most restless in American history.

This book is not the first one that I have written about the strange and unusual life of Abraham Lincoln, but it is the most complete. I have spent the last decade digging deeper into the supernatural life of our most haunted president and have found more material than I ever expected to find. There will be familiar stories -- although possibly presented in ways that you've never heard before - and stories that will be revealed for the first time in any of my books.

I am no Lincoln expert or scholar. You can trust in the fact that they would never want me in their ranks, but I am proud to say that I will introduce you to stories that you won't find in history books - eerie tales of mystery, spirits, seances, grave robbery, murder, death, and the supernatural.

Abraham Lincoln lived a troubled life. It was often filled with loneliness, despair, horror and, of course, ghosts. It is impossible for me to say whether I believe that he rests in peace, but when the final pages of this book have been turned, you can decide that for yourself.

Until then, keep an open mind and prepare yourself for something that is unlike any book about Lincoln that you have read before.

And make sure you leave the lights on as you do.

Troy Taylor
Fall 2020

1. SIGNS, OMENS, AND PORTENTS
The Early Life of Abraham Lincoln

Abraham Lincoln was born in Kentucky in 1809.

It was the beginning of an era that saw wide-ranging social changes in America. Many of those changes were religious ones. A steady stream of immigrants had been arriving on American shores. The land, with its wide-open spaces, offered opportunity and freedom - freedom that included the chance to worship as people saw fit. The new arrivals began leaving the crowded Atlantic coastline and began seeking wilderness lands in New York, Ohio, Indiana, and Kentucky. As they traveled west, they brought their religious fervor with them and a great revival began sweeping the young nation.

For many years, the staid Christians taught that the way to personal betterment was through God, raising mistrust about the extent to which people could make improvements in their lives unless they did so through the intervention of the Holy Spirit. The new revivalists offered the chance to be "born again," maintaining that people could take responsibility for their own deliverance from sin and damnation. This was groundbreaking in the early 1800s - completely different from the Puritan and Calvinist beliefs of the earlier era. It appealed to the simple, plain folk who had spread westward with the growing country.

As the people moved west to build new towns and start new farms, the religious men and women followed. They found fertile territory in the wilderness, actively converting as many people as possible to evangelical Christianity in the newly-settled regions. Some ministers preached fire and brimstone, hell and damnation, and the end of days.

Traveling circuit riders rode along the hills and valleys with news of the Holy Spirit. Itinerant ministers crisscrossed the mountains and hollows spreading the word of God. The preachers and their tent revival meetings ignited a fervent passion among the simple farmers and tradesmen. For days after they departed, without the prompting of the revivalists, men and women would speak in tongues or fall to the ground in religious ecstasy. Many reported visitations from angels and spirits. It was an unusual period in American history, which became known as the country's "Second Great Religious Awakening."

A painting of Nancy Hanks, Lincoln's mother

But the camp meetings and revivals were competing with other belief systems that were just as much a part of the daily lives of the backwoods people of places like Ohio, Indiana, and Kentucky -- and far stranger than the itinerant preachers could have ever dreamed of.

Abraham's father, Thomas Lincoln, had married Nancy Hanks, a tall, pretty, and poorly educated young woman three years before he built a log cabin for his family at a place called Sinking Springs Farm.

Nancy came from a family that Lincoln's friend and biographer William Herndon later referred to as "illiterate and superstitious," which he said was common in Kentucky at the time. He wrote, "They corresponded to that nomadic class still to be met throughout the South and known as 'poor whites.'"

It was their custom to only wear shoes when necessary and to gather with family to dance and drink whiskey. It was an isolated, rural life that revolved around food, fighting, drinking, and early death.

Abraham Lincoln was a Southerner by birth. He retained his rural twang throughout his life, often using it to his benefit when he felt that he could get listeners to underestimate him. The log cabin in which he was born was just a few miles away from the cabin where Jefferson

Davis was born. However, as the two men grew up, their families - and their politics - moved in opposite directions. Lincoln may have evolved intellectually, but he retained many of the core beliefs of his childhood - beliefs that included ghosts, spirits, and witches.

As William Herndon wrote:

Although gay, prosperous, and light-hearted, these people were brimming with superstition. It was at once their food and drink. They believed in the baneful influence of witches, pinned their faith in the curative powers of wizards in dealing with sick animals, and shot the image of a witch with a silver ball to break the spell she was supposed to have over human beings.

Virtually every community had a resident "water witch," or dowser, who could find sources of fresh water. Herndon noted, "they followed with religious minuteness the directions of the water-wizard, with his magic divining rod." In a time and place where actual medical doctors were few and far between, the "faith doctor wrought miraculous cures by strange sounds and signals from a mysterious agency."

For sick animals, settlers frequently resorted to the "horse whisperer." Lincoln's later benefactor and employer in New Salem, Denton Offutt, eventually left town and resurfaced some years later in Baltimore as a horse whisperer. Billing himself as a "veterinary surgeon and horse tamer," Offutt professed "to have a secret to whisper in a horse's ear that could tame the wildest beast." Horse owners often paid him the princely sum of $5 for this skill.

Whatever Lincoln's beliefs in these folk practices, we know for certain that he put great faith in the powers of what were called "mad stones." In frontier communities, folk remedies were often used to treat maladies and injuries and mad stones were one such treatment. A mad stone, more properly known as a bezoar, was a rocklike, concentrated hairball taken from the stomachs of animals like deer and dogs. A mad stone was often believed to possess miraculous powers, especially when it came to curing rabies. The stone would be boiled in milk until the milk turned green and then was applied to the wound.

Lincoln later confided to a friend in Illinois that "the people of the neighborhood of these stones were fully impressed with a belief in their virtues from actual experiment, and that was about as much as we could ever know about the properties of medicine."

More importantly, we know that when Lincoln's son, Robert, was bitten by a possibly rabid dog in Springfield, Lincoln rushed the boy to Terre Haute, Indiana, to be treated with a mad stone.

The settlers of the region had many beliefs involving the supernatural, including a whole host of signs and omens that could warn of misfortune. William Herndon wrote:

> The flight of a bird in at the window, the breath of a horse on a child's head, the crossing by a dog of a hunter's path, all betokened evil luck in store for someone. The moon exercised greater influence on the actions of the people and the growth of vegetation than the sun and all the planetary systems combined. Fence rails could only be cut in the light of the moon, and potatoes could only be planted in the dark of the moon. Trees and plants which bore their fruit above ground could be planted when the moon shone full. Soap could only be made in the light of the moon, and it must only be stirred in one way by one person.

Surrounded by people who believed in these things, Lincoln grew to manhood. With them he walked, he talked, and he labored, and from them he also absorbed whatever of superstition showed itself in him thereafter.

Throughout his life, Lincoln proved to be a man of two separate - seemingly contradictory - natures. He was known for his wide knowledge and power of reasoning. Close friends characterized him as an "intellect of mighty and exquisite mold... of a severely logical cast." Yet Lincoln was also well-known to his friends as a person who "believed also in the marvelous as revealed in presentiments and dreams." William Herndon stated that Lincoln possessed a "superstitious view of life which ran through his being like the thin blue vein through the whitest of marble."

There is no question that Lincoln's early life was influenced by the beliefs of his family, his friends, and those around him and his beliefs ranged from a fervent faith in God, to the spells of witches, cures by folk magic, and the spirit world.

But tragedy was coming to young Lincoln's life and it would change him forever.

Thomas Lincoln, later in life

Thomas Lincoln was a well-liked man in the community. He was a good storyteller and a man who was skilled at many things, although he never really settled down to try one thing in particular.

It was always assumed that Abraham would follow in his footsteps. He was a thin, spindly-looking boy who had a remarkable curiosity about everything. He walked into the nearby village of Elizabethtown and watched the travelers pass by along the Cumberland Gap trail. He was already much taller than other children by the age of seven when he and his older sister, Sarah, began attending "blab" school, which meant all of the students read their lessons aloud at the same time. Years later, Abraham would be remembered as being the best reader in school.

The exact reason why the Lincoln family decided to pull up stakes and move across the Ohio River to Indiana remains unknown. It has been suggested that Thomas lost his land because of bad property titles or that, as Abraham himself wrote in 1860, they had a desire to move from a slave state to a free state. Regardless, they settled along Little Pigeon Creek and Abraham began learning the ways of hard, outdoor work as he helped to clear the land around their new home. He earned a reputation as an honest, self-reliant boy with an interest in books and a love for learning, although his chores allowed him little time to do so.

In 1818, his life changed abruptly when the family was struck by the terrible frontier disease known as "milk sickness." The mysterious ailment - puzzling and incurable at the time - was caused by cattle eating a poisonous plant and then passing it on to people in their milk.

The illness swept through the community. Tom and Betsy Sparrow, close friends of the Lincolns, died first. Nancy Lincoln faithfully nursed them to their final hours, but she also came down with the ailment and soon, followed her friends to the grave.

Abraham helped his father build his mother's coffin, helped dig her grave, and laid her to rest in the ground. The boy held his head in his hands and wept for hours at her grave. Lincoln later said that from this point on, he felt completely alone in the world. The withdrawn, grief-stricken boy began to disappear into the woods for hours at a time. Drowning in his sorrow, he was never the same again.

In 1819, Thomas traveled back across the river to Kentucky and returned with the widow of an old friend. The widow's name was Sarah Johnston and she became Thomas's wife, as well as a new mother for Abraham and his sister, Sarah. The couple also brought three children from Sarah's first marriage and an orphaned cousin of Nancy's named Dennis Hanks. The family cabin was now packed to capacity and Abraham would later recall slipping off into the trees with his books for some peace and quiet or reading late at night by the dying embers of the fire while the rest of the clan slept.

An elderly Sarah Lincoln

There was no event in backwoods life that pleased Abraham as much as a trip to the local mill to have the family's corn ground into meal. The trip released him from a day's work in the field and gave him the chance to visit with other local boys who had also been sent there by their fathers.

The mill was a crudely constructed one that used an old dray horse that paced slowly round and round in endless repetition until dried corn was cracked and ground into something suitable for bread or sour mash. A man named Gordon had built the mill from suitable stones and gears that he had fashioned from wood. It was not the most efficient device. Lincoln once commented that his dog could eat the corn meal that came out faster than the worn stones could grind it. Gordon was not much of a miller - but he was a good businessman. Each man brought his own horse to power the mill, did the grinding himself, and then paid Gordon for the privilege.

One day, Lincoln left home and traveled the two miles to the mill in the company of a friend, David Turnham, a sack of corn, and an old gray unshod mare. They arrived late in the day, so there were already others waiting for their turn with the mill. It was almost sundown when Abraham hitched his mare to the arm of the gear that turned the millstone as the horse slowly paced in a circle.

The mill was slow, but the old nag was even slower. At frequent intervals, Abraham cracked a small whip and urged the animal on with a cry, "Get up, you old hussy!"

At a turn, Abraham lashed the animal again and the old mare, resenting the sting of the whip, kicked backward and struck the boy in the head, sending him sprawling on the ground.

Gordon, the miller, picked up the bleeding, senseless boy, believing he was dead - or soon would be - and sent someone to fetch his father. Thomas came as quickly as he could, loaded the bloody boy into his wagon, and drove him home. All night long, Abraham lay in his bed, breathing, but comatose. Curious neighbors came to the cabin to look at him. While death was common on the frontier, it never failed to capture the interest of the morbid curious.

Toward daybreak, the mourners in the Lincoln cabin noticed that Abraham was showing signs of life. His pale face began to show some color and several times, he jerked in his bed and called out, "Get up, you old hussy!" as if he was still urging the old mare to grind the corn.

Over the next few days, Abraham slowly recovered from his injuries, but throughout his life, he would always consider the injury that he suffered to have been a serious one. William Herndon later wrote that he and Lincoln discussed the "psychological phenomena" of the incident several times. Many Lincoln researchers have also discussed the psychological consequences of the injury and offered theories about how it affected his later life.

Analysis of Lincoln's later photographs have verified that he suffered a severe blow to the forehead, above his left eye, likely fracturing the skull at the point of impact. Judging from the size and depth of the depression left on his skull, medical experts agree that it was life-threatening.

At least one medical expert theorized that Lincoln suffered brain damage from the head wound - specifically to the frontal lobe. The most significant of the symptoms from this would be the "repetitive tendency to lapse automatically into a lower consciousness state of mental detachment or abstraction."

In other words, he went into trances.

Many who knew him in Illinois later recalled that he sometimes seemed "in a world by himself," ignoring his surroundings and visitors and guests in his office. He often sat for several moments, motionless, and staring straight ahead. Then, he would rejoin those around him "like one awakened from sleep." In Washington, many politicians and distinguished foreign visitors noticed this strange habit. While visiting in 1865, the Marquis de Chambron observed the president passing into this state multiple times in a single evening.

William Herndon referred to this as an "occult condition." He described Lincoln as a "peculiar, mysterious man with a double consciousness, a double life. The two states, never in a normal man, co-exist in equal and vigorous activities though they succeed each other quickly. One state predominates and, while it so rules, the other state is somewhat quiescent, shadowy, yet living, a real thing. This is the sole reason why Lincoln so quickly passed from one state of consciousness to another and a different state."

Lincoln's near-death experience as a boy was clearly the reasons for his trances, but also may have played a role in the deepening of the melancholy that he had been suffering since the death of his mother.

And it may have played another important role in his life, as well. It would not be long after his accident that Lincoln began to experience what was referred to as "a rent in the veil which hides from mortal view what the future holds," which, throughout the rest of his life "elated and alarmed" him.

Even after Lincoln's near fatal accident, he continued to excel in school. He composed poetry and wrote essays, and legend claims that he often mounted a tree stump for speeches about whatever he was interested in at the time. He knew how to appeal to people and to talk to them, and despite his gangly limbs and towering height, he charmed most people he met. He was a born talker, and, yet, he was also an expert log-splitter, a quick hand with a horse and plow, and a skillful hog butcher. By the age of 17, he was nearly six-feet-tall and could outwrestle any man in the surrounding counties. His physical strength was extraordinary.

Young Abraham Lincoln

His mental feats were also the stuff of local legend. Teachers and ministers admitted that the young man was better read than they were and that a life of hard labor on a farm would never suit him. Lincoln agreed and he dreamed of far-off places and adventure.

He knew that a life of tedious, hard work was not for him. He often worked along the Ohio River, cutting wood and stacking it on the banks for riverboat captains to buy or worked alone ferrying passengers across the Anderson River, but when his father rented him out with his axe for 25-cents per day, he started to grow resentful of the life that he felt trapped in. He went about his labors with a book stuck in his back pocket, but even this small escape did little to alleviate his boredom.

Lincoln's first view of the wider world was thanks to James Gentry, a man that he had done work for in the past. Gentry had outfitted a flatboat that was filled with grain, meat, and other goods and wanted to send Lincoln along with his son, Allen, to New Orleans.

They departed in March 1828 and little is known about Lincoln's first visit to New Orleans other than that the two young men had an encounter with a band of river pirates a few miles south of Baton Rouge. Lincoln, armed with an ax handle, easily fought off the attack.

Allen and Abraham sold their cargo in New Orleans for a profit and, after an undetermined time in the city, returned to Indiana. Little is known about what happened in New Orleans during Lincoln's first visit–perhaps deliberately so.

Claims have been made by mainstream historians that the two young men, visiting the most decadent city in America at the time, likely didn't visit the already famous brothels and saloons that could be found there. There are suggestions that Lincoln did nothing other than read newspapers and learn about local politics.

Who are they kidding?

Lincoln was not a drinking man, but many of William Herndon's unpublished notes make it clear that the description of Lincoln's "shyness in the company of women" was a fabrication created to sanitize his reputation after his assassination.

Abraham and Allen were two healthy young men with the same overabundance of hormones as any men of their age. While we can't be certain that Lincoln visited the sporting houses during his time in New Orleans, it would have been very out of character for any rural young man who was visiting the big city for the first time.

In addition, New Orleans in this era was well-known as a hotbed for the magical practice of Voodoo, a peaceful religious faith that was brought to Louisiana from Africa - via the Caribbean islands - by slaves, as early as 1719. Most of them came directly from West Africa, bringing with them their language and religious beliefs, which were rooted in spirit and ancestor worship. In the Fon language of West Africa, "Vodun" means spirit - an invisible and mysterious force that can intervene in human affairs.

Voodoo developed more prominently in Louisiana than in other parts of the new country, and one reason for that is largely because the French - then the Spanish, then the French again - colonized Louisiana. They were far more tolerant of the practices and the faiths of the slave population than were the British, who had come to America for religious freedom and then suppressed the faiths of anyone who didn't agree with them.

Voodoo in Louisiana was a blend of different cultures. One of the most important cultures was Catholicism. Over time, Catholic saints and icons became stand-ins for important Voodoo deities, which would have made it seem very exotic to two young men from Indiana who may have joined other visitors to the city in Congo Square, watching Voodoo ceremonies as entertainment.

Abraham and Allen may not have interacted with Voodoo during their first visit to the city, but they had to have been exposed to some aspect of its culture in New Orleans.

Voodoo would become part of Lincoln's legend a few years later.

After Abraham returned home to Indiana, he found that his father had become restless and wanted to move the family to Illinois. They arrived in the settlement of Decatur in March 1930, traveling in a party

An old newspaper drawing of the Lincoln home in Macon County, Illinois. Note: Accuracy not guaranteed.

of 13 people - Abraham; Thomas and Sarah; John S. Johnston, Sarah's son from her first marriage; and two daughters from the same marriage, Mrs. Dennis Hanks and Mrs. Levi Hall, who came with their husbands and children. They traveled by wagon, pulled by teams of oxen, and spent their first night camped in what later became the city's first town square.

On March 15, they sought out John Hanks, another cousin of Nancy's, who had encouraged the Lincolns to come to Decatur. John suggested that the family settle on a site along the Sangamon River that he had previously chosen for himself. He had already cut the logs for a cabin but had decided to build on the north side of town instead.

The Lincolns took his advice and Abraham helped to build the cabin. That spring, he worked for his father and labored on neighboring farms. He and John Hanks reportedly split more than 3,000 wooden rails from locust and walnut trees for William Warnick, the sheriff of surrounding Macon County.

That summer, Lincoln was working on the farm of William Hanks, Jr., near what is now downtown Decatur, and left his plowing to see what had attracted a crowd of people in the public square. He became so interested in the discussion that was taking place that he climbed onto a tree stump for a better view. He became passionate about the subject of the debate that he ended up offering what became his first political speech.

You'll understand the importance of this if you have ever heard the term "stump speech."

But Lincoln was still stuck in Decatur. He helped with the harvest that fall and endured the conditions of what was known as the winter of the "Deep Snow," thanks to the frigid temperatures and unusually heavy snowfall.

William Warnick, for whom Lincoln had split so many rails during the summer months, lived on a farm about two miles southeast and across the river from the Lincolns. Abraham was walking through a snowstorm to the Warnick home one day when he fell through the ice and into the bitterly cold river. He managed to make it to the Warnick farm, where he spent more than a week recovering from frostbite and a severe cold. Legend claims - and there are a lot of legends when it comes to Abraham Lincoln - that Lincoln read through the sheriff's copy of the Illinois statutes while in his sickbed and this is how he first became interested in the law.

By the following spring, Thomas had tired of the Decatur area and he decided to move with Sarah to Coles County, Illinois. The once restless farmer remained there for the rest of his life.

But Abraham did not follow his father. He was now 22-years-old and he wanted to strike out on his own. He had many decisions to make but, luckily, he was given some time by Denton Offutt, a "brisk and venturesome businessman," who operated flatboats on the Ohio and Mississippi River. Offutt came to Decatur to see John Hanks, who had worked for him in the past. He wanted John to take a boatload of stock and merchandise to New Orleans for him. John was interested and suggested that Abraham and his stepbrother, John Johnston, join him in the expedition.

In March 1831, the three young men met up with Offutt in Springfield at a place called the Buckhorn Inn. There, the three young men found Offutt seriously engaged in sampling the tavern's liquid refreshments. He was supposed to have the flatboat ready for them but his daily visits to the Buckhorn Inn had slowed down his progress considerably. So, the three young men decided to build the boat themselves.

It took them four weeks, but they finished it. In April, the boat was launched, loaded with barrels of pork, sacks of corn, and livestock. Once clear of the local mill dam on the Sangamon River, they made steady progress down the Mississippi, arriving in New Orleans in early May.

After selling their cargo, the three young men lingered in the city for a month "viewing the sights." Again, we don't know exactly what they experienced in a city with plenty to offer for healthy young men with money in their pockets, but we do know that Lincoln experienced at least two events on this trip that profoundly affected his life.

Abraham's cousin, John Hanks, later in life.

While a young boy in Kentucky, Lincoln had certainly seen slaves, but there, farmers were mostly small landowners who generally owned one or two slaves. They served as field hands whose labor was in addition to the work done by the farmer's sons or they were domestic labor to help the farmer's wife with her chores. The slaves were not the farm's only source of labor, but a supplement to the farmer's own efforts. Lincoln had never really witnessed first-hand the horrors of slavery and the slave trade before.

In New Orleans in 1831, Lincoln experienced a slave market for the first time. He saw African American men and women in chains, sold like cattle. He saw families torn apart when sold - husband from wife, mother from children - never to see one another again. One morning, he was out for a walk and saw an auction in progress. It was for a young, light-skinned slave girl who was being sold to the highest bidder. The prospective buyers touched her all over her body and made her walk back and forth to see how she moved. It was obvious that the bidders had something in mind for her that was not manual labor. The sight of this outraged Lincoln.

John Hanks later wrote, "Slavery ran an iron into him then and there."

At some point during the trip, Lincoln was moved by another experience. He paid a visit to an elderly black fortune-teller, described as an "old Voodoo negress." The fact that he would have his fortune told was not out of the ordinary. It was a common activity engaged in by Voodoo practitioners that served as a popular diversion for visitors to the city. What was out of the ordinary was what she told Lincoln during his sitting.

Slave markets in New Orleans in the 1830s

In the session, the woman went into a trance and passed along a series of vague predictions. Soon, though, she became excited and exclaimed to Lincoln, "You will be president and all the Negroes will be free!" While fortune-tellers are notorious for telling patrons what they want to hear it seemed exceptional that this "Voodoo seer should utter a prophecy that was so specific - and one so in line with Lincoln's own current train of thought," William Herndon later wrote.

Lincoln would soon come to believe that he was destined for some great purpose in life and it seems possible that it was during this second trip to New Orleans that he began to believe that it would have something to do with slavery. John Hanks later told one of Lincoln's biographers that he could tell how deeply the experience affected him. "His heart bled," John recalled. "He was mad, thoughtful, abstracted, sad, and depressed."

A great change was coming to America and Lincoln knew that he was going to be a part of it.

2. NEW SALEM

Heartbreak, Hauntings, and Lincoln's Political Rise

The town of New Salem was barely a speck on the map when Abraham Lincoln came to live there. In those days, it was home to only about 12 families and had begun as the dream of two entrepreneurs who envisioned it as a thriving Sangamon River community. It was in New Salem that Lincoln truly began to come into his own. He took a job working in a small store and watched the town begin to grow. Other stores opened, along with a tavern, sawmill, and school. It seemed that the dreams of the settlement's founders would come true when

New Salem

steamboats began navigating the river - but this turned out not to be. The Sangamon was simply too shallow for passenger travel and with no hope on the horizon, people began to leave.

Abraham Lincoln was one of those who left the village behind. Strangely, New Salem came to life about the time that Lincoln settled there, and it died soon after he departed.

The community was founded just before

Lincoln returned to Illinois from New Orleans. James Rutledge and his nephew, John Cameron, brought their families to the region between 1825 and 1826 and established themselves along Concord Creek. They had plans to build a mill on this small tributary from the Sangamon River but soon realized that the Concord would not be able to produce the water volume necessary to power the mill. The realization led to a search for a more promising location.

On July 19, 1828, Cameron purchased land along the Sangamon River and applied to the Illinois State Legislature for permission to build a dam across the river. The place was known as "Fish Trap Ford" and was where the road from Beardstown to Springfield -- the only major road in the area -- crossed the river. In anticipation of a favorable response from the legislature, the two men moved their families to a bluff overlooking the mill site and Rutledge soon converted his home into a tavern, providing food and lodging for travelers on the busy road.

In January 1829, permission for the dam was obtained from the legislature and work immediately began. Wooden bins were built in the river and local farmers provided wagons and teams to haul the hundreds of rocks needed to fill the structures. When the dam was completed, a mill to grind grain and to cut wood was constructed on a platform above the river. It was an immediate success and drew customers from across the area. It was later recalled that it was not unusual to see more than 40 horse-drawn wagons tied to the trees on the hillside as their owners waited for their grain at the mill.

Late that year, in the fall of 1829, Samuel Hill and John McNeil built a general store on a rise that was crossed by the Springfield Road. Around that same time, a tavern was built by William Clary above the mill and he began dispensing alcohol to the thirsty customers who waited for their orders to be cut or ground.

It wasn't long before the mill, store, and inn were the center of trade in the vicinity, so Rutledge and Cameron decided to build a town around them. On October 29, 1829, the community was platted, and lots were drawn up with the name of the settlement as New Salem. The first lot was sold on Christmas Eve and it slowly began to take shape. On Christmas Day, an official post office was established in the Hill and McNeil store and Samuel Hill was named as postmaster.

The town grew over the course of the next two years. Most prominent among the arriving settlers were Henry Onstott, a cooper or barrel-maker; the Herndon brothers, William, and James; and Dr. John Allen, a graduate of Dartmouth College. Each man left his mark on the small village but none to the extent of that left by the young man who arrived there in April 1831.

Abraham Lincoln's arrival in New Salem was anything but auspicious. Although accounts vary as to what happened, most agree that he was part of the crew of a flatboat that hung up on the dam below the village. From the shore, the townsfolk watched as he and the others struggled to save the boat from sinking. Lincoln was described as an "ungainly youth" but despite his appearance, his thinking was obviously quick. He ordered most of the cargo to be unloaded and taken to shore and then moved the rest of it to the stern of the boat. After borrowing a wood drill from one of the spectators, he opened a hole in the bottom of the craft and let out the water that had gathered in the bottom. When the vessel was free of water, he plugged the hole and the flatboat slipped effortlessly over the dam.

The reproduction of the Offutt store in New Salem, where Lincoln worked

Lincoln was not at New Salem for long that day, but he did return in July. He began running a store for his old boss, Denton Offutt, who later left town and turned the store over to Lincoln. Abraham became popular in the village and in the surrounding neighborhood. He had a good sense of humor and was an excellent storyteller. He was also a hard worker and his skill at wrestling - a popular pastime in frontier communities - earned him many friends and admirers.

Lincoln was considered a good man and, on the surface, seemed to be a simple one. But looks were deceiving when it came to the rugged outdoorsman. Most would never have predicted that he would join the New Salem Debating Society or that he would persuade the local schoolmaster, Mentor Graham, to loan him books with which to further his education. People in the community soon learned there was much more to Abraham that met the eye, and they realized that the tall young man was both intelligent and well-spoken. They encouraged his dreams of a career in law and politics and watched the transformation of a rowdy, fun-loving frontiersman into a deep-thinking intellectual with a tendency toward melancholy.

Ann Rutledge and Abraham Lincoln

There are many who believe, though, that it was not the continuation of Lincoln's education that changed his personality - it was an ill-fated love affair that again altered Lincoln's life and put him on track with his destiny.

If Ann Rutledge had lived, it's been said, Lincoln might never have changed American history in the way that he did.

When Abraham first met Ann, the auburn-haired beauty was being courted by the two shopkeepers, Samuel Hill and John McNeil. It was McNeil who eventually won the young woman's favor and they were engaged to be married. However, in 1832, McNeil sold his interest in the store to his partner and made plans to depart from New Salem for a short time. Before he left, though, he made a startling confession to Ann --- his real name was not John McNeil, but John McNamar, and he had changed it before leaving his home in New York so that he could escape from crushing debt owed by his family. Now that his future in Illinois was secured, though, he intended to return home, settled his affairs, and come back to New Salem and to Ann. She accepted the story and sent McNamar away with a promise to write. He wrote a handful of letters but eventually, his correspondence slowed and then stopped altogether. It was obvious that he wasn't coming back to Illinois.

After sufficient time had passed, Lincoln began courting Ann and a love affair blossomed between them. They began looking forward to a bright future together. Lincoln planned to open a law office and once he was firmly established as an attorney, the two planned to be married.

Tragically, though, the marriage never happened.

Before Lincoln could start his career as an attorney, he was sidetracked by friends, who persuaded him to try his hand at politics. He decided to make a run for the state legislature.

His first campaign got off to a good start when he was chosen to pilot the *Talisman* steamship on its first trip upriver to Springfield. The *Talisman* was to be the first steamboat to navigate the Sangamon River and many believed that it would open the city of Springfield for a booming river economy. The plan turned out to be a disaster. The riverboat became stuck in shallow water and the expedition was called off. No steamboat ever attempted to travel up the Sangamon again. Luckily for Lincoln, he wasn't blamed for the fiasco and it didn't hurt his run for office.

However, his campaign was interrupted a short time later by the Black Hawk War. Lincoln ended up serving two months during the campaign in the Illinois Militia.

The short-lived war was the result of trouble that had been brewing for years. When the number of white settlers in the Illinois country began to grow, it was only a matter of time before the native people who already lived in the region - the Illinois, Ho-Chunk, Fox, Sauk, and Miami - began to have a conflict with the new arrivals. To pacify the Indians, they were presented with various treaties that were designed, in most cases, to relocate them, usually across the Mississippi River. Many of the Native Americans refused to recognize the treaties. The most outspoken of them was a prominent war chief named Black Hawk.

That anger caused Black Hawk, along with most of the Sauk, Fox, and Ho-Chunk, to side with the British during the War of 1812. The British promised Black Hawk that if the Americans were defeated, they would create an Indian-controlled buffer between the eastern states and the western frontier. This would keep the Americans from expanding any further to the west if, of course, the British won the war. As it turned out, they were defeated a second time by the young, upstart nation and the earlier treaties remained in effect. In fact, in

1828, restrictions were stepped up and the government gave the Sauk and Fox one year to vacate all their lands in Illinois.

By the spring of 1829, nearly two dozen white families decided that they had waited long enough and moved into Indian lands at Saukenuck, Black Hawk's home village, which was located near present-day Rock Island. In the process, they tore down Indian lodges and put fences around Sauk farm fields. The Sauk reported the invasion to U.S. officials, but were ignored. In September, a young Sauk chief, Keokuk, decided that it was best to avoid the conflict and led most of the remaining Sauk to lands west of the Mississippi.

Black Hawk

Black Hawk, meanwhile, remained angry over the treaties and the indignities suffered by the Sauk. In the spring of 1831, he led a group of about 300 of his people back to Saukenuk and ordered the squatters to leave. His warriors burned several cabins, and word spread that the Sauk had declared war on the white settlers. Illinois Governor John Reynolds called up a militia of 700 men, and they were later joined by about an equal number of regular troops. The newly assembled army marched against the Indians, and facing this much larger adversary, Black Hawk agreed to return to Iowa. He even signed a treaty that promised he would not return to Illinois without permission.

But nature made it impossible for him to keep this bargain. The winter was bitterly cold, and the Sauk had no fertile grounds for planting, as they had in Illinois. Hunting was poor and Black Hawk's people were starving. Believing he had no choice, he led 500 men and nearly 1,000 women and children back home, across the Mississippi in April 1832. He planned to plant corn with the Winnebago near Prophetstown, about 50 miles up the Rock River, trying to stay away from the settlers in the region. But word spread and eventually reached

Governor Reynolds, who again called up troops, Abraham Lincoln. This time, 1,000 soldiers and nearly 2,000 militia volunteers marched against Black Hawk.

Black Hawk began negotiating with other tribes in the region, trying to gain support from them to help fight the approaching army, but his efforts failed. He decided to withdraw to Iowa, and sent a handful of his men, under a white flag of truce, to meet with the U.S. troops, hoping to reach an agreement that would avoid bloodshed. Black Hawk believed that the nearest company of troops was under the direct command of General Henry Atkinson, leader of the Illinois militia. Instead, Black Hawk's men encountered a batch of newly recruited militia members under Major Isiah Stillman. When the Sauk envoys reached the encampment, the undisciplined militiamen attacked and killed several of them. Black Hawk, who was close by with about 40 warriors, decided to counterattack. Although greatly outnumbered by the disorganized militia, the warriors fiercely charged them, and the surprised soldiers turned and fled.

This rout, followed by several subsequent attacks on settlers and the militia, emboldened Black Hawk and he became determined to outlast the soldiers. By June, the frustrated U.S. command called up a new army of about 4,000 soldiers and militia volunteers and began a dogged pursuit of Black Hawk and his people through Illinois and into southwestern Wisconsin. In August, the army finally caught up with Black Hawk at the Battle of Bad Axe. The Sauk and Fox were overwhelmed by numbers and, after being soundly defeated, Black Hawk surrendered. But even in surrender, he remained defiant, blaming the short-lived war on a government that lied and cheated the Indians.

Black Hawk and several of his chiefs were taken east and placed in prison in Virginia, where he met with President Andrew Jackson and Secretary of War Lewis Cass. He was eventually released, but then was forced to take part in parades through several American cities, where huge crowds turned out to see the exotic captives. Jackson and Cass had an underlying reason for sending Black Hawk on tour -- they wanted him to see the size of resources of the United States, and to realize that the Indians had no choice but to surrender.

After returning to Illinois, Black Hawk was again imprisoned, this time at Fort Armstrong, near Rock Island, where he told his story to an interpreter and writer. It became the first Native American autobiography published in the United States.

The Black Hawk War marked the end of the major conflict between Indians and white settlers in Illinois. The surviving Sauk and Fox, including Black Hawk, were sent to a reservation in southeastern Iowa, where Black Hawk died in 1838.

Lincoln considered his role in the war to be far from a heroic one. He was delighted when his fellow soldiers asked him to serve as captain of their company from New Salem, but often complained that there being more mosquitoes to fight than Indians. He was mustered out after the campaign and set out for home, only to have his horse stolen. Lincoln ended up walking most of the way back to New Salem from the Wisconsin border. By the time he arrived, he had only two weeks left to work on his political campaign. He managed to win his hometown, but he ended up coming in eighth in a field of 18.

While he was away, the store where he'd been working had closed but he took over the position of New Salem postmaster. This gave him the chance to read dozens of newspapers every week before he delivered them and soaked up all the information they contained. He also worked part-time as a deputy surveyor.

Lincoln used both jobs to campaign for the legislature again in 1834. He asked for votes on local farms, along his mail route, at dances, barbecues, cock fights, and at wrestling matches, where he usually served as referee because everyone refused to tussle with him. He ended up winning this time and was soon on his way to the state legislature.

In November, he left for the state capitol in Vandalia wearing the first suit that he had ever owned.

But bad news was coming for Lincoln - and for Ann Rutledge. In early 1835, Ann, now engaged to Lincoln, received a letter from the long absent John McNamar. He had met with unavoidable delays, he told her, including the death of his father and two brothers in New York and his own serious illness. He wrote that he was now returning to New Salem for their wedding.

Ann was distraught by this news. She loved Abraham but she felt honor-bound to marry McNamar, since she had still been betrothed to him when she accepted Lincoln's proposal. She saw no way out of the situation.

That summer, before McNamar returned, Ann fell ill with a fever that worsened until she was confined to her bed. Her health failed to the point that the doctor saw no hope for her recovery. Although the doctor had ordered strict silence and had forbidden outside visitors, Ann repeatedly called for Lincoln and her parents eventually summoned him to their farm. Abraham entered her sick room and closed the door behind him. What was said during their final meeting will never be known, but her family later recalled Lincoln leaving the house and falling to sob under a tree in the yard. He stayed there, unmoving, for hours.

A day or so after Lincoln's visit, Ann slipped into unconsciousness and never awakened. She died quietly on August 25, 1835, and while her death was listed as caused by "brain fever," her close friends and family claimed that she had died from a broken heart.

Ann's death drove Lincoln into the depths of despair. He was so distraught that a friend took away his pocketknife, fearing that Lincoln might try and take his own life. Lincoln recovered in time, but fate had dealt him another cruel blow. It was one he would never forget.

While dealing with his turbulent love affair with Ann Rutledge, Lincoln was also serving as a member of the Illinois Legislature in Vandalia, the state's second capital.

The previous capital, Kaskaskia, had been a thriving Mississippi River town in the days when Illinois was still a territory. After being granted statehood, a new site - closer to the middle of the state and at the end of the busy National Road - was chosen and legislators and state archives were moved into a temporary wood frame building in Vandalia in 1820.

Vandalia didn't seem a fitting place for the hub of state government. It was a shoddy, dirty little town that needed a lot of work, but the General Assembly soon put several renovation plans into action. A bridge was built east of town, new roads were constructed, and new businesses moved to the area. Vandalia grew rapidly, attracting new residents from around Illinois and beyond.

The Legislature - made up of 14 senators and 29 representatives - continued to meet in the wood frame building until it was destroyed by fire in 1823. Local residents built a two-story brick building to replace it, but that was torn down in 1836, and most of the wood and brick from it was used for a new capitol building a few months later. The sum of $16,000 was raised for its construction and the Legislature first convened there in December 1836. There was still a lot of work to be done, however, as noted in a letter that Lincoln wrote to his friend, Mary Owen: "The new State House is not yet finished and consequently, the legislature is doing little or nothing."

A later view of the Illinois capitol building that was located in Vandalia

Even after the new state house was finished, it was still considered a very plain structure, and unworthy of its use. It was not until 1859 that eight Doric columns were added to try and enhance the front of it - although that didn't really help. The building, which had been erected with such high hopes, was only briefly used as the Illinois capitol. When it was decided to move the state capital to Springfield, the Legislature voted to refund to Vandalia the money the city had spent on its construction.

The original agreement had stated that Vandalia would be the capital of Illinois for 20 years, but long before that, it was clear that population growth was taking place around the middle of the state, many miles north of Vandalia. It was clear that the capital would be moved so various towns and cities began scheming to become the next Illinois seat of government. In 1833, the Legislature submitted the question of a new capital to voters and Alton received the highest number of votes. The city began clearing land for a new state capitol building, but no money was made available for the move. When the question came up again, bills for the Illinois and Michigan Canal, along with other improvements, were being considered and it was placed on a back burner.

By the time it was considered again, things had changed. Alton had seen a decline after a series of national bank panics, and now, Sangamon County was regarded as the most populated county in the state. Springfield, its county seat, had been a distant third place as a capital site in the earlier vote.

But there were two senators and seven representatives from Sangamon County who were determined to bring the capital to Springfield, no matter the cost. These men - known as the "Long Nine" because all of them stood over six-feet-tall - cajoled, convinced, harassed, and threatened other legislators to vote with them and managed to get $50,000 for the construction of a state house, as long as the city of Springfield would raise a matching fund. It was agreed and the city became the third capital of Illinois.

The movement of the capital dealt a crushing blow to Vandalia. In the months that followed, the city's population dwindled to less than 300. Businesses closed and homes were boarded up. As the city declined, the former capitol building fell into disrepair. Part of the building was used as the Fayette County Courthouse, but the rest of it was abandoned. It deteriorated for decades until it was purchased by the county in 1889. The brick columns were replaced by iron pillars and a balcony was added to stabilize the structure. After a fire in 1930, the building was restored to its original condition and has been used as a historic site ever since.

Although forgotten today, the old state house is a place with a rich history - and perhaps a few ghosts, too.

Legend has it that Abraham Lincoln once jumped out of a second-story window of the building to keep from voting on a measure he didn't like. There's also a story that claims that Stephen Douglas - a man who would eventually become both friend and rival to Lincoln - once rode a donkey upstairs to the upper floor to celebrate a Democratic victory. It was in Vandalia that those two men first met.

At that time, Stephen Douglas, a native of Vermont who had also lived in Ohio before coming to Illinois, was teaching school in the town of Winchester, west of Springfield, and studying the law. He later opened a law office in Jacksonville and, in 1835, went to Vandalia to ask the Legislature to be appointed to the position of state's attorney. Lincoln, a representative for Sangamon County, voted against him.

This was their first disagreement but would not be their last. Douglas would also court Lincoln's future wife, Mary Todd, and then he and Lincoln would clash over a hotly contested Congressional seat in 1858, sparking a series of debates throughout Illinois. But Douglas was also an honorable man. He was not one to hold a grudge against Lincoln. He would later help shape the destiny of the United States when he split the Democratic Party with a stand against secession and assure Lincoln's election as president in 1860.

Over the years, the Vandalia capitol building has gained a reputation for being haunted, although no one seems to agree on the identity of the spirits that linger here.

Some have suggested a former governor like Shadrach Bond or Ninian Edwards, men who helped build the state in its early days. Others have suggested that it might be Abraham Lincoln - although this seems a bit of a stretch. He may have been the most famous legislator to serve in the capitol, but it seems an odd place for his spirit to have returned.

But, as we'll later see, Lincoln's ghost does have a habit of traveling.

Lincoln or not, stories maintain that there are ghosts within the building's walls and many people have had strange experiences there.

As far back as the 1960s, visitors at the Old State Capitol have heard voices echoing in empty rooms, have heard footsteps pacing back and forth, and have caught glimpses of figures moving about in rooms and hallways that are unoccupied by the living.

Years ago, a witness told me about an experience he had there in 1992. He was walking through the quiet building one afternoon and glanced up to see a man looking down at him from an overhead balcony. He was startled by the presence - but even more startled when he looked back a few seconds later and realized the man was gone. He searched through the place but found no one else was there.

Lincoln finished his term in Vandalia and was re-elected in 1836. He would now be serving in Springfield, where he would also practice law. He had completed his studies and passed his final exam in March 1837. Riding on a borrowed horse, he bid farewell to the dwindling town of New Salem. The remaining residents had given up on the idea of the river bringing prosperity to their own and three years after Lincoln left, New Salem was abandoned.

Abandoned, but not empty. Not entirely, anyway.

Author John Winterbauer has long maintained that if there is anywhere in Menard County that has ghosts, it's the small, reconstructed village of New Salem. Restored many years ago and designated as an Illinois state park, New Salem has been designed to reflect life in the small town while Lincoln was living there. Cabins, mills, and outbuildings have been carefully built on existing foundations and living history presenters demonstrate what life was like in early nineteenth century Illinois. These presenters are costumed to look like the inhabitants of the village from years past -- which is a bit eerie considering that many of those past residents are still believed to be lingering behind.

John has recounted many stories of ghostly lights that burn in windows at night, the eerie face of a woman that peers from the window of the cabin that once belonged to Samuel Hill, and even an unidentified specter that is believed to haunt a cabin that once belonged to the Isaac Burner family.

The ghost in the Burner cabin may be unknown but there is one spirit in New Salem whose identity is almost without question. She remains behind at her former home for a very good reason.

A small piece that appeared in the Springfield newspaper, the *Sangamo Journal*, for January 25, 1833 tells a tragic story:

TERRIBLE ACCIDENT --- We learn that on Wednesday last, while Mr. R. Herndon of New Salem was preparing his rifle for hunting excursion it went off, and the ball, striking his wife in the neck, separated one of the principal arteries, and in a few moments she was a corpse. It is hardly possible to conceive the anguish of the husband on this melancholy catastrophe. The community in which he lives deeply sympathize with him in this afflicting event.

The home where this horrific event occurred is located on the edge of New Salem village. The reconstructed cabin belonged to John Rowan Herndon and his wife, Elizabeth, the sister of village schoolmaster, Mentor Graham. She had married John in Kentucky in 1827 and in the spring of 1831, the couple moved to New Salem. Rowan, or "Row" as he was affectionately called, and his brother, James, opened a store in the village the following autumn but the business didn't last long. By that summer, James had moved away and had sold his half of the business to William Berry. Row Herndon and William Berry did not get along and Herndon later sold his interest in the store to Abraham Lincoln.

The reconstructed John Herndon cabin at New Salem, where the ghost of his wife, Elizabeth, is still believed to linger.

Herndon remained in New Salem, however, until the tragic accident recounted in the newspaper gave him reason to leave. The incident occurred on the morning of January 18, when he was cleaning his gun. As it happened, Abraham Lincoln was at the nearby Rutledge Tavern that morning, helping to repair a broken bed. He needed a certain tool to finish the work and he sent 10-year-old Nancy Rutledge to Herndon's house to borrow it.

Nancy later recalled: "When I arrived there Mr. Herndon was loading his gun to go hunting, and in getting ready to go out, his gun accidentally discharged, and his wife, who was sitting near talking to me, was shot right through the neck, her hands fluttered for a moment; then I flew out of the house and hurried home and told Annie and Mr. Lincoln what had happened."

Elizabeth Herndon slumped over to the floor and died immediately in a pool of her own blood. Not long after, her husband moved away, unable to deal with the haunting rumors that her death might not have been accidental. New Salem cooper Henry Onstott recalled the incident many years later and stated that residents were divided on whether

Herndon had killed his wife or whether the gun had fired by mistake. But regardless, he said, "he was fooling with a loaded gun and it went off and killed her."

No matter how Elizabeth died, the question remains as to whether she has ever left New Salem. In recent years, there have been many sightings of a woman in an old-fashioned dress - who promptly disappears - around the site of the old Herndon cabin.

One afternoon, two tourists - a man and his daughter -- were walking near the cabin and the little girl saw a woman on the steps, who vanished a few moments later. The father never saw the figure but was so convinced by his daughter's story that he investigated the history of the house and discovered the tragic tale of Elizabeth Herndon. He became convinced that she was the woman that his daughter spotted that day.

A summer volunteer at the park told John Winterbauer that she saw the ghost of a woman at the far end of the village on two separate occasions over three years. The first time, the volunteer was alone and walking down the path from the second Berry-Lincoln Store when she saw a woman on the path in front of her. The ethereal figure took a few steps and then blinked out of sight. "Her back was toward me," she remembered, "so I didn't see her face at all... I'm positive she vanished. It was early afternoon and sunny. I'm sure I saw her."

She saw the woman again sometime later but on this occasion the volunteer was not alone. She and another staff member were walking down the path together. Once again, it was a bright and sunny day. As they were walking toward the Herndon house, her companion pointed to the porch and asked who was working there that day. The volunteer looked up to see a woman on the porch of the cabin, in full pioneer costume, holding a broom. As the two volunteers drew closer, they realized that they didn't recognize the woman as anyone on the staff. They decided to walk over and talk to her but before they reached the cabin, the woman turned and vanished - walking directly through the locked wooden door. Shocked, but curious, they hurried to the cabin and tried the doors. They were locked, so they peered into the windows but saw no sign of the mysterious woman. Whoever she had been, she had simply vanished without a trace.

The wide variety of ghost stories told about New Salem, from floating lights to spectral cold spots and phantom figures, leads many to believe that Elizabeth Herndon does not walk here alone. There is at least one other substantiated ghost that has been spotted here and John Winterbauer believes that he knows this specter's identity. John believes that this lingering spirit is that of a man who had a closer connection to New Salem than just about anyone else, a pioneer named Jack Kelso.

Little is known about Jack Kelso, other than he was a man of many skills but no fixed trade. He hunted the forests, fished the streams, and acted as a general handyman around the village. Kelso was well-liked by his neighbors and it was he who introduced Lincoln to the works of Shakespeare and the poetry of Robert Burns. He would be remembered fondly in all the accounts that mentioned him. A former resident named Thomas Reep wrote of Kelso: "No one at New Salem lived better than he, nor was any family more forehanded. He led a happy and contented life."

By 1840, the village of New Salem had all but faded away. Kelso departed in 1841 for Jasper County, Missouri, near Joplin, and then moved again in 1850 to Atchison County, Missouri, where he eventually vanished from history. The last record of him that exists was in 1868 when he acknowledged a deed for some land that he sold.

John believes that Kelso may still roam the forests around New Salem because he loved the place so much. Even after the town was dying, he stayed behind, and it was not until the last house was shuttered and the last store closed that he reluctantly departed.

But did he return after death?

Many believe so, including a former Menard County teacher, who used to jog through New Salem each day in the early morning hours. One morning, she was passing one of the cabins and spotted a man standing on the porch who was only there for a few moments before disappearing. The cabin that she passed is a unique structure in New Salem -- a "dogtrot" cabin, which is essentially two cabins joined together by a shared porch. This cabin once belonged to Jack Kelso and his brother-in-law, Joshua Miller, who was the town blacksmith. The two men had married sisters and, upon arriving in New Salem, they constructed their home so that the two women could be near one another. They remained together the rest of their lives, moving to Missouri after New Salem was abandoned.

Another possible sighting of Jack Kelso was experienced by a man who worked at the park for many years. He claimed to have seen a man wandering about near the cabin, dressed in clothing from the 1830s. The man walked about the yard, seemingly contented, and then disappeared.

John collected another story of Jack Kelso in the summer of 2004. The story was told to him by a retired couple, Jan and Rex, from Jacksonville, who camped at New Salem for a week and liked to stroll through the village just before the park closed at dusk. On the fourth night they were there, they spotted a man in costume along the path. He was wearing dark pants, a long white shirt, boots, suspenders, and a strange, floppy looking hat. He seemed completely at ease and there was nothing out of the ordinary about him. He appeared to be just another living history presenter from the park, enjoying the evening.

"We got right up on him," Jan recalled, "and Rex nodded and said, 'good evening,' then this man opened his mouth as if to answer but then he was gone. He didn't fade away or anything like that, he just wasn't there anymore."

John asked the couple if they could point out the location of this strange encounter on a map of the park. They both agreed that it had taken place just a short distance down the road from the blacksmith's shop --- only a few feet away from the Kelso-Miller dogtrot cabin.

Was it Jack Kelso they met that evening, still roaming the landscape of New Salem, a place that he was so passionate about in life?

I'd like to think that it was.

3. ABRAHAM AND MARY
The Springfield Years

Premonition: An antecedent impression or conviction of something that is about to happen.

Abraham Lincoln was not a stranger when he arrived in Springfield. The former New Salem wrestler, business owner, and public speaker was respected for his time in the Legislature, having made a name for himself in Vandalia. This sent many people to the door of his new law office in the city.

Lincoln had many acquaintances but few true friends. While always friendly, he was an introvert, uncertain of himself and his country manners in the city. Springfield was not exactly cosmopolitan at the time - it still had unpaved streets, roamed by wild pigs into the 1870s - but it was quite a change from the quiet life of New Salem. He often described himself as "desperately lonely" in his early days in his new home.

One of his first close friends was a local merchant named Joshua Fry Speed. Lincoln may have been quiet and difficult to get to know, but Speed was the ideal man to get past his reserved nature and become his friend. They shared many things in common, including a worry about finding lasting love and marriage. Lincoln roomed with Speed for a time and they spent hours talking, laughing, telling stories, and discussing anything that came to mind. Lincoln would always refer to Speed as the best friend that he ever had in his life.

Joshua Speed

His friend's store attracted many of the young businessmen, politicians, and lawyers who came to Springfield and it was there that Lincoln began to meet new arrivals, share his political beliefs, and make a name for himself in the city. According to Speed, "Mr. Lincoln was a social man, though he did not seek out company; it sought him. After he made his home with me, on every winter's night at my store, by a big wood fire, no matter how inclement the weather, eight or ten choice spirits assembled, without distinction of party. It was a sort of social club without organization. They came here because they were sure to find Lincoln."

At that time, Springfield was a growing city of about 1,500 people but it was still only a few steps above the rough settlement that had been carved out of the wilderness less than two decades before. Even so, Springfield did manage to have a social circle and one of the members of the city's elite was Ninian Edwards, the son of a prominent politician. His wife, Elizabeth Todd Edwards, was the reigning queen of Springfield's social life and a born matchmaker. Nothing delighted her more than to find husbands for her sisters among Ninian's wealthy and prominent friends.

In 1839, her sister, Mary, came to visit. The petite, attractive young woman had a reputation for her engaging personality and quick wit, and she became the center of attention in the Springfield social set. She soon had many suitors to choose from, including Stephen Douglas, who was the most insistent in his pursuit of her.

And then, at the Christmas cotillion in December 1839, Mary met a young attorney and political hopeful named Abraham Lincoln. And the rest was history, right? Not exactly - although many would insist that Abraham and Mary were destined to be together.

When mainstream historians dismiss the links that Abraham Lincoln has to the supernatural, they do so by placing the blame on

Mary Todd Lincoln. In fact, just about any negative aspect of the Lincoln presidency has used Mary as a convenient scapegoat.

This criticism isn't new. Almost from the day she arrived at the White House, Mary was criticized and abused. Born and raised an upper-class Southern woman, the social circle of Washington, then almost overwhelmingly secessionist in sentiment, regarded Mary as a traitor to her class and region. In addition, the Virginia socialites also looked down on her as an uncouth Westerner who was lacking in social graces.

On the other hand, Northerners, particularly the Radical Republicans, regarded her as a secret Southern sympathizer and a traitor to the Union. The fact that many of Mary's relatives were soldiers in the Confederate Army caused rumors to spread that she was a spy for the South. Gossip and rumors turned into outright lies - and Mary was never good at remaining silent about the stories.

A young Mary Todd, who Lincoln met at a Christmas party in 1839

A female cousin of Mary's once described her personality as "like a spring day." This was not a compliment. She explained that Mary was liable to have outbursts "like a sudden spring thunderstorm, but then the anger would pass, and Mary would be all sunny once more."

In Washington of the 1860s - just like it is today - honesty and candor were not regarded as virtues. Mary was rarely able to disguise her feelings. She was outspoken in an era when women were expected to hold their tongue. Well educated and cultured at a time when most were not, Mary often spent more money than Abraham made, plus her sense of entitlement and vanity made her vulnerable to flattery and to those seeking favors from the White House.

For these reasons, it has made it easy for historians to demonize Mary as a selfish, neurotic shrew and to portray Abraham as a long-suffering husband. For those who have considered Lincoln's interest in the supernatural to be a negative aspect of his life, it's been easy to blame everything on Mary.

But Abraham and Mary's relationship, both with the supernatural and with each other, was more complex than most believe.

Even if one doesn't believe in destiny or fate, the law of averages was certainly on Mary Todd's side that she would one day become the First Lady of the United States. No less than three of the four men who campaigned to become president in 1860 had courted Mary. They included Abraham Lincoln, Stephen Douglas, and John C. Breckenridge of Kentucky. This may be a coincidence, but it seems a strange one.

There would seem to be no couple as mismatched as Abraham Lincoln and Mary Todd. Lincoln's humble beginnings, his lack of formal education, his series of low-paying jobs, and his career as a rural lawyer and politician are all well known. When he was first introduced to Mary, he was lacking in social graces and both his financial and political prospects were poor.

By contrast, Mary had been born into a distinguished Kentucky family. Her father, Robert Todd, was not only wealthy but politically well-connected. He spoiled his daughters, provided extravagantly for them, and hired the best tutors. Mary attended finishing school at Mrs. Ward's Academy, a prestigious institution for young ladies of quality. Mary and her sisters were better educated than most men of the era.

Mary was regarded as quite attractive but, more importantly, was charming, witty, and very personable - when she chose to be. Even William Herndon, who generally had little good to say about Mary, noted that when she arrived in Springfield, "her trenchant wit, affability, and candor pleased the young men, not less than her culture and varied accomplishments impressed the older ones with whom she came into contact." Most men were undoubtedly also impressed with her father's wealth and political influence, too.

To put it bluntly, Mary Todd was everything that Abraham Lincoln was not.

Even so, the two of them met and something strange happened. Mary, who could have had the pick of the most eligible bachelors in Illinois and Kentucky, set her sights on the country lawyer - a "poor nobody" in Lincoln's own words. Introduced to her by a fellow attorney, Lincoln was immediately charmed by her intelligence and beauty.

Mary's sister, Elizabeth, soon noted with disapproval that when Lincoln would sit with Mary in the Edwards' drawing room, he paid rapt attention to everything the young woman said. She said that Lincoln "gazed on her as if irresistibly drawn towards her by some superior and unseen power."

Friends of relatives of both Mary and Abraham remarked on how ill-suited they were for one another and yet, something drew them together. While cynics might argue that Lincoln was attracted to Mary because her social and political connections would further his career ambitions, it remains difficult to see what Mary saw in Lincoln - unless we look beyond the practical and delve into the mysterious.

Elizabeth Edwards later wrote that when Mary was a girl, she often said to her friends that "she was destined to marry a president." She often said this in her presence growing up and, she added, "in Springfield, she said it in earnest." Elizabeth assumed this was "a seemingly absurd and idle boast," but Mary also told her that she had many dreams about dancing at the White House in a cotillion.

Elizabeth's comments about her sister's innate belief - perhaps a prophetic one - about Lincoln was later confirmed by another of Lincoln's close friends, Ward Hill Lamon. Only a few months after meeting Lincoln, Lamon attended a reception held at the Lincolns' home in Springfield. After Abraham introduced Lamon to Mary, he left them alone to talk.

Lamon was chatting with Mary about her husband's popularity. At the time, Lincoln was still a hard-working lawyer, hardly known outside of Central Illinois. However, Mary blurted out, "Yes, he is a great favorite everywhere. He is to be President of the United States someday; if I had not thought so I never would have married him, for you can see he is not pretty."

Lamon, who had not known Lincoln for very long, was taken aback by Mary's bold statement. He wrote, "I felt convinced that Mrs. Lincoln was running Abraham beyond his proper distance." Time would

William Herndon, Lincoln's friend and law partner

prove him wrong, of course, but at that moment, Mary's belief seemed both foolhardy and bizarre.

Mary's decision to accept Lincoln as her husband was clearly not based on any pragmatic considerations. Rather, it was some inner voice that told the ambitious young woman that this unlikely candidate for her hand in marriage would one day be the president and that if she wanted to fulfill her own destiny, she needed to latch onto him and not let go. It was an inner knowledge that she couldn't explain and yet, even through their "stormy" courtship, she persisted until she had what she wanted.

There is no question that the course of their love did not run smoothly. After their initial meeting and courtship, Mary was still being pursued by other men. Finally, in the fall of 1840, Lincoln decided that he wanted to make her his wife. Then, without explanation, on New Year's Day 1841, he changed his mind.

No one can say what happened. Some have speculated that Lincoln feared the loss of his freedom, even though he was in love with Mary. William Herndon, his friend and law partner, said that Lincoln acted as "crazy as a loon." He didn't eat, didn't sleep, let his work slide, and refused to meet and dine with friends. A friend, Dr. Anson Henry, suggested that Lincoln take a trip out of town and try to decide what he wanted.

Lincoln decided to visit his friend Joshua Speed, who had moved to Louisville, Kentucky. But things were no better there. Speed was also in the middle of a turbulent relationship with a young woman named Fanny Henning and had little sympathy to offer his friend. After a short visit, Lincoln went back to Springfield and Speed went with him so that he could wrap up some outstanding business and settle in Louisville permanently. He would soon be marrying Fanny and before he left, he offered Lincoln some advice - either give up Mary for good or marry her.

In the summer of 1842, Abraham and Mary rekindled their romance. The fact that Mary was so easily won over by him again speaks volumes about her passion for the young man and about her belief in his future greatness. Otherwise, it would be impossible to explain how a woman so proud and quick to anger would tolerate repeated slights from any man, much less from a poor country lawyer. Mary's patience with him can only be understood if we accept her absolute certainty that Lincoln would one day ascend to the highest office in the land.

Ward Hill Lamon later wrote that from the day he met Mary to the day of her husband's inauguration, she "never wavered in her faith that her hopes in this respect would be realized."

Abraham and Mary were together throughout the summer of 1842 and by that fall, were talking of marriage. On the morning of November 4, the couple announced that their marriage plans were official. They were getting married - that same evening.

Their friends, surprised by the announcement, worked quickly to make plans for the ceremony. Lincoln asked his friend, James Matheny, to stand with him as his best man. Matheny later wrote that during the ceremony, Lincoln "looked and acted like a lamb being led to slaughter." While he was getting dressed, his landlord's son asked him where he was going. Lincoln replied, "To hell, I suppose."

Mary's faith in Lincoln never wavered, but Lincoln wasn't so sure about marriage.

The couple had their honeymoon at the Globe Tavern, where they lived during the first years of their marriage. There was every indication that the marriage was a happy one, although it was quite different from the average marriage of the time. Wives were then supposed to be docile and not speak up, but Mary

The Globe Tavern in Springfield, where the Lincolns lived after getting married

In the early 1840s, Lincoln began making a name for himself in political circles.

had her own opinions and Lincoln paid heed to what she had to say - whether about business, friendship, or the supernatural.

In many of the paranormal incidents that occurred in Lincoln's life, it was usually that he would experience something uncanny - like a disturbing dream or omen - and then tell his wife about it. Even if he didn't outright tell her, Mary, always attune to his state of mind, would notice something was wrong and pry it out of him.

Lincoln would often begin to tell her of his premonition or vision and then just as quickly drop the subject, dismissing it as unimportant. This, of course, upset Mary and would not rest until Abraham told her fully about the incident. Lincoln had the experience, but it would be Mary who interpreted it. By the time they were living in the White House, they had been married for years and Mary was well-acquainted with her husband's prophetic mind, as we'll see in the pages ahead. I have no doubt that there were many other incidents that transpired in the years they were together that were never committed to paper.

In addition to courting Mary in the summer of 1842, Lincoln was also making a name for himself in political circles, although that summer was marred by an affair that Lincoln would always consider one of the most embarrassing mistakes of his life.

That summer, the Illinois banking system collapsed, and state officers were forced to suspend the collection of taxes when it became obvious that citizens were only able to pay them with depreciated or worthless bank notes.

The Illinois State Auditor at the time was a man named James Shields and Lincoln, with Mary as his conspirator, decided to poke fun at the Democrats then running the state. They singled out James Shields for torment and began writing letters to the *Sangamo Journal* that came from a fictious woman named "Rebecca." The letters berated Shields for his fiscal policies, questioned his honesty, and challenged his manly courage. The letters were obviously satire but many Democrats, already feeling public pressure, did not take them well. Shields himself

Illinois State Auditor James Shields

was enraged. He demanded to know who had written the letters, and when confronted, Lincoln admitted responsibility. Shields then demanded that Lincoln confess to writing the letters and retract them or he would face "consequences which no one will regret more than myself."

Lincoln laughed the whole thing off. It had been a silly joke and the joke was over - but not for James Shields. He didn't get the apology he wanted so he spread the word that a duel was going to take place between the two men. Lincoln laughingly suggested that they fight it out with cow pies in a pasture, but Shields was having none of it. He was serious. His honor had been challenged and the only way to satisfy that challenge was a fight to the death - a not uncommon practice among politicians at the time.

Duels were "affairs of honor" and were violent and often to the death. They were carried out covertly, although if the fight was considered to be fair, the participants were usually safe from arrest. The quarrels often began in newspaper columns, in speeches, or in off-handed remarks. Strangely, duels were often seen as a continuation of business or politics and often the negotiations involved in a duel could be more complicated than the quarrel that prompted the affair in the first place.

Lincoln had no desire to fight with Shields. Hoping to cool tensions, he sent the man a letter and offered to confess to writing the letters as political farce, not as something meant to defame Shields' character. But if Shields still wanted to have a duel, then Lincoln stipulated that it must be held with cavalry broadswords while standing on a wooden plank that was 10 feet long and 12 inches wide.

Again, Lincoln was not serious. His stipulations were meant to show just how ridiculous the whole thing was. Or, it might be said that Lincoln was making a point to Shields that if he persisted in forcing a duel, it would be deadly to Shields. He may have wanted him to realize that Lincoln's long arms - with blade in hand - would reach the smaller man very easily.

Still, though, Shields demanded that the duel be fought. He arranged for the two men to meet in Alton, Illinois, and hold the duel on "Sunflower Island," on the Mississippi River. Dueling was illegal in Illinois, and so by meeting on neutral ground, they would be able to avoid the authorities.

On the morning of September 22, 1842, Lincoln and Shields, along with their "seconds," a physician, and a number of friends, met on Sunflower Island. Asked to choose weapons, Lincoln, who was much taller than this prospective opponent and with much longer arms, picked up a broadsword and began using it to hack at tree branches that were well out of Shield's reach.

After what must have been a chilling demonstration, Shields decided that he would accept Lincoln's apology and accept his explanation. The fight was called off, but if the duel had proceeded, two promising political careers could have ended. Shields later became a Brigadier General in the Mexican and Civil Wars and a U.S. Senator from Illinois, Minnesota, and Missouri. The two men became friends and Lincoln often relied on Shields during the war.

After the matter was settled, the party rowed back to Alton. A small crowd of friends was gathered on the dock, waiting to hear the outcome of the duel. As the boat carrying the group returned to the river landing, many anxious spectators were startled to see a "bloody corpse" on the floor of the boat. One of the women fainted but Lincoln and Shields burst into laughter because the "corpse" was just a log that was wearing a red shirt. After the "duel," the parties were hosted at the Old '76 Tavern in town.

And while the matter ended on a light note, Lincoln was so ashamed of the affair that he never talked about it again. After that, he never published cruel or embarrassing letters either, even for satire. He also became very opposed to physical violence and when insulted, or if someone tried to pick a fight with him, Lincoln simply laughed and walked away. He would remember how badly things could have turned out in Alton for the rest of his life.

The Lincolns' first son, Robert, was born just three days short of nine months after the wedding. At that time, they were still living at the Globe Tavern, but they wouldn't be for much longer.

By 1844, Lincoln was able to afford to purchase a home in Springfield. It was a one-and-a-half story cottage at the corner of Eighth and Jackson Streets, not far from Lincoln's law office in the downtown district. The Lincolns lived in the house from a period shortly after Robert was born until they moved to Washington in 1861. Lincoln would later make improvements for this growing family and it would be the only house that Lincoln ever owned during his lifetime.

Family life, a new home, and a law office put many demands on Lincoln's time. Work and travel caused tension in his marriage in those early years. He was active in court cases all over Illinois and was away from home several days every week. Mary, left at home with a toddler, was convinced that something terrible was going to happen while he was away.

Their second son, Eddie, was born in 1846 but only lived to the

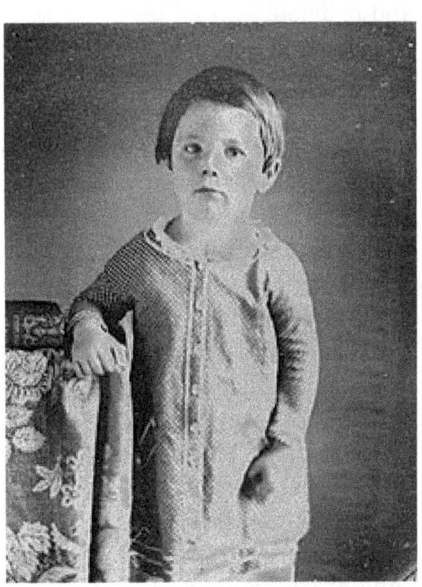

Eddie Lincoln was the first of the Lincoln sons to die in 1850

age of four. Shortly after Eddie's birth, Lincoln won a seat in the House of Representatives, taking him further away from home, but by late 1849, he was back in Springfield. Eddie became sick around Christmas with either tuberculosis or diphtheria and never improved.

The little boy had been named after Edward D. Baker, a man who had preceded Lincoln in Congress. Lincoln had met him shortly after moving from New Salem to Springfield. They became close friends and Mary loved the exuberant Baker so much that she agreed to name their second son after him.

Eddie was a sweet child and was much lankier than his older brother. There is a good chance that he would have taken after his father, but fate intervened, and Eddie was, as Mary put it, "called to die." None of the local doctors' cures worked on the boy and he died just one month after his fourth birthday.

Lincoln had an eerie dream on the night before this new tragedy in his life occurred. It was a dream that he'd had before and knew that something unusual was going to follow it. In the dream, he was in a ship that was sailing quickly into the night, carrying him into darkness and oblivion.

Lincoln would have the dream again shortly before his assassination.

The Lincolns had more children, of course. Willie was born in 1850, not long after the death of his brother, and Thomas "Tad" Lincoln was born in 1853. The children drew Lincoln closer to home, but his marriage was still sometimes rocky. He was nine years older than Mary and almost a foot taller. She often complained that he treated her more like a child than a wife.

Lincoln's law practice was based in Springfield, where most people in Central Illinois had to bring their grievances for settlement. However, twice each year, a judge took justice out to the people. At fixed sessions of two days each week, this special magistrate sat at county seats that were scattered all over the prairie and tried to mete out rulings on the crimes and cases of each locale. Joining the traveling tribunal across what was known in Illinois as the Eighth Circuit, was a band of lawyers who sought out clients at each stop and defended them with skill.

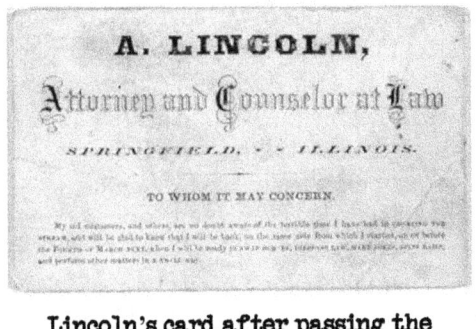

Lincoln's card after passing the Illinois Bar Exam

(Right) Lincoln during his days on the law circuit across Illinois

Lincoln was one of the attorneys who could be found on the circuit. The travel appealed to him, as did meeting the people, and he endured long rides, harsh weather, and uncomfortable beds so that he could provide advice and a legal defense for those who needed it. In those days, few of Illinois' county seats could be reached by the new railroads. Most were accessible only by the muddy paths that passed for roads, across bridges that were often washed out, and wooded trails that had to be traversed by horseback because they were impassable by carriage or wagon. Lincoln usually traveled at the head of the caravan that was made up of other lawyers and the judges. His long legs made an excellent marker for what streams could be crossed safely by the other men. They slept in farmhouses, in barns, hotels, and tavern beds. Some of the courthouses were ornate structures of stone and brick, while others were primitive log cabins. Legal strategies often had to be dreamed up on the spot because defendants weren't used to the idea that they had to tell their attorneys the truth.

Lincoln was all business during his trials, listening attentively when not involved in the case, assisting other lawyers with advice and pleading his own cases in the slow drawl that he became famous for, always with care and common sense. Unfortunately, Lincoln never fared well in criminal trials and although he tried 13 murder trials, he lost about half of them.

When the workday ended, the lawyers usually gathered around the fire at the local tavern to play cards, swap stories, and sing songs.

There was also usually some liquor or hard cider involved. Lincoln would later be recalled as the center of attention, whether he was telling jokes or recounting the courtroom antics of himself and his fellow lawyers. He also mingled with the folks that he met in the small towns and backwoods communities, visiting their homes, talking about their crops and livestock, discussing politics, or bouncing their children on his knee. The shy, introverted young man had been replaced by one who enjoyed meeting and talking with people.

Many memorable incidents occurred during Lincoln's time on the law circuit. While in Decatur, he had a chance to visit with his cousins, the John Hanks family, and usually stayed at the Macon House, one of the most popular hotels in town.

It was at the Macon House that he met Jane Martin Johns, a woman who would later become one of his greatest supporters and who would rally all the Decatur women to make food, roll bandages, and provide care for Union soldiers during the Civil War.

Jane and her husband, livestock owner and future state legislator H.C. Johns, were living at the Macon House while her grand home was being built on what became known as Johns Hill. She was waiting on the delivery of the first piano in the city and Lincoln became an important part of the story. The piano had traveled down the Ohio River on a steamboat. It had then been sent up the Wabash River to Crawfordsville, Indiana, and then carried by wagon to Decatur. To move the heavy, crated instrument into the Macon House was quite a chore and interrupted the dinner that was being eaten by the gathered attorneys. The men, organized by Lincoln, managed to wrestle the piano into the hotel. Mrs. Johns was so grateful that she made sure that she was on hand each night when the men returned from court so that she could take requests, sing, and play for them. In the years that followed, Lincoln was a frequent guest at the Johns' home.

During his trials, Lincoln was all business, listening attentively when not involved in the case, assisting other lawyers with advice and pleading his own cases in the slow drawl that he became famous for, always with care and common sense. Unfortunately, Lincoln never fared well in criminal trials and although he tried 13 murder trials, he lost about half of them.

This was undoubtedly a somber thought for the man that he ended up defending in his last murder trial, but Lincoln felt honor bound to step in and try and help.

The accused killer was an old friend.

It was a hot, humid night in late August 1857 when James Metzker was fatally beaten just a short distance from a Methodist camp meeting. The people at the religious service didn't know there had been a murder until a few days later, when Reverend George Randle, received word from town that a man had died at the "whiskey camp."

Camp meetings - outdoor religious revival meetings - were an important part of spiritual life in rural American in those days. The meetings, which often lasted for several days, attracted not only the faithful but young men who saw the gatherings as a place to drink, fight, and socialize. This rowdy element became so disruptive that a law was passed in Illinois against "disturbing a worshipping congregation." Methodist ministers often tried to keep the young men away from the meetings, so the hellraisers set up their own tents and wagons and made a "whiskey camp."

On Saturday night, August 29, James Metzker, a farmer in his mid-twenties who lived in Menard County, was hanging around the whiskey wagons. He was there with James Norris, a farmer in his late twenties who had a wife and four children, and William "Duff" Armstrong, 24, another farmer from Menard County. The three men were acquaintances, but after some heavy drinking, both Norris and Armstrong began bickering with Metzker. There was likely nothing meant by it - just three men with strong opinions and too much liquor.

A little before midnight, one of the arguments turned physical and Metzker was struck in the head with a "slung-shot" - a weight tied to a leather thong that was a lot like an early blackjack. He managed to get home from the camp the next morning, falling off his horse several times. When he was examined by a doctor, he discovered that Metzker's skull had been fractured in two places. He died from his injuries two days later.

Norris and Armstrong were arrested by the Mason County sheriff, but the local jail turned out to be unsafe for them. Public anger over the case was heated and the jail was insecure, so they were taken to

Lewiston and locked up in the Fulton County jail to await trial. Armstrong's trial would later be held in Beardstown.

In October, the two men were indicted by the Mason County Circuit Court. Both men were indicted for murder. Norris had killed a man years earlier but was cleared of charges after he claimed self-defense. Things did not go as well this time - the jury found him guilty and he was sentenced to eight years in the state penitentiary.

William "Duff" Armstrong

While Duff Armstrong was awaiting trial, his father, Jack, died. On his deathbed, Jack had urged Duff's wife, Hannah, to do everything she could to save her husband, even if she had to sell their farm. She initially hired the same attorneys who had defended Norris but, after he was sent to prison, had second thoughts. Friends urged her to call on an old friend of the family, a lawyer who dabbled in politics, named Abraham Lincoln.

Lincoln had known Jack Armstrong since his New Salem days, nearly three decades before. At the time they met, he had been working as a store clerk for Denton Offutt. Offutt had always liked Lincoln and often bragged about him to his customers, claiming that Lincoln could outrun or outfight any man in the county.

Bill Clary, whose family was the namesake of a settlement southwest of town called Clary's Grove, was skeptical of all the boasts - mostly because Clary's Grove was home to a group of young toughs led by Jack Armstrong. They were a loud, rowdy, hard-drinking bunch who often came to New Salem to drink, gossip, and trade. They had been besting young men in fights in other settlements for quite some time and Clary figured that Lincoln couldn't whip any of his boys - especially Jack Armstrong. So, tired of Offutt's big talk, Clary bet him $10 that Jack Armstrong would prove to be a better man than Lincoln in a wrestling match.

Lincoln didn't want to take part in the match, but he eventually gave in to Offutt's pleas. The match took place right in front of the store and everyone in New Salem came out to watch and wager on the winner.

Most of the onlookers bet on Armstrong but within a few minutes, they realized - according to attorney John T. Stuart - Armstrong realized that "he had got hold of the wrong customer." The two men fought hard, doing their best to throw the other, but remained on their feet. Unable to throw Lincoln fairly, Armstrong tried a cheap shot that only caused Lincoln's temper to flare. Angry, he grabbed Armstrong by the throat, lifted him off the ground using his long arms, and shook him like a rag doll.

The rest of the Clary's Grove boys rushed Lincoln, kicking and punching him in an effort to knock him down. Lincoln barely flinched. In fact, he laughed as they tried to pry him loose from their friend. When the others finally stopped, Lincoln let Armstrong go free. The two men shook hands, Lincoln having proved that he had the strength and the courage to best anyone in town. Armstrong later called Lincoln "the best fellow who ever broke into camp."

Lincoln became close friends with Jack and his wife, Hannah. He often stayed in their home, where he split rails, helped the Clary's Grove boys with their work, and even studied surveying so that he could help them establish the lines of their land.

When Lincoln heard about Duff Armstrong's troubles from Hannah, he wrote to her. Despite the fact that he was busy preparing for his Senate campaign against Stephen Douglas - and the fact that he had never fared well with murder trials - he offered to take Duff's case pro bono.

In his letter to Hannah, he wrote:

I have just heard of your deep affliction, and the arrest of your son for murder. I can hardly believe that he can be guilty of the crime alleged against him. It does not seem possible. I am anxious that he should have a fair trial, at any rate; and gratitude for your long continued kindness to me in adverse circumstances prompts me to offer my humble services gratuitously in his behalf. It will afford me an opportunity to requite, in a small degree, the favors I received at your

Hannah Armstrong

hand, and that of your lamented husband, when your roof afforded me grateful shelter without money and without price.

Yours truly,
Abraham Lincoln.

Hannah traveled to Springfield to meet with Lincoln and see if he could get Duff out on bail before his trial. Lincoln tried, but was unable to secure his release. He went with Hannah to the county jail to break the bad news to the young man that he would have to stay in jail until his trial, which would be the following spring.

At the jail, Hannah met Duff's cellmate, a former schoolteacher who was serving a sentence for larceny. He proposed to her that if she bought him a new pair of eyeglasses and some books to pass the time, he would teach Duff to read while he waited for his trial. Hannah agreed and the following May, a literate Duff Armstrong left his jail cell to be put on trial.

The Circuit Court of Cass County convened in Beardstown on May 3, 1858, to begin Armstrong's trial. When Lincoln arrived, he discovered that his star witness, a man named Charles Allen, was missing. When Lincoln asked Duff's friends about Allen, he learned that they had made an agreement with the man. He was going to stay at a hotel in the nearby town of Virginia during the trial and wouldn't testify. In exchange, Duff's friends would pay his living expenses. But Lincoln explained to them that if Allen didn't appear, the case would be continued, and Duff would have to wait in jail for the trial to be rescheduled. Realizing their mistake, two Armstrong cousins hurried to Virginia to bring Allen back with them. The trial was finally ready to begin the next morning.

State's Attorney Hugh Fullerton prosecuted the case, assisted by a private attorney named Collier who had been hired by Metzker's brother. Lincoln was assisted by William Walker, the attorney who had defended Duff's friend Norris the year before.

During the early parts of the trial, Collier offered what appeared to be a solid case. Lincoln only asked a few questions of Collier's witnesses, called several of his own, and only spoke up occasionally to double-check some dates and names.

Until Charles Allen took the stand.

Allen testified for the prosecution that he had seen Duff Armstrong strike the blow that killed Metzker. On cross-examination, Lincoln pushed Allen for more details.

How far away had he been standing? About 150 feet.
What time was it? Approximately 11:00 p.m.

How could he be sure that the assailant was Armstrong if it was the middle of the night and he was so far away from the action? "By the light of the moon," Allen testified. He said it had been shining high in the sky and offered more than enough light for him to plainly see the attack take place. During his questioning, Lincoln kept going back to these details and Allen had to repeat his testimony about the moon several times.

Lincoln purchased an 1857 almanac from a nearby drug store and asked that it be entered into evidence. The judge allowed it and Lincoln opened the book to the calendar for the previous August. He showed the pages to the jury and explained that on the night of the assault, the moon had only been in the first quarter - and it had set at three minutes after midnight. At the time Allen claimed he'd seen the attack, the moon would have been low on the horizon, not directly overhead. It's size and position did not match Allen's testimony.

When Lincoln explained this to the jury, a ripple of laughter went through the spectators in the courtroom. Even some of the jurors had a hard time hiding their grins. The moon, low on the horizon an hour before setting, probably still could have offered enough light for Allen to see the assault, but Lincoln had distracted them by pointing out the problems with the man's testimony.

Years later, a juror recalled, "The jury thought Allen was telling the truth. I know that he impressed me that way, but his evidence with reference to the moon was so far from the facts that it destroyed his evidence with the jury."

Lincoln didn't rely solely on the almanac to defend his client. He also had a doctor testify that the blow that Norris struck to the back of Metzker's head could have been the fatal blow. Lincoln even performed this for the court during his closing arguments.

And that was not his only performance that day. On the afternoon of final remarks, it was hot in the courthouse. As Lincoln stood to speak, he took off his coat, his vest, and necktie. As he talked and paced in front of the jury box, one of his suspenders slipped off his shoulder and fell to his side. Lincoln left it there until he finished talking. Looking disheveled and fresh from the farm, Lincoln spoke at length about his feelings for the Armstrong family and how much they meant to him. He even went so far as to plead for the life of the son of his old friends.

The jury deliberated for just one hour, took only one vote, and then delivered a unanimous acquittal. After the verdict was returned, Lincoln shook hands with Duff, led him to his mother, and told him to care for her and try to be as good of a man as his father had been. He left the courthouse, returned home, and went back to preparing for his Senate campaign.

Lincoln had gotten an acquittal for Duff Armstrong largely just by poking a hole in a witness's testimony with an almanac. His part in the trial would soon come back to haunt him as his adversaries would use it against him in the Senate race and, two years later, when he ran for President.

During the Senate campaign, his critics accused him of using an altered almanac in the trial. It was a serious charge but an absurd one. Lincoln would have had to put a lot of effort into such a ruse, since he had three copies of the almanac at the courthouse. After he cross-examined Allen, he gave one to the judge, one to the prosecutor, and one to the jury so they could inspect it. The prosecutor even sent his assistant to the store to buy a few more of them and he returned with several copies, some published by different companies than the one Lincoln used. They all said the same thing and agreed with Lincoln's almanac about the position of the moon. If Lincoln had tried to fool the court, he would have to have been involved in a massive conspiracy with several almanac publishers.

But politics weren't much different then than they are today. If people are willing to believe the lies, then there is always a politician who is willing to broadcast them.

As it turned out, this was not the only time that Abraham Lincoln saved the life of Duff Armstrong.

Duff and three of his brothers enlisted in the Union Army at the start of the Civil War. In 1862, Duff became seriously ill and was laid up in a military hospital. His mother wrote to Lincoln, explaining his condition, and asked for a discharge so that he could recover at home. Lincoln granted the discharge immediately and Duff returned home to Hannah, who nursed him back to health. He died in Illinois in May 1899 at the age of 66.

4. FIRE ON THE PRAIRIE
The Lincoln and Douglas Debates

Lincoln continued riding the law circuit during the early 1850s. His practice - and the travel that went with it - kept him too busy to think much about his political career. But that would change, and his attention began to be focused on the vile institution of slavery. His empathy for the people held in chains began to alter the course of his life - perhaps just as that New Orleans fortuneteller had told him it would more than two decades earlier.

But Lincoln was far from perfect when it came to how he saw the African American race. In mostly white Indiana and Illinois, Lincoln had little experience with black people. The terrifying problems of slave unrest and violence were far away in states like Virginia and the Carolinas, where slaves had been bought and sold for generations. In Illinois, people were plagued by both prejudice and ignorance and Lincoln was not immune to either. He believed - as most whites did at the time - that Negroes were, by nature, inferior to whites. They were not allowed to vote, serve on juries, or marry outside their race. People were taught these things by society and it was usually reinforced by the teachings of the churches they belonged to. Lincoln had no qualms about referring to black men as "boys" or telling stories about "pickaninnies" and "darkies." It took years for Lincoln's views about race to evolve but eventually, they did.

By the time that he was 28, he and his friend, Dan Stone, were the only state legislators in Illinois to take a stand against slavery. They called slavery an "injustice" and condemned the lynch mobs that terrorized blacks and abolitionists. However, they also condemned the radical abolitionists, stating that they increased rather than abated slavery's evils. Lincoln was still content to believe that slavery would eventually die out on its own. He hated the institution, but he didn't endorse abolishing it - not yet, at least. Lincoln was only opposed to the further spread of slavery in the country and supported the Missouri Compromise, which outlawed slavery in the west, where America's future would be built.

But in 1854, a congressional act, pushed ahead by Lincoln's longtime personal and political rival, Stephen Douglas, threatened to allow slavery in the new territories. Lincoln was incensed by this reversal and he made the decision to largely abandon his law practice and return to the political arena.

That summer, Lincoln decided to campaign for a seat in the Illinois State Assembly. He easily won the election but didn't serve long. He had his eye on a seat in the U.S. Senate, where he believed he could really make a difference for the country. He ran in February 1855 but lost. In early 1856, though, a new political party emerged from the ruins of the Whigs - the Republican Party. Its first political move was to try and keep Democrat James Buchanan out of office. They failed but gained favorable attention among voters.

Buchanan's time in office managed to reverse the course of the anti-slavery movement. It was during his term that the U.S. Supreme Court ruled in the Dred Scott case, effectively ruling that blacks could not - and never would be - American citizens. The case, along with the rising tide of the abolitionist movement, ignited passions across the country and dire predictions began to be made about the possibilities of secession and even civil war.

Perhaps realizing which way the winds of change were blowing, Stephen Douglas abruptly changed his mind about slavery and announced that he was now opposed to allowing it into the western territories. Illinois Republicans were unconvinced by his change of heart and in June 1858, nominated Abraham Lincoln to run against Douglas for a seat in the Senate.

On the night of his nomination - during the exciting convention - Lincoln made what became his famous "House Divided" speech. He declared that the country could not endure as a divided nation. It was a speech that had been months in the planning, and it has endured over the years as one of the most eloquent and thought-provoking in American politics. Lincoln told the assembled Republicans:

A house divided against itself cannot stand. I believe this government cannot endure permanently half slave and half free. I do not expect the Union to be dissolved — I do not expect the house to fall — but I do expect it will cease to be divided. It will become all one thing, or all the other. Either the opponents of slavery will arrest the further spread of it, and place it where the public mind shall rest in the belief that it is in the course of ultimate extinction; or its advocates will push it forward, till it shall become alike lawful in all the States, old as well as new — North as well as South.

But Lincoln would not have an easy path to victory. He would first have to - once again - face his rival, Stephen Douglas.

Stephen Douglas arrived in Illinois nearly penniless in 1833. He lived in Jacksonville for a short time but the 20-year-old, who had been born in Brandon, Vermont, found little opportunity in the city. He spent the next few months in the nearby town of Winchester - where he taught school, earning $3 per pupil, and studied law - and then returned to Jacksonville, where he opened a practice. He later served as the state's attorney and began dabbling in politics. In 1834, he made his first public speech at the Morgan County Courthouse, where he defended President Andrew Jackson's removal of government money from the Second Bank of the United States. Jacksonville citizens carried the short, fiery man on their shoulders around the square, declaring that he was a "Little Giant." The nickname stuck throughout his entire career.

Douglas' popularity led to his election to the State Legislature in 1836, and in the next year, he was appointed Register of the Land Office at Springfield. In was in this city that he truly began his political career. In 1841, at the age of 27, he was appointed an Associate Justice of the Illinois Supreme Court. However, he resigned from the court after being elected to the U.S. House of Representatives in 1843. He was re-elected in 1844. In Congress, he championed territorial expansion and supported the Mexican War. In 1846, the Illinois General Assembly elected him a U.S. Senator.

While beginning his political rise, Douglas briefly courted Mary Todd, but in March 1847, he married Martha Martin, the 21-year-old daughter of wealthy Colonel Robert Martin of North Carolina. The year after their marriage, her father died and bequeathed Martha a 2,500-acre cotton plantation with 100 slaves on the Pearl River in Lawrence County, Mississippi. He appointed Douglas the property manager but, as a Senator from the free state of Illinois, and with presidential aspirations, Douglas found the Southern plantation presented difficulties. He created distance by hiring a manager to operate the plantation, while using his allocated 20-percent of the income to advance his political career. Douglas privately told friends that he believed slavery was a "cancer on the nation," but he would not offend southerners by publicly condemning it. He also didn't mind profiting from it either.

Illinois Democrat and Lincoln's **personal and political rival, Stephen Douglas.**

In 1848, Douglas moved his family to Chicago. He and Martha had two sons, Robert and Stephen, Jr. but Martha Douglas died in January 1853, after the birth of their third child, a daughter. The girl died a few weeks later, leaving Douglas alone with his sons until he remarried in 1856. His second wife, 20-year-old Adele Cutts, was the daughter of James Madison Cutts of Washington, D.C., nephew of President James Madison.

Senator Douglas was a strong supporter of popular sovereignty, a doctrine which asserted that residents of territories had the right to decide whether they wanted to have a free state or a slave state. His beliefs, his ties to the south, and his support of the Kansas-Nebraska Act of 1854, which applied popular sovereignty to those territories, made him a favorite target of criticism from the new Republican Party. His support of the act made him so unpopular for a time that Douglas joked that he could travel from Washington back to Illinois by the light of burning effigies of him.

In 1856, Douglas was a candidate for the Democratic presidential nomination, and while he received strong support at the convention, he was passed over.

Douglas continued to steer a middle course on the slavery issue. His "popular sovereignty" doctrine that slavery should be decided on locally by states and territories was satisfactory to southerners who didn't want outside interference with slavery and Northerners who didn't want to take sides over it. It was famously said of him that he didn't care "whether slavery was voted up or voted down," as long as it was voted on by the people.

Then in 1857, the U.S. Supreme Court issued the Dred Scott decision, which declared that under the Constitution, neither Congress nor a territorial legislature created by Congress had the power to prohibit slavery in a territory. This struck down key elements of the Missouri and 1850 Compromises, made the Kansas-Nebraska Act irrelevant, and denied the basis of "popular sovereignty." Pro-slavery Southerners had praised Douglas for relaxing restrictions on slavery in the Kansas-Nebraska Act, but now, ardent pro-slavery radicals denounced him for supporting any restrictions at all. At the same time, some Northerners, seeing "popular sovereignty" apparently dead, went over to the Republicans. Douglas faced a dilemma. If he rejected Dred Scott, he would lose Southern support he needed for the presidential election of 1860. If he embraced Dred Scott, he would lose northern support. He tried to avoid both hazards by issuing a tepid endorsement of the decision, while continuing to state that he believed in popular sovereignty without explicitly saying the Court was wrong.

Another issue came up at the same time and Douglas was forced to take a side in the matter. President James Buchanan and his Southern allies tried to get Kansas admitted as a slave state. But the anti-slavery majority in Kansas rejected this, despite efforts to rig the voting there. Douglas strongly opposed Buchanan's maneuvers, and the

The clashes between Lincoln and Douglas on the Senate campaign trail led one reporter to write, "The prairies are on fire."

two became bitter enemies. Even his Republican critics praised him for this stand, and he restored his standing with the moderates of the north. This was critically important, because his Senate term ended in 1859, and he wanted to be re-elected.

It was during this campaign in 1858 that Douglas came up against his friend and political and romantic rival, Abraham Lincoln, who had been picked to run for the Senate seat by the Republicans. Douglas tried to avoid meeting Lincoln directly. He traveled the state, making speeches and was provided with a private train from the Illinois Central, which was then run by his friend and future Civil War General George McClellan. Lincoln followed Douglas around the state, answering each Douglas speech with one of his own a day or two later.

After several such incidents, Lincoln proposed that he and Douglas meet for a series of seven formal debates in front of audiences all over the state. Douglas agreed and the two began a series of appearances that have become legend in Illinois for their volatile content. "The prairies are on fire," wrote one reporter, after witnessing a clash between Lincoln and Douglas.

The events were held in Ottawa, Freeport, Jonesboro, Charleston, Galesburg, Quincy, and Alton. In the debates, Douglas reiterated his support of popular sovereignty. He demanded to know whether Lincoln would ever vote to admit a new slave state, even if the majority of settlers favored slavery. He denounced Lincoln for his insistence that slavery was a moral issue that had to be resolved by the entire nation. Douglas described this as causing an unnecessary conflict between free and slave states, which threatened to boil up into disunion and war. He also asserted that Lincoln supported civil and social equality between the races, and insinuated that Lincoln even accepted racial intermarriage.

For his part, Lincoln criticized Douglas for his moral indifference to slavery, but denied any intention of interference with slavery in the South. He evaded Douglas' question about the admission of a slave state. Lincoln disclaimed the radical views on racial equality attributed to him by Douglas, arguing only for the right of Negroes to personal liberty and to earn their own livings. Like most debates throughout history, the two men attacked each other for allegedly extreme or irresponsible statements by supporters or colleagues and accused each other of bad faith in denying responsibility for such statements or for inconsistency in their own statements.

In other words, politics has changed very little between 1858 and the present day.

By the time the two men arrived in the Mississippi River town of Alton for the final "Lincoln-Douglas Debate" on October 15, 1858, their battle had been raging for nearly four months. During the campaign, Lincoln had followed Douglas in speaking on 23 of 80 days. Douglas had traveled more than 5,277 miles of muddy back roads and had made 130 speeches. Lincoln had traveled 4,350 miles and had spoken 63 times. When they arrived in Alton, Douglas was exhausted, and his voice was failing, but Lincoln's harsh tenor was clearer and stronger than ever.

The candidates arrived at dawn on the morning of the debate. They came from the river aboard the steamship *City of Louisiana* and first went to the Alton House, Douglas' headquarters, which was located at Front and Alby Streets. A committee of local Republicans then escorted Lincoln to the Franklin House, which years later would be renamed the Abraham Lincoln Hotel. Mary and Robert joined him later that day and the family had dinner and then spent the night at the hotel. Both hotels were filled with supporters for the two men, and many prominent citizens from Alton and the surrounding area were present when the debate got underway.

It was held on the east side of

The Lincoln Hotel in Alton was still known as the Franklin House when Lincoln stayed there before his debate with Stephen Douglas in 1858

Alton's new city hall. The building had been hastily readied for the debate, but actual construction would not be completed until 1874. By prior agreement, no slogans or banners were allowed on the podium, but the streets and buildings around the site were decorated with signs of support for either Douglas or Lincoln. The estimated crowd of between 5,000 and 10,000 that gathered that day were mostly Democrats, turning out to support Stephen Douglas. He spoke first, his voice obviously worn down and tired, repeating his stand that it was the right of each individual state to do as it pleased on the question of slavery. He spoke on other issues as well, but this subject was a lightning rod of controversy between the candidates.

Lincoln argued that the fundamental difference between his supporters and those who supported Douglas was whether slavery was wrong. Lincoln repeated his prior statements and belief that a house divided against itself could not stand and that the United States must be all slave or all free. He believed that a crisis was approaching that would make the country move in one direction or another.

Lincoln was described by the reporters present, as well as the casual listener, as a powerful public speaker. His enemies often painted a portrait of him as a gangling, backwoods lawyer, but even the most cynical admitted that he came to life when behind the podium. Francis

Grierson, one of many who heard Lincoln speak in Alton, was astonished that "the moment he began to speak, the ungainly mouth lost its heaviness and the half-listless eyes attained a wondrous power." Grierson later wrote that there was something "elemental and mystical" about Lincoln as a public speaker, and as a result, "Before he had spoken 20 minutes, the conviction took possession of thousands that here was the prophetic man of the present."

Lincoln may have won the debate that day in Alton but, in the end, he lost the Senate election. Two years later, however, he won the presidency - and faced Stephen Douglas once again.

Douglas was the obvious nominee for the Democrats in the election of 1860, despite opposition from President Buchanan. Unfortunately for Douglas, he had lost support in the south and southern Democrats ran their own candidates against him, essentially splitting the party between north and south. During his campaign, Douglas broke the unwritten rule of campaigning in person. In those days, it was considered beneath the dignity of a presidential candidate to go out and appear before the voters. The candidate had speakers to do that for him. But Douglas, seeing the dangers facing the country, went on speaking tours across the country. He campaigned energetically, attacking both abolitionism in the north and talk of secession in the south. Despite the vigor of his campaign, Douglas was defeated.

After losing to Lincoln, Douglas immediately came out in support of his old friendly rival. He urged the south to accept the results of the election and tried to do what he could to avert secession, which he denounced as criminal. He was one of the strongest advocates of maintaining the integrity of the Union at all hazards.

He also turned out to be a loyal friend. He was present at Lincoln's first inauguration. Lincoln took the oath of office, then took off his stovepipe hat in preparation for giving his inaugural address. But he had nowhere to place it. Douglas, who was on the platform, stepped forward and took the hat from Lincoln's hands. Moving back, he remarked, "If I can't be the President, at least I can hold his hat." It was a symbolic gesture that showed the true character of Stephen Douglas. Though he and Lincoln had long been political rivals, his respect for the man - and the office that he held - overcame any bad feelings he might have had.

After the bombardment of Fort Sumter, Lincoln decided to proclaim a state of rebellion and call for 75,000 troops to suppress it. Douglas looked over the proclamation before it was issued and endorsed it completely. He suggested only one change: Lincoln should call for 200,000 troops, not just 75,000. "You do not know the dishonest purposes of those men as well as I do," he said. He then left on a mission to the border states to raise spirits for Union support, appearing in Virginia, Ohio, and Illinois

It was during this trip that Douglas was infected with typhoid fever, and he died in Chicago on June 3, 1861. He was only 48 years old, and his death left a terrible void in American history. Although condemned today for his support of slavery, Douglas was in the unique position of supporting the Union while also understanding the South.

I have to wonder if the Civil War would have lasted as long as it did - ending with Lincoln's assassination - if Douglas had lived to perhaps broker an earlier peace.

We will never know.

Abraham Lincoln worked hard to win the Senate seat from Stephen Douglas. He traveled, gave speeches, studied his notes, and astounded audiences with his eloquence and intelligence. Oddly, though, on September 14, 1858, the night before the third debate, Lincoln spent it with a reporter from Chicago, gazing up at the night sky. According to Horace White from the *Chicago Press and Tribune*, the two men sat on the porch of the hotel where Lincoln was staying and watched a comet cross the sky. White wrote, "Mr. Lincoln greatly admired the strange visitor and he and I sat for an hour or more in front of the hotel looking at it."

In another part of Illinois that night, a prairie preacher told his congregation that the comet was a divine sign. As he looked out at the crowd, gathered for a revival, he said, "The Lord has opened the roof of Heaven so you can see what's coming... Under the stars air begins to shift and wonder. Destruction will overtake those on the wrong side of this fight."

He then concluded his sermon with a prophecy: "He shall send them a savior, and a great one, and he shall deliver them... Ask yourself who it is that's crying for deliverance? There ain't but one people crying for deliverance and they are the slaves down in Egypt."

In 1858, Lincoln was only starting to emerge on the national scene, but the arrival of the comet made some connect it to the great issues of the day. The preacher's prophecy of freedom for the slaves was made without knowing that Lincoln already believed that some great task awaited him.

Lincoln's own thoughts about this comet were not recorded, but he was clearly interested in it and knew that, throughout recorded history, the arrival of such a celestial event was believed to usher in a period of famine, death, and war. The sun, moon, and stars had always been consulted to guide men's destinies - to predict peace and war, planting and the harvest, fair weather and foul, and every kind of human endeavor.

But only the comet had been consistently taken as a bad omen.

The advent of Christianity did nothing to allay people's fears about omens in the sky. Constantine the Great, the first Christian emperor, died soon after the appearance of a comet in the sky. One Pope event went as far as to excommunicate a comet that appeared at the time that Constantinople fell to the Turks.

Three years after the comet that Lincoln observed from a hotel porch in Northern Illinois, another "bad star" appeared in the night sky. It was seen first in Australia on May 13, 1861, crossing into the northern hemisphere around the end of June. It came to be known as the "War Comet."

Word spread of the ominous portent in both the north and the south. Given the state of the country at that time, it was widely observed and written about. Union propaganda used the comet as a sign that the rebellion was going to be repressed. One image depicted Lincoln as the "Star of the North" hurtling through the sky like a comet. Another image portrayed General Winfield Scott descending from the heavens with the caption: "About this time you will hear thunder."

The comet certainly seemed to be a bad omen. The southern states were already in open rebellion and both sides were busy preparing for war.

In Washington, Lincoln's government seemed isolated from the rest of the country. Virginia was firmly part of the Confederacy and Maryland teetered on the edge of secession. If Maryland fell, the nation's capital would be completely cut off. Even within the city of

Washington, the residents were of dubious loyalty. When Lincoln was inaugurated, General Winfield Scott made sure there were sharpshooters on every roof and a battery of artillery was placed to guard the new President's route to the inauguration.

One person who was aware of events inside the White House at that time was Julia Taft. Her father was Horatio Taft, a Democrat who was nonetheless loyal to Lincoln and the Union cause. Julia's younger brothers were about the same age as Tad and Willie Lincoln, so they were often invited to play at the White House.

Mary never had daughters of her own and the teenage Julia soon became her favorite guest. Julia's recollections of her visits to the White House are just part of the unique chronicles that are not a part of official or mainstream history. This is especially true of certain uncanny incidents and supernatural beliefs from inside the Lincoln White House.

The "War Comet" that began appearing in the skies in 1861 was seen as a dire omen of things to come.

Julia took note of the "War Comet's" arrival. She wrote that, "While fear of an attack thus held the city in its grasp, the Negroes cowered under the great War Comet blazing in the sky."

A neighbor of the Tafts - a family named Woodward - owned an elderly slave name Oola. The other servants in the neighborhood were terrified of the old woman and believed she could "conjure spells." Even as the comet blazed in the night sky, Julia and her brothers dared to have their fortunes told by Oola. Julia recalled it as a "terrifying yet fascinating experience."

But then Julia heard more than she had bargained for from the old woman. She told Julia that a war was coming between the North and the South and the North was going to take a sword and "cut the South's heart out." She also added something that sent a chill down the young woman's spine - that if Lincoln raised the sword, he would perish by it."

Julia told the Lincolns about her experience and about Oola's prophecy concerning the "War Comet," carefully leaving out the part about the president's death. Mary laughed off the tale, Julia later said, but the President "seemed strangely impressed" by it. He stated that he hoped that the prophecy wasn't true, adding, "I hope it won't come to that."

A few evenings later, Julia was back at the White House and saw Lincoln looking out the window, intently studying the comet in the sky. He was apparently still thinking over the words that Julia had passed on to him - and he may have been thinking of the woman that he had met so many years ago in New Orleans who had told him of his role in freeing the slaves.

Lincoln didn't need a prophet to tell him what the "War Comet" meant. War and death were already on the minds of everyone who gazed up into the sky that summer, but for Lincoln, the old woman had just confirmed something he already knew.

War, devastation, and death - perhaps his own - were coming. It was his destiny to play a role in them.

5. THE FACE IN THE MIRROR
Lincoln and the Presidency

Lincoln's loss to Stephen Douglas for the U.S. Senate seat in 1858 was the best possible outcome for the country - and for Lincoln himself. Political analysts on both sides of the aisle had watched the race closely and saw how it had galvanized the people of Illinois and drew interest from all over the country. Republicans began to favor Lincoln as their choice for President in 1860.

He began traveling across the country with a small delegation of Illinois Republicans, making his name known and becoming a recognizable entity. However, it was at home in Illinois where he earned his first presidential nomination.

In 1860, Decatur was chosen as the site of the Illinois State Convention for the Republican Party. The convention attracted more than 700 delegates to the city, along with party leaders, candidates, newspaper reporters, and scores of interested citizens. There was some question, especially in Chicago, as to whether Decatur could actually handle a convention of such size. Since the city was served by two railroads at the time, and had many hotels, the biggest problem seemed to be the lack of a hall in which to hold the gathering.

A citizens' committee was soon formed and began planning a hall for the event. DeWitt C. Shockley, a leading contractor, was given the task and began immediate plans for a convention hall or "Wigwam." It was an antebellum custom to call a political campaign headquarters a Wigwam and this one was no exception.

Richard J. Oglesby – Lincoln supporter and future Illinois governor – was instrumental in getting Lincoln the presidential nomination in Decatur

The hall was built along South Park Street, occupying not only the street but vacant lots on each side of it. Plans called for a structure that was 100-feet wide and 70-feet deep but there was not enough lumber to complete it. Enough wood was found for the framework, the support pillars, and roof stringers but that was all. Richard J. Oglesby, a Lincoln supporter and future Illinois governor, rented a circus tent that provided a covering for the roof and walls for three sides. A platform was built at the back wall and planks were laid out to serve as seating. Seats for the delegates were arranged by congressional districts and signs identified the individual counties.

The convention had been called to nominate Republican Party candidates for state office in the November 1860 election. However, the most important and historic event to occur was officially unscheduled -- although it was secretly the agenda of Oglesby and his close associates.

The convention began on the morning of May 9. Lincoln had arrived in Decatur the day before, accompanied by two delegates and friends from Sangamon County, John Moses and N.M. Knapp. They were unable to find lodgings at the Macon House, where they usually stayed, but managed to find a room at the Junction House, the railroad depot hotel, that all three of them were forced to share.

The convention began in a routine fashion with Judge John A. Palmer of Macon County as the temporary chairman. He called out the roll of the delegates and after that, the convention adjourned for dinner. When it reconvened at 2:00 p.m., Joseph Gillespie of Madison County was elected as the permanent chairman. He was escorted to the platform and his acceptance speech drew the standard round of applause.

Then, Richard Oglesby, who was not a delegate, rose from his seat and addressed the chair, "I am informed that a distinguished citizen of Illinois, and one whom Illinois will ever to delight to honor, is present; and I wish to move that this body invite him to a seat on the stand ... Abraham Lincoln."

Lincoln was reported to have been sitting on his heels just inside the entrance to the Wigwam, which was jammed with more than 3,000 people while another 1,000 or so stood outside. Ward Hill Lamon reported, "Not a shout, but a roar of applause, long and deep, shook every board and joist of the Wigwam."

The motion was seconded and approved, and Lincoln was "seized and jerked to his feet," Lamon wrote. An effort was made to "jam him through the crowd" and that failing, the six foot, four-inch Lincoln was passed over the heads and shoulders of the crowd where, after acknowledging the cheers of the audience, he took a seat.

After that came a call for nominations for governor and an informal ballot. But as the convention prepared for a formal ballot a short time later, Oglesby rose again and addressed the chair. He announced that an old Democrat desired to contribute to the proceedings and into the tent walked Lincoln's cousin, John Hanks, and another man, Isaac Jennings. The men carried two wooden rails between them with a banner stretched between the rails that read:

Abraham Lincoln, the Rail Candidate for President in 1860. Two rails from a lot of 3,000 made in 1830 by Thos. Hanks and Abe Lincoln, whose father was the first pioneer of Macon County.

The banner contained two errors in that it was John, not Thomas Hanks, who split the rails and that Thomas Lincoln was certainly not the first pioneer in the county, but no one seemed to care.

The rails and banner were met with shouts of approval and thunderous applause. The roof was literally "cheered off the building" as men threw hats, canes, and books into the air and then jumped and screamed with wild abandon. They howled until part of the canvas awning over the platform fell onto their heads, nearly wrecking the Wigwam. The enthusiastic response to Lincoln's candidacy would only be matched by the reception that the young lawyer received in Chicago a few weeks later, when he earned the nomination for president by the entire party.

Ironically, Lincoln was not even in the Wigwam at the time of the "rail-splitter" demonstration. He had gone over to Jim Peake's jewelry store to take a nap and had to be awakened and rushed back to the site. When he arrived, he spoke briefly to the still cheering crowd.

Although some believe that the convention's endorsement of Lincoln as the Republican Party's presidential nominee came immediately after the "rail-splitter" furor, it really did not come until the following day, after Richard Yates, who had been nominated as governor, told the convention that he had a "preference" for Lincoln and would support him at the national convention in Chicago.

This launched Lincoln's "rail-splitter" candidacy for President in 1860.

But there was still a battle ahead of him. Lincoln may have won the nomination by the Republicans of Illinois, but he had to face the national convention in Chicago the following week. Of course, he prevailed but the nomination almost didn't happen and there are many who are still pondering the mystery of how a minor contender in the presidential race managed such a sweeping victory in the convention's third ballot.

It's a mystery that will never be solved, but perhaps we can once again accept that it was Lincoln's destiny to lead the country through the war.

The convention was held at Chicago's Wigwam, a convention and meeting hall that was located at Lake Street and what is now Wacker Drive, near the Chicago River. This location had previously been the site of the Sauganash Hotel, the first hotel in the city. The two-story building was a temporary, wooden structure, built by Chicago business leaders to attract the convention. It was constructed to hold between 10,000 and 20,000 attendees.

Lincoln's supporters - who were portraying him accurately as an honest, upstanding, backwoods rail-splitter - were thrilled that the convention was held in Chicago. The city was only two decades past being little more than a frontier town and Lincoln had many friends and most of the newspaper support on the Illinois prairie.

The 1860 event was only the second national convention held by the Republicans, and for the first time, they believed they had a chance

The Chicago Wigwam as it looked in 1860

to put one of their candidates in the White House. The Democratic Party, which dominated politics for years, was split over the issue of extending slavery into the territories and this division gave the Republicans hope.

Before Chicago, the favorite to win the nomination was New York Senator William H. Seward. His supporters and delegates were so certain of his victory that they focused more on his choice of a running mate than on the actual nomination. That turned out to be a costly mistake.

The convention opened early on the morning of Wednesday, May 16. Over 10,000 people packed into the Wigwam while another reported 20,000 lingered outside. Four years earlier, at the first Republican convention in Philadelphia, the party had drawn less than 4,000 people.

The meeting was called to order and began with a stirring address by David Wilmot of Pennsylvania. The remainder of the day was spent electing a chairman and constructing a platform that was modified and adopted the following day. The first vote was scheduled for Thursday evening. Many expected Seward to be chosen by a landslide, so a chorus of groans greeted Chairman George Ashmun when he announced that the printers had failed to deliver the tally sheets in time. With no vote possible, a motion was raised and seconded to adjourn until Friday.

David Davis, Lincoln's friend and campaign manager

(Below) Ward Hill Lamon

Lincoln's campaign manager, David Davis, was thrilled. He and his compatriots - including Ward Lamon, William Herndon, and Stephen T. Logan - saw the delay as a sign from God. Led by Lamon, scores of Lincoln's friends began scrawling the names of convention officers on admission tickets while another supporter, Norman B. Judd, a railroad attorney, arranged for special trains to bring more Lincoln backers to Chicago.

While Lincoln's men were working feverishly behind the scenes, William Seward's followers publicly declaring their man the winner and they even hired a brass band to lead the Seward supporters from their hotel to the Wigwam on Friday morning. But when they got there, they found the hall was so crowded that few people other than official delegates could find seats.

The bogus tickets that Lamon, Herndon, and Logan had created had been handed out to those arriving in the city by train and now the hall was packed with Lincoln supporters.

The first roll call of state delegations gave Seward 173 votes, but he needed to have 236 to win. Lincoln followed behind him with 102 votes and Simon Cameron of Pennsylvania, Salmon P.

Chase of Ohio, and Edward Bates of Missouri each received about 50 votes each.

Recognizing that Pennsylvania would be crucial in winning the nomination, David Davis arranged for the delegates from that state to be seated between those from Illinois and Indiana, who strongly backed Lincoln. He then convinced the delegates from Pennsylvania that if Seward won the nomination, the party would lose the election. Simon Cameron agreed and withdrew from consideration.

Lincoln's opponent Salmon P. Chase would go on to serve as his Secretary of the Treasury

A second roll call was held and when the ballots were tallied, they offered a stunning surprise - especially to the Seward supporters. Their candidate had only gained 11 additional votes, but Lincoln's count had increased by 79. That left Salmon Chase in third place with 42 votes.

Lincoln operatives had been approaching delegates from every state and used a deceptively simple strategy with them. Instead of asking for votes on the first ballot, they persuaded as many of them as possible to make Lincoln their second choice.

They also stressed the differences between Lincoln and Seward. Lincoln had been very guarded in his campaign at that point, carefully not offending anyone. Seward, though, had made his position clear on most national issues. He was the only nationally-known Republican who had allegedly praised the attack on Harper's Ferry, Virginia, by the radical abolitionist John Brown and hinted at a civil war by warning that an "irrepressible conflict" seemed to be coming because of slavery.

This was not what most Republicans wanted to hear at that point. In 1860, actual abolitionists in the north were a small but vocal minority and many feared they would push the country into war. Lincoln knew this, and while on record as opposing the extension of slavery into the territories, he admitted that slavery was lawful where it now existed and should not be challenged. It would, he believed, die out on its own.

It was plain that there was a sharp contrast between the familiar candidate with the controversial views and the little-known rival who was not as well-known nor as eager to enter a war, but this was not enough to allow Lincoln to win on just those merits. There was more work that needed to be done.

Lincoln's supporters seemed willing to promise almost anything to those who would back him - something that worried Lincoln. He sent a telegram to Davis from Springfield that told him to make no deals. "Make no contracts that bind me," he wrote. Davis used the telegram to show those who hesitated in backing Lincoln that the candidate was not flagrantly offering positions in his administration -- unless someone really deserved it, of course. And Davis spent a lot of time during the second day of the convention persuading delegates who deserved a seat at the table to abandon their candidates for positions in Lincoln's cabinet.

Or those are the stories, at least. Some historians will insist that nothing untoward happened in the "smoke-filled rooms" in Chicago during the convention. No promises were made, no positions were guaranteed - it was all aboveboard. And perhaps it was, but there's no argument that it's almost impossible to explain how Seward lost four votes in the third ballot and Lincoln gained 53. The little-known candidate was now just two votes short of the nomination.

The interior of the Wigwam became deafening with shouts, cries, and laughter. As soon as he could be heard above the commotion, David K. Carter of Ohio jumped up and shouted that five of the delegates from his state wanted to switch their votes to Lincoln. Amidst the noise, other states began to call for Lincoln. After the 466 votes had been cast, Lincoln had 364 of them - 128 more than he needed to win.

How did Lincoln manage such a sweeping victory? Were votes traded for positions in Washington? There's nothing documented that says either way. Charles H. Ray, a journalist in Lincoln's inner circle, later said that he heard campaigners promising delegates from Indiana and Pennsylvania anything they asked for. Carter of Ohio, who started the third-ballot uprising, was said to have been promised a cabinet position and while rumors abound, nothing unseemly has ever been proven.

It is clear, however, that many of those who stepped aside for Lincoln, or worked for him behind the scenes, were chosen for important posts in his administration. William H. Seward became Secretary of State. Salmon Chase ran the Treasury Department. The fourth contender for the nomination, Edward Bates, became Lincoln's Attorney General. David Davis became a federal judge and he was appointed to the U.S. Supreme Court in 1862. Ward Hill Lamon, creator of bogus admission tickets, became Marshal of the District of Columbia. William P. Dole, who was credited with securing the Indiana and Pennsylvania votes, was named Commissioner of Indian Affairs.

Edward Bates, Lincoln's Attorney General

And the list went on.

The news of Lincoln's nomination was greeted with skepticism in many parts of the country, but not in Springfield. When the news reached the candidate's hometown, he was given a 100-gun salute. That evening, a huge crowd gathered at Lincoln's home and he spoke to them from the front steps and then invited as many of them into the house as he could crowd inside.

But outside of Illinois, Lincoln was not viewed as warmly. Many saw him as nothing more than a "country lawyer" and a "huckster." Even abolitionists, who should have seen Lincoln as their best hope, bemoaned the fact that he was a backwoodsman from Illinois and was "half-horse, half-alligator."

By later that summer, the nation's attention was focused on Springfield. Politicians from all over the country were traveling there to size Lincoln up. He had become a very real threat to southern politicians because if Lincoln won the election, they knew that slavery could be abolished, which meant the end to their treasured way of life. But Lincoln met with all of them, discussed the issues, and offered them hospitality in his home.

Springfield, Illinois around 1860

Unlike Stephen Douglas, who traveled the country during his campaign, Lincoln followed the political custom of the day and allowed others to go out and speak on his behalf. His advisors told him that they wanted him to stay home and focus on the issues. In reality, though, they wanted to keep him out of the public eye as much as possible. Republican leaders had great faith in Lincoln as a candidate but were hesitant about letting the public get a look at his lanky frame in his wrinkled suits, frumpy hat, and sweat-stained shirts. He did not, they decided, look like a future president, even though he had all the knowledge, skills, and intelligence to be one.

The political delegations, well-wishers, and critics gave Springfield a carnival-like atmosphere that summer, highlighted by a huge Republican rally at the fairgrounds on the hottest day of the year. A parade that was part of the celebration took more than eight hours to pass the Lincoln home and it ended with a picnic, where tubs of lemonade, liquor, and several entire roasted steers awaited the revelers.

It was a day like no other in the history of the city and a preview of the excitement that would come to the city in November.

November 6, 1860 - Election Day - dawned with rousing cannon blasts, music, and excitement in the streets of Springfield and across the country. Unlike today, Election Day was considered a holiday in the nineteenth century. Men took the day off work, children were usually allowed to stay home from school, and it was a celebration of drinking, eating, and, of course, voting at the local polling place.

Lincoln spent most of the day in his office with a few friends. Around 3:00 p.m., he walked over to the polling place at the courthouse, where a throng of people were congregating. Most of them were supporters and rushed to greet him when he was spotted in the crowd. Lincoln shook hands and accepted warm wishes as he pushed through those milling about and entered the courthouse. Inside, he cut his own name off the ballot and then voted straight along the party line.

After the polls closed, Lincoln left his office and joined his friends at the telegraph office. Thanks to the telegraph, news traveled faster than it ever had before. Election returns used to take weeks but now results could be sent out all over the nation in a matter or hours. Lincoln stayed at the telegraph office until it closed at midnight. Mary came to fetch him, and they went to a supper in his honor and then went home.

By the next morning, election returns were pouring in from all over the country. District by district, state by state, the news of who led in the votes changed every hour. Lincoln spent most of the day at the telegraph office - which had become his unofficial campaign headquarters - closely following the race.

As state after state fell in line behind Lincoln, Lincoln's friends and supporters cheered, drawing large crowds around the office. Finally, by 4:45 p.m., it was clear that Abraham Lincoln has been elected President of the United States. Springfield residents cheered and guns were fired in celebration throughout the night.

Lincoln won the day but, by today's standards, he didn't fare well in the popular vote -- receiving just 40-percent of votes cast. However, there were three other candidates in the race, including Stephen Douglas. Splitting the race in four directions, Lincoln received the majority of the popular vote and won in the Electoral College.

A celebration outside the Lincoln home after the 1860 Election

Of course, this was mostly in the North. He had no support at all in southern states. The outgoing president had a cabinet filled with secessionists. Southern politicians were spewing in angry rhetoric in the U.S. Senate and the House and stirring up passions across the south.

On Election Day, Lincoln had been hanged in effigy in Florida.

From the telegraph office, Lincoln went to the House Chambers at the State Capitol, where he made a brief statement announcing victory. He told the crowd, "We expected it would be so, and so it is."

Although Lincoln seemed outwardly calm and relaxed, the two days of following election returns, combined with months of campaigning and preparing, finally took their toll on him. He managed to return home late in the evening, although telegraphs of congratulations were still being wired to the office.

Exhausted, he went into his bedroom for some much-needed rest and collapsed onto a settee. Near the couch was a large bureau with a mirror on it and Lincoln stared for a moment at his reflection in the glass. His face appeared angular, thin, and tired. Several of his friends suggested that he grow a beard, which would hide the narrowness of his face and give him a more "presidential" appearance. Lincoln pondered this for a moment and then experienced what he would come to believe was a prophetic vision.

In the mirror, he saw two separate, distinct versions of his face. The tip of one nose was about three inches away from the tip of the other one.

Startled by the strange sight, Lincoln got up and walked over to inspect the mirror. When he got up, the two faces vanished, and he was left with an ordinary reflection of his lanky frame and tired features.

Assuming he imagined the odd sight, he settled back onto the couch, only to see the vision return, reflecting back at him in the mirror. He said it was "plainer, if possible, than before."

This time, Lincoln observes that one of the faces is much paler than the other - "five shades paler," he said. It had the coloring of death.

Again, though, as Lincoln got up from the couch, "the thing" disappeared. Unable to rest with this disturbing vision bothering him, he left his bedroom and found rest elsewhere. He dismissed the whole thing and credited the hallucination to the excitement of the day and his lack of sleep.

For a time, the weird incident is pushed out of Lincoln's mind by the post-election frenzy. He forgot about the vision "nearly, but not quite." He later confessed that "the thing" would appear again in the days that followed and give him "a little pang, as though something uncomfortable had happened."

Clearly, though, the incident bothered Lincoln more than he admitted since he mentioned it to at least four other people in the days that followed. While all three of those people differed on particulars in their recounting of the incident, there is no doubt that Lincoln believed the vision to be real - and that it made a profound impression on him.

The fourth person that Lincoln told about the incident was, of course, Mary. Soon after it occurred, he described the "illusion" to her.

After nearly two decades of marriage, Mary was very aware that her husband had prophetic visions and dreams, and she became quite concerned.

Lincoln attempted to conjure up the vision again in the days that followed. The faces always returned to him and while Mary never saw them, she believed her husband when he said that he did. She also believed she knew the significance of the vision. The healthy face was her husband's "real" face and indicated that he would serve his first term as President. The pale, ghostly image of the second face, however was a sign that he would be elected to a second term --- but would not live to see its conclusion.

Lincoln's rational side wanted to believe the double image was merely an optical illusion, an imperfection in the glass. However, as one friend said, "the flavor of superstition which hangs about every man's composition made him wish he had never seen it." Like Mary, several of those close to Lincoln believed "the thing" was a warning of death.

In the many years since Lincoln's vision, debunkers have written off the incident as nothing more than Lincoln's exhaustion, his imagination, or a flaw in the glass of the mirror. These were all the same things that Lincoln himself said about the vision - at first, anyway. But it's obvious that he was clearly disturbed by the experience. If he really believed it was easily explained away, it's doubtful that he would remember a "mere trick of the mirror" four years later. It came back to haunt him during the turbulent years of the war.

The First Lady's interpretation of the incident was very much in keeping with Lincoln's own previous premonitions of his future fate. Just a few days before the election, he spoke to some friends as they were discussing the possibilities of a civil war in the country. "Gentlemen," he said to them, "you may be surprised and think it strange, but when the doctor here was describing a war, I distinctly saw myself, in second sight, bearing an important part in that strife."

That the incident of the double image actually happened to Lincoln is unquestionable. Whether it was a trick of the glass or a true premonition remains in question, but the fact that Mary's interpretation of the uncanny event eventually proved true is one more link in a chain of strange circumstances in Lincoln's life.

No matter what we might believe about what happened in Lincoln's home in Springfield in November 1860, there is no arguing with Ward Hill Lamon's description of the event as "an ominous incident of mysterious character."

6. PERILOUS JOURNEY
Mr. Lincoln Goes to Washington

Lincoln spent the remainder of the year in Springfield, growing a beard and preparing for the move to Washington. As the new year approached, he found himself beleaguered by the sheer volume of mail that was landing on his desk. On one occasion, he was seen at the post office filling a "good-sized market basket" with the latest batch of letters and then carefully navigating his way along icy streets back to his office. Soon, Lincoln hired John Nicolay, a bookish young Bavarian immigrant as his private secretary.

John found himself immediately troubled by the growing number of threats and hate letters that crossed Lincoln's desk. He later wrote, "His mail infested with brutal and vulgar menace, and warnings of all sorts came to him from zealous or nervous friends. But he had himself so sane a mind, and a heart so kindly, even to his enemies, that it was hard for him to believe in political hatred so deadly as to lead to murder." To John Nicolay, though, it was clear that not all warnings could be easily brushed aside.

Major David Hunter wrote the president-elect from Fort Leavenworth, warning him of several young Virginians who had taken a solemn oath to assassinate him after he was elected president. There was also talk in Kentucky of tarring and feathering him and then setting him on fire so that he could lead a torchlight procession. A local clergyman visited Lincoln three times to warn him about murderous plots that he imagined the Jesuits were creating against him.

Some of the warnings were even stranger.

A woman from Tennessee wrote to Lincoln about a dream that she had revealing how he could prevent a civil war. On December 11, 1860, an anonymous letter arrived from Cleveland that warned Lincoln of a plot to poison him when he arrived in Washington. The letter writer had learned of the conspiracy from a young girl who was a somnambulist and clairvoyant. During a trance, she had informed him of the scheme and requested that he pass on the information to Lincoln.

Lincoln was concerned by these letters and by the outpouring of hatred -- especially from the southern states -- but refused to let anyone know he was worried. Every afternoon, he met people in an office at the State Capitol building, where he talked and laughed and let his friends and supporters know that he was one of them. This continued day after day, but when the crowds never seemed to stop coming, John Nicolay cut down the visits to only an hour or so each day. It wouldn't serve anyone to have Lincoln exhausted before he was even sworn into office.

In January 1861, Mary went east to New York. A delay in her travel plans meant that she didn't make it back to Springfield until the night before Lincoln's departure. By this time, their belongings had been packed away and their steamer trunks had been moved to the Cherney House, a local hotel, before being loaded onto the train to Washington.

Two weeks earlier, Lincoln had traveled to Charleston, Illinois, to say goodbye to his elderly stepmother, Sarah. After bidding farewell to the Springfield friends who would not be accompanying them to Washington, Lincoln's plans were complete.

He bid goodbye to the city where he'd made his home on a rainy morning on February 11, 1861. Lincoln rode alone in a carriage to the train station. Mary and the boys would meet him in Indianapolis. Lincoln requested that there be no public demonstration during his departure, but several hundred friends and well-wishers lined the streets near the station anyway.

Lincoln knotted a rope around his traveling cases and when they were bundled, he quickly scrawled an address on the tag --"A. Lincoln, White House, Washington, D.C."

At 8:00 a.m., the train bells sounded. The train was leaving. Lincoln faced the crowd from the rear platform. "My friends," he said, "no one, not in my situation, can appreciate my feeling of sadness at this parting. To this place, and the kindness of these people, I owe everything...I now leave, not knowing when or whether I may return, to a task before me greater than that which rested upon Washington."

His face was filled with emotion as he waved and then boarded the train. He didn't look back as it steamed away to the east.

He would never see his adopted hometown again.

Abraham Lincoln was a simple, plain-spoken man. He was honest and expected others to be honest with him. He had little interest in fancy dinners, parades in his honor, or for anyone to make a fuss over him. So, it's likely that he never realized that his dislike of "ostentatious display and empty pageantry" - and refusal to accept a military escort to Washington - had created a logistical and security nightmare to the men who wanted to make sure that he got their safely.

Samuel Morse Felton, the president of the Philadelphia, Wilmington & Baltimore Railroad, was one of those men - and he believed the president-elect had failed to grasp the seriousness of the situation he was in. Rumors had reached Felton that secessionists were building a "deep-laid conspiracy to capture Washington, destroy all the avenues leading to it from the North, East, and West, and thus prevent the inauguration of Mr. Lincoln in the Capitol of the country."

Felton's railroad formed a crucial link between Washington and the north and the threat against Lincoln was also a threat to the railroad that he had been building for the better part of his life. He became determined to investigate the matter and realized that he needed an independent operative who had worked for the railroads before - Allan Pinkerton. He dashed off a letter at the end of January and it was received in Chicago just two weeks before Lincoln departed Springfield.

Pinkerton was a Scottish immigrant who had started out as a cooper making barrels on the Illinois prairie until he helped his neighbors snare a ring of counterfeiters and decided he had a knack for battling crime. The fearless, quick-witted man went on to serve as the first official detective for the city of Chicago and earned a reputation as incorruptible - which was saying a lot in Chicago. By the time Felton wrote to him, the 41-year-old was running the Pinkerton

National Detective Agency and serving major clients across the country, including the Illinois Central Railroad.

He didn't hesitate when Felton's letter reached him. He immediately left for Philadelphia and was in Felton's office two days later. The railroad man outlined his concerns and, shocked by what he was hearing, Pinkerton listened in silence. He later wrote that Felton's pleas for help, "aroused me to a realization of the danger that threatened the country, and I determined to render whatever assistance was in my power."

Allan Pinkerton

At this point, Felton was mostly worried about his railroad. Neither man, at this early stage, considered the possibility of violence against Lincoln. They realized that secessionists wanted to prevent the inauguration, but they had not grasped, as Felton later wrote, that if the plan succeeded, Lincoln's life would "fall a sacrifice to the attempt."

At this point, the inauguration was only six weeks away, which meant that an attack on the railroad could come at any time. Pinkerton departed immediately for Baltimore, which he believed was "the seat of danger." Virtually any route that Lincoln chose between Springfield and Washington would pass through the city.

Pinkerton didn't go to Baltimore alone. He took with him a crew of his best agents, including a recent recruit named Harry Davies. The unassuming young man had a razor-sharp mind, spoke many languages, and could swiftly resolve any problem that was thrown at him. Best of all, for Pinkerton's needs in this case, he had traveled widely throughout the south, had lived in New Orleans, and had a deep knowledge of southern customs and prejudices. He would provide insight into their opponents for Pinkerton.

The arrived in early February and took rooms at a boarding house near the Camden Street train station. Once settled, the agents spread out across the city, mixing with locals in saloons, hotels, and restaurants,

Barnum's Hotel in Baltimore, where Harry Davies went undercover to find the extremists who wanted to stop Lincoln's inauguration

gathering evidence as they went. They soon discovered there was bitter opposition to Lincoln's inauguration in the city and Pinkerton realized that was a great danger to the president than he first assumed.

Pinkerton created a cover identity for himself as a newly arrived southern stockbroker named John Hutchinson. This gave him the opportunity to get acquainted with Baltimore's businessmen, whose interest in cotton and other southern commodities spoke volumes about their political leanings. In order to be convincing, he hired a suite of offices in a building at 44 South Street.

Harry Davies assumed the character of an anti-Union extremist who was also new to the city from New Orleans. He booked a room at Barnum's, the best hotel in the city, and made it known that he was willing to pledge his loyalty and his pocketbook to southern interests.

Before Lincoln had departed from Springfield, he had offered the details of his itinerary to the press. He made it clear that he would travel to Washington in an "open and public" fashion, with stops along the way to greet the public. His route would cover 2,000 miles and he planned to arrive in Baltimore on the afternoon of Saturday, February 23. His train would arrive at the Calvert Street Station and his next train would leave from the Camden Street Station about two hours later. Pinkerton noted with concern that the "distance between the two stations is a little over a mile."

After the travel announcement, Lincoln's imminent arrival became the hottest news in Baltimore. Of all the stops on the president-elect's itinerary, Baltimore was the only city that allowed slavery within its borders, aside from Washington itself. There was a distinct possibility that Maryland might vote to secede from the Union before Lincoln arrived. Pinkerton heard the talk and grew increasingly worried for Lincoln's life. "No man's life was safe in the hands of those men," he later wrote.

From the moment his train left Springfield, anyone who wished Lincoln harm only needed to follow the itinerary that had been provided to the press. It gave the location of the train - and Lincoln - sometimes down to the minute.

To make matters worse, Lincoln was still receiving daily threats on his life - promising death by knife, bullet, poison, and, in one odd note, by spider-filling dumpling.

In Baltimore, Davies set to work building a friendship with a young man named Otis Hillard, a heavy drinker who liked to hang around at Barnum's. Hillard was a rabid secessionist. He always wore a glad badge stamped with a palmetto, the symbol of South Carolina's secession. He had also recently signed on with the Palmetto Guards, one of several secret military organizations in Baltimore.

Davies told his new friend that he had come to Baltimore on business but, as much as he could, he insinuated that he was far more interested in matters of "rebeldom." The two young men soon became inseparable.

On February 12 - the day after Lincoln left Springfield -- a significant break occurred for Pinkerton and Davies. He had been talking to Hillard until the early morning hours and Hillard had asked Davies if he had "seen a statement of Lincoln's route to Washington City." This got Davies' attention. Hillard spent most of his time drunkenly bragging and this was the first hard evidence that Davies had heard that pointed to anyone wanting to stop the inauguration, or worse, to cause harm to Lincoln.

Hillard explained a coded system that would allow Lincoln's train to be tracked from stop to stop, even if telegraph communications were being monitored for suspicious activity. The codes, he said, were only a small part of the bigger plan. Hillard told him grimly that he was unable to tell him anything else and cautioned Davies to say nothing of what he had shared with him.

Pinkerton was also making headway. He had become friendly with a businessman named James H. Luckett, who occupied the office next to his. Pinkerton managed to steer their conversation toward Lincoln's impending passage through Baltimore and Luckett turned cautious. He told Pinkerton, "He may pass through quietly, but I doubt it."

Seizing an opportunity, the detective pulled out his wallet and counted out $25 with a dramatic flourish. He said that he had no doubt that money was needed for a patriotic cause and asked that his donation be used "in the best manner possible for Southern rights." Pinkerton also offered the man some advice. He warned him to be "cautious in talking with outsiders." You might never know, Pinkerton said, when Northern agents might be listening.

The plan worked. Luckett took the advice - along with the money - as proof that his new friend was trustworthy. He told Pinkerton that only a few men, part of a secret group, knew the full extent of the plans that had been made to stop the inauguration. He suggested that Pinkerton go with him to meet the "leading man" of the organization, Captain Cypriano Ferrandini.

The name was familiar to Pinkerton. He knew him as an Italian immigrant who worked as a barber in a shop in the basement of Barnum's. A few days earlier, Hillard had brought Davies to the barber shop to also meet the man.

Luckett explained that Ferrandini had "a plan fixed to prevent Lincoln from passing through Baltimore." He would see to it that Lincoln would never reach Washington - and never become president.

The plan was to kill him.

Pinkerton was stunned. He had come to Baltimore to protect Samuel Felton's railroad but now - with Lincoln's train already en route - he had to consider the possibility that it was Lincoln himself that was the target.

He needed to get a warning to Lincoln. Pinkerton knew the best way to do it was through his acquaintance, Norman Judd, the former Illinois State Senator who had helped Lincoln get elected. Pinkerton knew that Judd was now aboard Lincoln's train, so he fired off a terse telegram to him:

I have a message of importance for you. Where can it reach you by special messenger?

Allan Pinkerton

Later that evening, Pinkerton went to meet James Luckett at Barr's Saloon, where he planned to introduce him to Captain Ferrandini. Luckett presented the detective as a resident of Georgia and an "earnest worker in the cause of secession, whose sympathy and discretion could be implicitly relied upon."

Luckett's introduction had the desired effect on the Italian. Ferrandini warmed to the detective immediately and after ordering drinks and cigars, they moved to a quiet corner to talk. Right away, Ferrandini announced that he had been outraged by the election of Lincoln and believed the south was justified with their efforts to keep Lincoln from the presidency.

Pinkerton had seen many charlatans in his time, but he believed Ferrandini was the real thing - his angry rhetoric and harsh resolve made him a dangerous adversary. "Never, never shall Lincoln be president," Ferrandini vowed. "He must die–and die he shall."

But Pinkerton was unable to get even an inkling of the man's plans. He was only assured that they were arranged and could not fail.

This was disheartening news to Pinkerton.

It took nearly five days for the clever detective to be able to piece together Ferrandini's plan on his own, using rumors and reports from his operatives. The plan was for a large crowd to meet Lincoln at the Calvert Street depot. Nearby, a disturbance would start that would draw away the police officers that were there on duty. As Pinkerton wrote, "It would be an easy task for a determined man to shoot the President, and, aided by his companions, succeed in making his escape."

Pinkerton was convinced that Otis Hillard was the weak link in Ferrandini's chain of command, and he believed they could use him to uncover the final details of the plot.

On February 18, Davies and Hillard had supper together and Hillard confirmed that his military unit was going to "draw lots to see who would kill Lincoln." If the responsibility was his, he boasted that, "I would do it willingly."

Davies demanded to be taken to the meeting where the choice would be made, insisting that he should have the chance to "immortalize

Captain Cypriano Ferrandini's plot to kill Lincoln in Baltimore was a hastily arranged plan with several weak links that Pinkerton was able to exploit

himself" by murdering Lincoln. Two nights later, Hillard returned to tell Davies that if he would swear an oath of loyalty, he could join Ferrandini's group of "southern patriots" that very night. He was taken to the home of a local secessionist, where he found 20 men waiting for him. Ferrandini instructed Davies to raise his hand and swear allegiance to the cause of southern freedom. He did so and a few moments later, he was embedded with the enemy.

Ferrandini reviewed his plan to divert the police at the Calvert Street station and then led the men in cheers for Lincoln's death. Afterward, they drew lots to see who would "assume the task of liberating the nation of the foul presence of the abolitionist leader." Slips of paper - one of which was marked with a red X - were placed into a wooden chest and then each man drew from the box. To keep the identity of the assassin a secret, the lights were put out and the men were asked to leave the house after drawing their lot.

One by one, the "solemn guardians of the south" filed past the box and withdrew a folded slip of paper. Neither Davis nor Hillard drew the fateful lot. As they went off in search of a drink, Davies told Hillard that he was worried that the man who had been chosen to carry out the attack - whoever he might be - would lose his nerve at the crucial moment.

But Hillard told him that Ferrandini had anticipated this possibility and had confided to him that the wooden box had contained not one, but eight ballots marked with a red X. Each man would believe that he alone was charged with the task of killing Lincoln, and that the southern cause rested solely on his "courage, strength, and devotion." If one or two of the chosen assassins failed to act, there were others to strike the fatal blow.

Later that night, Davies burst into Pinkerton's office with this unsettling news. It was now clear that Pinkerton's period of surveillance and undercover work was over.

As he later wrote, "My time for action had now arrived."

On the morning of February 21, Lincoln departed New York City for the first leg of that day's travel, which would take him to Philadelphia - where Pinkerton was waiting for him. Before he left Baltimore, he had put together a plan of action that he was going to present to the president-elect. He believed that if he could get Lincoln through Baltimore ahead of schedule, the assassins would be unprepared and caught off guard. On February 23 - when Lincoln was supposed to arrive in Baltimore - he would already be safe in Washington.

Pinkerton knew it was a risky plan. Even if Lincoln departed ahead of schedule, he still had to pass through Baltimore. If any hint of a change of plan leaked out, Lincoln's life could be in even greater danger. Instead of traveling with his large group of friends and protectors, he would be relatively alone and exposed, with only one or two men at his side. Secrecy was more important than ever if he wanted to get Lincoln to the capital alive.

But for that, Pinkerton had a secret weapon.

Her name was Kate Warne and he had known her since 1856. The young widow had stunned Pinkerton when she walked into his office one day and asked him to hire her as a detective. At first, he refused to consider exposing a woman to danger in the field, but Kate convinced him that she would be invaluable as an undercover agent. She soon

Pinkerton agent Kate Warne

displayed extraordinary courage, helping to apprehend all kinds of criminals, from killers to train robbers.

When Pinkerton returned to his hotel, the St. Louis, he told Kate to be prepared - he would soon have an important job for her.

Pinkerton sent a message to his friend, Norman Judd, who was staying with the Lincoln party at the Continental Hotel. He arranged a meeting with Judd and railroad president Samuel Felton in his hotel suite that evening. The two men arrived just after 6:45 p.m.

Pinkerton told Judd that if Lincoln followed his current itinerary, he would be reasonably safe while still on board the train. But as soon as he arrived at the Baltimore depot - especially riding through the city in an open carriage - he would be in mortal danger. Pinkerton's next words sounded ominous to Judd, "I do not believe it is possible he or his personal friends could pass through Baltimore in that style alive."

The detective proposed that Lincoln leave Philadelphia that very night, aboard the late train. This would get him through Baltimore unnoticed, before the assassins had completed their plans. Pinkerton believed it was the only way to get Lincoln through the city alive.

But Judd shook his head. "I fear very much that Mr. Lincoln will not accede to this," he said. He explained that Lincoln had a great faith in the goodness of people and didn't believe there would be an outbreak of violence in the country. He still believed that through negotiation, he could convince the secessionists to rejoin the Union.

The only way that Lincoln could be convinced to follow Pinkerton's plan was for the detective to present it to the president-elect himself. There is nothing to suggest that Pinkerton ever expected to meet with Lincoln, nor is it likely - thanks to his passion for secrecy - that he welcomed the idea.

But he would do what had to be done, and since it was now nearly 9:00 p.m., he had barely two hours to act if he was going to get Lincoln onto the 11:00 p.m. train.

Lincoln had already gone to bed by the time the men arrived at the Continental. Regardless, Judd dashed off a note and asked him to come to his room "so soon as convenient on private business of importance." Lincoln arrived a few minutes later and had a kind word of greeting for Pinkerton. The two men had once worked

Norman Judd

together when Lincoln was a lawyer for the Illinois Central Railroad and Pinkerton was its chief of security. "Lincoln liked Pinkerton," Judd later noted, and "had the utmost confidence in him as a gentleman—and a man of sagacity."

The detective began his story, carefully reviewing what he and his agents had uncovered and explained that the men in Baltimore were "ready and willing to die to rid their country of a tyrant, as they considered Lincoln to be." Pinkerton bluntly stated that if the president-elect kept to his published scheduled, "an assault of some kind would be made upon his person with a view to taking his life."

Lincoln listened calmly, with no agitation whatsoever, and when he spoke it was only with feelings of profound regret that these southern sympathizers considered his death necessary to further their cause. He would not, he told Pinkerton, leave that night. He had promised to raise the flag over Independence Hall the next morning and to visit the legislature in Harrisburg in the afternoon. "Any plan that may be adopted that will enable me to fulfill these promises I will accede to, and you can inform me what is concluded upon tomorrow," he told Pinkerton, wished him goodnight, and left the room.

With no other options, Pinkerton immediately set to work on a new plan. He was still working at 8:00 a.m. when he left his suite to meet Judd at the Continental. He was secretive about the details of his new plan, but he made it clear that the broad strokes were still the same - Lincoln would pass through Baltimore ahead of schedule.

Lincoln's train left Philadelphia at 9:30 a.m. and as it neared Harrisburg, Judd told Lincoln that he believed they should tell the other men in the party about the danger that Pinkerton said was waiting for the president-elect in Baltimore. Lincoln agreed. "I reckon they will laugh at us, Judd, but you had better get them together." Pinkerton would have been horrified at the lack of secrecy, but Judd was resolved to explain the matter to Lincoln's inner circle before they sat down for dinner.

They arrived in Harrisburg at 1:30 p.m. Lincoln went to the Jones Hotel with his host, Governor Andrew Curtin, and decided to increase the number of people in on the secret by sharing the threat with Curtin. The governor was a Republican who had forged a close alliance with Lincoln during the presidential campaign and he pledged his full cooperation. He later wrote that Lincoln "seemed pained and surprised that a design to take his life existed." Even so, he remained "very calm, and neither in his conversation or manner exhibited alarm or fear."

Lincoln dined with Governor Curtin and several other prominent Republicans at the Jones House that evening. Around 5:45, Judd stepped into the room and tapped Lincoln on the shoulder. He rose, excused himself - claiming to be tired - and, with Judd and Curtin, left the dining room.

Upstairs in his suite, Lincoln gathered a few articles of clothing, including a new beaver hat that a friend had given him in New York. He put on an old overcoat, stuffed the hat in his pocket, and walked out the back door of the hotel without causing any interest in him. He then put on the soft hat and joined his friends, "without being recognized by strangers, for I was not the same man," he said.

Meanwhile, in front of the hotel, Governor Curtin was creating a distraction to allow Lincoln to slip away. A large crowd had gathered - perhaps hoping to hear one of Lincoln's balcony speeches - but Curtin appeared and began greeting people and suggesting that Lincoln might soon come out and when he did, he told his carriage driver, he was to be taken to the Executive Mansion.

Curtin went back inside, where he was joined by Ward Hill Lamon, Lincoln's friend, and now self-appointed personal bodyguard. Curtin asked him if he was armed and Lamon showed him "a small arsenal of deadly weapons. In addition to a pair of heavy revolvers, he had a slung-shot and brass knuckle and a huge knife nestled under his vest."

Curtin and Lamon quickly joined Lincoln and the others, leaving the throng in front of the hotel craning their necks for a look at Lincoln. Curtin led the group toward the side entrance of the hotel, where a carriage waited. As they made their way toward it, Judd whispered to Lamon, "As soon as Mr. Lincoln is in the carriage, drive off. The crowd must not be allowed to identify him." Lamon nodded, climbed into the carriage first, then helped Lincoln and Curtin inside.

The first part of Pinkerton's plan had gone off without a hitch.

But the gears of Pinkerton's scheme were turning in other places, too. Railroad crews received some unusual orders concerning the 11:00 p.m. train from Philadelphia on the night of February 22. Samuel Felton himself had directed the train's conductor to hold the train at the station until a special courier arrived, who would hand over a vitally important parcel. Under no circumstances was the train to depart without it. Felton told him, "This package must go through to Washington on tonight's train."

The package, though, was a decoy. It was part of an elaborate web of bluffs and tricks that Pinkerton had designed to make his entire plan work correctly. The train had to be delayed and only orders from the railroad's president could make that happen.

They assembled a parcel, wrapped it in heavy paper, and closed it with an impressive wax seal. Inside it was a stack of useless old railroad reports. Felton marked it, "Very Important - To be Delivered, Without Fail, by Eleven o'clock train."

In Harrisburg, Lincoln was rushed toward a private train, which had to take him 200 miles to meet the late train from Philadelphia. The revised version of Pinkerton's plan was to not only get Lincoln through Baltimore early, but to bring him into the city on a different rail line and arrive at a different station.

The first leg of the trip was by private train, but Pinkerton could not risk using anything that might draw attention for the last two parts of the journey. So that he could travel anonymously, Lincoln would have to ride on regular passenger trains, taking the chance that the privacy of an ordinary sleeping car would be enough to keep his identity secret.

Felton's decoy parcel managed to keep the Baltimore-bound train in the Philadelphia station longer than usual, without causing any suspicion. Next, they had to smuggle Lincoln aboard and, if all went according to plan, he would arrive in Baltimore in the dead of night. His sleeper car would be unhitched from the train and drawn by horse to the Camden Street Station, where it would be added to the train bound for Washington.

Getting Lincoln onto the Baltimore-bound train would be tricky because it would have to be done in plain view of the crew and other passengers. For this, Pinkerton put a second decoy into play - Kate Warne. In Philadelphia, Kate reserved four double berths in the sleeper car at the back of the train. She had been instructed to stay in the car until Pinkerton arrived with Lincoln.

Thinking on her feet, Kate flagged down a conductor and - after putting some money in his hand - asked him for a special favor. She would be traveling with her "invalid brother," she said, and he would need to retire immediately to his compartment and remain there for the duration of the trip, with the blinds closed. She asked him to hold a group of spaces at the back of the train to ensure his comfort and privacy. The conductor, touched by her concern for her ailing sibling, took up position at the rear door of the train, to keep any arriving passengers away from the compartments at the rear.

Arrangements for the private train were made in Harrisburg by a last-minute addition to the network of operatives - George C. Franciscus, superintendent of the Pennsylvania Railroad. Pinkerton had confided his plan to him the previous day since Lincoln was going to have to use his railroad to get to Philadelphia and board the southbound train to Baltimore. Pinkerton had worked with Franciscus before and, as he wrote, "knew him to be a true and loyal man."

A train was prepared for emergency duty, although all the men aboard knew was that it was to carry a group of railroad executives to Philadelphia. The two-car special train was run one mile south toward Front Street, where it was to idle at a track crossing and wait for its passengers.

Franciscus was the last man to join Lincoln's carriage at the Jones House as it sped away toward the Front Street crossing. When the carriage arrived, Franciscus quickly alighted and escorted a tall man down the tracks to the saloon car.

Lincoln's dash to Washington was now underway.

As the special train steamed off into the darkness, a lineman directed by a Pinkerton agent climbed a wooden utility pole south of town and cut off telegraph communication between Harrisburg and Baltimore. Pinkerton was taking no chances.

Meanwhile, Governor Curtin had returned to the Executive Mansion and spent the evening turning away callers, giving the impression that Lincoln was there and that he was resting.

The special train roared toward Philadelphia, making excellent time. All trains had been shunted off the main line to allow the special an unimpeded run.

In the saloon car, Lincoln and his fellow travelers sat in the dark, reducing the chance that the president-elect might be spotted from outside when the train stopped for water.

Allan Pinkerton waited anxiously for the train to arrive in Philadelphia. It finally pulled into the station just after 10:00 p.m., well ahead of schedule - a major problem for Pinkerton. As he exchanged hushed greetings with Lincoln, he was forced to tell him that the early arrival of the train had left him too much time. The Baltimore-bound train was not scheduled to leave for nearly an hour and Felton's depot was only a few miles away.

Unable to linger at the train station or on the streets, where Lincoln might be spotted and recognized, he believed it best to place the president-elect into a moving carriage. To avoid rousing the carriage driver's suspicions, Pinkerton gave him a set of confusing, time-consuming directions that would send them, "driving northward in search of some imaginary person." The convoluted orders sent them cruising in aimless circles through the streets while Lincoln was sandwiched in the cab between the small, wiry Pinkerton and the tall, stocky Ward Lamon.

Finally, after checking his pocket watch, the detective banged on the roof of the carriage and ordered the driver to go straight to the train depot. When they arrived, Lamon kept watch from the rear while Pinkerton walked ahead, with Lincoln "leaning upon my arm and stooping...for the purpose of disguising his height." He was still wearing the soft hat and overcoat and had a blanket over his shoulders, bunched around his neck and face to disguise him further.

When they reached the train, Kate Warne stepped down from the sleeper car and greeted Lincoln as her brother. The conductor that she had placed on duty didn't look twice at what appeared to him to be a feeble, elderly man.

Pinkerton later said that only two minutes elapsed between the arrival at the station and the departure of the train. He had perfectly timed his deception. He later wrote, "So carefully had all our movements been conducted, that no one in Philadelphia saw Mr. Lincoln enter the car, and no one on the train, except his own immediate party—not even the conductor—knew of his presence."

The trip from Philadelphia to Baltimore was expected to take just over four hours. Kate had managed to secure the back half of the sleeping car, four pairs of berths in all, but there was no privacy to speak of. Only a curtain separated them from strangers in the car's front half, so they were forced to do all they could not to draw attention. Lincoln remained out of sight behind a curtain, but there was little chance that he would get any rest. As Kate noted, he was "so tall that he could not lay straight in the berth."

Pinkerton, Lamon, and Kate all settled into their berths and Lamon later recalled that Lincoln tried to ease the tension by offering a few quiet jokes. None of them slept, even though the others, unlike Lincoln, found the berths to be comfortable. Quite simply, as Kate said, "The excitement seemed to keep us all awake."

Pinkerton's nerves kept him from lying still for more than a few minutes at a time. At regular intervals, he stepped through the rear door of the car and kept watch from the back platform, watching the tracks behind them for any sign of trouble.

The train arrived in Baltimore on schedule, at 3:30 a.m. Kate bid goodbye to Lincoln. Her job as the "sister to an invalid" was over.

Pinkerton listened as the railroad workers uncoupled the sleeper car and hitched it to a team of horses. The car lurched forward, starting its slow, creaking journey to the Camden Street Station, just over a mile away. Pinkerton later wrote, rather poetically, "The city was in profound repose as we passed through. Darkness and silence reigned over all."

Pinkerton's plan called for Lincoln to stay no longer than 45 minutes in Baltimore. When they arrived at the Camden Street Station, though, they found that the incoming train was running late. For the detective, who feared that even the smallest problem could upset his entire plan, the waiting was agonizing. At dawn, the busy station came to life with the usual activity. With every moment that passed, discovery seemed more likely.

Camden Street Station in Baltimore, around the time of Lincoln's arrival

The only person not bothered by the situation was the man they were trying to protect. Pinkerton later wrote, "Mr. Lincoln remained quietly in his berth, joking with rare good humor."

As the delay dragged on, however, even Lincoln's mood darkened. The tension in the sleeper car could be cut with a knife. As the skies began to brighten, Pinkerton spent more and more time peering through the blinds for the late-arriving train that would take them the rest of the way to Washington. Unless it came soon, their advantage would be lost to the rising sun. If Lincoln were discovered by the assassins - pinned in the car at Camden Street and cut off from all reinforcements - he would have only Lamon and Pinkerton to defend him. They were a formidable pair, but they would be unable to stand off a mob.

Pinkerton had just started to consider his limited options when he heard a commotion outside - a team of railroad workmen arriving to hook up the sleeper car to the Baltimore & Ohio train that would take them on the final leg of their journey. The train was soon on its way and Pinkerton was able to let out a sigh of relief. He would later write, rather stoically, perhaps not wishing to suggest the outcome of the plan was ever in doubt, "In due time, the train sped out of the suburbs of

Baltimore, and the apprehension of the President and his friends diminished with each welcome revolution of the wheels."

The train carried Lincoln the last 38 miles of his perilous journey, arriving at the depot in Washington at 6:00 a.m. When it came to a stop, three passengers - one of them tall and lanky, wrapped in a blanket and wearing a soft, low-crowned hat - emerged from the sleeper car at the end of the train.

Mr. Lincoln was finally in Washington.

Later that morning, in Baltimore, Pinkerton agent Harry Davies accompanied Otis Hillard to the site where the assassination was supposed to take place. But they found that rumors were already spreading through the city, claiming that Lincoln had already arrived in Washington.

"How in hell," Hillard asked," had it leaked out that Lincoln was to be mobbed in Baltimore?"

What happened to Harry Davies in the years that followed is unknown. He likely continued to work for Pinkerton but all the records that documented his dates of service were lost during the Great Chicago Fire in 1871.

Kate Warne tragically died from a lingering illness in 1868, when she was only 35. She was buried in the Pinkerton family plot in Chicago's Graceland Cemetery.

Decades later, in 1883, Pinkerton quietly penned an account of his exploits in 1861. "I had informed Mr. Lincoln in Philadelphia that I would answer with my life for his safe arrival in Washington," Pinkerton wrote, "and I had redeemed my pledge."

But Pinkerton continued to serve Lincoln in the years that followed. He became chief of the Union Intelligence Service later that year. When news eventually reached him of Lincoln's assassination in 1865, he wept. "If only I had been there to protect him, as I had done before," he mourned.

He presided over the Pinkerton National Detective Agency until his death at age 63 in 1884.

7. "THE UNION WILL ALSO CONTINUE"

When Lincoln reached the capital at dawn on February 23, he went straight to the Willard Hotel. He had not slept at all in the cramped sleeper car berth and he was exhausted. However, his first view of Washington as the president-elect likely did nothing to make him feel better.

Looking out over the city from the carriage that he rode in, he saw only scenes of cold desolation. Down on the banks of the dirty Potomac River, he saw a white shaft of marble against the horizon. It was the unfinished monument to George Washington, which looked toward the uncompleted dome of the Capitol Building. Scaffolds covered the cupola and cranes stretched over the dome. There were stacks of building material all around the Capitol and the unfinished Treasury Building.

Washington was filthier than Lincoln remembered, with stinking livery stables and rancid saloons at every corner. Pigs rooted in the muddy streets off Pennsylvania Avenue and sewage swamps lay just steps away from the White House. Not far away, near land strewn with garbage, was an open drainage ditch, "floating with dead cats and all kinds of putridity and reeking with pestilential odors," wrote one visitor to the city. Even now, in the early morning hours, Lincoln could smell the foul reek that hung over the city.

Lincoln soon arrived at the Willard Hotel -- a castle-like structure that boasted of running water in every room -- and he checked into a

When Lincoln arrived in Washington in 1861, he found an unfinished capitol building, filthy streets, drainage ditches filled with sewage, and pigs that rooted in the muddy streets

suite, where he and his family would stay until the inauguration. Inside, Lincoln found a letter waiting for him: "If you don't resign, we are going to put a spider in your dumpling and play the Devil with you." This statement was followed by lines of obscene abuse and ended with "you are nothing but a goddamn Black nigger."

Mary arrived with the boys that afternoon, still shaken from an ordeal in Baltimore. Frenzied crowds had greeted the Presidential train and had shouted for Lincoln. No violence had occurred, but Mary had been terrified. She collapsed at the hotel with one of her legendary headaches and did not stir again until late in the evening.

The opposition press noted with sarcasm that the Republican President had arrived without fanfare. And when details of the secret arrival leaked out, newspapers mocked Lincoln without mercy and published scathing cartoons about the "flight of Abraham." It was the beginning of a merciless smear campaign against the "backwoods President" and his "boorish" wife. Their taunts about his crude behavior and illiterate education wounded Lincoln badly, but he never replied to journalistic abuse, writing it off as part of the job.

Mary, however, was mortified and permanently wounded. She was from a proud and cultured family, with impeccable manners, and was also proud of her gifted and intelligent husband. Her hurt and her anger were intensified when the leading ladies of Washington began to snub her, as if she were truly the country bumpkin the papers claimed she was. She became determined to prove she was the best First Lady that Washington had ever seen. She would dress better, furnish the White House better, and entertain better than any of the Washington ladies could ever hope to do. She did not realize at the time that such plans would backfire on her and she would never earn the place in Washington society that she so desperately craved.

Mary Lincoln was determined to prove she was the best First Lady that Washington had ever seen with her clothes, manners, and parties. She was disappointed when society did not respond as she wanted.

Lincoln had won the election fairly in 1860. But the slave states - led by South Carolina - refused to acknowledge his victory and began leaving the Union. Lincoln, as president-elect, had watched powerless for four months as one by one, the southern states seceded.

James Buchanan, a weak president for the past four years, chose to do nothing. There were many who suspected that Buchanan was even in league with the secessionists.

All this - and more -- turned inaugural week into a nightmare for Lincoln. Rabid and persistent office seekers refused to leave him alone and, to make matters worse, the endless delegations from outgoing President Buchanan's office and his cabinet filed in and out of his hotel suite. Lincoln was also plagued by groups of congressmen and senators who harassed him about his Cabinet choices and his policy of dealing with the south.

There were also delegations from Virginia and the border states. One group came from the Virginia secession convention, wanting to see what Lincoln would do and whether they should secede or adjourn. The Virginians urged Lincoln to give them a "message of peace" to take home with them but he would only say that southerners would be protected in all their legal rights.

Another delegation, consisting of border state Union loyalists, told Lincoln that he must avoid coercion at all costs. He must evacuate Fort Sumter, whose Union flag aggravated the situation with the secessionists, and that he must offer "satisfactory guarantees" to the eight slave states still loyal to the Union. Seward had assured the border Unionists that the crisis would disappear within 60 days of Lincoln being in office, but the delegation now wanted assurances from Lincoln himself. Lincoln was blunt with them. He would, he told them, support a slave amendment for loyal states in the Constitution but he would never guarantee slavery in the territories. He also refused to give up any of the military forts the Union held in the south.

Or so he told the committees from the border states. He had already made an offer to the delegation from Virginia, telling them that if they could persuade the Virginia secession convention to disband, he would give up Fort Sumter. But the Virginians refused his proposal. Every delegation departed Washington with no solution in sight.

Even with all the commotion that week, Lincoln somehow managed to complete his Cabinet - although rival factions fought him down to the last appointment. He also realized that he was going to have his hands full with Secretary of State William Seward.

After Lincoln ignored his suggestion for the appointment of Postmaster General, Seward submitted his resignation on the eve of the inauguration. Lincoln was unsettled by this but quickly came to the realization that Seward, believing himself to be the greater politician, hoped to try and gain control over Lincoln's Cabinet and his administration. Seward believed that Lincoln, unable to do without his superior abilities, would try and get him to stay by allowing him to have his choice for the Cabinet position. But Lincoln wasn't in the mood for playing games and he wasn't going to let Seward bully him. He told John Nicolay that he couldn't "afford to let Seward take the first trick" in their struggle for administrative leadership. Lincoln had a confidential chat with Seward and said that if he was going to start replacing his choices for Cabinet positions, he might consider finding a new Secretary of State, too. Could Seward recommend anyone? Seward quickly withdrew his resignation and Lincoln took "the first trick."

As Inauguration Day approached, Lincoln carefully crafted his speech. A lot was at stake and Lincoln polished and rewrote with great care. On March 3, he asked Seward to look it over and Seward suggested that Lincoln should offer greater concessions to the south. He insisted also that Lincoln remove one offensive sentence -- stating that he would recapture all the federal forts and arsenals that the secessionists had already taken over. Lincoln believed this was necessary and while Seward didn't disagree, he thought leaving it in the speech would alienate the southern Unionists, which they depended on.

Secretary of State William Seward believed he could manage Lincoln to his advantage. He quickly discovered he was wrong

Lincoln reluctantly agreed but didn't cut out much else. In his mind, the future of the country depended on him standing firm. He had been freely and fairly elected and had not lied in any of his pledges to the people who voted for him and his party. If the southerners did not like him, they were free to vote him out of office in 1864. But they had no right to separate the Union and he was not going to let them. The Union was the authority of the land and could not be wrecked by some disaffected minority. The principle behind secession was one of destruction and no government had ever been established that allowed for its own demise. Lincoln was not going to see the government that he loved end up being destroyed.

March 4, 1861 was a grim day in Washington. Heavy storm clouds hung low in the sky and soldiers marched through the crowded streets of the city, watching for the trouble that so many predicted was coming. There were assassination rumors in the wind and for all of

Lincoln's first inauguration in March 1861

those who feared for Lincoln's safety, there were many others who hoped that terror would strike.

Lincoln stayed in his suite at the Willard Hotel that morning. He read his inaugural address to his family and then asked to be alone. When the clock chimed noon, he dressed in a new black suit and stovepipe hat and departed for the lobby. President Buchanan called on him for the traditional carriage ride to Capitol Hill, but the two men said little to one another during the journey.

The clouds had lifted over Washington and the sun was now brightly shining over the grand parade of horse-drawn floats and military bands. Double rows of cavalry rode along the flanks of the carriage and lines of infantrymen filed along behind it. Hundreds of soldiers had been deployed by General Winfield Scott throughout the crowd, guarding against violence. They mingled with the sidewalk crowds and sharpshooters peered over rooftops on both sides of the avenue. As Lincoln looked out over the throng, his eyes landed on the soldiers and he was dismayed to see that it already looked like the country was at war.

The carriage pulled up to the Capitol steps and at least 30,000 people surged about the East Plaza, where an enormous platform extended from the building's east wing. Pinkerton detectives stood about, watching for any signs of trouble and soldiers watched from the windows of the Capitol and stood in profile on the rooftops of adjacent buildings. On a nearby hill, artillerymen manned a line of cannons, prepared to rake the streets with deadly fire at the first sign of assassins.

Lincoln walked out onto the giant platform with about 300 dignitaries. He faced Chief Justice Roger Brooke Taney as he took his oath as the Sixteenth President of the United States and then prepared to deliver his Inaugural address. With a brisk wind blowing, he stood at the podium and looked out over the sea of faces below.

Until that day, Lincoln had been so absorbed with political affairs and drafting his speech that he had forgotten that the Capitol building was still under construction. Just minutes before the inauguration, workers had been busy sawing and hammering, working diligently on the building's huge dome.

As he stood there at the podium, he surveyed the building and the workers who also stood watching the excitement. He seemed deep in thought. To his close friends, Lincoln had remarked that he was glad that the laborers were still busy at their work. "I'll take it as a sign," he commented. "So long as work continues on the Capitol, the Union will also continue."

Lincoln slowly unrolled the manuscript that contained his speech, placed a pair of steel-rimmed spectacles on his nose, and began to read in a nervous but clear voice. He spoke at length to the concerns of the southerners and assured them that he would not endanger their property, their peace, or their personal security. He would not menace the institution of slavery as he had, according to the Constitution, no right to do so. But Lincoln also spoke about the supremacy of the national government and vowed to enforce federal law in all states. The Union was perpetual, he said, and could not be destroyed and he promised to shed no blood in its defense unless he was forced to do so.

He would, he vowed, "hold, occupy, and possess" those southern forts still in Union possession.

Despite these proclamations to use whatever force necessary to save the Union, Lincoln went on to say, "We are not enemies, but friends. We must not be enemies. Though passion may have strained, it must not break our bonds of affection. The mystic chords of memory, stretching from every battlefield and patriot grave, to every living heart and hearthstone, all over this broad land, will yet swell the chorus of the Union, when again touched, as surely they will be, by the better angels of our nature."

Up on the hill, cannons fired into the wind and a cheer went up from the assembled crowd below. Lincoln had triumphed, it seemed, but inside, he knew that America was at the precipice of the most troubled and dangerous time in her history.

8. WAR COMES TO WASHINGTON

Omens of War and Portents of the Supernatural

On March 5 - as southerners condemned Lincoln's inaugural address as a declaration of hostilities - the War Department produced an unsettling report from Major Robert Anderson, the commander of Fort Sumter, a Union fort sitting in the Charleston, South Carolina harbor. The fort was surrounded by secessionist guns and Anderson had serious doubts about whether he could hold it against the growing ranks of enemy troops and cannons. Their supplies were running out and would be exhausted within a few weeks. He feared that any attempt to rescue his men would require a force of several thousand soldiers.

Lincoln was disheartened by the news but hoped it might be wrong. Officials from the War Department assured him that it was not - Anderson was a man whose opinion could be trusted. Lincoln was unsure what to do next. He was not a military man and he had never commanded any troops other than a handful of frontiersmen during the short-lived Black Hawk War. Not trusting himself to assess Anderson's situation, he called on General Winfield Scott for his opinion.

Scott was a hero of the Mexican War and a professional soldier at a time when the United States didn't have many of those. In March 1861, there were only 16,367 men in the U.S. military, including 1,108 commissioned officers. Despite his age, General Scott - who suffered from dropsy and vertigo and was so feeble that he could no longer mount a horse or even climb the White House steps without assistance

General Winfield Scott

- was the Army's General in Chief. He was a legendary soldier, though, and Lincoln had great respect for him.

General Scott believed that it was too late to save Fort Sumter and he told Lincoln that it would be wise to let it go. Lincoln thanked him but didn't want to follow the general's advice. He spent the next several days consulting with the Cabinet, with his advisers, and with high-ranking officers in the Army and Navy. After countless hours of deliberation, a consensus was reached - Sumter had to be surrendered. It would be disastrous to try and reinforce it. With secessionist batteries lining the harbor and troops and politicians crowding into Charleston, an aggressive move by the government was sure to ignite a war.

But still Lincoln hesitated. He and several others believed it would be a grave mistake to abandon the fort. Lincoln had stated publicly that he would not surrender Fort Sumter or any other federal fort. If he did so now, he would be going back on his word to the people who had elected him to office.

Lincoln waited. He demanded written opinions from his Cabinet and from his generals and commanders, but then decided that he couldn't count on them to make up his mind for him. He had to decide for himself. He was, after all, the nation's Commander in Chief.

On the night of March 28, he locked himself in his office and stayed up all night, pacing the floor. He finally made a decision at dawn. He informed the Cabinet that he would dispatch a re-supply fleet to Fort Sumter and leave it up to the secessionists as to whether they wanted to start a war. The War and Navy Departments were ordered to begin outfitting a relief expedition to go to Charleston.

Every member of the Cabinet - except for Seward - supported Lincoln's plan. Seward, thanks to promises that he had made to the new Confederate government, had a serious dilemma. He had promised them, along with the Virginia Unionists, that Sumter would be abandoned. And yet now, Lincoln was insisting that he was going to hold the fort. Once again, the "prairie lawyer" who had taken away Seward's chance to be president was rejecting his counsel and now was threatening to upset the negotiations that Seward had been working on privately. Seward complained that Lincoln was incompetent and had "no relative ideas and no concept of the situation." As a result of his anger, on April 1, he sent Lincoln a memorandum with some thoughts for the President's consideration.

Seward wrote that after one month in office, the administration had no policy, either foreign or domestic. Since the Union faced disaster without a policy, Seward offered one for Lincoln to adopt. First, the government must assure the public that slavery was not an issue in the present situation. The matter concerned union or disunion and slavery must be left out of it. Second, the government must abandon Fort Sumter. This policy then must be pursued energetically by the President or "by some member of his Cabinet" --- in other words, by Seward himself. After that, all debate had to stop and everyone in the administration had to agree with the policy and execute it without question.

Lincoln was shocked and enraged by the letter. The Secretary of State was not only criticizing the President but was offering to take over his administration and run it for him. Lincoln immediately wrote Seward a harsh reply - but then didn't send it. This was no time for a letter. Instead, he took Seward into his office and privately told him exactly what the policy of his administration would be. Furthermore, it would be Lincoln who would carry it out. Seward quickly realized that he had pushed Lincoln too far and it was likely this moment that caused him to reassess his position in the White House. While the two men would spar many times in the years to come, it never rose to the level of disrespect that Seward showed Lincoln in the early days of the presidency. He would serve him faithfully until the end.

"Executive force and vigor are rare qualities," Seward wrote to his wife soon after the incident. "The President is still the best of us."

Fort Sumter in Charleston harbor after the 1861 bombardment by Confederate forces

On April 4, Lincoln directed Assistant Navy Secretary Gustavas Fox to command the Sumter expedition and sent him south with three warships, a gunboat, and a steamer that held 200 soldiers and a year's worth of provisions. He also sent a special messenger to inform Major Anderson that a relief fleet was on its way.

Unfortunately, it wouldn't arrive on time.

On April 13, telegraph messages began arriving at the White House. Southerners, who felt betrayed by the false promises that had been made to them by Seward, had opened fire on Fort Sumter and were pounding the garrison with harbor guns.

Then came more news. Fox's expedition had arrived but was unable to provide support. Instead, secessionists allowed Fox to evacuate Anderson and his men from the fort. The battle was brief, but Fort Sumter had fallen.

America was at war with itself.

On April 14, with an air of solemn resignation, Lincoln announced to his Cabinet that the south had fired the first shots, forcing on him the decision of "immediate dissolution, or blood." The Union would not fall, Lincoln repeated, and, therefore, he would mobilize a militia of 75,000 men to suppress the rebellion and call for Congress to convene in a special session on Independence Day.

Lincoln announced that he would not officially view the conflict as a war between the states but as an insurrection against the government. Since secession was constitutionally illegal, he refused to concede that any of the states had left the Union. Rather he contended that rebellious citizens established a false, Confederate government that

Washington would never recognize. Lincoln's objective now was to suppress the southern rebels as quickly as possible and restore order in the sections of the country they had seized.

The following day, Lincoln's call for 75,000 militiamen went out to the states and it forced those in the north and the south who had been undecided before to choose sides. In the border states, secession conventions sprang into action, for the thought of invading armies from the north, attacking rebels and freeing slaves was more than even the southern Unionists could stand.

War had come to America and the country was splintered apart.

Southern secessionists moved quickly to separate from the Union. Not just in Charleston, but throughout the south, arsenals and forts were seized by radicals, often before their states had even voted to secede. But the votes were coming. On April 17, the Virginia convention adopted a secession ordinance that was approved by the voters. Virginia joined the Confederacy and the rebels moved their capital to Richmond.

The small federal army, not yet buoyed by Lincoln's militia, was scattered from coast to coast and was too weak to resist the capture of weapons and garrisons. Worse, some army officers even aided and abetted the secessionist seizures.

In the weeks that followed the inauguration, Washington became more and more isolated. The Capitol was almost defenseless, and it seemed that the situation became more dangerous with each passing day until finally, loyal soldiers began trickling in to defend the city.

Other states also seceded and even in those slave states that tried to remain neutral - like Maryland, Missouri, and Kentucky - rebel sympathizers used violence to try and drag them into the fray. For example, southern militants in Baltimore cut the telegraph lines and burned the bridges leading into Washington. They also attacked a Massachusetts militia regiment as it was marching from one train station to another. Both soldiers and rioters were killed in the skirmish.

Near the end of April, one of the many visitors to the White House was politician Carl Schurz, who had come from Wisconsin to offer help in rallying German immigrants to the Union cause. During Schurz's meeting with Lincoln, the President confided in him about a strange incident that had occurred about two weeks before.

One afternoon, soon after he issued the call for the militia troops to defend the Union, Lincoln was alone in his office when a feeling

Carl Schurz

suddenly came over him that he described as "if he were utterly deserted and helpless."

Lincoln's melancholy was justified. As he told Schurz, "Any moderately strong body of secessionist troops, if there were any in the neighborhood, might come over the Long Bridge across the Potomac and just take me and the members of the Cabinet - the whole lot of them."

As Lincoln was sitting at his desk, brooding about the predicament that the Capitol was facing, he was startled by the sound of a booming cannon that was fired much too close for comfort.

"There they are," Lincoln thought to himself.

At any moment, Lincoln expected someone to rush into his office with news that the city was under attack - but nothing happened. Finally, Lincoln left his desk and asked the staff if they have heard news, or if they had at least heard a cannon fire. None of them had. Lincoln was the only one to hear the sound - and he knew he had not imagined it.

Perplexed, the President did what he could to investigate the mysterious cannon fire. He left the White House, went out to the street, and started walking in the direction from which he believed the sound had come. There was no one running in the streets and no sound of battle. Only the usual sounds of the city can be heard around him.

Lincoln finally reached the Federal Arsenal. He walked up to the entrance and found it unguarded. The doors were unlocked, and no soldiers were in sight. As Lincoln told Schurz, "Anyone might have gone in and helped themselves to arms."

Lincoln returned to the White House, deeply unsettled by the whole experience. His fear of a surprise attack turned out to be unfounded, but his intuition of danger was very real. With the federal supply of military stores unsecured, anyone who wished to harm the government was free to pillage the city. Washington had been safe and secure for so long that the security of some of its most volatile sites had become lackluster.

Lincoln made immediate changes to the security procedures at the arsenal and other locations. Later in the war, there were many secessionists in the city who were more than willing to harm the government and its leaders. As arsenal of explosives, powder, shot, cannons, and rifles left open and unguarded was like an open invitation to a slaughter. But, of course, that couldn't happen because Lincoln made sure the army was prepared - all because of a "phantom" cannon that didn't exist.

In the days, months, and years that followed the start of the Civil War, the personality of Abraham Lincoln was altered considerably by the horrible pressures of leadership. Although he had always been prone to moodiness and melancholy, his periods of reflection became longer and more pronounced. As the death toll of the war mounted on both sides, Lincoln became more and more obsessed with his destiny. He was convinced that he had been born to guide the United States through the deadliest and most heartbreaking conflict in its history. Thanks to this, his leadership during this period - although often questioned - never faltered and the events of his presidency both strengthened and destroyed the man that Lincoln was.

The great loss of life and the bitter turmoil of the war took their toll on him. He changed and he became more bitter and dark. Gone was the humorous man who was apt to take off his shoes during staff meetings to "let his feet breathe." He had been replaced by a sad, often gloomy man who was prone to days of isolation and depression. It was as if the weight of the entire nation had fallen on his shoulders.

Lincoln turned inward during his quiet times of contemplation, staring out the window at the Potomac and walking the nighttime streets of Washington, much to the chagrin of Ward Lamon, who would chastise the president for slipping away unguarded. He spoke more often about destiny and seeing the "hand of God" at work in some battles. It was almost as if his uncanny perception somehow strengthened as the war raged on.

By the time the first year of the war had come to an end, Lincoln had finally taken on the mantle of America's military commander. The doubts and worries of the early days were over. Lincoln orchestrated the Union Army during the bloodiest times of the war, enduring complaints and criticisms from ineffective generals about this "meddling." The inexperienced soldier who once looked for help from Cabinet members and aging generals had been replaced by a Commander in Chief who seemed to sometimes have an almost supernatural insight into events that were occurring hundreds of miles away.

War Department documents contain at least one occasion when Lincoln burst into the telegraph office late one night in a restless state. He had visited earlier, looking for the latest news, but when he came back, he was in a panic. He ordered the operator to get a line through to the Union commanders. He was convinced that Confederate soldiers were just about to cut through the Federal lines.

The telegraph operator asked where he had obtained such information and Lincoln reportedly answered, "My God, man! I saw it."

He had been dozing in his office, he said, and the vision had been sent to him in a dream. Much to the telegraph operator's surprise, a return message that was sent to him some time later informed him that Lincoln's vision had been true. When soldiers in the field asked him where he came by such knowledge, the operator was unable to provide them with an answer that he thought they would believe.

And Lincoln was not the only military leader to depend on the supernatural during the war. In 1862, a Copperhead plot to seize the Philadelphia Navy yards was foiled by spirit communications from the beyond. The Navy yard commander had received an anonymous letter that warned him of a plot to seize his command and turn the guns of the yards on the city. Some of the traitors were in his employ, the message said, and were recruiting others to rebellion. Once the gun boats were taken, they would be used to attack Philadelphia, New York, and Boston. The letter writer claimed that the warning came from none other than the spirits of Generals George Washington, Zachary Taylor, and Andrew Jackson.

The letter had been written to the Navy yards commander by someone who heard the message relayed to a Spiritualist medium in a public hall, in front of a large audience.

We will never know what truly convinced him of its authenticity, but the commander decided to take the message seriously. Guard patrols were doubled, and cannons were placed at the gates. Soon after, the commander employed a detective who visited the medium and questioned him carefully. The medium told him that the warning had been dictated from the spirit world and that he had written it down word for word. The detective asked for the names of the men who were traitors in the Navy yards and to supply them, the man recommended another medium, a woman, who he believed could learn them.

The commander sent his private secretary, in disguise, to visit the other medium. She went into a trance and called out 60 names of employees in the yards, all of whom were personally unknown to her. Every one of the men named by the medium was discharged and other evidence was gathered against them, revealing the widespread plot that the commander had been warned of.

He came to believe that the Navy yards rebellion was defeated by spiritual means.

9. THE DEATH OF WILLIE LINCOLN

"Do you ever find yourself talking with the dead? I do... ever since Willie's death. I catch myself involuntarily talking to him as if he were near me..... And I feel that he is!"

Abraham Lincoln, speaking to the Secretary of the Treasury, Salmon P. Chase

The war took a terrible toll on President Lincoln, but there is no doubt that the most crippling blow that he suffered during his time in the White House was the death of his son, Willie, in 1862. Lincoln and Mary grieved deeply over Willie's death. Their son Eddie had passed away a dozen years before and while they didn't know it at the time, Tad would only live to be 18. Robert was the only Lincoln son to see adulthood.

Lincoln was sick at heart over Willie's death and it was probably the most intense personal crisis of his life. Some historians have even called it the greatest blow he ever suffered. Even Confederate President Jefferson Davis sent a letter to Washington to express his condolences over the boy's death.

Lincoln felt that all the good in his life was ripped away by Willie's passing. The boys, Willie and Tad, had been Lincoln's antidote to the perils of the war. As the conflict dragged on, and he fell deeper and deeper into depression, it was only the two boys who brought light back

This print of the Lincoln family was produced by New York engraver John Chester Buttre in 1873. He relied on a photograph by Matthew Brady that had been taken in his studio in 1864 for his representations of President Lincoln and Tad. The images of Mary, Willie, and Robert were his own creation.

into his life. He treasured the moments that he could spend with them, when he could forget about the generals and their mistakes and the bickering politicians and relax with his sons, reading them stories and sharing their wild fun and antics. He loved to beleaguer his visitors with tales of his "two little codgers" and he bragged about them to all who would listen.

Both Willie and Tad found the White House to be a place of constant revelry and Lincoln let them run wild with very few restraints. They played and shouted in the corridors and burst into Lincoln's office in the middle of conferences, chasing one another through the room and darting in between stiff politicians who were not amused. Tad, who instigated most of the mischief, once fired his toy cannon at a Cabinet meeting and also liked to stand at the front of the grand staircase and collect a nickel "entrance fee" from those who came to see his father. Also, with Lincoln's help, the boys converted the White

Lincoln with his son, Tad

House lawn into a zoo, with animals consisting of ponies, kittens, white rabbits, a turkey, a pet goat (which often slept in Tad's bed), and a dog named Jip, who had a habit of sleeping in Lincoln's lap during meals. When the boys were not chasing animals through the Executive Mansion, they were holding fairs and minstrel shows in the attic. One day, Tad discovered the White House bell system, which had cords running to various rooms so that Lincoln or the staff could summon servants whenever they needed anything. Tad set all the bells clanging at once, sending the White House into bedlam. It took a few minutes for them to figure out what was going on, but eventually members of the staff climbed into the attic and found Tad yanking all the bells and giggling madly.

Inspired by the martial atmosphere in Washington, the boys waged mock battles with neighborhood children on the White House lawn. They also held military parades through the corridors of the mansion, with the boys and their friends marching in a single line, blowing on old horns and banging tin drums. They carried out secret missions on the White House roof, hiding out, and watching for "Johnny Rebs" with their telescopes.

On another occasion, they held a solemn court martial for a soldier doll named Jack, found him guilty, shot him for desertion, and buried him in the White House garden. One day, though, they burst into Lincoln's office during a meeting and explained in a breathless voice that they had shot Jack for desertion and buried him but that the White House gardener wanted the doll removed because they had dug up some roses. So, they wanted their father to fix up a pardon for Jack. Lincoln said that he reckoned that he could do that and took out a piece of official stationery and wrote, "The Doll Jack is pardoned by order of the President" and signed it "A. Lincoln."

Because the boys loved the Army, Lincoln often took them along when he went to visit General George McClellan's camps across the Potomac. They looked up to the soldiers with wide-eyed reverence and watched the marching bands and the drilling regiments in awe. When Lincoln was presented to the troops, the boys rode with him in his carriage and tipped their hats to the soldiers just as their father did.

Despite how it sounds, though, life for the Lincoln boys was not all play. Tad was a nervous boy, like his mother, and a hyperactive child with a speech impediment. He was slow to learn and many did not believe that he could read. Mary hired tutors for the boys, but Tad had "no opinion of discipline" and teacher after teacher resigned in frustration. But Lincoln refused to worry about Tad, insisting that he would learn his letters over time. The boys might be a little spoiled, but he was determined to let them have as much fun as they could. They would have to grow up far too soon.

In contrast to Tad, Willie had a serious side and often behaved like a small adult. He had turned 11 in December 1861 and many of the Lincolns' friends and staff members commented on his precociousness. The young man would sit in church, listening to the minister with rapt attention while Tad played with a jackknife on the floor of his mother's pew. When he was tired of romping with this younger brother, Willie liked to lock himself in his room, where he would curl up in a chair and read a book or write stories on a writing pad, just as his father used to do when he was growing up. He also kept scrapbooks about historical and significant events, filled with clippings on his father's inauguration, the war, and deaths of important people. Willie was much like his father in so many ways and because of this, was his father's special favorite. He and Willie shared many interests, especially reading, humor, and a love for animals. Lincoln had bought Willie a pony for his birthday and it became the pride of the boy's life. Mary loved Willie's gentleness and he was so affectionate that she often counted on him desperately for family companionship. He would, she prayed, "be the hope and stay of her old age."

Tragically, this was not meant to be.

By spring of 1862, the tide of the war was slowly starting to turn for the Union. Lincoln's generals were finally starting to triumph on the battlefield. Buell had actually managed to defeat the rebels in a battle in eastern Kentucky and Halleck had finally come alive and had sent a column down the Tennessee River. Neither man was cooperating as Lincoln had directed but at least they were fighting.

Even better news soon followed. A Brigadier General named Ulysses S. Grant had driven into northwestern Tennessee and had captured Fort Henry on the Tennessee River and then had stormed Fort Donelson on the Cumberland. He pounded the garrison until it met his terms of unconditional surrender.

Lincoln and Stanton congratulated one another when they read the news and Lincoln noted happily that Grant and many of his men hailed from Illinois. Subsequent reports also maintained that Grant's victories had broken the Confederate line in Kentucky and forced the rebels to retreat into Tennessee. Though Halleck, who was sitting behind a desk in St. Louis, claimed most of the credit, Lincoln himself nominated "Unconditional Surrender" Grant for a promotion to major general. After a long and dismal winter, Grant had given the president a little bit of hope.

While Grant was busy hammering the river garrisons in Tennessee, both Willie and Tad became sick. The onset of their sickness occurred during the last days of January 1862. The boys were out playing in the snow and both developed a fever and a cold. Tad's illness soon passed, but Willie seemed to get worse. He was kept inside for a week and finally put into bed. A doctor was summoned, and he assured Mary that the boy would improve, despite the fact that Willie's lungs were congested, and he was having trouble breathing. Day after day passed and Willie grew more and more sick. He developed chills and soon his fever spiked out of control. White House secretaries later told of hearing his cries in the night.

The cause of Willie's death varies by account. In the end, it remains a mystery. He was said to have been a delicate child, despite his rough play with friends and his many outdoor activities. Like his brother Eddie, he may have suffered from "consumption" or, according to some accounts; he contracted either an acute malarial infection or typhoid. In either case, the lack of proper sanitation was probably a factor. During this period, Washington had open sewers and a filthy canal for drinking water. Worse, the city's garbage was dumped into the water just a short distance from the White House.

Before Willie had gotten sick, the Lincolns had planned a large reception at the White House with more than 800 people in attendance. The lavish party included dinner, music, and dancing and the invitations had already gone out, leaving Mary no opportunity to cancel. The evening turned out to be a dismal affair for the worried parents as they continually took turns climbing the stairs to check on their son.

Willie's condition did not improve. The doctor was summoned back and by then, everyone in the household and the offices knew that Willie was seriously ill. More doctors were called in to consult and soon, Willie's illness made the

Willie Lincoln

newspapers. The reporters conjectured that he may have contracted bilious fever. One parent always stayed with the frightened and sick boy and a nurse came to help them from one of the local hospitals. After a week of this, Mary was too weak and exhausted to rise from her own bed, but Lincoln never left the boy's side, sleeping and eating in a chair next to his bed. All he could do was to bathe Willie's face with a wet cloth and look on helplessly as his son's life slowly slipped away. The doctors had no hope for the child as he grew worse. Soon, Willie's mind wandered, and he failed to recognize anyone, including his beloved father.

Death came for Willie on the afternoon of February 20, 1862. Lincoln covered his face and wept in the same manner that he had for his mother many years before. He looked at Willie for a long time, refusing to leave his bed side. "My poor boy," the President said. "He was too good for this earth. God called him home. I know that he is

Mary's friend and confidante, seamstress Lizzie Keckley

better off in heaven, but then we loved him so. It is hard.... hard to have him die."

Mary fell apart. She collapsed and cried out with a heartbreaking wail. Her closest confidante, her black seamstress Lizzie Keckley, led her away to comfort her. The talented Mrs. Keckley, a former slave who previously worked for Mrs. Jefferson Davis, had become an almost constant companion of Mrs. Lincoln after completing her ball gown for the inauguration. She was one of the few people who possessed the patience and strength needed to deal with the high-strung First Lady. Mary trusted her implicitly, confided in her, and called the woman her best living friend. Lizzie listened to Mary, sympathized with her, and advised her as best she could. She would soon influence Mary greatly when it came to her beliefs in Spiritualism.

After Willie's death, it was Lizzie who washed the boy's body and dressed him in a plain brown suit of clothes for the funeral. She herself had lost her only son and understood Mary's pain.

President Lincoln was unable to stomach his own loss. He managed to stand after Mary was led away by Lizzie Keckley and stumbled into John Nicolay's office to share the horrible news. Then, sobbing, he walked to Tad's room. He sat down with the boy and tried to tell him that Willie would not be able to play with him anymore; that his brother had died. Tad refused to believe it for a time and then he too began to cry.

Orville Browning, one of Lincoln's longtime friends from Illinois, and his wife, Elizabeth, immediately came to the White House when they heard the news. Elizabeth stayed with Mary throughout the night and Orville began taking care of funeral arrangements.

It was a tragic time in the White House and according to the tradition of the day, the mirrors in the house were covered and the mansion was draped in black. The Lincolns hardly stirred from their rooms. If not for their friends and Lincoln's most trusted staff, the White House would have come to a standstill.

On February 24, a minister conducted the funeral in the East Room, while Willie lay in a metal coffin in the nearby Green Room. It was said that the boy only appeared to be sleeping as his friends and family passed slowly by him, their faces twisted in grief. Lincoln stood with Robert by his side, but Mary did not attend the funeral. She was in such a state of shock that she was unable to leave her room. Most of official Washington was there, including William Seward, who wept openly. Lincoln's Cabinet, his secretaries, dozens of politicians and lobbyists filed past the casket. So did General George McClellan, who was so moved by the President's suffering that he later sent Lincoln a compassionate note expressing his sorrow and thanking him for standing by him after his many failures during the ongoing war. When the service was concluded, the pallbearers and a group of children from Willie's Sunday school class carried the coffin outside to the waiting hearse.

The day of the funeral was a stormy one, as if the forces of nature reflected the anguish in the Lincoln's hearts. The procession to the cemetery was several blocks long and it ended at Oak Hill Cemetery in Georgetown. Throughout the day, rainstorms wreaked destruction upon the city. Steeples had fallen from churches, roofs had been torn form houses, trees and debris littered the roadways, and the funeral procession cowered under the torrents of rain. But as soon as they reached the cemetery, the storm passed over and the air became silent, almost as in deference to Willie Lincoln.

The service was short. Willie had originally been embalmed to make the trip back to Springfield and be buried beside his brother, but Lincoln changed his mind about that at the last minute. He accepted an offer made to him by a friend, William Thomas Carroll, to place the body of Willie in one of the crypts in the Carroll family tomb. He would remain there until Lincoln retired from the presidency and returned to Illinois. He could take the boy's body back to Springfield with him then.

The Carroll family tomb in Georgetown's Oak Hill Cemetery, where Willie was temporarily laid to rest

He couldn't send him back alone. Lincoln could not bear the idea of having Willie so far away from him just yet.

In fact, Lincoln returned to the cemetery the next day to watch as the body was moved from the cemetery chapel to the crypt itself. The tomb was located in a remote area of the cemetery and was built into the side of a hill. It was a beautiful and peaceful spot, but Lincoln wouldn't be able to leave his son unattended there for long.

Word spread that Lincoln returned to the tomb on two occasions and had Willie's coffin opened. The undertaker had embalmed Willie so perfectly that he appeared to be merely resting. The President claimed each time that he opened the casket that he wanted to look upon his boy's face just one last time.

After the funeral, Lincoln tried to go on about his work, but his spirit had been crushed by Willie's death. One week after the funeral, he closed himself up in his office all day and wept. It has often been said that Lincoln was on the verge of suicide at this point, but none can say for sure. He did withdraw even further into himself, though, and he began to look more closely at the spiritual matters that had interested him for so long.

10. SEANCES IN THE WHITE HOUSE

Mary Lincoln was visited by a succession of "spirit ministers" after Willie's death. Their impact was palpable. One night she knocked on the door of the Prince of Wales bedroom, where her half-sister Emilie Helm was staying, to talk about Willie. "He lives," Mary said, her voice trembling. "He comes to me every night and stands at the foot of my bed with the same sweet, adorable smile he has always had." Sometimes he brought other departed family members with him, like his brother Eddie. "You cannot dream of the comfort this gives me." Mary's eyes were wide and shining and otherworldly as she spoke, and Emilie grew alarmed. "It is unnatural and abnormal," she wrote in her diary. "It frightens me."
Terry Alford

After Willie died, Lincoln was lost - at least for a time. He treasured small toys, objects, and drawings that Willie had given to him, sometimes placing them on his desk while he worked, as if hoping to capture his essence. He often placed the toys on his fireplace mantel, next to a photograph of the two of them together. When he displayed Willie's artwork, he explained to visitors that it had been painted by "my boy, who died." John Nicolay stated that Lincoln would often watch the door while he worked, as if expecting the boy to run through it and give his father a hug, as he often did in life.

Willie's death left a permanent hole in Lincoln's heart. Often he would dream that Willie was still alive and would see the boy playing in the leaves on the White House lawn and calling out to him --- only to awaken in his darkened bedroom and realize that it was only a dream.

Lincoln also began to speak of how Willie's spirit remained with him and how his presence was often felt in his home and office. Some mediums theorized that Lincoln's obsession with the boy's death may have caused Willie's spirit to linger behind, refusing, for his father's sake, to pass on to the other side.

After days of mourning, Mary's older sister, Elizabeth Todd Edwards, became so alarmed over Lincoln's state of mind that she arranged for the Reverend Francis Vinton of Trinity Church in New York to visit the President. Imperious and opinionated, Vinton, who was also once a lawyer and a soldier, told Lincoln that he was fighting with God by indulging his grief in such a manner.

Lincoln heard Vinton out, barely listening to what he said, until the minister stated, "Your son is alive."

"Alive? Alive?" Lincoln repeated, jumping up from a sofa. "Surely you mock me."

Vinton responded, "Seek not your son among the dead. He is not there. He lives today in Paradise."

Vinton's words were meant to be hopeful but for Lincoln, they brought cold comfort. Lincoln was a fatalist. As he explained to his old law partner, William Herndon, "Things were to be, and they came, irresistibly came, doomed to come."

It was the relentless demands of the war that brought Lincoln back from the depths of despair. He attached a wide black ribbon around his hat in Willie's memory and tried to move on. The ribbon was still there when he was assassinated three years later.

The black pall continued to hang over the White House. Lincoln's grief turned inward, and he tried to escape his despair through work, but that was something that Mary was unable to do. Even Tad was distraught. Until his brother's death, he was a loud, playful boy, but now he broke into bouts of weeping because "Willie will never speak to me anymore."

Mary was overwhelmed with her grief. Emotional at even the best of times, she was broken by Willie's death. She shut herself in her room for the next three months, crying into her pillow, and begging Willie to come back to her. Lizzie Keckley would later recall how tender President Lincoln was with his anguished wife, but he worried for her sanity. One day, he gently led her to the window of her bedroom and pointed to a distant structure that was the asylum for the insane. He told her, "Mother, do you see that white building on the hill yonder? Try and control your grief, or it will drive you mad, and we will have to send you there."

Mary Lincoln in her mourning dress after Willie's death

The warning seemed to reach Mary and with care from her husband, love from her son, and friendship and kindness from Lizzie, she slowly began to improve. However, it was still some time before the mere mention of Willie's name - or some small reminder of him - didn't reduce her to violent tears. Unable to bear any memory, she gave away all his toys and anything that might make her think of him. She never again entered the guest room where he died or into the Green Room where he had been laid out in his coffin. She canceled all but the most important social functions and lived in veritable seclusion for weeks, trying anxiously to hold on. Five months after her son's death, she was still so shaken that she could barely write to her friends in Springfield about "our crushing bereavement." Sometimes, she wrote, when she was alone, she realized again that "he is not with us" and the terror of the thought "often for days overcomes me."

Mary searched for small ways to alleviate her grief. Following Lizzie's advice, she began visiting the military hospitals in Washington, distributing food and flowers to the wounded soldiers. She also developed a deep compassion for the refugees who arrived in Washington, who were mostly "oppressed colored people." These "contraband Negroes" were streaming into Washington and Mary helped care for them and tried to find them jobs. She even convinced President Lincoln to donate $200 to her cause because "humanity requires it."

This eased her pain and provided her with stability - during the daylight hours at least. After night fell, or when she found herself alone because her husband was working late, she remained unstable. Her mood swings, headaches and explosive temper were worse than ever. She began to see political conspiracies against her husband everywhere, especially on the part of William Seward, who she referred to as the "dirty sneak" who had tried, and was still trying, to take her husband's job. She despised the man and hated him even more for the fact that he cheerfully ignored her hatred for him. She believed that all the Cabinet members were evil and was bothered by the fact that her husband seemed to be so unaware of it. Mary also fretted about his safety, begging Lincoln to take guards along when he went out on his nocturnal walks to the War Department. She begged him to be careful and worried about him so much that it seemed to Lizzie that Mary "read impending danger in every rustling leaf, in every whisper of the wind."

Mary continued to search for comfort and had difficulty finding it. More conventionally religious than her husband, she was still unable to accept the teachings of her Presbyterian faith that Willie had gone to God in peace and rest. She did not want to part with him. Perhaps she didn't have to, friends told her. They explained that Willie was still here–anxious to see her, in fact–and simply waited on the other side of a veil that could be lifted by those with the proper gift.

This was finally what it took for Mary to find some peace. She found it in Spiritualism, a movement had only been founded about a dozen years before, in the tiny community of Hydesville, New York. The Fox family was living in a rented cottage that they grew to believe was haunted. One day, two of the Fox sisters, Maggie and Kate devised a system with which to communicate with the resident spirit. Word spread and the Spiritualist movement was born. It revolved around the belief that life existed after death, that spirits continued to exist without a physical body, and, most importantly, that these spirits could - and did - communicate with the living.

Spiritualists believed that the dead communicated through "mediums" -- sensitive men and women who slipped into trances and passed along messages from the other side. Sometimes, during sittings -- referred to as séances -- the dead produced not only messages but physical phenomena like mysterious lights, unearthly music, levitating objects, disembodied voices, or actual apparitions.

Spiritualism was very appealing in the nineteenth century and the movement's influence soared with the suffering produced by the war. Thanks to Spiritualism, lost loved ones were no longer lost at all. They could speak and be spoken to as if they were still alive. Spiritualism filled the huge void that death had made in the lives of the everyday person. They now had something to cling to and a belief that their family members and friends had gone on to a better place.

Spiritualism had been popular since 1849 but saw a resurgence after the start of the Civil War. Mary Lincoln was just one of the millions of people who attended seances in the 1860s and beyond

Spiritualist newspapers proclaimed the faith, and circles of believers established themselves in the leading cities. The Washington circle counted among its members a number of government officials. Many believed there was more interest in Spiritualism in the nation's capital than in any other city in the country.

The possibility of communicating with the dead makes it easy to understand the draw that Spiritualism had for Mary Lincoln. And, by extension, for President Lincoln, as well. He was a man known for his belief in the mystic, fate, and meanings behind dreams, portents, and omens. He may not have publicly embraced the Spiritualists in the way that Mary did, but there is little doubt that he became involved with prominent members of the movement in Washington and - if the stories and first-hand accounts are true - actively participated in seances at the White House and other locations in the city.

It should also be noted that this period was not the first time that the Lincolns had been exposed to Spiritualism or even contact with the dead. Mary had spent her entire childhood exposed to the beliefs of the African Americans who helped to raise her. It was common for her maids and nannies to "see spirits and foretell events" and they often recognized their influences as "the spirits of their deceased friends." Mary's nursemaid, known only as "Mammy Sally," always told her tales of spirits and of the dead returning for friendly visitations.

Lincoln had also been exposed to Spiritualism in the early days of the movement. There were more than 800 Spiritualists in Illinois in the 1850s and in 1852, author G.K. Nelson - writing about the spread of Spiritualism on the western frontier - noted, "it was at this time that Abraham Lincoln's name was first associated with Spiritualism."

An affidavit, sworn to by Dr. J. Ridgeley Martin, stated, "I was a close neighbor for a period of three years at Springfield, Illinois, studied law in a building where he had his office... and the medium's name was Thorp... Mr. Lincoln received messages from his mother and Ann Rutledge."

Lincoln may not have spoken casually about these experiences. Mary Lincoln once said that her husband was not a demonstrative man; that when he felt something most deeply, he expressed his feelings about it the least. William Herndon, his friend and law partner, when asked about Lincoln's spiritual beliefs, replied that Lincoln made no real revelations to him on the subject, but added, "I have grounds... of the probability that he did sometimes attend here, in this city, séances. I am told this by Mr. Ordway, a Spiritualist... He craved light from all intelligences to flash his way to the unknown future."

Dr. Anson G. Henry, Lincoln's Springfield physician and friend, was a confirmed Spiritualist. Dr. Henry was a great supporter of Lincoln during his romantic troubles of 1841 and spent several hours each day with his severely depressed patient. Dr. Henry once wrote to him, "I believe our departed friends hover over and around us, and are fully cognizant of all that transpires, while we are not sensible of their presence."

By the summer of 1862, Mary was meeting with a number of different Spiritualist mediums and invited many to the White House, as each claimed to be able to "lift the thin veil" and allow Mary to communicate with Willie.

Many believe that Mary was introduced to Spiritualism by Lizzie Keckley, but no one knows for certain. Lizzie was not the only person caring for Mary during this difficult time. Mary Jane Wells, the wife of Secretary of the Navy Gideon Welles, was a close friend to Mary. After Willie's death, she came to the White House to assist the family. Mary Jane was a committed Spiritualist who began attending seances after the death of her daughter in 1854. It's likely that she shared her beliefs with Mary, who then sought out Spiritualism to ease her grief.

Satisfied by what she saw and heard at the seances she attended; Mary became an ardent believer in the movement. Through the spirit raps and trance messages relayed by mediums, she became convinced that she was speaking to the spirit of Willie. For her, it was indisputable proof that an afterlife existed and that her children were there, waiting for the day when the family would be reunited.

Through friends, Mary made the acquaintance of a Miss Bonpoint, a journalist who was writing about Spiritualism in the papers. It was she who introduced Mary to the Lauries, a husband and wife medium team that lived in Georgetown. After that, the black presidential carriage was often seen outside of the Lauries' brownstone.

By then, Washington had become a mecca for Spiritualists. They came from all over the country to conduct seances for government officials, members of the Union Army, and for families who had lost loved ones in the war.

Mary immersed herself in the Spiritualist community and eagerly shared her newfound beliefs with her husband. It kindled his interest in the arcane and bizarre as he was still struggling with his grief over Willie's death.

William Carpenter, a painter who lived in the White House for six months during the war, claimed that after Willie's death, the president would lock himself away every Thursday, the day the boy had died.

Three months after Willie's death, Lincoln expressed his grief by reciting a passage from Shakespeare: "That we shall see and know our friends in heaven. If that be true, I shall see my boy again." Turning to a military officer that was in his office for a meeting, Lincoln asked him, "Did you ever dream of some lost friend, and feel you were having a sweet communion with him? That is the way I dream of my lost boy."

One day, Lincoln asked Secretary of the Treasury Salmon P. Chase, "Do you ever find yourself talking to the Dead? I do, ever since Willie's death. I catch myself involuntarily talking to him as if he were near me. And I feel that he is!"

Mary saw Spiritualism as the perfect outlet for her husband's grief - and perhaps it was. Rumors swirled that Lincoln began consulting with mediums and clairvoyants as the pressures of the war increased. He allegedly found that the information they gave him about matters as mundane as Confederate troop movements often matched not only his own reports from the War Department but also the dreams and precognitive visions of his own. Years later, some Spiritualists displayed accounts and diaries that detailed Lincoln's interest in the spirit world. One even claimed that Lincoln's plans for the Emancipation Proclamation, which freed the southern slaves, came to him from the ghost of Daniel Webster and other abolitionists of the spirit world.

This was likely not the case - but only because Lincoln was waiting for another miraculous sign that would tell him that it was time for him to free the slaves.

Despite his aversion to slavery, when Lincoln ran for the presidency in 1860, he made it very clear that he had no plans to abolish it. In the early days of the war, he resisted pressure from northern abolitionist and Radical Republicans in Congress to do so. He even publicly reprimanded Federal officers who openly recruited African Americans as soldiers or provided shelter for runaway slaves in their camps.

Lincoln was morally opposed to slavery, but he was not an abolitionist. In October 1859, a militant abolitionist named John Brown and a band of followers staged a failed raid on the federal arsenal at Harper's Ferry, Virginia. Their plan was to arm the slaves of the South and start a bloody insurgency. But Brown's plan failed, and he was hanged in December. In the north, he became a martyr to the abolitionist cause - but not to Lincoln. He condemned Brown and anyone else who advocated violence to end slavery.

And then there was Harriet Beecher Stowe's novel *Uncle Tom's Cabin*. It sold more than 300,000 copies in 1852, the year it was published, while another million and a half unauthorized copies were also sold. Its portrayal of the evils of slavery was so emotionally effective that it touched the hearts - and enraged the passions-- of millions of people in the north. The book had more power than Stowe, or any of the abolitionists, could have imagined. Soon after the Civil War began, President Abraham Lincoln met Mrs. Stowe for the first time. He smiled kindly as he shook her hand and then sighed softly, "So, you're the little lady who started this war."

Lincoln tried hard to steer a moderate path between two political extremes and besides, when the war started, there were very few people in the north who were willing to go to war to end slavery - and Lincoln knew it.

As the war dragged on, the battles became bloodier and public attitudes became more bitter. Lincoln, as well as many others, began to change his mind about the issue of freeing slaves. Union soldiers on the front lines were not inclined to return runaway slaves to the very masters who were in rebellion and trying to kill them. Radicals in Congress and in the press were speaking out and clamoring for action on the slavery issue.

More importantly, men like Frederick Douglass were now educating Lincoln about how slavery could be used as a powerful weapon against the south. By late 1862, Lincoln saw that freeing the slaves could be idealistic and practical at the same time.

When he finally came to the decision that the slaves needed to be set free, he expressed the belief that it was fate that finally forced his hand in the matter. Writing to an ally, he stated, "I claim not to have controlled events, but confess plainly that events have controlled me."

A friend of Lincoln, Joseph Gillespie, later wrote, "After he became President, he gave unmistakable indications of being a believer in destiny. Mr. Lincoln had a strong faith that it was the purposes of the Almighty to save this country as Moses had that God would deliver the Israelites from bondage, and he came to believe that he himself was an instrument foreordained to aid in the accomplishment of this purpose as well as to emancipate the slaves."

In late July 1862, Lincoln presented a draft of the Emancipation Proclamation to his Cabinet. Only one member opposed the idea outright, although many others offered suggestions to improve or strengthen it. Seward, though, raised objections as to the timing and suggested that Lincoln delay it until there was a time that was more favorable to its cause. He wanted it to come from a position of strength, not weakness and, in that, he had a valid point. The Union wasn't faring well against the Confederacy at that time. Lincoln had been dealing with one ineffectual general after another and the north had been losing ground. In the end, Lincoln concurred with Seward and the proclamation was postponed.

He was resolved to wait for a sign that would let him know that the time was right to make the announcement.

But rumors spread that a document had been prepared that would free the slaves. Pressure mounted from the abolitionist press - and even from within his own administration -- to release it. William Lloyd Garrison, the fiery abolitionist publisher said that Lincoln was "nothing better than a wet rag." Others called Lincoln a tool of "traitors and rebels."

But Lincoln waited. He knew a sign was coming.

It finally came in September 1862. Confederate General Robert E. Lee and his Army of Northern Virginia crossed the Potomac River and began an invasion of the north, hoping to circle around and attack Washington from the northwest. If he succeeded, another Union defeat could cause Britain and France to finally recognize the Confederacy as a sovereign nation, which would put extensive military and economic resources at their disposal.

The only defense that the Union had was spearheaded by General George McClellan, the latest commander of the Army. He had proven himself to be so concerned about not losing battles that he seemed incapable of winning them. Time after time, his timidity had cost the Union chances for victory.

Things seemed dire and then a curious event occurred. It is one that has never truly been explained, and it changed the course of the battle to come. If it had not taken place, it's entirely possible that the outcome of the war could have been much different.

Copies of Special Order No. 191, which was Lee's plan for the invasion of the North, were sent out to all of Lee's generals. Thomas "Stonewall" Jackson received his copy of the order, copied it, and then sent it out to his brother-in-law, Harvey Hill, who also received a copy

The aftermath of the battle at Antietam

from Lee. Not realizing that Jackson had sent him an additional copy, Hill never knew that the second copy had not arrived.

On September 13, Union troops moved into a camp that had been recently abandoned by Hill. A corporal with the 27th Indiana Volunteers found an envelope containing three cigars wrapped around a piece of paper lying in the grass. The paper was a copy of Lee's orders. McClellan, upon being presented with the document, realized that he was now privy to Lee's secret plans. He is reported to have jubilantly stated, "Here is a paper with which, if I cannot whip Bobby Lee, then I will be willing to go home."

But even though he now possessed a step-by-step outline of the Confederates' plans for invading Maryland and attacking Washington, McClellan did nothing. His failure to act in such situations had previously cost the Union Army dearly and he was frequently criticized by President Lincoln for being overly cautious. This time was no exception. Instead of starting out immediately in pursuit of Lee's forces, McClellan waited overnight and then started west to South Mountain. He was convinced that Lee's dirty, tired, hungry army still outnumbered him. Ironically, the Union Army outnumbered Lee by more than 35,000 men.

On September 14, Lee tried to block McClellan's pursuit at South Mountain, but he was forced to split his army and send troops to aid Stonewall Jackson in his capture of Harper's Ferry. He was able to delay McClellan for one day, and by September 15, battle lines had been drawn west and east of Antietam Creek, near the town of Sharpsburg.

When the smoke finally cleared after the battle that occurred two days later, Lee was in retreat back to Virginia and McClellan was left with empty fields of the dead and dying. It is considered the bloodiest single day of the war - but the Confederacy's invasion was stopped.

Lincoln considered this the divine sign that he had been waiting for.

Only five days after Antietam, on September 22, he called a Cabinet meeting and formally announced his decision to issue the Emancipation Proclamation. He explained that, shortly before the battle, he had made a sacred vow to wait for a sign that would be an indication of "Divine Will that it was his duty to move forward in the cause of emancipation." After the battle was won, he said, he believed that "God had decided the question in favor of the slaves."

During this time, Lincoln began to show his first interest in the Spiritualist movement and began attending seances with Mary. A statement from Jack Laurie, the son of Cranston Laurie and his wife, Margaret, established that both Lincolns were present at the Laurie home for séances. He wrote:

I have on several occasions seen Mr. Lincoln at a circle at my father's house... take notes of what was said by mediums. At one circle... a heavy table was... raised and caused to dance about the room... Mr. Lincoln laughed heartily and said to my father, "Never mind, Cranston, if they break the table, I will give you a new one." On one occasion, my father asked Mr. Lincoln, if he believed the phenomena was caused by spirits, and Mr. Lincoln replied, that he did so believe. This was on a Sunday evening late in 1862. I fix the time by the fact that I was injured that same evening by a runaway horse. In 1862, I was fifteen years of age...

J.C. Laurie

Another observer, Mrs. Elvira M. Debuy, also participated in séances with the President. She wrote, "I have always known from my husband and others that Mr. Lincoln attended circles and séances and was greatly interested in Spiritualism. My husband was a visitor to séances where Mr. Lincoln was present, and he told me of many interesting occurrences. In the winter of 1862-1863, I attended a séance at Mrs. Lauries' in Georgetown, where Mrs. Lincoln was present. She was accompanied by Mr. Newton, Commissioner of Agriculture. At the séance, remarkable statements were made, which surprised Mrs. Lincoln to such a degree that she asked that a séance might be given to Mr. Lincoln."

Colonel Simon Kase also wrote about his experiences with Lincoln during seances that took place during the war. Writings by Kase were later used against him by a critic of Spiritualism named Fayette Hall. Hall was a Confederate sympathizer and claimed that "demonically possessed Spiritualists" had influenced Lincoln to free the slaves and destroy the South. He believed this had been accomplished by introducing Lincoln to celebrated medium J.B. Conklin, but I really don't think Kase had anything nefarious in mind.

Kase came to Washington in late 1862 as a lobbyist on behalf of his nephew's railroad. One afternoon, he took a walk past a building where he used to work and discovered that Conklin had set up shop in his old office. According to Kase, he had the overwhelming urge to enter the building and he found the medium writing a letter while in a trance. After he returned to consciousness, Conklin - who had no idea who Kase was - urged him to take the letter to President Lincoln immediately. Although shocked by the strange request, Colonel Kase decided to go along with it, and he took Conklin with him to the White House.

A couple of things need to be noted here. First, it was a lot easier to meet with the President in those days than it is now. Just about anyone could get a meeting if they waited long enough. Secondly, this was not Conklin's first attempt to get the attention of President Lincoln. Earlier in the year, he had sent him a letter that allegedly contained a spirit communication from Lincoln's old friend, Edward Baker. There's no way to know if Lincoln saw the letter or not, but if he did, he didn't extend an invitation to the medium to visit the White House. Kase, though, was able to get him inside.

At the White House, Colonel Kase managed to get a meeting on the books with Lincoln, but Conklin was left behind in the gentlemen's parlor. After a greeting between the two men, Kase handed Lincoln the letter. The letter from Conklin read: "Sir, I have been sent by the spirit world to speak with you upon matters of vital importance to the nation. I cannot return to New York until I have seen you."

Kase later said that Lincoln was "stunned" by the message. In my opinion, he'd probably seen a lot of letters just like it. However, before Kase left, Lincoln agreed to meet Conklin on the following Sunday morning at 10:00 a.m. To Kase, this meant that Lincoln was interested in Spiritualism, but to others it was simply in keeping with the man's curiosity. A friend of the President later wrote, "He has an orbit of his own, and no one can tell where he will be or what he will do, from anything done yesterday."

It is unknown if Lincoln kept his appointment with Conklin. If he did, he never became part of the Lincolns' inner Spiritualist circle and was never mentioned in writings from any of those who were. He simply became just another medium who contacted the President - and there were plenty of them.

Even God had messages for the President. Writing through the mediumistic powers of Lydia Smith, God told him, "Now Abram Lincoln, I want you to call together six of your best men in the army on the first day possible... I want you to have this medium present and I will tell you and the six beside yourself just what to do that will speedily terminate this devilish war now existing in your midst." If Lincoln ignored this summons, God warned, there would be dreadful punishments. Lincoln decided to take his chances and he never summoned Lydia Smith to Washington.

It wouldn't be long, and Lincoln wouldn't have to look for messages from outside the city - soon they would be coming from inside the White House.

Among the hundreds of Spiritualist mediums who flocked to Washington during the war was a young woman named Nettie Colburn Maynard, a trance medium from upstate New York.

In the 1850s, a teenaged Nettie became aware of her mediumistic abilities when she discovered that she could induce spirit rappings -- knocking sounds purported to be communications from the other side. Her ability manifested itself during the 1856 James Buchanan and John C. Fremont presidential election, in which Nettie's father, a staunch Fremont supporter, found out how accurate his daughter's talents could be. Too young and inexperienced to comprehend the political differences between the two candidates, she was nevertheless "seized by a power that I could not control" on the day before the election. Grabbing a piece of paper, Nettie scrawled the word "Buchanan" on it and as she did "loud raps came upon the table". Her startled father asked if this meant that Buchanan would win the election. Nettie said that it did and the next day, her prediction proved to be accurate. Her father became convinced that she could help others with her talents.

Nettie Colburn Maynard

With her father's approval and support, Nettie went on to become a "spirit lecturer," mainly in New England towns and villages. When the Civil War began in April 1861, despite northern boasts of a quick victory, she predicted otherwise. "Our spirit friends," she said, "reply ... it would continue four years and require five practically to end it."

By 1861, the 21-year-old had become a successful and popular speaker on the Spiritualist lecture circuit. During one lecture, she went into a trance and claimed that her spirit guide informed her there was a "Congress of Spirits" -- comprised of leading Americans who had died - who had selected her for an important mission. They wanted her to travel to Washington so that she could relay messages and advice to President Lincoln. After learning what the spirits wanted her to do, Nettie balked at the idea, believing she would receive "poor reception in the presence of the first ruler of the land."

As it happened, though, Nettie was in Washington in December 1862. While lecturing in Baltimore, she received a letter from her youngest brother stating that he was seriously ill in a military hospital and that he needed her help in getting a furlough so that he could return home to recover.

After arriving in Washington, Nettie quickly found herself immersed in the city's Spiritualist community, who welcomed her into their ranks. She took up residence in the home of a friend, Mrs. Anna Cosby, whose father had been Robert Mills, the architect who had designed the capitol building. While living in the Cosby home, Nettie met many prominent people, including General Simon Cameron and other military officers with an interest in the spirit world. She was also introduced to Spiritualist lecturer and War Department official Thomas Gales Foster, former Congressman Daniel E. Somes, and Cranston and Margaret Laurie. In addition to being one of Washington's leading Spiritualists, Laurie was also an official with the U.S. Postal Service.

At the Laurie house, Nettie gave public and private seances and met one of the Lauries' clients, Mary Lincoln. In 1891, Nettie recalled that meeting in her memoirs. She wrote, "Some new and powerful influence obtained possession of my organism and addressed Mrs. Lincoln, it seemed, with great clearness and force, upon matters of state."

Whatever Nettie said to Mary at this meeting - and Nettie always claimed that while in a trance she had no memory of what was said - it struck a chord with the First Lady.

After the séance, Mary was so impressed with Nettie that she told the Lauries, "This young lady must not leave Washington. I feel she must stay here, and Mr. Lincoln must hear what we have heard. It is all-important, and he must hear it."

To keep Nettie in the city, Mary used her clout to arrange for her to be employed as a clerk for the Department of Agriculture, where she filled packets of seeds. She also arranged for Nettie's brother to receive the furlough that he needed so he could go home and recover from his illness.

According to Nettie, she first met President Lincoln on February 5, 1863, during a séance in Georgetown that he was not scheduled to attend. The medium would later claim that her "spirit guide" told her that Lincoln would be in attendance. The host of the party declared that this was unlikely to happen, as Lincoln rarely attended séances away from the White House. To his surprise, though, the President did come, and the host exclaimed upon seeing him that he had been expected. Lincoln was reportedly shocked and stated that he had not been planning to come but only accompanied Mary that night on a whim.

During the séance, Lincoln was allegedly contacted by an "old Dr. Bramford," who is said to have given him information about the state of the war. Nettie later quoted the spirit as saying, "a very precarious state of things existed at the front, where General Hooker had just taken command. The army was totally demoralized; regiments stacking arms, refusing to obey orders and do duty; threatening a general retreat; declaring their purpose to return to Washington."

An illustration of Lincoln at one of Nettie Maynard's seances

She wrote that the vivid picture of this terrible state of affairs seemed to surprise everyone but Lincoln, who spoke up to the spirit. "You seem to understand the situation," he said. "Can you point out the remedy?"

Dr. Bramford replied that he had one, but only if Lincoln had the courage to use it. The President smiled and challenged the eerie voice that was coming to him from the darkness. According to the spirit, the remedy for success lay with Lincoln himself. He spoke: "Go in person to the front; taking with you your wife and children; leaving behind your official dignity, and all manner of display. Resist the importunities of officials to accompany you and take only such attendants as may be absolutely necessary; avoid the high-grade officers and seek the tents of the private soldiers. Inquire into their grievances; show yourself to be what you are -- 'The Father of Your People.' Make them feel you are interested in their sufferings, and that you are not unmindful of the many trials which beset them in their march through the dismal swamps, whereby both their courage and numbers have been depleted."

Lincoln is said to have replied that if this would do the soldiers good, that such a thing was easily done. The mysterious voice explained that it would do all that was required to unite the soldiers again.

In April, Lincoln paid a lengthy visit to the Army of the Potomac, arriving at Aquia Creek and traveling by train to Falmouth where Hooker's men were camped. From there, Lincoln could see with a spy glass across the Rappahannock to Fredericksburg, where Robert E. Lee's Army of Virginia waited, less than a half mile away. A short time later, the overconfident Hooker led the Union to one of the costliest defeats of the war at Chancellorsville. Amid this disaster, though, his men followed him bravely into battle. It was believed that their courage had been restored by the visit from President Lincoln.

Nettie Maynard later recalled that after the advice given by Dr. Bramford, the spirit and the President continued to speak about the war and other affairs of the state. The spirit also told him that "he would be re-nominated and re-elected to the Presidency."

This was more unusual than most modern readers might believe because, at that point in history, no President had ever been elected to a second term. Lincoln was not shocked by the news. He smiled sadly, however, and said, "It is hardly an honor to be coveted, save one could find it his duty to accept it."

It was during the same séance where Lincoln's second term was predicted by the spirits that perhaps the most famous incident connected to the President and the Spiritualists took place. A prominent local medium named Belle Miller was playing the piano and, under her influence, the piano "rose and fell" off the floor, keeping time to her fingers on the keys.

It was an amazing display of the power of the spirts, everyone agreed, but someone suggested that as an added test of the invisible power causing the instrument to move, Belle should place her hand on the piano and stand at an arm's length from it. This would show that she was in no way connected to it except as an agent of the mysterious power.

President Lincoln then placed his hand underneath the piano, at the end that was closest to Mrs. Miller, who placed her hand upon his

An illustration of the "floating piano" that allegedly occurred at a séance that Lincoln attended with medium Belle Miller at the keyboard

to demonstrate that neither strength nor pressure was being used. In this position, the piano rose and fell several times, seemingly at their bidding. Lincoln even changed places to stand on the other side of the piano, but the same thing continued to happen.

Lincoln was reported to have grinned at the display and said that he believed he could hold the instrument to the floor. He climbed up onto it, sitting with his long legs dangling over the side, as did a Congressman Somes, Colonel Simon Kase, and an unnamed Federal officer. The piano, ignoring the enormous weight now upon it, continued to wobble up and down until the sitters were obliged to "vacate the premises."

The audience was, by this time, satisfied to the fact that no mechanical means had been used to move the instrument and Lincoln himself declared that he was sure the motion was caused by some "invisible power."

Mr. Somes spoke up, "Mr. President, when I have related to my acquaintances that which I have experienced tonight, they will say, with a knowing look and a wise demeanor, 'you were psychologized and as a matter of fact, you did not see what you in reality did see.'"

"You should bring that person here," Lincoln quietly replied, "and when the piano seems to rise, have him slip his foot under the leg and be convinced by the weight of the evidence resting upon his understanding."

Nettie Maynard held many seances for the Lincolns during the latter days of February and early Match 1863. The séances all took place by appointment and after the close of each session, Mary made another appointment to come at a certain hour of another day, usually around the time that the President took his lunch in the afternoon.

Mary and Nettie had formed a relationship based on the young woman's ability to channel the spirits. Because of the services she offered, she was trusted by Mary - and by the President, too - and was given full access to the White House. There is no record to say that Nettie was paid outright for her services, but there is no question that she received material advantages and influence from her close relationship with the First Lady. She was publicly discreet but her activities at the White House were well-known in Spiritualist circles.

And among them were those who took advantage of Nettie to try and reach the President for their own purposes. In one instance, it wasn't just Nettie who was used, but Lincoln's old friend, Joshua Speed, as well.

Lincoln's relationship with Speed had cooled somewhat since they became close friends in Springfield in the 1840s. Speed had moved back home to Kentucky and still owned slaves. Even though he professed loyalty to the Union, he openly disagreed with his old friend's political policies in print. Throughout the war, Speed made several visits to Washington, and it was during one of these visits that he was apparently recruited to reach out to Lincoln on behalf of Nettie and especially for her friend, Anna Cosby, with whom she had been living. Anna's husband had recently lost his position as consul to Switzerland after being accused of associating with Confederate officials who were looking for European aid.

Nettie was worried that because of her friend's fall from grace, Nettie's own access to the Lincolns and to the White House might be affected - or so she had been convinced.

Nettie was a naïve young woman who often found herself taken in by people who didn't have her best interests at heart. For instance, she had once been summoned back to Washington during a trip to New York by Colonel Morgan H. Chrysler because he needed her help in acquiring the command of a brigade. He was so convinced that Nettie could influence President Lincoln - and convinced of the "unseen powers" that controlled her, he said - that he covered all her expenses for her return trip.

In this situation, the attention-seekers who used Nettie to reach out to the President on their behalf were worried that she might be tainted by her association with the Cosbys. They convinced her that she needed to try and smooth things over with the Lincolns and managed to also convince Joshua Speed to help her.

Nettie needn't have worried about the President. When she arrived at the White House the next time, he accepted her into his office and greeted her warmly, just as he always had.

I'm sure this was a relief to all the favor-seekers who would continue to use Nettie in the years to come. Was Lincoln aware of what was happening with the medium? It's hard to say. Lincoln could certainly be shrewd when he wanted to be, although there were times when her requests were brushed off or, in the case of anything to do with the military, he directed her to take matters to the Edwin Stanton, the Secretary of War. In such cases, it was easy for Stanton to dismiss her requests and allow Lincoln to maintain his friendly relationship with Nettie.

It's possible, though, that Lincoln knew things about the young medium that no one else did.

There is the account of Nettie being summoned to a séance at the White House one evening by Congressman Somes, who told her that the meeting was of such a private nature that he was not at liberty to say more. Somes picked her up in a carriage and explained that while at the War Department that afternoon, he had met President Lincoln coming from Secretary Stanton's office. Somes spoke to him briefly and Lincoln asked him if he knew if Nettie was in the city and if she was, would it be possible for her to visit the White House that night. When Somes told him that Nettie was indeed in Washington, Lincoln asked that she come that evening, but that the matter should be kept confidential.

By the time that Somes had finished explaining what had occurred, the carriage had arrived at the White House. A waiting servant ushered them inside and they were hurried up to the President's office, where Lincoln and two other men were waiting. The President sent the servant out of the room and a few moments later, Mary entered the chamber. Lincoln told Nettie that he wished for her to give the visitors an opportunity to witness something of her "rare gift" and he added, "you need not be afraid, as these friends have seen something of this before."

Nettie described the men as being military officers, although their coats had been buttoned to conceal any insignia or rank. One of the men was tall and heavily built, with auburn hair and dark eyes. He had thick side whiskers and carried himself like a soldier. The other man was of average height and she had the impression that he was of a lesser rank than his companion. He had light brown hair and blue eyes and was quick in manner but deferential towards his companion.

The group sat quietly for a few moments and then Nettie entered a trance. One hour later, she became conscious of her surroundings and was standing at a table that had a large map of the Southern states lying on it. She held a lead pencil in her hand and Lincoln and the two men were standing close to her, bending over the map. The younger man was looking curiously and intently at her.

"It is astonishing," Mr. Lincoln was saying to the other officer, "how every line she has drawn conforms to the plan agreed upon."

"Yes," answered the other man. "It is astonishing."

Looking up, both men saw that Nettie had slipped out of her trance was awake again and they instantly stepped back. Lincoln took the pencil from Nettie's hand and eased her into a nearby chair. Mary soon appeared at her side to offer some comfort.

"Was everything satisfactory?" Somes asked the assembled men.

"Perfectly." Lincoln replied. "Miss Nettie does not seem to require eyes to do anything."

Shortly after, the conversation turned to more mundane matters and after a brief time, the military men left the room. Before Lincoln also departed, he carefully shook Nettie's small hand and said to her in a low voice: "It is best not to mention this meeting at the present."

This was the last time that the private séance was ever mentioned and Nettie never learned the identity of the two men who were with President Lincoln that night --- or just what the spirits may have revealed with the map of the Confederacy.

And this was reportedly not the only time that Nettie's contact with the spirit world provided answers for Lincoln.

In May 1863, she came to the White House to see Mary, arriving at the same time the battle of Chancellorsville was being fought. Nettie was brought into Mary's bedroom and she found the First Lady wearing only her dressing gown. Her hair was loose, and she was pacing back and forth in a distracted manner.

"Oh Miss Nettie," Mary cried, "such dreadful news; they are fighting at the front; such terrible slaughter; and all our generals are killed and our army is in full retreat; such is the latest news. Oh, I am glad you have come. Will you sit down a few moments and see if you can get anything from the beyond?"

Nettie was surprised by the news. Word of the battle had not yet reached the public. She put her things aside and sat down with Mary to let her "spirit guide" take control of her. In a few moments, she was able to reassure Mary that her fears were groundless. A great battle was being fought, but the Union forces were holding their own and while many thousands had been killed, none of the generals, as she had been informed, were slain, or injured. She would, Nettie assured her, receive better news by nightfall.

This calmed Mary somewhat but when President Lincoln entered the room a short time later, it was obvious that he was still anxiously worrying about what was occurring at the front lines. He greeted Nettie with little enthusiasm, but Mary insisted that he listen to what the medium had to say. Lincoln listened attentively to what had been passed on from Nettie's "spirit guide," recounting the true conditions at the front and assuring him of the good news that he would receive before nightfall. The battle would be costly, the spirits said, but not disastrous, and though not decisive in any way, it would not be a loss to the Union cause.

Lincoln brightened visibly under the assurances that he was given, and he later learned that Nettie's information had been correct. Chancellorsville resulted in the lives of many men lost and effectively ended the career of General Joseph Hooker, but no real ground was lost by the Union. Hooker had marched into a Confederate controlled area and his outnumbered army was sent into retreat but regrouped to fight another day.

One military man who did not keep his association with Nettie Maynard private was General Daniel Sickles, one of the most notorious men to attend seances at the White House.

Sickles was an eccentric and unusual man. Born to a wealthy family in 1819, he rose to political power thanks to Tammany Hall, the political machine in New York City. When he was 33, he married a woman less than half his age, which was only one of the many scandals in which he became embroiled during his lifetime.

When he discovered that his wife, Teresa, was having an affair, he shot and killed her lover on February 27, 1859. The dead man was Phillip Barton Key, a U.S. Attorney and the son of Francis Scott Key, author of "The Star-Spangled Banner." After slaying the man in broad daylight, Sickles turned himself over to the law.

General Daniel Sickles

In a matter of weeks, Congressman Sickles was on trial and he put forward a novel defense - temporary insanity. Witnesses backed up the wild claim, which had never before been used in an American courtroom. A former senator, Robert Walker, described Sickles moments after the shooting. Sickles made "unnatural and unearthly sounds," according to Walker. "The most remarkable I ever heard - something like a scream interrupted by violent sobbing."

Sickles brought seven defense attorneys to court. One of them, John Graham, spent two full days just giving his opening statement. He told the jury, "It may be tragical to shed human blood; but I will always maintain that there is no tragedy about slaying the adulterer. Philip Barton Key seduced the wife of Daniel E. Sickles, and for that, in a transport of frenzy, Daniel E. Sickles sent him to his long account."

After 20 days of testimony, the jury debated Sickles' sanity and were split. Two religious jurors insisted that taking life was wrong, no matter what the reason, and yet, after an hour of argument and prayer, the jury decided to let Sickles go free.

Chaos erupted in the courtroom and one of Sickles' attorneys even danced a jig. That attorney, by the way, was Edwin Stanton, Lincoln's future Secretary of War. Outside the courthouse, a crowd cheered Sickles and treated him like a hero for escaping the charge. A parade was even arranged in his honor. But the city was less accepting of Sickles' decision to take his wife back. "I shall strive to prove to all that an erring wife and mother may be forgiven and redeemed," Sickles declared.

With the public turned against him, Sickles expected to lose his next congressional race. Instead of running, he finished his term and made plans to return to New York and turn his attention to the brewing Civil War. He began raising fighting men for the Union, earning himself an officer's position, even though he had no formal military training. Congress initially turned down his appointment until President Lincoln interceded and made the former congressman a general.

He became one of the most prominent political generals of the Civil War, and at the battle of Gettysburg, Sickles disobeyed his commander, General George Meade, who ordered Sickles and his troops to hold their position. He disagreed and wanted to move to higher ground. Without permission from Meade, Sickles moved his troops, and broke the Union line. In the clash that followed, Sickles suffered a serious injury. A cannonball struck his leg, which had to be amputated. While recovering, Sickles escaped a court-martial for disobeying orders.

But he didn't leave his amputated leg on the battlefield. Instead, he donated it to the Army Medical Museum in Washington, and he reportedly visited it every year on the anniversary of the Gettysburg conflict.

Sickles' wife, Teresa, died when she was only 31 and he went on to get involved in several scandalous affairs, including high-profile liaisons with Fanny White, a famed New York madam, and with Queen Isabella II of Spain. Their affair became even more embarrassing after Sickles married one of her attendants.

In his early '90s, Sickles still had a government position overseeing the building of Civil War monuments in New York. But in 1912, officials discovered that $28,000 was missing from the commission's funds and Sickles was arrested. Once again, he managed to avoid prison. His supporters raised enough money to pay back the misappropriated funds. Daniel Sickles died two years later.

Sickles interest in Spiritualism began years earlier, before the war. In fact, on the night that he learned Teresa was having an affair with Phillip Barton Key, Sickles was giving a party in his Washington home that was enlivened by the presence of the Scottish wife of *New York Herald* editor James Gordon Bennett, an ardent Spiritualist. Mrs. Bennett had attended many séances in Washington and spoke openly of them.

In the summer after Willie Lincoln died, Sickles became a frequent guest at Mary Lincoln's seances. He returned to Washington after losing his leg at Gettysburg and continued the regular visitations. In early 1864, Sickles decided to concoct a ruse to test the spiritual powers of Mary's young medium, Nettie Maynard. Mary agreed to go along with the ruse, perhaps to teach a lesson to the general.

Nettie had recently returned to Washington after a brief absence and was living at the home of Mr. and Mrs. Somes. Nettie called at the White House, to pay her respects to the President and the First Lady and was warmly received. Lincoln expressed the hope that she had come to Washington to spend the rest of the year.

A few days later, Nettie, along with Somes and his wife, were invited back to the White House to meet a friend -- Daniel Sickles in a disguise. Mrs. Lincoln, in her invitation to Nettie, mentioned her desire to see if Nettie's "spirit guide" would be able to tell who the friend was.

The party arrived at 8:30 p.m. and was welcomed by the First Lady, who introduced them to a distinguished, soldierly gentleman, who was wrapped in a long cloak, completely concealing his person. Mrs. Lincoln did not call him by name, apologizing for not doing so, and explained that she wanted to see if her spirit friends could recognize him. She promised to present him afterward. Mr. Somes recognized Sickles immediately but gave no hint of the general's identity.

President Lincoln had a late-night Cabinet meeting and after joining the group, asked that the proceedings be brief. Silence fell on the group and Nettie entered into a trance. The spirits that spoke through her turned all their attentions on Lincoln. Their remarks related to the condition of free black people in Washington, declaring that their condition was deplorable -- they were half-fed and half-clothed --- and stated this should be an embarrassment to the country. The spirits called on Lincoln to form a special committee to investigate the condition of their people, and to organize a bureau to control and regulate the affairs of the free men and women of color. The Bureau of Freemen was eventually formed in March 1865, but if Nettie really influenced its creation, those notes are missing from its history.

When the spirit was finished communicating with Lincoln, Nettie turned to Sickles and referred to him as "General" and praised him for the "noble sacrifice" of his leg at Gettysburg. A few moments later, another presence took control of Nettie -- her usual "spirit guide", who was an Indian woman -- and she turned to Sickles and addressed him as "Crooked Knife," her Native American name for him, which was close enough to "Sickles" that everyone present was satisfied.

After Lincoln hurried off to his meeting and Nettie awoke, Mary made the promised presentation of General Sickles, who put aside the cloak, revealing his uniform and concealed crutch. Sickles had no choice but to confess that he was impressed with Mary's young medium.

Abraham Lincoln had spent most of his adult life under a dark cloud. He always believed that a portent of doom hung over him. Even when he told Mary about the visions that he experienced on Election Day in 1860, he was not surprised to learn that she interpreted them to mean that death awaited him in his second term.

As the war continued, there were constant threats of death and violence. He received frequent letters that were filled with hate and these missives kept his friends and personal bodyguards constantly on edge.

But Lincoln chafed at what he felt was their overprotection. "I cannot be shut up in an iron cage and guarded," Lincoln irritably told those who worried that his security was inadequate. A president must go among the people, Lincoln tried to explain. "One man's life is as dear to him as another's, and if a man takes my life, he may be reasonably sure that he will lose his own," he told a friend, Congressman Cornelius Cole. Lincoln had thought of assassination, yes, "but I do not believe it is my fate to die in this way."

But this did nothing to ease the worry of Lincoln's friends. As the Civil War entered its final months, the Confederacy became desperate, making plans to rob northern banks, wreck trains, raid prison camps, and even send disease-infested clothing to Washington. One night, Rebels tried to burn 19 hotels and public buildings in New York. After the Union targeted Jefferson Davis for capture or worse, many now wondered if the south, in response, might suspend the unwritten rules that protected Lincoln from a bullet.

In addition to the constant warnings from his friends, loved ones, and bodyguards about his life being in danger, Lincoln also received letters and messages from Spiritualists who feared that he might be killed. This was nothing new. Since he was nominated by the Republicans to run for president in 1860, there had been letters of warning sprinkled in with the hate mail that arrived for him each day. The letters carried warnings from the spirits, from long-dead American statesmen, and even from angels, Jesus Christ, and the Almighty himself. Even though Lincoln's thoughts about the validity of Spiritualism had likely changed by the end of the war, he still didn't put much stock in the warnings that he received from the other side.

Although maybe he should have.

Charles J. Colchester was one of the men who warned Lincoln that his life was in danger. He wasn't a close friend, like Lincoln's bodyguard Ward Lamon, or a member of his Cabinet, like Edwin Stanton. In fact, Lincoln hardly knew him, even though he was a frequent visitor to the White House. Colchester was a Spiritualist, a medium who had become important to Mary since Willie's death, and he was probably the one person whose warning Lincoln should have heeded. Colchester didn't need psychic powers to know the president was in danger, though. His information probably came from another source - from his friend, an actor named John Wilkes Booth.

After Colchester arrived in the city, he quickly ingratiated himself in Spiritualist circles. He was a young, red-faced, blue-eyed Englishman with a large mustache. Alleged to be the illegitimate son of a duke - he wasn't - he claimed to have remarkable powers. Among his many gifts were his ability to read sealed letters, see spirits and cause them to appear, and produce words on his forearm in blood-red letters.

A Cincinnati newspaper reported, "Colchester is regarded as the leader of Spiritualism in America and, as a consequence, his votaries, believers, and visitors are counted by the hundreds."

To believers, he was an extraordinarily gifted medium, but to skeptics, he was a con artist who employed sleight of hand, hypnosis, and sideshow magic in darkened rooms to make money off the grieving and brokenhearted. It should perhaps be noted that, in the fall of 1865, he was convicted in upstate New York of practicing sleight of hand without a license and died in Iowa a few years later.

Colchester set up shop in Washington during the war and before long was becoming well-known to other Spiritualists and to those in mourning, like Mary Lincoln. He was introduced to her - as most other mediums were at the time - by a Spiritualist that she trusted. He was soon performing seances for her at the White House and at the Soldier's Home, where a presidential summer cottage sat on a hill north of downtown.

The first séance took place at the Soldier's Home. Mary was eager to experience it because Colchester told her that he was going to produce messages from Willie. She didn't want to go alone, so she invited family friend Noah Brooks to join her.

Brooks was a journalist who had written and edited newspapers in California, New Jersey, and New York. He would also later write an extensive biography of Abraham Lincoln. The two men had become friends when Brooks was living in Dixon, Illinois in 1856, where he became involved in the first Republican presidential campaign for John C. Fremont. After the death of his wife in 1862, Brooks moved to Washington as a writer for the *Sacramento Daily Union* and was accepted into the Lincoln household as an old friend. He maintained a close friendship with both Mr. and Mrs. Lincoln until their respective deaths.

Mary had tried hard to convert Brooks into a believer in Spiritualism - especially with the death of his wife - but he remained skeptical and only accepted Mary's invitation to the séance to watch out for her interests. He was not impressed by what he saw there. He later wrote, "By playing on her motherly sorrows, Colchester actually succeeded in inducing Mrs. Lincoln to receive him in the family residence at the Soldier's Home, where, in a darkened room, he pretended to produce messages from the boy by means of scratches on the wainscoting and taps on the walls and furniture."

But while Brooks was dismissive, Mary was enthralled. She refused to listen to anything Brooks tried to tell her about what was going on. Instead, she only wanted to share the news of the séance with her husband, who agreed to sit down with the medium in the White House.

After a few sittings with Colchester, Lincoln became particularly intrigued by his eerie ability to create noises in different parts of a room. He wanted to understand what was happening, so he asked the medium to submit to being examined by Joseph Henry, the Secretary of the Smithsonian Institution. Colchester agreed and a chagrined Joseph Henry reported back to the president that he had no immediate explanation for what was causing the phenomenon - but he believed the noises were not coming from the room, but from Colchester himself. He was unable to find anything out of the ordinary on the man, however.

Later, Henry's suspicions would be proven right. While on a train, Henry met a man who sold instruments to Colchester and other fraudulent mediums to aid them in their presentations. Colchester, for instance, wore a specially designed electric noisemaker strapped to his biceps. Henry wasn't able to expose the man as a charlatan to the Lincolns, but it didn't matter because by then, Noah Brooks had already done it.

Meanwhile, Colchester was moving in some questionable circles that went behind just Spiritualist mediums. As a regular on the Washington social circuit, the medium met and became acquainted with popular stage actor John Wilkes Booth. He was also living in Washington at the time and was plotting to abduct President Lincoln as a hostage for the Confederacy.

Booth formed a close friendship with the medium. His own interest in Spiritualism had started in 1863, when his sister-in-law, Molly, died. He and his widowed brother, Edwin, attended many seances together, but it was John who became particularly fascinated with the movement.

He became attached to the remarkable brothers Ira and William Davenport, who were more magicians and escape artists than actual spirit mediums. They did bring a sense of sensationalism to the movement, though, and inspired a legion of followers. Their act introduced the idea of a "spirit cabinet" to future seances. At each

The actor John Wilkes Booth had a developed an interest in Spiritualism after the death of his sister-in-law. He was also fascinated by the Davenport Brothers, who became famous as spirit mediums.

performance, they were tied up inside a sealed box with musical instruments - that audiences could then hear playing. Yet, when the box was opened and the brothers were revealed to be still tied in their original positions, it seemed as if they had summoned a ghostly orchestra to perform. Booth loved the Davenports and had private sittings with them whenever he could.

In the spring of 1865 - just weeks before Lincoln's murder - Booth was living at the National Hotel on Pennsylvania Avenue, just six blocks from the Capitol and even closer to Ford's Theatre. Colchester often visited him there. The two men drank together, and Colchester would often use his "psychic skills" to his friend's advantage. In addition to being able to communicate with the dead, Colchester also claimed to be able to foretell the future - a useful ability to a man with the kind of plans that Booth was making. According to George W. Bunker, the National's room clerk, the two men spent a considerable amount of time at the hotel, and often went out in one another's company. Bunker stated that Colchester was not merely Booth's friend - he was Booth's "associate."

At this same time, Colchester was causing trouble at the White House. Most likely, he was a fraud, but even if he wasn't, he turned out to be a man who was receptive to the distilled kind of spirits, not just the ethereal ones. Most of the money he earned from his seances was spent on whiskey. Chronically short of cash, he was greedy, dishonest, and a lot of trouble.

Having gained the trust of Mary Lincoln, he demanded that she get him a free railroad pass from the War Department. He made it clear that if she refused, then he would go public with some of the embarrassing things he had learned about the Lincolns during his seances. Frantic, Mary went to Noah Brooks and told him about the blackmail attempt.

Friend of the Lincoln family, journalist Noah Brooks

Brooks decided to confront the medium. He paid $1 to attend a Colchester séance "at the house of a Washington gentleman who was a profound believer in the pretentious seer," he later wrote. He took a friend with him who was also a reporter. Neither man was impressed by what he experienced in the séance room.

The group was instructed to sit holding hands around a table on which a banjo, drum, and bell were placed. When the lights went out, music began to play from the instruments. Breaking his hands free, Brooks grasped in the direction of the sound and cracked his head on something hard. He held his grip, however, and when his friend struck a match, Colchester's hand -- holding a bell and a drum that had left a gash on Brooks' head -- was in his grasp.

Colchester left the room and refused to return, saying he was "so outraged by this insult."

Even after he was exposed, Colchester went after Mary again. It's likely that he had no idea who Brooks was, or that he was a close friend of the Lincolns. A few days after the interrupted séance, Brooks received a note from Mary, asking him to come to the White House. When he arrived, he found her frazzled and upset. She showed him a letter she had gotten from Colchester, demanding the railroad pass - or else.

Furious, Brooks arranged for Mary to invite the medium to the White House the next day. He arrived with the expectation that he would receive the rail pass but found Noah Brooks waiting for him instead. After formally introducing Colchester to Brooks, Mary left the room. Brooks lifted his hair from the unhealed scar on his forehead and asked the medium if he recognized it. "You know that I know you are a swindler and a humbug," Brooks growled at him. He warned him to leave the Lincolns alone and Colchester fled from the building.

A short time later, John Wilkes Booth abandoned his plot to kidnap Lincoln and began to plan his assassination instead. In front of many of his trusted friends in Washington, he threatened to kill the President. It is more than likely that Colchester was there for these threats, but there are no definitive records of his presence.

However, we do know that Colchester - whatever else he might have done - did warn President Lincoln that trouble was coming. A few days after the incident with Brooks, a Lincoln staff member urged the president to be mindful of his safety and he responded, "Colchester has been telling me that." While warning Lincoln of impending doom had become a standard routine for mediums at the time, this was one mystic who knew what he was talking about. For all his faults, Colchester's crimes were always misdemeanors - he had no murder in his heart. Even so, he didn't betray his friend Booth either. He probably felt that he had done what he could, and it was up to the president to act on the information.

But those who knew Lincoln knew that he wouldn't. Lincoln "was too intelligent not to know he was in danger," wrote his secretaries John G. Nicolay and John Hay. "But he had himself so sane a mind and a heart so kindly, even to his enemies, that it was hard for him to believe in a political hatred so deadly as to lead to murder."

Lincoln routinely disregarded all the warnings he received, which led to his death on April 14, 1865. After the assassination, the search for the killer and his accomplices immediately began. Colonel Henry H. Wells, a top military policeman, went to the National Hotel to look for information about Booth. Bunker, the room clerk, told him about Booth's association with Colchester and said the medium had been staying at the Washington House.

But Wells didn't find him there - nor anywhere else in Washington. Like the spirits that were said to swirl about his séance table would do when exposed to the light of day, Colchester vanished.

By the late winter and early spring of 1865, the war was nearing its end. In late February, Washington was filled to capacity with people who had come to witness the second inauguration of President Lincoln. But Nettie Maynard found herself summoned out of town. Her father had become extremely ill and she was asked to come home at once. Her trip was going to interfere with an appointment that she had with Mary Lincoln, so she made a trip to the White House to tell her that she had to leave town. Mary was away so Nettie went upstairs to leave word with the President instead. This is another indication of how much access the young medium had to the White House and the First Family.

It was the early part of the afternoon, and during the last days of the expiring Congress, and the waiting room was filled with members of both the House and the Senate, all anxious to get a word with the President. Nettie soon became doubtful that she would obtain any time with Mr. Lincoln, especially because many of the prominent men had been waiting for several hours. Edward, Lincoln's devoted usher, was walking back and forth and collecting calling cards to take in to the President and Nettie called him over. She explained that she needed only a moment with Lincoln and asked for any opportunity to tell him why she would have to cancel her appointment the following week.

Half an hour went by and Edward appeared and asked Nettie to follow him. Several of the senators that Nettie knew laughed when she was led away to Lincoln's office and asked with a smile that she put in a good word for them. She was soon in the presence of the President. He stood at his desk, looking over some papers but laid them down and greeted her with a genial smile. In as few words as possible, knowing how precious his time was, she informed him of her unusual call and told him that she had been summoned out of town because her father was seriously ill. Lincoln looked at her with a curious smile. "But cannot our friends from the upper country tell you whether his illness is likely to prove fatal or not?"

Nettie replied that she had already consulted with her "friends" and they had assured her that his treatment was wrong and that her presence was needed to affect a cure.

Lincoln laughed and turned to his secretary. "I didn't catch her, did I?" he teased Nettie and then seriously added that he was sorry that she would be away during the inauguration.

"I would enjoy it," she assured him, "but the crowd will be so great that we will not be able to see you, Mr. Lincoln, even if I remain."

"You could not help it," he answered, drawing his lean figure to its full height and glancing at her in an amused way. "I will be the tallest man there."

"That is true, in every sense of the word."

Lincoln nodded pleasantly at the compliment and then asked Nettie what her "friends" predicted for his future.

"What they predicted for you, Mr. Lincoln, has come to pass and you are to be inaugurated for the second time." He nodded his head and she continued. "But they also reaffirm that the shadow they have spoken of still hangs over you."

Lincoln shook his head impatiently. "Yes, I know," he said quickly. "I have letters from all over the country from your kind of people --- mediums, I mean --- warning me against some dreadful plot against my life. But I don't think the knife is made, or the bullet run, that will reach it. Besides, nobody wants to harm me."

A feeling of sadness overwhelmed Nettie. It was a feeling that she could not account for and one that she could not conceal. She spoke to the President boldly: "Therein lies your danger, Mr. President --- your overconfidence in your fellow men."

The old melancholy look that Nettie had grown so used to in her time of friendship with the President and his wife descended over his face. His voice was quiet and subdued. "Well, Miss Nettie," he said, "I shall live until my work is done and no earthly power can prevent it."

Then, brightening a little, he extended his hand to her. "Well, I suppose that I must bid you goodbye, but we shall hope to see you back again next fall."

"I shall certainly come," Nettie told him, "if you are still here."

With another cordial shake of the President's hand, Nettie passed out of Lincoln's presence for the last time.

"Never again," she later wrote, "would we meet his welcome smile."

11. DREAMS OF DEATH

Inaugural Omens and Portents of Doom

The bloody tide of the Civil War had finally turned in favor of the Union during the autumn of 1864. It was just in time to secure the re-election of Abraham Lincoln. On November 8, northern voters overwhelmingly voted to keep him in office, although with his re-election, any hope for a negotiated settlement with the Confederacy vanished.

Even if you believe in omens and portents, Lincoln's re-election hardly seems to have been preordained. By the time people went to the polls, Lincoln was facing many challenges to his presidency. The war was now in its fourth year, hundreds of thousands of men had died, and many questioned if the south could ever be beaten by military strength alone. General Ulysses S. Grant mounted a massive campaign in the spring of that year to finally defeat the Confederate Army led by Robert E, Lee, but after sustaining losses at the Wilderness, Spotsylvania, and Cold Harbor, the Union bogged down around Petersburg, Virginia. As autumn approached, Grant seemed no closer to beating Lee than his predecessors. In addition, Union General William T. Sherman had fought his way to Atlanta but was unable to take the city. Some of the Radical Republicans were unhappy with Lincoln's conciliatory plan for reconstruction of the South. And many northerners had never been happy with Lincoln's 1862 Emancipation Proclamation, which changed the war from a battle to reunite the states to a crusade to destroy slavery. Weariness with the war caused many to start calling for a compromise with the states that had seceded.

Believing that Lincoln was vulnerable, Democrats had nominated George B. McClellan, former commander of the Army of the Potomac, to run against him. McClellan was regarded as a brilliant soldier, but he had failed to defeat Robert E. Lee in Virginia. He and Lincoln quarreled constantly - mostly over his delays and fears of defeat - and Lincoln finally replaced him after he failed to pursue Lee into Virginia after the battle at Antietam Creek in September 1862.

Things were not looking well for Lincoln in the months leading up to the election but then the tide finally turned. While Grant remained stalled at Petersburg, Mobile Bay fell to the Union Navy in August, Sherman captured Atlanta in September, and General Phil Sheridan secured Virginia's Shenandoah Valley in October.

On Election Day, Lincoln won all but three states - Kentucky, New Jersey, and Delaware - and won 55-percent of the vote. He won 212 electoral votes to McClellan's 21. Perhaps more importantly, Lincoln won the majority of the votes cast by Union troops, including those from the Army of the Potomac, McClellan's old command.

Perhaps most important of all, though, was the fact that the election was held at all. Before this, no country had ever held elections during a military emergency. But Lincoln was determined that an election be held, stating, "We cannot have free government without elections; and if the rebellion could force us to forego, or postpone a national election, it might fairly claim to have already conquered and ruined us."

Five months after Lincoln's re-election, the collapse of the Confederacy was complete.

Lincoln's second inauguration took place on March 4, 1865, a stormy morning that was plagued by rain and cold winds. A drenching downpour fell throughout the morning, finally letting up around noon, when Lincoln rose to his feet and prepared to speak.

Just as he did, the clouds overhead suddenly spread apart, and a brilliant burst of sunlight came through and illuminated Lincoln as he stood in front of the Capitol building. A roar of applause welled up from the crowd and took Lincoln's breath away. He had to pause for a moment before he could speak.

A photograph taken during Lincoln's second inauguration

(Left) a detailed look at the same image showing Lincoln in the lower center and John Wilkes Booth on the raised platform above and behind him

Lincoln later remarked to a journalist that attended the ceremony, "Did you notice that sunburst? It made my heart jump. I am just superstitious enough to consider it a happy omen."

Later, in a note that accompanied the Bible on which Lincoln had taken his oath of office for the second time, Salmon P. Chase, who was now Chief Justice of the Supreme Court, also commented on the sun that ripped through the clouds at just that moment. He called it "an auspicious omen of the dispersion of the clouds of war and the restoration of the clear sunlight of prosperous peace."

Looking back today, neither Lincoln's first inaugural sign or his second inaugural omen may seem that important to us, but they do offer a glimpse into the mind of the President. At those two momentous moments of time, even as Lincoln assumed a role of power, he could not help but see affirmations of his pre-ordained mission to guide the United States.

The speeches that Lincoln wrote for these events also reveal his thoughts. His second inaugural speech in particular was laden with biblical imagery, interpreting the war in terms of God's divine judgement. A reporter from a British newspaper described the speech as being "something of a sacred and almost prophetic nature."

Clearly, Lincoln was looking for signs that the war was coming to an end and when it did, then perhaps this also meant that Lincoln's own divine destiny was also coming to an end.

Lincoln chose to focus on the bright omen of that day, but it would turn out that the burst of sunshine from the heavens also helped to illuminate a much darker foreshadowing of Inauguration Day.

It was during this bright moment that famed photographer Alexander Gardner took a photograph that has since become one of the most chilling images in American history.

After the plate developed, it was discovered that President Lincoln himself had been completely blotted out by a careless thumbprint that was pressed on the wet negative. This was considered unfortunate, but it wasn't a complete loss since many other photographs were taken that day that captured the scene. It would be many years later, though, when closer examination of the photograph revealed a group of men not far from the President who would be implicated in his murder less than six weeks later.

To the left of President Lincoln and under the platform on which he spoke stands Lewis Payne - or Powell - who tried to stab Secretary of State Seward on the night of Lincoln's assassination; David Herold, who helped John Wilkes Booth escape; George Atzerodt, who was assigned to kill Vice-President Andrew Johnson, but lost his nerve; John Surratt, a Confederate spy whose mother owned a boarding house where the conspirators to kill Lincoln met; and Edman Spangler, a laborer at Ford's Theater, who helped the killer to escape.

But to Lincoln's right, above the platform and standing in front of a pillar, was John Wilkes Booth. His face stands out in the crowd and he used his engagement to a senator's daughter to obtain a spot close to the President as he spoke. Booth later complained, "What an excellent chance that would have been to kill the President."

We'll never know why he didn't choose to take it.

Vivid dreams were nothing new to President Lincoln.

He had been experiencing them - including many he believed were prophetic - throughout his entire life. He often dreamed of sailing off into a dark sea, which he first experienced in Springfield, just before the death of his son, Eddie.

More often, though, he dreamed of Willie. He had spoken of the boy in his dreams when he quoted from Shakespeare, who had written of loved ones visiting us in our dreams. Lincoln said this was "the way I dream of my lost boy Willie."

How many times Willie visited his father in his dreams is unknown but apparently it was frequent in the year after he died. For Lincoln, such dreams were a bittersweet reunion.

Mary was also visited by Willie after his death. With Mary, though, it's not entirely certain whether Willie came to her in her dreams or in visions that can be linked to her Spiritualist beliefs. When her sister Emilie visited the White House in the fall of 1863, Mary confessed to her that Willie came to her on a regular basis. "He comes to me every night," she said, "and stands at the foot of the bed with the same sweet, adorable smile he has always had."

According to Mary, Willie was sometimes accompanied by his little brother, Eddie, and at least twice by Mary's brother, Alexander Todd, a Confederate Army lieutenant that had been killed in August 1862. "You cannot dream of the comfort this gives me. When I thought of my little son in immensity, alone... it nearly broke my heart," Mary told her sister.

But Lincoln's dreams could be far stranger.

In June 1863, Mary had left Washington with Tad to do some shopping in Philadelphia. While they were away, Lincoln had a disturbing dream about a pistol that Tad carried with him. He'd had a "terrible longing for a real revolver - one that could shoot." In those days, even young boys were expected to know how to safely handle a gun, but it's thought perhaps Tad was not up to the task. The details of Lincoln's dream are unknown but they were apparently unsettling enough to cause Lincoln to send his wife an urgent telegram on June 9 that read: "Think you better put Tad's pistol away. I had an ugly dream about him."

Another time, Lincoln was visiting City Point, Virginia, the Union's base of operations during the final stages of the war, when the city of Richmond was under siege. While there, he had another vivid dream.

In the dream, Lincoln saw the White House consumed in flames. He was so upset that he sent Mary, who had come with him, back to Washington so that she could make sure the White House was undamaged and still standing. Once she did, she telegraphed her husband to let him know all was well.

Neither of these dreams came true. Were they only projections of Lincoln's anxiety? Not everyone thinks so. Many believe that predictive dreams "anticipate the trajectory of current events and picture the likely outcome." In other words, this sort of a dream shows a "probable future" so that the dreamer can prevent it from happening.

Dreams like the ones mentioned can be explained away by modern psychology, of course, but towards the end of Lincoln's life, he experienced several uncanny and prophetic dreams that are not quite as easy to dismiss.

In the spring of 1865, Lincoln experienced several dreams about his own death, which he had started to feel was looming over him. But Lincoln was not the only person who experienced a foreshadowing of that dire event. Spiritualists from all over the country still deluged the White House offices with letters that warned the president of danger. But Lincoln continued to refuse to take them seriously.

As the war dragged on, threats of death and murder seemed to multiply. Lincoln's bodyguards, as well as the soldier assigned to his protection, were still constantly being thwarted from their duty by Lincoln himself. He often slipped out of the White House at night for solitary strolls and refused to take precautions that were necessary to keep him protected.

The man most frustrated by Lincoln's foolhardy behavior was his old friend Ward Hill Lamon, who had assigned himself the position of the president's chief bodyguard. Lamon worried constantly over

Lincoln's seeming indifference to threats and warnings of death. This was a man who would have unquestionably taken a bullet to save the life of his president and friend and yet, he resigned his position repeatedly because Lincoln did not take danger seriously. Lincoln always convinced him to stay on, promising to be more careful ---- then vanished out of the White House at night, or attended the theater without protection.

Lamon became obsessed with watching over Lincoln and many believe that the president would not have been killed at Ford's Theater had Lamon been on duty that night. As it happened, the security chief was in Richmond, Virginia, on an errand for the president, when disaster struck. He never forgave himself for what happened --- especially since he believed that he had a forewarning of the event, from Lincoln himself.

Years later, Lamon would remember that Lincoln had always been haunted by the strange vision that he experienced in the mirror in 1860. In April 1865, Lamon was present when the President recounted an eerie dream of his death.

They were on a river steamer, traveling to City Point, and Lincoln was in a particularly "melancholy, meditative mood" that morning. Concerned, Mary tried to stir him from his somber mood, but it was no use, something was deeply troubling him.

Finally, he began to talk, rambling on about the subject of dreams in the Bible. "And if we believe the Bible," he told them, "we must accept the fact that in the old days God and the angels came to men in their sleep and made themselves known in dreams." However, then Lincoln added, "Nowadays dreams are regarded as very foolish, and are seldom told, except by old women and young men and maidens in love."

"Do you believe in dreams?" Mary asked him.

Lincoln hesitated. At first, he said he didn't, but then said, "But I had one the other night which has haunted me ever since."

And then he recounted the dream.

"About ten days ago, I retired late. I soon began to dream. There seemed to be a death-like stillness about me. Then I heard subdued sobs, as if a number of people were weeping. I thought I left my bed and wandered downstairs. There the silence was broken by the same pitiful sobbing, but the mourners were invisible. I went from room to room; no living person was in sight, but the same mournful sounds of distress met me as I passed along.

"It was light in all the rooms; every object was familiar to me, but where were all the people who were grieving as if their hearts would break? I was puzzled and alarmed. What could be the meaning of all this? Determined to find the cause of a state of things so mysterious and so shocking, I kept on until I arrived at the East Room, which I entered. Before me was a catafalque, on which rested a corpse wrapped in funeral vestments. Around it were stationed soldiers who were acting as guards; and there was a throng of people, some gazing mournfully upon the corpse, whose face was covered, others weeping pitifully.

"'Who is dead in the White House?', I demanded of one of the soldiers.

"'The President', was his answer, 'He was killed by an assassin.'

"Then came a loud burst of grief from the crowd, which awoke me from my dream. I slept no more that night; and although it was only a dream, I have been strangely annoyed by it ever since."

Mary was shocked by the story and told her husband that she wished he had not told it.

Trying to soothe her, Lincoln assured her that it was only a dream. "Let us say no more about it," he said calmly," and try to forget it.

But no one would forget it.

A short time later, Lincoln was shot to death and his body was displayed during his funeral in the East Room of the White House. On the night of Lincoln's fatal attack, recalling this incident, the first words uttered by Mary were, "His dream was prophetic."

On April 13, 1865, only a short time after his terrifying dream of a shadowy funeral at the White House, Lincoln experienced another portentous dream. This one was familiar, more reassuring than disturbing, although it, too, proved to be a warning of what was to come.

The following morning, the usual Friday morning Cabinet meeting was held at the White House and yet the meeting turned out to be anything but ordinary.

The mood was upbeat. Lee had surrendered to Grant on April 9. In Charleston harbor, the American flag had again been raised over Fort Sumter, the battered garrison where the war had begun. And news was expected anytime from General Sherman, whose men were running the last major Confederate force - the Army of Tennessee - to ground in North Carolina.

General Grant attended the meeting in person so that he could offer a first-hand account of Lee's surrender. The meeting had been scheduled to start at 9:00 a.m. but it was postponed for two hours. It was then delayed even further because Secretary of War Stanton was running late. He was still in the department's telegraph office, hoping for word from Sherman so that he could announce it at the meeting.

While waiting on Stanton to arrive, the men made small talk. General Grant said that he was waiting hourly for word from General Sherman.

"It will no doubt, come soon," Lincoln replied, "and come favorable, for I had the usual dream last night. Before every great national event I have always had the same dream. Generally, the news has been favorable which succeeded this dream, and the dream itself is always the same."

"What could this remarkable dream be, Mr. President?" asked Secretary of the Navy Gideon Welles.

"It relates to your element Mr. Welles - the water. I seem to be in some singular, indescribable vessel, and I am moving with great rapidity toward an indefinite shore. I have had this dream preceding the surrender of Fort Sumter, the battles of Bull Run, Antietam, Gettysburg, Stone's River, Vicksburg, Wilmington..."

Grant interrupted him. "Stone's River was certainly no victory; I know of no great results that followed it. A few more such fights would have ruined us."

"We may differ on that point, General," Lincoln said. "At all events, my dream preceded it. I had this strange dream again last night, and we shall, judging from the past, have great news very soon. I think it must be from Sherman. My thoughts are in that direction, as are most of yours."

Lincoln remained in a happy mood throughout the day, even though no news had yet arrived from General Sherman. After the

Cabinet meeting, Lincoln and Mary took a carriage ride and Mary commented on his mood.

He told her that he felt that this was the day when the war was finally coming to a close. He believed that his dream was a presentiment of victory - even if he had also had the same dream before terrible things had occurred. He refused to believe it was a portent of anything bad that was going to happen.

This isn't a surprise, considering that he had also dismissed his dream about the funeral in the White House as a warning for someone else. He told Ward Lamon, "In this dream, it was not me but some other fellow that was killed. It seems that this ghostly assassin tried his hand on someone else."

Of all the portents and predictions connected to Abraham Lincoln, these two dreams - documented by other people - that occurred within two weeks of his death remain the clearest evidence that Lincoln may very well have possessed paranormal gifts.

Although the various primary accounts of the Cabinet meeting do vary in detail, the basic things that Lincoln said at the meeting remain remarkably consistent. The men who heard Lincoln's words that day were not mystics or even believers in the fantastical. They were hard-headed, serious politicians and soldiers - men who dealt with facts and realities. Whatever their spiritual beliefs, they were not men inclined to exaggerate - and certainly not to fabricate - such an incident.

Abraham Lincoln was given a glimpse of the other side. Those men witnessed it but they, like the President himself, failed to recognize the event that they were being warned about.

After the Cabinet meeting, Lincoln became resolved to go to the theater that night. It was a diversion that he dearly loved and with Washington in a general state of celebration, he felt some entertainment was called for. He made plans to attend a comedy that night at Ford's Theater called "Our American Cousin."

General Grant and his wife, Julia, were invited to attend the play with the Lincolns that night. After all, who better than to share the victory with than Grant? However, at the last minute, they declined the invitation, mostly at Julia's insistence.

Earlier in the afternoon, Julia began to be overtaken by an uneasiness that consumed her mind. She kept feeling like something

Ulysses and Julia Grant, who were supposed to accompany the Lincoln's to Ford's Theater on April 14

was wrong and when she was told about the invitation to the theater, she became even more agitated. She wanted to leave Washington immediately, even though the entire city was celebrating her husband's victory over Lee and the surrender of the Confederacy.

She was sure that something terrible was about to happen.

She was so convinced of it that even while her husband was still at the White House, she not only sent a note to Grant, but also sent three of his staff officers to reinforce the message.

Julia later wrote in her memoirs, "I do not know what possessed me to take such a freak but go home I felt I must."

As it turned out, Julia's premonition of danger was correct. General Grant was also targeted for assassination that night and his absence from Ford's Theater probably saved his life.

That same afternoon, one of Lincoln's bodyguards, Colonel William H. Crook, also had an odd experience. In retrospect, he took it for an omen of what was to come.

Crook was a no-nonsense man. Like Ward Lamon, he took his task of protecting the President very seriously. He stayed awake all night, sitting outside the bedroom while Lincoln slept. He refused to even read the newspaper while on duty. He wanted to be ready for any emergency that came along.

Crook and Lincoln had spoken in the past about the strange dreams the President sometimes experienced. Unlike Lincoln, Crook was not feeling celebratory on April 14. The cautious man was worried that danger was not yet past. The recent attacks in New York and Baltimore, carried out by Confederate guerilla fighters, had unnerved him. He feared trouble still might come to Washington. His advice to the President was that he should not go to the theater that night. But Lincoln, as usual, brushed aside his concerns. He promised Mary that they would go. In that case, Crook asked if he might accompany the Lincolns as their security detail, but Lincoln refused. Crook could not work around the clock, he told him.

Colonel W.H. Crook served on Lincoln's security staff and later achieved notoriety out west during the Indian Wars

Lincoln had a habit of bidding Crook a "good night" each evening as he left the office and went to the private residence. It was as regular as clockwork and the President had not varied it so long as Crook could remember.

On that fateful day, though, according to Crook, Lincoln paused as he left for the theater and turned to the bodyguard. "Good-bye, Crook," he said significantly.

Crook later wrote, "It startled me. I remember distinctly the shock of surprise and the impression, at the time, that he had never said it before. It was the first time that he neglected to say 'Good Night' to me. And it was the only time that he ever said 'Good-bye'. I thought of it at that moment and, a few hours later, when the news flashed over Washington that he had been shot, his last words were so burned into my being that they can never be forgotten."

And these were not the only omens that occurred that day, suggesting that something evil was afoot in the city.

A named Sister Thomas had a reputation as a "conjure woman" in Washington. She lived with her children not far from Ford's Theater.

According to stories, ghosts were always dropping in at the home of Sister Thomas, although she never minded their presence. She knew how to talk to them. However, when dogs kept howling for several days in a row and the rooster kept crowing, she began to get upset - and more than a little spooked.

Finally, "when a large picture of President Lincoln fell off the wall, just as a bird flew in the window," she later explained, "I just knew someone was going to die in the neighborhood."

Her prediction soon turned out to be true.

After the President was pronounced dead at 7:00 a.m. on April 15, news of his death spread quickly by telegraph and by courier. And yet, somehow, word reached some people faster than any earthly method could have done.

Far south of the city, Sherman's troops were still wiping out the last of the Confederate resistance. Major George Putnam of the 176th New York Volunteer Infantry, was part of a division linked to Sherman's army. They had no direct telegraph lines to the outside world, but they generally received dispatches by courier around noon each day from a rider that came from Wilmington.

In his memoirs, Major Putnam told a chilling story about his experience on the day after the Lincoln assassination. He had gone to see the local barber, an African American man who had a shop near the camp, so that he could get a shave. When he arrived, the barber's hands were visibly shaking. He explained that he was unable to shave Putnam that day. When the Major asked what was wrong, the man told him that "something's happen to Mr. Lincoln."

Putnam tried to reassure him, explaining that they'd had no news of anything amiss up north. The army would have received the word first if anything was wrong.

The barber shook his head, though, insisting that the "colored folk get news in other ways" and that "something had gone wrong with Mr. Lincoln."

Disturbed by this, Putnam walked over to headquarters to see if any news had arrived that he might not have heard. When he got there, he found he was not alone. Several other officers and soldiers had experienced similar encounters with the local African American residents and were equally perplexed about what was going on.

But there was no news at headquarters.

Then, at noon, the courier was seen racing across the field. From the man's face, they could see that he had an important message - and that it was bad news. His saddle bags carried the regular mail, but he handed a special envelope directly to the camp commander.

The officer opened the letter and read the dispatch inside. He tried but was unable to read it aloud. A lieutenant took it out of his hands. The young man, too, was overcome with emotion.

He could only blurt out a few chilling words, "Lincoln is dead."

We'll never know how word of Lincoln's death reached poor local residents in North Carolina before they reached the U.S. military. We can only assume that the telegraph they used was a spiritual one - and not a device of this earth.

12. "SIC SEMPER TYRANNIS"

Now he belongs to the ages.

Edwin M. Stanton, U.S. Secretary of War, at President Lincoln's deathbed on April 15, 1865

Five days before that final Cabinet meeting, on the cool Sunday evening of April 9, 1865, Abraham Lincoln was returning home from a visit to the bedside of Secretary of State Edwin Stanton, who was recuperating from a broken jaw. As he reached the White House, he was intercepted by a messenger with a telegram from General Grant. The war was over - the Confederate Army had surrendered.

The terrible war was finally ended. But Lincoln's work was not done. Now he could only think about the best ways to repair the divide between the victorious north and the defeated south. He knew that the radicals in Congress would want to seek revenge against the Confederate states but for now, they would hold off. They were fearful of Lincoln's popularity with voters. Lincoln knew that when things calmed down, he would have to announce a policy of mercy towards the south. For tonight, he had to think calmly and coolly about what he would say to the crowds that would surely arrive at the White House the next day, demanding a reaction from Lincoln.

But Lincoln wasn't ready when they came. They called out for him so loudly that he was unable to deny them. He appeared on the balcony for a moment, joked with them, put them off, and told them he was unprepared. He managed to slip out of the situation by asking the White House band to strike up "Dixie."

On Tuesday, the crowd returned. It was now even larger and more insistent than the night before. The President appeared before them; his face not jubilant but saddened by the loss of so many lives over the previous four years. He spoke with a voice that was quiet and yet piercing, sharing merciful thoughts to those gathered on the White House lawn. He spoke of the joys of peace, saying nothing of punishment for the Rebels. He spoke of God and thanksgiving, not of vengeance. He wanted his wayward brothers and sisters to return home. He had no desire to cast them out into the darkness.

Lincoln said, "We all agree, that the seceded states, so called, are out of their proper practical relation with the Union, and that the solid object of the government, civil and military, in regard to those states, is to again get them into that proper relation. I believe that it is not only possible, but in fact easier, to do this without deciding or even considering whether these states have ever been out of the Union, than with it. Finding themselves safely at home, it would be utterly immaterial whether they had ever been abroad."

These were the first words that Lincoln spoke concerning reconciliation with the former Confederacy, but they would not be the last. Over the three days that followed, he spoke often of peace and reconciliation and of "smoothing out the Mason and Dixon line."

Lincoln's mood was high. He was exhilarated knowing that the war had finally ended. No more lives needed to be sacrificed. He saw only good things on the horizon for America and, at last, he felt a lifting of the dark cloud that surrounded him for so many years. He was starting to feel that those portents of doom that had haunted him for so long had gone away. The frightful melancholy that seemed "to drip from him as he walked" might finally be safely relegated to his past.

Lincoln was feeling optimistic by the time the curtain rose at Ford's Theater on the night of April 14, 1865.

The people of Washington, wanting life and laughter in the chaos of victory, crowded into the theater to celebrate. It was Good Friday - usually a terrible night for theater owners because most ministers preached that it was sacrilege to attend the theater on a holy day - but this night was different. The city was celebrating, and Ford's was packed because word spread that President Lincoln and General Grant were going to be in the audience that night. Everyone wanted to see the men who were being called the "saviors" of the Union.

The theater floor was packed when the curtain went up and the play began, but the audience gave only half its attention to the actors on the stage. They were also watching the President's empty box and waiting for him to arrive.

When the Civil War ended, it did not end for everyone in Washington. There were many, in the north and the south, who refused to believe the Confederacy had fallen.

One of the men who professed his undying devotion to the Confederacy was John Wilkes Booth, the handsome actor who was then one of the most acclaimed performers in the country.

Booth's parents were noted Shakespearean actors Junius Brutus Booth and his mistress, Mary Ann Holmes, who came to America from England in 1821. They purchased a farm near Bel Air, Maryland, where John was born, the ninth of ten children. Junius Booth's wife, Adelaide, was granted a divorce from him on the grounds of adultery in 1851 and he and Holmes were legally wed on May 10, 1851, which was John's thirteenth birthday. It's been suggested that the shame and ambition of Junius's actor sons, John and Edwin, spurred both of them to strive for great acclaim and, in John's case, infamy.

Booth received a good education at the Bel Air Academy but was an indifferent student, more interested in horses than classes. He later attended the Milton Boarding School and later St. Timothy's Hall, an Episcopal military academy.

Legend has it that while at the Milton School, Booth had his palm read by a gypsy fortune teller who told him that he had a grim destiny. He would lead a grand but short life, she told him, doomed to die young after "meeting a bad end." His sister later recalled that he wrote down the palm-reader's prediction, showed it to his family and friends, and often talked about its meaning in moments of melancholy.

By age 16, Booth had become interested in theater and aspired to follow in the footsteps of his father and brother, Edwin. He made his stage debut in a supporting role in *Richard III* on August 14, 1855 in Baltimore. It did not go well. The audience jeered at him when he missed some of his lines. However, he quickly improved and began appearing in more shows in other cities and theaters. He soon had a following. Author Jim Bishop wrote that Booth, "developed into an outrageous scene stealer, but he played his parts with such heightened enthusiasm that the audiences idolized him."

Critics began calling him "the handsomest man in America" and a "natural genius" and noted his having an "astonishing memory." He was 5-feet 8 inches tall, had jet-black hair, and was lean and athletic. Civil War reporter George Alfred Townsend described him as a "muscular, perfect man" with "curling hair, like a Corinthian capital." His acting wasn't as precise as his brother Edwin's, but his strikingly handsome appearance enthralled women - and in the case of George Townsend, many men, as well. By the start of the 1860s, Booth had become wealthy as an actor, earning about $20,000 a year.

In 1865, John Wilkes Booth was one o the most famous men in America

Booth embarked on his first national tour as a leading actor after finishing the 1859-1860 theater season in Richmond, Virginia. He engaged Philadelphia attorney Matthew Canning to serve as his agent and began playing theaters and winning admirers in cities like New York, Boston, Chicago, Cleveland, St. Louis, Montgomery, and New Orleans. In October 1860, while performing in Columbus, Georgia, Booth was shot accidentally while in his hotel. The wound was thought bad enough that it might end his life, but he recovered.

When the Civil War began on April 12, 1861, Booth was performing in Albany, New York. He was outspoken in his admiration for the south's secession, publicly calling it "heroic." This so enraged local citizens that they demanded that he be banned from the stage for making "treasonable statements." He wasn't, but he learned to keep his inflammatory statements to himself - most of the time.

Booth had been sympathetic to the south since 1859, when radical abolitionist John Brown had raided the federal armory in Harper's Ferry, Virginia, or perhaps even longer. He was there on the day that Brown was hanged and afterwards expressed great satisfaction with his fate.

After Abraham Lincoln was elected in November 1860, Booth drafted a long speech, apparently never delivered, that criticized northern abolitionism and made clear his strong support of the south and the institution of slavery. He was unhappy with he decision of his native Maryland when the legislature voted against secession but pleased when it voted not to allow federal troops to pass south through the state by rail, requested that Lincoln remove the growing numbers of federal troops in Maryland. The legislature wanted to remain in the Union but also wanted to avoid involvement in a war with its southern neighbors. In response, Lincoln suspended the writ of habeas corpus and imposed martial law in Baltimore and other parts of the state. He also imprisoned many Maryland political leaders and stationed federal troops in Baltimore. Booth, like scores of other Maryland citizens, were enraged by what they saw as Lincoln's unconstitutional overreach.

Booth continued to travel extensively and perform during the early 1860s. According to his sister, Asia, Booth confided to her that he used his fame to avoid checkpoints and to smuggle the anti-malarial drug quinine into the southern states. It was crucial there, especially along the coasts, but was in short supply because of a northern blockade.

Booth fully supported the Confederacy - just as much as he hated Abraham Lincoln. After the war began, he quarreled often with his brother Edwin, who declined to make stage appearances in the south, remained loyal to the Union, and refused to listen to John's rabid denunciations of Lincoln. Edwin would be haunted for the rest of his life by John's murderous actions.

In early 1863, Booth was arrested in St. Louis after a performance when he was overheard saying that he "wished the President and the whole damned government would go to hell." He was charged with making "treasonous" remarks against the government but was released when he took an oath of allegiance to the Union and paid a substantial fine.

Booth's accomplices in the kidnapping plot – Samuel Arnold (Left) and Michael O'Laughlen

When the tide of the war began to turn in 1864, prospects for a Confederate victory began to wane. As a Union victory seemed more likely, so did the re-election of President Lincoln. Booth was filled with rage. He blamed Lincoln for the war and for all the south's troubles. At the start of the war, Booth had promised his mother that he would not enlist as a soldier, but he became increasingly angry about his failure to be more important to the war effort. In a letter he wrote to his mother, he said, "I have begun to deem myself a coward and to despise my own existence."

Booth brooded about his lack of courage and dedication to the Confederacy and knew that he had to act. He began to formulate a plan to kidnap Lincoln from the summer residence at the Old Soldier's Home and smuggle him across the Potomac River to Richmond. Once in Confederate hands, Lincoln would be exchanged for prisoners of war held in northern camps and, Booth believed, bring an end to the war by forcing the Union to recognize the Confederate government.

Booth recruited two friends - Samuel Arnold and Michael O'Laughlen - and they met often to plan the kidnapping at the home of Confederate sympathizer Maggie Branson in Baltimore.

Booth conspirators David Herold (Left) and George Atzerodt

In October, Booth made an unexplained trip to Montreal, Canada. Throughout the war, the Confederacy had maintained a network of spies in southern Maryland that smuggled recruits across the Potomac into Virginia and relayed messages for Confederate agents as far north as Canada. Montreal had become a center for clandestine activity.

Booth stayed in the city for 10 days, spending a portion of that time at St. Lawrence Hall, a rendezvous point for the Confederate Secret Service. There is no conclusive proof that the Confederate government was linked to the kidnapping plot or the assassination, but many historians believe that at least some of the lower levels of the Confederate spy agency may have been involved.

In early November 1864, Lincoln won a landslide re-election, running on a platform that advocated the abolishment of slavery. Booth, meanwhile, devoted even more time and money to his kidnapping plan. He assembled a loose-knit band of southern sympathizers to help him, including David Herold, George Atzerodt, Lewis Powell - or Payne - and Confederate agent John Surrat. They began meeting regularly at the boarding house owned by Surratt's mother, Mary.

By this time, there had been a complete falling out between brothers John and Edwin. Booth was finally told that he was no longer

Booth conspirators Lewis Powell (Left) and John Surratt, Jr.

welcome in Edwin's New York home. Booth also complained about Lincoln in conversations with his sister, Asia. She recalled one comment when he said, "That man's appearance, his pedigree, his coarse low jokes and anecdotes, his vulgar similes, and his policy are a disgrace to the seat he holds. He is made the tool of the North, to crush out slavery."

She said he also decried Lincoln's re-election where he was "making himself a king," and went on wild tirades against the north as the Confederacy's defeat became more certain.

In February 1865, Booth began courting a young woman named Lucy Lambert Hale, the daughter of U.S. Senator John P. Hale of New Hampshire. They later became secretly engaged, although Lucy had no idea of Booth's hatred for Lincoln. If she had, she likely would not have gotten him the ticket to attend the President's second inauguration on March 4 as her guest. Booth watched Lincoln speak from only a few feet away. Powell, Atzerodt, and Herold were in the crowd. Later, Booth remarked about his "excellent chance...to kill the President, if I had wished."

On March 17, Booth was ready to put his plan into action. He learned that Lincoln would be attending a play at a hospital near the Soldier's Home and assembled his team to kidnap him while he was on

Booth's secret fiancée, Lucy Hale

his way to the hospital. They waited for hours but Lincoln didn't show. Booth later learned that Lincoln changed his plans and attended a reception at the National Hotel - the same hotel where Booth was staying.

Less than a month later, when Booth learned that Robert E. Lee had surrendered to Grant, he gave up on his plans to kidnap the president. After the surrender, such a scheme was no longer feasible.

Booth was in the crowd at the White House when Lincoln gave his speech from the balcony. He left enraged and declared that it would be the last speech that Lincoln would ever make.

The kidnapping plot had been abandoned in favor of assassination.

At 7:30 p.m., just a half hour before *Our American Cousin* was supposed to start at Ford's Theater, Lincoln was still in his office with House Speaker Colfax. It was not a meeting of importance. It was a discussion of Colfax's trip out west.

Just before 8:00 p.m., Mary Lincoln appeared in the office doorway. She was wearing a black and white striped silk dress with a matching bonnet. Over the dress, she wore a black velvet, floor-length cloak.

"Well, Mr. Lincoln, are you going to the theater with me or not"? she asked.

Lincoln smiled at the man across from him. "I suppose I shall have to go, Colfax," he said.

Lincoln gathered his coat and his top hat - still with a mourning ribbon around it in Willie's honor - and left the room. On the way downstairs, Lincoln stopped at Robert's door. "We're going to the theater, Bob," he told his son. "Don't you want to go?"

The young Army captain politely declined. He was tired from his recent military exploits, although, thanks to his mother, he had never seen combat in person. He told his father that he just wanted to get some sleep.

"All right, do what you most feel like. Good night," Lincoln said.

"Good night, father," Robert replied - not knowing it would be the last words he would ever say to his father.

A final visitor appeared just as Lincoln was walking with Colfax down the staircase. His name was George Ashmun, and he was the Massachusetts attorney who had presided over the 1860 Republican Convention that had nominated Lincoln as the party's presidential candidate. He was waiting in the Red Room and Lincoln agreed to see him.

As he and Colfax walked toward the Red Room, Colfax again mentioned that many people had been worried when the president had recently gone to Richmond. They feared an angry southerner might shoot him.

Lincoln shrugged off the concern but thanked him for it. As he told him goodbye, he asked Colfax for a second time if he would like to accompany him and Mary to the theater, but the Speaker - and Ashmun a few minutes later - declined. Colfax was leaving on a trip the next morning and didn't want to be out late. Ashmun had a previous engagement.

For some reason, the Lincolns had a lot of difficulty getting anyone to go with them to the theater that night. Mary and the President had invited no fewer than 15 people to go with them that night, but all had declined, except for young Clara Harris and her beau, Major Rathbone.

Before Lincoln could get into the carriage, the doorman informed him of two more visitors, but Lincoln dashed off notes to them to return the next day. He also told Ashmun to come back the next morning, too.

The Lincolns' trusted household servant, Charles Forbes, helped the President into his topcoat. The young Irishman served as Lincoln's personal assistant was often a companion for Tad. As be brushed off the shoulders of Lincoln's coat, he spoke, "Mr. President, Tad gave me a photograph this afternoon, and I wish you would put your name on it."

"Certainly, Charlie," Lincoln said and scrawled his name on it.

**Ford's Theater in Washington
The Star Saloon is directly next door to the right**

Finally, he climbed into the carriage seat next to his wife, the door was slammed shut, and they were on the way to Ford's Theater.

It was now after 8:00 p.m. and the play had already started. The evening had turned cold and damp and rain seemed likely.

There was no security detail on the trip. The two-man cavalry escort that had accompanied the presidential carriage earlier in the day was nowhere to be seen. Even though his staff protested, Lincoln refused to have an armed military escort at the theater. He had agreed only to some inconspicuous bodyguards. His usual protector, Ward Lamon, was away and Lincoln had insisted that Crooks get some rest.

As a consequence, there was a Washington police officer assigned to protect the President that night. His name was John Parker and he had gone ahead of the carriage to Ford's Theater.

Parker was a poor choice for a bodyguard. He was a sloppy drinker and had been reprimanded several times for being drunk and visiting brothels while on duty. Assigned to stand guard outside of the presidential box, he was not at his post when John Wilkes Booth arrived there. He was last seen at a saloon next door with a drink in his hand.

He would eventually be charged with dereliction of duty, yet remained on the police force for another three years and even served as a White House bodyguard for months afterward. In 1868, he was finally dismissed for sleeping on duty - three years too late to save the life of President Lincoln.

The dark green presidential carriage exited the White House grounds and clattered toward the Harris home at H and Fourteenth Streets, just four blocks away. Major Rathbone lived in a nearby brick townhouse, just off Lafayette Square. It still stands today. After picking up Rathbone and Clare Harris, the carriage sped towards Ford Theater.

The Lincolns were very late. The carriage arrived at the main entrance to the theater at 8:35 p.m. The entrance had five double doors, each below a curved archway. There was a special wooden platform that made it easier for guests to alight from their carriages and stay out of the muddy street. Two men were waiting outside for the carriage - doorman John Buckingham and police bodyguard John Parker.

After helping the two ladies out of the carriage, Buckingham waited for the men and led the party into the theater's small lobby. The usher, James O'Brien, then led them up a curving staircase on the left side of the lobby. It led to a second-story balcony that overlooked the stage. There were eight private boxes in the theater and the cost for each was $10. In deference to the president, none of the other boxes were in use that night.

To reach their box, the Lincolns and their guests crossed the back of the balcony from left to right and made their way along the right wall to enter the box. The actors on stage would later disagree about what point in the play was interrupted by the arrival of the party. As was his custom - painfully aware that he was late - Lincoln tried to slip inconspicuously into the box without interrupting the play, but he couldn't do it. As soon as Lincoln was spotted, a murmur went through the audience and the actors, who could see what was happening from the stage, immediately paused.

For the first time at Ford's Theater, the orchestra leader, William Withers, led the musicians in a rendition of "Hail to the Chief" as the

Lincoln's Presidential Box

(Right) An advertisement for the play attended by the Lincolns on April 14

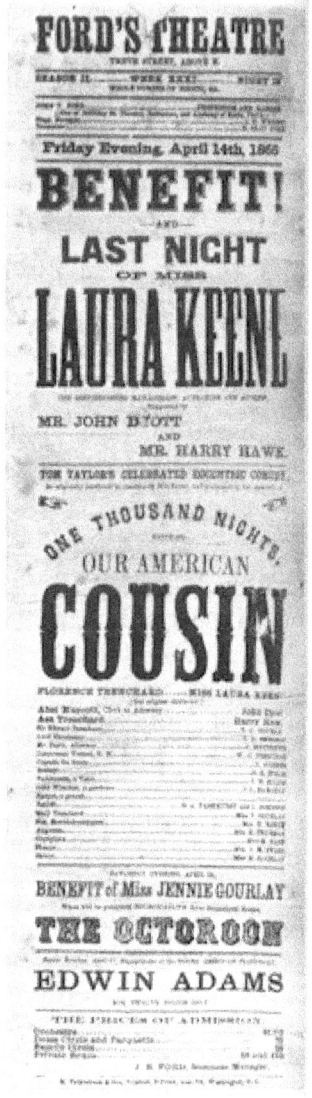

houselights were raised to full. With a pained smile on his face, Lincoln bowed humbly as the crowd rose to their feet and gave him a standing ovation. As the applause continued, Lincoln placed a hand over his heart and bowed again. On the stage, actress Laura Keene curtsied.

The audience continued to clap as the Lincolns and their guests took their seats. Lincoln slumped into a red upholstered rocking chair that had been provided by the management to fit his lanky frame and Mary sat beside him. Clara Harris and Major Rathbone were seated on the other side of a pillar that divided the box, about seven feet from the president.

Having left the Lincolns at their seats, the bodyguard, John Parker, left the box. He found a seat in the balcony, perhaps at Lincoln's suggestion. He later left the theater with the president's assistant, Charles Forbes, to have a drink next door.

Finally, the houselights were lowered again, and the actors started back from where they left off. In honor of the president's visit, though, the cast improvised a little. There was a line in the play that spoke of cold drafts, but Laura Keene, aware that the government had ended conscriptions the day before, said, "The draft has been suspended." Harry Hawk, the male lead, ad-libbed a line: "This reminds me of a story, as Mr. Lincoln would say..." The audience roared and clapped each time and Lincoln grinned and whispered to Mary. The war-weary leader was enjoying himself, chuckling at the play's corny one-liners. It was just the sort of thing that took his mind off his problems.

The first act ended around 9:00 p.m. The stagehands lowered the curtain and raised the houselights again. There was a brief intermission as the crew changed the sets on stage.

Around 9:10 pm., as the second act was about to start, a stagehand named Will Ferguson went out the back door to fetch any actors smoking or getting fresh air. While there, he saw that it was raining - and saw that the stage carpenter Ned Spangler was outside talking with the famous actor John Wilkes Booth.

Booth had arrived at the theater a little earlier. He had retrieved his rented horse from the stables and led it into the alleyway at the back door of the building. He ran into Ned Spangler there and Will Ferguson saw them talking.

"Ned, help me all you can, will you?" Booth asked the man. The remark, overheard by other crew members, would cost the hapless carpenter dearly in the days, months, and years that followed. He had nothing to do with Booth's sinister plan, but he'd be a suspect for decades.

As Act II began, Booth handed the reins of his horse to Spangler and asked him to hold them for a few minutes. Booth then met up with a crew

Stage carpenter Ned Spangler

The alley behind the theater where Booth left his horse and by which he would later make his escape

member named John DeBonay, just 17-years-old, and another man, John Selectman. They went inside and to the right side of the stage, where a trapdoor offered a passage across the stage while the show was going on. Booth and DeBonay were able to cross underneath the stage without being seen, coming up in the wings beneath the presidential box.

Meanwhile, Ned Spangler, who was needed for the many scene changes in the play, didn't have time to stand around and hold Booth's horse, no matter how famous the actor might be. He asked another stagehand to do it, who refused, and then turned to a boy named John Burroughs, who was in charge of the back door. Spangler promised him that Booth would give him 50-cents if he watched his horse. The boy sat outside in the rain for the next 45 minutes, waiting for his reward.

Inside, Booth and DeBonay walked along the narrow passages that ran along the south wall of the theater and came out on Tenth Street, directly in front of the Star Saloon. Witnesses saw Booth inside the saloon, where he ordered a whiskey and water and quickly drank it. If he was nervous, no one noticed it.

Booth walked out the saloon's front door, smoking a cigar, and went next door to the theater. There, he chatted with doorman John Buckingham and asked him what time it was. By this time, Booth was likely a little drunk. He had been drinking on and off all day.

Around 9:45 p.m., Booth walked over to the ticket booth on the right side of the lobby, chatted with young Harry Ford, who was counting receipts and then brushed off a ticket taker who demanded a ticket from him. He asked again what time it was and then wandered over to the theater door and watched part of the play over the heads of the audience. He was heard quietly humming to himself.

On stage, the players hammed it up in silly and melodramatic scenes and laughter rolled through the audience. Harry Hawk was playing a homespun American woodsman named Asa Trenchard and Laura Keene, a stunning actress with thick auburn hair, was his young English cousin, Florence Trenchard. A scheming English matron named Mrs. Mountchessington, convinced that Asa was a rich Yankee, was out to snare him for her daughter, Augusta.

Booth seemed at ease and yet his presence did arouse some suspicion. A former police officer who helped in the ticket booth, Joe Sessford, walked over to the boy that was taking tickets. "I wonder what he's up to," Joe muttered. "He was in here this afternoon, too."

Act II ended at 9:50 p.m. and the houselights were raised for another brief intermission. About half of the audience, as well as many members of the cast, left their seats to get a quick drink at the Star Saloon.

As Spangler and the other stagehands moved the set, Booth walked back over to the ticket boy and bummed some tobacco from him. He was also keeping a close eye on the clock in the lobby. He knew the play by heart and knew that, at roughly 10:15, Harry Hawk would be onstage to deliver the biggest laugh line of the evening.

Shortly before Booth made his way to the Lincoln box, two of his conspirators - former Confederate soldier Lewis Powell and former pharmacist David Herold - were about a mile away from the theater, taking part in another element of Booth's plan to destroy the leadership of the U.S. government.

They were outside the home of Secretary of State William Seward, about 10 blocks from Ford's Theater. Seward was widely considered to be the most powerful man in the government after the president. Even though he was a lawyer, committed abolitionist, former New York governor, and friend to Catholics and immigrants, he had a reputation as the most ruthless man in Washington. He was despised by Confederate sympathizers for his willingness to arrest and even execute spies, couriers, and blockade runners. Seward had been badly injured just one week earlier after a carriage accident. When the surrender of the south had been announced, he was at home recovering from a concussion, a broken jaw, and other injuries. His treatment required a special metal splint.

Booth had ordered Powell, also known as Lewis Payne, to kill Seward but the Maryland man didn't know his way around Washington. As a result, David Herold, who had been born and raised there had to guide Powell to Seward's house. The plan was for Herold to remain outside with the horses while Powell went inside.

As it turned out, Booth picked the wrong man for the job. Powell was a Confederate deserter who had met Booth in a Baltimore hotel. Over dinner, Booth recognized a kindred spirit and recruited the young man to his kidnapping plot that later turned to murder. The two men became close and worked tirelessly to plan the attacks that would cripple the government and punish the south's enemies for their roles in the war. While Booth killed Lincoln, Powell would murder Seward, and George Atzerodt would shoot Vice President Andrew Johnson.

But every part of the plan - aside from Booth's, of course - went wrong from the start. Atzerodt, overcome by fear, only got as far as the bar in the hotel where Johnson was staying. He ended up drinking all night and never shooting the vice president.

Powell knocked on the front door of the Seward house. He had an excuse for being there so late - he was delivering medicine for the secretary. However, when the door opened, a servant refused to let him into the house. Ignoring him, Powell pushed his way inside. This frightened Herold, who immediately fled the scene.

Powell dashed up the stairs, where he was confronted by the secretary's son, Frederick. Powell again tried to use his excuse about delivering medicine but when he realized that Frederick didn't believe him, he drew a large, .38-caliber Whitney revolver and aimed at Frederick's face. He pulled the trigger, but nothing happened. The revolver had misfired. Powell beat him to the floor with the butt of the gun and made his way to the room where Seward was recovering.

The Secretary of State was being tended to by his daughter, Fanny, and by Sergeant George F. Robinson, an army nurse. Powell slashed Robinson with a large knife and punched Fanny in the face. He then climbed atop Seward and stabbed and slashed at him, badly cutting his face, neck, and arms. He tried to slit Seward's throat but because of the carriage accident, Seward was wearing a metal splint around his jaw. This protected him from any fatal blows, although his scars would remain with him for life.

As Powell was trying to stab the secretary, Sergeant Robinson recovered his feet and leapt onto Powell's back, pulling him away and allowing Seward to escape. Moments later, Seward's other son, Augustus, burst into the room. He had been sleeping in the bedroom next door.

Augustus and Robinson wrestled with Powell. The would-be killer was pinned for a moment but managed to get away, although not before encountering a state department messenger in the hallway. Powell stabbed him and ran.

He escaped from the house but was a stranger in the city. He was expecting to find Herold waiting outside for him, holding his horse for a getaway - but he was gone.

"I'm mad! I'm mad!" Powell shouted as he threw himself on his horse and rode away.

Hopelessly lost without Herold, he disappeared for three days, wandering the streets, and trying to hide. Finally, he returned to the boarding house where Booth and the other conspirators had met before the assassination. When he arrived, the police were taking the owner of the house and others away for questioning. Powell claimed that he was just a laborer there to dig a gutter, but the police didn't believe him. He was taken into custody and was positively identified a short time later.

Vice President Andrew Johnson was asleep in his room at the Kirkwood House Hotel when all this was happening. Word of the attack on Seward quickly spread and it was immediately feared that a plot might be happening against the U.S. Government. It was former Wisconsin Governor Leonard J. Farwell who rushed over to Johnson's hotel to warn him.

After waking Johnson and telling him what had happened, Farwell convinced someone to post a guard outside the vice president's room as a precaution.

He really didn't have to bother. George Atzerodt was, by then, too drunk to shoot anyone.

During the intermission, Booth returned to the Star Saloon. He was drinking again and, unbelievably, so were all three of Lincoln's attendants for the night - police bodyguard John Parker, carriage driver Ned Burke, and Charles Forbes.

The audience members only had a few minutes for their drinks, and they rushed back to the theater for the start of the third and final act.

Only Charles Forbes had enough sense of duty to return to his post outside the door leading to the presidential box. Burke eventually returned to his carriage outside. Parker remained in the saloon. He only discovered what happened to the president when he staggered into the police station after midnight with a prostitute named Lizzie Williams.

As theater patrons were leaving the tavern, Booth ran into an old friend, Edwin Brink, who became the last man to speak to him before the assassination. He later claimed that Booth told him, "I'm going to hang my name in a place where my father's never was."

The two men walked back to the theater lobby together. Brink went to the left and Booth followed him up the narrow staircase to the balcony. At the top of the stairs, Booth walked quickly along the south wall towards the president's box. Directly in front of the outer door to the presidential box, watching the play, sat two Army officers, Alexander Crawford and Theodore McGowan. The men's chairs were blocking Booth's way. Booth insisted on getting past them and the two men reluctantly moved their chairs, believing the actor was drunk.

Booth paused for a moment, removed his hat, and looked down at the stage, which was about 20 feet away. For a moment, Booth caught the eye of actress Helen Truman, who played Augusta, and she subtly nodded a greeting at him.

On the opposite side of the theater, James Ferguson, the owner of the Greenback Saloon, where Booth often ate lunch, spotted the actor. Ferguson had come to the theater hoping to see General Grant and using his girlfriend's opera glasses, he'd been watching the presidential box all evening. He knew Booth well and couldn't understand why he'd be lurking outside Lincoln's box.

Charles Forbes had returned to his seat outside the president's box. It was the seat that Ward Hill Lamon would have been in that night if Lincoln had not sent him on an errand to Richmond. There was a single step down from the aisle where Booth stood to the level of the doorway, and Booth took it. Forbes looked up at him. "This is the president's box, sir, no one is permitted to enter," he said. Charlie was not a guard - the guard was nowhere to be found -- but he was loyal to Lincoln.

Booth reportedly replied, "I am a senator. Mr. Lincoln has sent for me."

Booth reached into his pocket and pulled out a calling card. His secret fiancée, Lucy Hale, would later say that it was likely one that belonged to her father. Whatever it said on the card, it worked. Forbes, assuming Booth had permission to be there, nodded at him to enter. Again, it was not Charlie's job to guard the box. In the past hour, two other men had come to the presidential box bearing messages for Lincoln and both had been allowed to enter.

On stage, Mrs. Mountchessington finally discovered the shocking truth about Asa, that he was poor and no catch at all for her daughter. In stiff British rage, she sent Augusta to her room, reproached the American for his ill-mannered impertinence and then marched haughtily into the wings, leaving Harry Hawks alone on the stage to deliver his most comical line.

Booth reached for the doorknob and tried to open the door. It was stuck. He had to lean into it and give it a little shove with his knee before it opened. He quickly entered the narrow passage leading to the private boxes and closed the outside door behind him. He jammed the door shut with a piece of wood so that no one could enter from the outside. Later, it had to be removed by Major Rathbone before anyone could enter.

It was now 10:20 p.m.

Booth was now inside the short, narrow hall that led to the two inner doors that opened to two boxes. Both of these inner doors usually had locks on them, but at least one was broken. The theater crew had recently mislaid the keys and the lock had to be forced open. The door on the left, which was closed and locked, let into box 7. The door directly ahead of him led into box 8. It was open and slightly ajar. Booth could hear the actors on the stage through the open door. He paused just outside of it. When he peered in, he could see Lincoln about four feet from the opening. He was in a rocking chair, a small distance from the balcony railing.

The back of Lincoln's head was directly in front of Booth. Mrs. Lincoln sat next to him, on his right. Further over, on the other side of

One of the many images of the assassination that were circulated at the time

(Left) The derringer that Booth used to shoot Lincoln in the back of the head

the column that divided the box, were Clara Harris and her fiancée, Major Rathbone. Clara sat in an upholstered chair and Rathbone sat on a small sofa next to her. All four were watching the action on the stage.

No one saw John Wilkes Booth behind them.

Booth held a single-shot .44-caliber derringer in his right hand. In his left, he held a long dagger with the word "Liberty" engraved on it. It was a backup weapon in case the derringer misfired. He was determined not to fail. The actor waited patiently for his cue, waiting for Harry Hawk to say the laugh line.

And then he did. "Don't know the manners of good society, eh? You sockdologizing old man trap!" Predictably, the audience exploded with laughter.

And Booth pushed the narrow door open and stepped silently into the box.

During the evening, the Lincoln party had been discussing the Holy Land. The President made a comment about wanting to visit Jerusalem someday as he leaned forward and noticed General Ambrose Burnside in the audience of the theater.

Booth stepped forward. Major Rathbone caught movement out of the corner of his eye and bolted from his seat to confront the intruder. But he was a step too slow.

The derringer was just six inches from the back of Lincoln's head when he pulled the trigger. The gunshot echoed in the theater and Lincoln slumped forward, his head dropping to his chest.

The bullet had entered the lower half of Lincoln's skull, slightly to the left of the centerline, lodging behind one of his eyes.

The explosive laughter in the theater had been silenced by the sound of the shot. White smoke filled the box, briefly blinding Major Rathbone, who sprang forward anyway. He grabbed Booth from behind and pulled him back from the balcony railing.

Booth dropped the tiny pistol on the floor and twisted around, raising the dagger. "Let go of me or I will kill you!" he hissed at Rathbone. But Rathbone held him tighter, reaching for Booth's throat. The two men struggled, and the actor broke free. He stabbed at Rathbone's chest with the dagger and the soldier instinctively raised his left arm to parry the blow. The knife slashed into Rathbone's forearm and cut upwards from his elbow to his shoulder, narrowly missing his brachial artery. In seconds, there was blood everywhere.

Booth shoved the other man away from him and without hesitation, stepped up onto the velvet-covered balustrade that overlooked the stage. He did not "vault like a gymnast" over the rail. In truth, he awkwardly lowered himself part of the way down the front side of the box, holding onto the decorative flags with both hands, and then dropped the last six or seven feet onto the stage.

Although badly hurt, Major Rathbone managed catch hold of Booth's coat as he was going over the railing. He was knocked off balance and then one of his spurs caught on a flag. Because of this, he landed hard on the stage and fractured his left leg about two inches above the ankle. He managed to get up and he bellowed, "Sic semper

A *Harper's Weekly* illustration of Booth fleeing the stage after President Lincoln's assassination

tyrannis!" - "Thus always to tyrants," the motto of the Commonwealth of Virginia.

Once on the stage, Booth couldn't resist getting a little more attention. He spun around, faced the audience, and raised the bloody dagger into the air. "The South shall be free!" he cried out, according to actor Harry Hawk, who was a few feet away. Others heard him say, "The South is avenged!"

Major Rathbone shouted at the stunned audience, "Stop that man! Stop that man!"

And yet no one moved. Not realizing what was happening, the audience simply sat there, stunned. Most of the men in the audience carried revolvers on them. Others were Union soldiers, fresh from combat. However, they assumed the gunshot and Booth's wild entrance were just part of the show.

Booth rushed to his right, toward Hawk, with the dagger in his hand. As he did so, he glanced up into the audience and according to the saloon keeper, Booth caught James Ferguson's eye, raised the dagger, and mouthed words to him that looked like "I have done it!"

Harry Hawk took one look at Booth with the knife in his hand and fled for his life from the stage. The two men had quarreled over a woman named Ella Starr in the past and Hawks, not realizing what was happening, may have thought Booth was there to kill him.

Booth limped quickly offstage toward the exit, roughly bumping into Laura Keene as he passed her. He leaned against the wall for a second to catch his breath and then hurried toward the alley. As he made it to the back door, he found orchestra leader William Withers and his girlfriend - neither of whom had any idea of what had just transpired - blocking his path.

"Let me pass!" Booth shouted at them.

Withers froze and Booth ran into him. "Damn you!" the actor snarled and slashed at Withers with the dagger. He nicked him on the side of the neck and shoved him out of the way. Another stagehand, Jacob Ritterspaugh, tried to block Booth's exit but backed away when the actor swung the knife in his direction.

Booth slammed open the door and ran into the alley. A cold rain was falling as he looked around for Ned Spangler and his horse. Booth spotted young John Burroughs with the mare.

"Give me that horse!" Booth demanded, startling the boy, who didn't know who Booth was. Before he could speak, Booth cracked him in the head with the butt of the dagger and tore the reins out his hands.

His left foot screaming with pain, Booth struggled into the saddle and prepared to flee.

"Won't somebody stop that man," Clara Harris pleaded. "The President is shot!"

It was Clara's scream that finally snapped the audience out of its stupor. Almost immediately, voices began to take up the call of "Booth!" Many of them had recognized the famous actor as he landed on the stage. The theater erupted into pandemonium. There were more screams, groans, and the crashing of seats.

Above it all was Mary Lincoln's shrill and terror-filled scream for her husband.

Only a few of the audience members instantly understood what had just happened. An Army colonel named Joseph B. Stewart had leapt to his feet the moment he saw Booth crossing the stage with the dagger in his hand. Stewart had clambered onto the stage and chased Booth down the dark passageway toward the alley. He saw Booth go through the outside door but, unfamiliar with the theater and unable to see clearly in the dim light, he fumbled around looking for the outside door. He plunged out into the rain as Booth was trying to gain control of his skittish horse. Stewart reached for the reins of the mare - and barely missed them.

Booth jerked the horse away and kicked the animal with his spurs. The mare exploded away down the alley at a full gallop.

In seconds, Booth vanished into the dark and stormy night.

Army surgeon Dr. Charles Leale was one of the first to rush to Lincoln's aid after the shooting

Inside, the scene was chaotic. People were shoving into the aisles and rushing for the exits, with Laura Keene yelling at them from the stage: "For God's sake, have presence of mind and keep your places, and all will be well."

Mary was still wailing a piercing shriek that was echoing off the walls of the theater. She was trying to hold her husband upright as he slumped over toward the balcony rail. Major Rathbone, with his arm bleeding profusely, turned toward the wounded president, trying to understand what was happening. He could hear someone banging loudly a short distance away and he ran toward the sound. It was coming from the outer door - it had been jammed shut with a piece of wood. With considerable effort, thanks to his mangled arm, he succeeded in knocking the wood free and opening the door.

In the theater's audience was a young doctor named Charles Leale, who rushed upstairs to Lincoln's aid. The 23-year-old had been a surgeon in the Army and had come to the theater that evening with the express purpose of seeing President Lincoln, who he greatly admired. With the lower orchestra seats all filled, Leale had taken a seat in the balcony.

When he heard Clara's cry that the president had been shot, he didn't hesitate. He fought his way to the president's box, where a weeping Clara Harris tried to console Mary, who was holding Lincoln in the rocker and weeping hysterically.

Right behind Leale was Dr. Albert King, who had also been sitting in the balcony. The two men reached the box in a matter of minutes. Leale felt for Lincoln's pulse and was alarmed when he couldn't find it. The men lifted Lincoln from the rocking chair and laid him out on the floor of the box.

Right at that moment, a third doctor, Charles Taft, an experienced Army surgeon, announced himself from the stage below. He was boosted up the box by theater patrons, eager to help. Taft wasted no time. Using a borrowed knife, he cut off Lincoln's collar and tore open his shirt. But the doctors could see no bleeding or any sign of a wound.

Leale examined Lincoln's eye by lifting the president's eyelid and saw that his pupils were dilated, which was not a good sign. With his fingers, he probed around Lincoln's head and quickly found a wound - a clean hole in the back of his skull. Using his finger, he probed the hole and removed a blood clot, relieving the pressure on the president's brain. Immediately, Lincoln began to breath more easily.

At that moment, actress Laura Keene inexplicably walked into the presidential box. Down below on the stage, she had heard Clara cry for water. With a natural performer's instinct for publicity, she grabbed a water pitcher from the theater's greenroom and directed her stage manager to get her upstairs to the box by any means necessary. Somehow, she made it upstairs, got through the crowd, and pushed her way to where Lincoln was lying unconscious on the floor.

Actress Laura Keene

Laura Keene - likely knowing that she was witnessing history - knelt on the floor and cradling Lincoln's head, oozing blood and brains, in her lap. She kept the bloodstained dress for many years afterward as proof that she had held Lincoln's head as he lay dying.

But the three doctors were determined not to let Lincoln die. Leale reached into his mouth, opened his throat, and applied artificial respiration in a desperate attempt to save him. Taft joined him as he continued his efforts. Taft raised and lowered the president's arms, while Leale massaged his chest, and then he forced his own breath into Lincoln's lungs again and again. Lincoln somehow began to breathe on his own, his heart beating with an irregular flutter. Lincoln was failing fast --- but he was still alive.

They knew that Lincoln could not be moved to the White House. Travel by way of the muddy, pot-holed streets of Washington would only hasten his demise. But they had to get him someplace where he might be treated. The doctors, with help from bystanders, managed to get the President out of Ford's Theater. Soldiers cleared a path through the crowd outside, where people rushed madly back and forth and milled about in confusion. As the group moved slowly forward, Leale would occasionally pause to pick open the scab that was forming on the bullet hole, allowing it to drain.

A man named Henry Safford, who worked as a clerk at the War Department, beckoned to the doctors and they carried the President across the street to a three-story brick boarding house that was owned by a German tailor named William Petersen.

Lincoln was taken into a small bedroom at the back of the house. His lanky frame was too long for the bed and they were forced to lay him down at an angle. Clara Harris and Major Rathbone, with his untreated arm bleeding profusely, brought Mary to the house. When she saw Lincoln in the back room, Mary ran to him, falling sobbing to her knees and calling him intimate names. She begged Lincoln to speak to her until finally the doctors led her to the front parlor, where she broke into convulsive weeping.

The doctors returned to the bedroom for a more thorough examination. They removed all of Lincoln's clothing and went over his body, inch by inch, looking for any other trauma. Only the bullet hole in his head was found. They covered his near-lifeless body with mustard plasters to keep him warm, drew blankets over him, and did their best to make him comfortable.

Soon, the Surgeon General, Joseph K. Barnes, and Lincoln's personal doctor, Robert Stone King, arrived and examined the President. They also realized that it was no use - there was nothing that could be done for him.

Mary was allowed to return to the room. She sat down in a chair next to the bed and again, begged her husband to speak to her. Lincoln remained silent and Mary began to weep once again.

The Petersen house, located across the street from Ford's Theater

As word spread through Washington of Lincoln's fate, a procession of government officials came running to the boarding house, crowding into the room where Lincoln lay with a cluster of doctors and a sobbing Mary at his side.

Outside, all hell was breaking loose on the streets. Word of the assassination attempt on Lincoln, and the earlier attack on Secretary Seward, spread like wildfire across the city. Large crowds that had been drunkenly celebrating the end of the war rushed to Ford's Theater, loudly crying that they should burn the place to the ground. It was still raining but the streets were packed with the morbid curious.

Tad Lincoln, watching a play about Aladdin at the Grover's Theater, heard the manager announce that President Lincoln had been shot. Aides rushed the boy to the White House, even though Mary had asked that he be brought to the boarding house so that he could see his father one last time. Robert Lincoln, asleep at the White House, was awakened by John Hay and told of the news. They hurried together to his father's deathbed.

Rumors swept the city, including that all the telegraph wires out of Washington had been cut. They hadn't, but many citizens were terrified believing they were witnessing a coup d'état against the government that had been engineered by the fallen Confederacy. In truth, if George Atzerodt had killed Vice President Johnson as Booth had ordered him to, a coup might have been possible. As it was, the political leaders of the Confederacy were on the run, certain they would be tried for treason. It seemed believable that a last-ditch effort to destabilize the federal government was taking place.

Secretary of War Stanton had received a report of the attack on Seward and rushed to his home. He found him wounded but alive, so he left him in the care of the doctors already there and hurried to Ford's Theater. Within 30 minutes of the attack, he was in the parlor of Petersen's boarding house, turning it into both a war room and the temporary headquarters of the executive government. For all intents and purposes, he was the acting president. When Andrew Johnson eventually arrived, he stepped aside and allowed Stanton to continue running the country in the midst of the crisis.

Secretary of War Edwin Stanton, the man who would unofficially be running the country in the wake of Lincoln's murder

Stanton's first objective was to try and piece together exactly what had happened. He quickly found a secretary named James Tanner and drafted him into duty taking notes for a three-man board of inquiry that was made up of top judges. They proceeded to interview one witness after another through the night. From the testimony of literally dozens of eyewitnesses, they soon identified John Wilkes Booth as the main suspect.

Stanton declared martial law in the city and as he issued orders that mobilized troops and police officers, Mary lay on the sofa in the front parlor, going back and forth between eerie quiet and fits of weeping. When she recalled Lincoln's dreams of mournful voices in the White House, she cried miserably that his dream had come true. She begged God to take her too, or to trade her life for her husband's.

Robert Lincoln arrived with John Hay, barely hearing the words of the doctor who told them at the doorway to the room that there was nothing that could be done for the President. When Robert saw his father lying diagonally across the bed, his brain destroyed, and his eye swollen and broken with blood, the usually calm and collected young man broke down in despair and disbelief. Finally, in shock himself, he went into the front parlor to try and comfort his mother. Mary had been sedated by one of the doctors, though, and in her stupor, hardly knew he was there.

As Robert left the room, Senator Charles Sumner entered, his face twisted in anguish. The senator took Lincoln's hand and spoke to him, but a doctor assured him that Lincoln was beyond hearing, that he was dead.

"No, he isn't dead," Sumner protested in anger. "Look at his face, he is breathing."

The other physicians assured him that Lincoln would never regain consciousness and, at that, Sumner clasped Lincoln's hand tightly, bowed his head close to the pillow and began to weep.

Senator Charles Sumner

Booth had spent months planning his escape from Washington. Originally, he would have had Lincoln with him as his captive but now, riding alone, he followed the same roads and knew precisely where to go. His plan was to get out of Washington as quickly as possible, ride south into rural Maryland, and then cross the Potomac into Virginia.

Booth's quickest way out of the city was across the bridge that was next to the Navy Yard. He made it to the Washington side of the bridge around 11:00 p.m. The sentry on duty immediately challenged him and then called for his sergeant. It was a suspicious situation - both the late hour and a horse breathing heavily from a hard ride - but Booth used his skills as an actor to bluff his way across, even though the bridge was supposed to be closed after 9:00 p.m.

David Herold was just as lucky. He arrived at the same bridge a short time after Booth, gave a false name, and said he'd been visiting a woman in the city and time got away from him. The soldiers let him pass over the bridge, too.

Herold caught up with Booth on the dark road and they proceeded together to their meeting place - Mary Surratt's tavern in the small town of Surrattsville, which is now Clinton, Maryland. They arrived just after midnight, waking the proprietor, John Lloyd. They collected guns, a bottle of whiskey, and some binoculars that Booth had left with Mary Surratt earlier in the day and rode on.

Behind them, in Washington, the federal government, convinced it was under attack, reacted with remarkable speed. Armed guards were immediately stationed outside the homes of Cabinet members and other officials. Roads were closed and all transportation out of the city was immediately stopped.

Within an hour after the shooting, Stanton's aide, Major Thomas Eckert, had sent a telegram to General Grant, informing him of events and ordering him back to the city.

In the hours and days that followed, hundreds of people were arrested and interrogated, often with little or no cause. That included most of the cast and crew of Ford's Theater, including the owner, John Ford himself. Those arrested were held at the Old Washington Penitentiary or the Navy Yard and were ruthlessly questioned.

The government showed remarkable restraint, though. Most of those arrested were released quickly and only those who conspired with Booth eventually faced justice.

But Booth and one of those conspirators were on the run together, heading south of Surrattsville in the pre-dawn hours. There were no soldiers on the road. They didn't see anyone as they rode silently in the darkness. Around 4:00 a.m., they arrived at a farmhouse just outside of the village of Bryantown in Charles County, Maryland.

It was the home of Dr. Samuel A. Mudd and Booth had been there before. Now, he needed help with his broken leg, and he sent Herold to try and raise someone in the dark house. Herold pounded on the door. When a voice answered, he said that they needed a doctor.

Dr. Mudd, 32-years-old with a bald head and thick goatee, was a respected physician in the area and a well-known Confederate sympathizer. He had earned his medical degree from Georgetown College and with his wife, Sarah, and their four children Mudd managed a 218-acre tobacco farm with the help of 11 slaves.

Dr. Samuel Mudd

Mudd would later claim that he didn't know, or didn't recognize, John Wilkes Booth when he treated his broken leg that night, but this wasn't true. Even his own attorney would later admit that he knew Booth well and at the very least, knew about his plan to kidnap Lincoln. Booth had been to Bryantown twice in the past six months and had even attended mass with Mudd and his family in the nearby parish church. It was Mudd's lies, evasiveness, and nervousness, that later made investigators suspicious of him.

Mudd helped Booth into the farmhouse and, after getting him into a chair, examined his leg. He tried to remove Booth's boot, but it wouldn't move. The swelling above his left ankle made the boot impossible to pull off, so he carefully cut it away with a scalpel. He found that Booth's injury was a clean break, not a compound fracture. Mudd found some wood to use as a splint and fashioned some crude crutches for him out of an old plank.

Dr. Mudd offered to let the two men rest at his house but Booth was anxious to leave. He knew the authorities would soon be looking for him - if they weren't already - but he also realized that riding out in the daylight would be a serious mistake. The sun was starting to rise, so Booth took the doctor up on his offer. Mudd and Herold helped Booth to the staircase, and, with a lot of effort, he climbed the stairs to the second-floor guestroom.

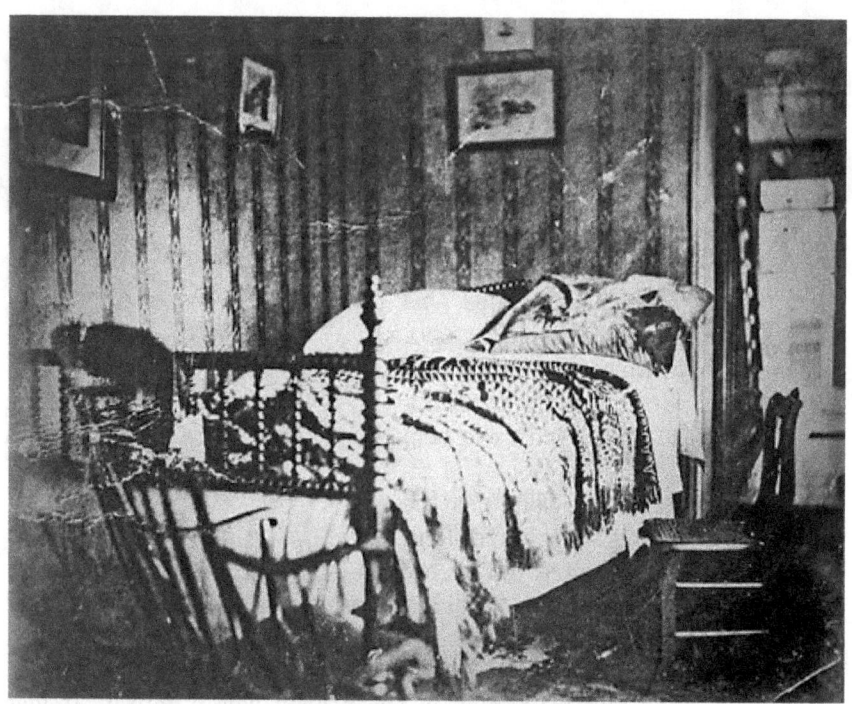

The bed at the Petersen house where Lincoln died. The dying man was so tall that he had to be turned at an angle so that he could fit on it

In Washington, Stanton and the doctors stood watch over Lincoln at the Petersen house.

Detectives had raided Booth's room at the National Hotel, searching for clues, and found a letter from a friend named Sam Arnold that made it clear that there had been a conspiracy of some kind against the president. He had urged Booth to "not act rashly or in haste." The two men had eaten dinner together a month earlier and Booth's conversation - which hinted at assassination - had filled Arnold with dread and fear. He had been willing to go along with Booth's plans to kidnap Lincoln, but he'd wanted nothing to do with murder.

By 6:00 a.m., around the same time that Booth was lying down in a warm bed at Mudd's house, the doctors were anxiously watching the life drain from President Lincoln. Thousands of people, both black and white, filled the streets outside the house, waiting desperately for news.

They stayed there, keeping a constant vigil, and asking the officials who came and went if there was any word - or any hope.

As the first gray light began to appear at the windows, a heavy rain began to fall, as if the heavens were weeping. Mary came to see Abraham one last time. She kissed his face and whispered to him, "Love, live but one moment to speak to me once" but then she looked at his shattered face and realized, perhaps for the first time, that he was beyond hope. She wept as she was led away.

With the end now close, Lincoln's friends and colleagues gathered at his bedside. Stanton and Robert Lincoln came in from the front room and Robert, giving away to his agony, put his head on Sumner's shoulder. At that, many of the others present also began to cry. Finally, Lincoln took one great breath, his face relaxed, and then he was gone.

The Surgeon General carefully crossed the lifeless hands of Abraham Lincoln at twenty-two minutes after seven on the morning of April 15, 1865.

Edwin Stanton stood by the bedside of the slain president. He raised his head and with tears streaming down his face, uttered the most unforgettable words that a man not known for his poetic soul could ever manage... "Now, he belongs to the ages."

13. SPIRITS OF THE ASSASSINATION

The Aftermath of Lincoln's Death and the Spirits that Linger From It

At the same time that life was draining away from Abraham Lincoln, John Wilkes Booth and David Herold were having breakfast with the Mudd family at their Maryland home. Herold joined the family at the table, but Booth took his breakfast in bed. His broken leg was throbbing with pain.

Later in the day, Dr. Mudd and Herold rode to the farm of Mudd's father to see if he had a carriage that he could spare so that Booth could be taken into Virginia. Mudd's younger brother told them they didn't and suggested they look for one to rent in nearby Bryantown.

The two men were riding toward town when Herold suddenly stopped short on the road. A unit of soldiers were up ahead from the Thirteenth New York Cavalry. They were precisely what Herold feared they were - riders in pursuit of the man, or men, who had assassinated President Lincoln. Without saying a word, Herold turned his horse around and galloped at full speed back to Mudd's farm.

Dr. Mudd, though, kept on riding toward them. At this point, he may not have known what Booth had done and so he had no reason to fear the soldiers. He soon found out, however. As he entered the town, which had long been known for its sympathy for the Confederacy, he saw Union soldiers going from house to house asking questions. When he asked what was going on, he was told that the actor John Wilkes Booth had killed President Lincoln.

Meanwhile, Herold had returned to the farm. He hurried upstairs and a few minutes later, he was in the kitchen with Booth. Both men were dressed for travel with gun belts around their waists. They had to run. If Dr. Mudd betrayed them, soldiers would be at the door within the hour. Yet Booth hesitated. They would be fleeing in broad daylight and had no idea where to go next. They decided to take a chance and wait for Mudd to return.

Mudd returned to the farm around 6:00 p.m. He did not betray Booth, but he was ready for him to leave. Booth had placed Mudd and his family in mortal danger and he had to get away from the farm. But the doctor still offered to help. He was going to have to report Booth's visit to the authorities, but he would give Booth and Herold a large head start. He also gave them the names of other Confederate sympathizers who might help them, as well as directions to their homes.

The fugitives left the Mudd farm after dark, staying away from Bryantown, and searching for the farmhouses that Mudd had told them about. They missed the first one, owned by a man named William Burtles, but eventually made it to the home of Colonel Samuel Cox, a Confederate courier. They approached the house long after midnight and when Cox came out to meet them, Booth told him who he was and why they needed help.

Like Dr. Mudd, Cox knew that he was placing himself and his family in danger by helping the assassin, but it was as though he was unable to resist one last act of defiance for the Confederacy. He couldn't let the men in the house, but he did offer to hide them in a nearby pine thicket where they could avoid detection.

They were safe - for now.

On Monday morning, Dr. Mudd sent his cousin to the military headquarters that had been set up in Bryantown to tell them about the two strangers who had stopped by his house on Saturday morning. When investigators inevitably searched the Mudd home, the doctor showed them the boot that had been removed from the injured man's leg. Inside it, the soldiers found a name engraved in the leather - K. Wilkes.

A short distance away, Booth and Herold were still hiding on the Cox farm. Cox sent his son to visit a neighbor, Thomas A. Jones, who had been one of the most successful river smugglers the Confederacy had. The boy brought Jones back to the farm and Cox explained the situation. Jones, even though he knew the odds were against them, was also intrigued by helping Booth and Herold escape.

Jones rode out to the pine thicket to see the two fugitives in person. Using a special whistle that Cox had worked out with Booth, he approached their camp. He found Booth in considerable pain. He was lying on a blanket on the damp ground, but he greeted Jones warmly and admitted that he had, indeed, killed Lincoln. He asked Jones if he could help them escape.

Thomas A. Jones, the former river smuggler who assisted Booth and Herold

With Union troops scouring the area, Jones said that Booth's best chance was to remain where he was, hidden in the pine thicket. When the soldiers didn't find anything, they'd move on. He promised to keep the fugitives supplied with food and other provisions, as long as they didn't light a fire or draw attention to themselves. They could fill their canteens from a nearby spring. Once the search parties moved on, Jones would get them across the river to Virginia.

The largest manhunt in American history took place in the days that followed. While literally thousands of soldiers and detectives searched every farmhouse, henhouse, and outhouse for hundreds of miles around Washington - storming into homes and arresting anyone suspected of aiding the assassin - Booth and Herold simply waited in a dense pine thicket and kept quiet.

As Jones believed, the disappearance of Booth into that pine thicket made it seem as if he had vanished without a trace. The country assumed he was racing to Virginia, trying to escape to the south and perhaps even leave the country, but after being seen at Mary Surratt's tavern on the night of the assassination, he'd vanished. Stanton and other government officials were frantically directing the searchers to find him.

On Monday, they got their first break. One of the conspirators put himself right into their hands. With Booth's trail gone cold, Stanton and other top men were going over what they knew, hoping for fresh leads - and they kept coming back to a mysterious boarding house owned by the equally mysterious Mary Surratt. This was not the tavern outside the city but the boarding house that she operated at 541 H Street in Washington. Booth had visited there many times, they knew, and Mary's son, John Surratt, Jr., was a suspect in the assassination.

The Surratt boarding house on H Street in Washington

Around 11:00 p.m. on Monday night, soldiers raided the boarding house with the intention of arresting every man, woman, and child they found there. Led by Major W.H. Smith, a contingent of soldiers stormed into the place and informed Mary Surratt that all the occupants were under arrest.

As they began searching the house, something unexpected happened. While waiting for a wagon to transport the prisoners to military headquarters for questioning, an unknown man walked up the stairs to the boarding house, apparently oblivious to the large group of soldiers in the street. He was dressed in good clothing but was dirty and unshaven and was carrying a large pickaxe. He knocked on the front door and was immediately allowed inside - where he found himself face-to-face with five armed soldiers.

Lewis Powell had just made a big mistake.

Powell, after trying to kill the Secretary of State and his two sons, had fled from Seward's home only to discover that David Herold had panicked and ridden away, leaving Powell to his fate. For two days, he'd been lost in the city, eventually hiding out in a cemetery. Cold and hungry, he made his way back to one of the only places he knew - the boarding house where the conspirators often met. He just happened to show up there at a very bad time.

Thinking quickly, he claimed that he was at the house to dig a trench for Mary Surratt, ignoring the fact that it was nearly midnight. For her part, Mary insisted that she had never seen the man before in her life. After a few more questions, Major Smith decided that Powell was suspicious enough that he should be arrested, too. Knowing his deception was over, Powell put down the pickaxe and gave up without a fight. A short time later, detectives working the case would discover exactly who he was.

The second most wanted man in the country had literally walked right into their arms.

The same thing was almost true of another of Booth's conspirators, George Atzerodt. Like Powell and even David Herold, Atzerodt could have left Washington and vanished. In the era before fingerprinting and other methods of identification, he could have picked a new name, traveled west, and become someone else. But he didn't. After he lost his nerve and failed to kill Andrew Johnson, he spent the rest of the night getting drunk.

He eventually stumbled into the Pennsylvania House hotel, a little after midnight. He rented a shared room, at first declining to sign the guest book, and spent the night there. The next morning - perhaps a little more sober - he walked down F Street and tried to throw away his knife, which he feared might implicate him. Unfortunately for him, someone saw him trying to dispose of a dangerous weapon, picked it up, and turned it over to police.

Atzerodt traveled to Georgetown, where he tried unsuccessfully to borrow some money and was forced to pawn his pistol for $10. He used that money to journey about 20 miles north of the city to the home of a friend in Montgomery County, Maryland. He had dinner with his friend's family and then went to stay with his cousin, Hartman Richter, who lived nearby. He stayed there for the next four days, not realizing that he was being hunted by every police officer in Washington.

It was Atzerodt's brother, John, who turned him into the authorities. On April 20, six cavalrymen arrived at Richter's home and found Atzerodt asleep in an upstairs bedroom. He was arrested without a struggle and then proceeded to confess to everything he knew - the kidnapping plan, Booth's last-minute decision to kill the President, his failed plan to kill Andrew Johnson, everything.

Only one of the conspirators got away - John Surratt, Jr. Although he abandoned Booth when it became clear that the actor was planning murder instead of kidnapping, Surratt was initially suspected of being one of the assassins. The famous $100,000 wanted poster that Stanton had made listed Surratt along with Booth and Herold as the three wanted men. There was a $25,000 price on his head and Surratt knew he had to get out of the country.

For five long days, Booth and Herold waited in the pine thicket. During that time, soldiers conducted house-to-house searches and patrolled the area but found nothing. They finally considered that Booth had eluded them and vanished into Virginia.

Booth was in great pain when Jones appeared on Thursday, April 20, and announced that they should leave. He had been passing the time in the local general store, listening to the troops as they came in to buy supplies. He had just overheard that a report had come in saying that Booth and Herold were spotted in another county. The entire force had moved out in pursuit and it was now safe for Booth to escape.

After dark, Jones led the fugitives along three miles of forest paths and marshy areas to the Potomac River, where he had hidden a boat. He instructed them on the best way to navigate the river and gave them a candle, matches, and a compass. If they followed the heading he gave them, they'd make it to Machodoc Creek on the Virginia side. There they would find help at the home of a woman named Elizabeth Quesenberry, who lived in a farmhouse along the creek.

They shoved off and Herold rowed them out into the fast-moving river. Booth sat in the stern, trying to navigate in the dark with the flickering candle, which he held down low so that it wouldn't be spotted. They went badly off course. The river was too strong, and Booth had no idea how to direct Herold. They spent most of the night on the river and ended up going in the wrong direction. They eventually made it to shore near an inlet called Nanjemoy Creek, northwest of where they started.

They had gone sideways. They still weren't in Virginia.

However, Herold knew someone in the area, a man named John Hughes, who took them into his home and gave them a hot meal. He sent them to hide in a marsh near the river. They should have pushed off that night and tried to cross the river again, but for some unknown reason, they didn't. They chose to stay hidden in the marsh for another 24 hours, allowing their pursuers to gain ground.

While sitting in the wet mud along the riverbank, Booth had time to curse his predicament in his diary. He was angry that he had no support from the Confederate cause after "striking down the great tyrant" and was reduced to hiding in pine thickets and swamps. He had been "abandoned, with the curse of Cain" upon him. He would try to escape, he wrote, but had no intention of dying like a criminal. He prayed that God would let him "die bravely."

The following night, better prepared, Booth and Herold once again shoved off in the little skiff and heading out into the rushing waters of the Potomac, narrowly missing a federal gunboat that was searching the shoreline.

They rowed for hours - in the right direction this time - and the little boat made it across the river, although they missed their destination of Machodoc Creek - again. They beached the skiff near Gambo Creek instead.

They were now in Virginia. It was Sunday morning, April 23, 1865.

The events that happened next were a series of bizarre happenings that eventually set the stage for Booth's final capture. Amazingly, the fugitives were helped by many people and likely could have escaped if not for these weird incidents that led them into a trap.

Herold left Booth at the boat and went to find Elizabeth Quesenberry's house. He quickly found it and explained who he was. He appealed to her sense of Confederate loyalty but, unsure of what to do, Elizabeth sent for the top Confederate agent in the area who turned out to be an acquaintance of Booth named Thomas Harbin. He had been one of the early conspirators in the kidnapping plot.

Along with another spy, William Bryant, Harbin agreed to help the two men. They arranged for horses and brought them, along with food from Elizabeth Quesenberry, to the boat after darkness had fallen. They now needed a place where Booth and Herold could hide out. The first place they tried was the home of Dr. Richard Stuart, but the physician refused to hide them. He immediately realized who they were and ordered them off his property.

The four men left the house and then forced their way into a cabin that was owned by William Lucas, a free black man. They terrorized Lucas and his wife and stayed the night there. The couple spent the night on their front porch rather than share quarters with Booth and his friends.

The next day, they forced Lucas to have his son, Charles, drive Booth in their buggy to Port Conway, a ferry crossing on the Rappahannock River, about 10 miles further south. Booth offered to pay them $20 for the trip, which turned out to be uneventful. The fugitives arrived at Port Conway around noon and Booth took the time to write a hateful letter to Dr. Stuart about his lack of southern hospitality.

Herold tried to talk a fisherman into taking them across the river and even as far as Bowling Green, where they could catch a train to Richmond, but he was busy mending his nets so they moved on to look somewhere else for help.

And that was when they ran into a trio of Confederate soldiers that were not just any soldiers - they were members of the guerilla unit known as Mosby's Rangers. After spinning an unconvincing tale about also being soldiers on their way home - which the rangers didn't believe - Herold decided to take a chance and tell them who they really were. The young soldiers were startled but impressed. Booth told them that there was a large reward for the man who captured him, but the soldiers agreed to help him.

After sending Charles Lucas back home with his wagon - and Booth's ridiculous letter to Dr. Stuart - Booth, Herold, and the three rangers boarded a ferry that took them across the river to Port Royal. From there, the soldiers began trying to find a farm that would house the two fugitives, who were now pretending to be a returning Confederate soldier and his cousin, both with the last name of Boyd. Two farms sent them on their way because their men were not home, and it wouldn't be proper - or safe - for women to take strange soldiers into their homes.

But finally, in the late afternoon of Monday, April 24, they found a farmer willing to help. His name was Richard Garrett, and he was the owner of a 500-acre piece of land called Locust Hill. He had two sons who had recently returned safely from the war and he felt it was his duty to help two Confederates who were also returning home. He said that he would allow them to stay for a day or two.

With their mission accomplished, the three rangers left and said they were heading to the nearby town of Bowling Green. Herold went with them, saying that he wanted to visit an old friend who lived there.

Booth stayed behind at the Garrett farm, where he was treated like an honored guest, given good food and wine, and treated to a warm bed to sleep in.

The Garrett home, where Booth spent his final days. He would eventually die on that front porch

At the same time that Booth was arriving at the Garrett farm, detectives working in Washington received what amounted to a false tip about two men crossing the Potomac into Virginia on April 16. The men who had been spotted were not Booth and Herold, but someone else - but there was no way for the detectives to know that. The false report led the detectives to organize a military unit - the Sixteenth New York Cavalry regiment - to track down the men. Led by two of the detectives, Luther Baker and Everton Conger, and Lieutenant Edward Doherty, 26 soldiers and their horses boarded a river steamer at the Sixth Street wharf that same day.

They planned to ride south toward Fredericksburg, but to get there, they had to leave the steamer at Belle Plain and travel by road to Port Conway, where they would cross the Rappahannock by ferry.

In other words, they were hot on the trail of Abraham Lincoln's assassin without even knowing it.

The next day, April 25, Booth slept late in the comfortable guest room bed. When he went downstairs for breakfast, he felt comfortable enough to leave his guns behind. It was a warm spring day and he limped outside to find a place to relax on the grass and watch the Garrett children play.

At the noon dinner table, those gathered there discussed the news of the Lincoln assassination and the reward that was being offered for the capture of the president's killer and his two accomplices. Booth, of course, feigned ignorance of these events. No one suspected a thing.

But their friendliness toward Booth wouldn't last.

After dinner, Booth was sitting on the porch when he and some of the younger Garrett children heard a loud noise from the road. An advance guard of the Sixteenth New York Cavalry, which had just crossed on the Rappahannock ferry, was galloping past the farm. Booth went into a panic. He yelled for the Garrett children to bring him his guns from upstairs. The children were startled by his sudden change in behavior and the older boys began to wonder just who this man was that they were sheltering in their home. He claimed to be a soldier returning home, but was he really?

When David Herold returned to the Garrett farm a little while later, the older children were no longer as welcoming as they had been. They informed Herold that his "cousin" was no longer welcome there. Only a few minutes later, two of the Confederate soldiers that had brought the fugitives to the farm came running up the road - a unit of Yankee cavalry was on its way from the ferry!

Booth and Herold didn't hesitate. They immediately ran to the woods behind the Garrett home, which was another act that convinced the Garretts that the two men were not who they claimed to be.

The main cavalry force came thundering down the road - and passed right by the Garrett farm. They vanished in the distance, leaving behind only a cloud of dust. With the danger passed, Booth and Herold emerged from the woods, but they could see immediately that the mood of the Garrett family had changed. The older boys, both Confederate veterans, told the two men that they couldn't stay another night. They wanted them to leave right away.

But after some tense and increasingly hostile negotiations, the Garretts eventually agreed to allow Booth and Herold to sleep in their old tobacco barn. The ramshackle building wasn't much, but at least it was safe and dry. They led the men there, settled them inside, and then closed the doors.

As the Garretts walked back to the house, though, they began to worry. What if the fugitives decided to steal their horses, or even rob them in the night? They had younger siblings, elderly parents, and unmarried sisters to protect. After they talked about this for a few minutes, the Garretts did something that would change history - they silently closed the big metal lock on the barn door, securing Booth and Herold inside. The two men in the tobacco barn never heard a thing and they soon fell asleep.

When the Sixteenth New York Cavalry had raced past the Garrett farm that afternoon, it had seemed as though they had no idea where they were going. In truth, though, they had a lot of information about Booth's whereabouts. When they had reached the ferry at Port Conway, detectives Baker and Conger had questioned the very same fisherman that had initially agreed to take Booth and Herold across the river. The fisherman confirmed that a man with a limp had crossed the river the day before and even identified the fugitives from their photographs.

The fisherman was joined by his wife and she told the detectives the names of the three Confederate soldiers who had befriended Booth and where they were likely staying in Bowling Green. It turned out that one of the soldiers, Willie Jett, was courting the daughter of the proprietor of the Star Hotel in town.

Baker and Conger couldn't believe their luck. They passed the information on to Lieutenant Doherty and went in pursuit of the soldiers. When the soldiers of the Sixteenth passed by the Garrett farm, they were headed directly to where they believed the three men were staying. The two detectives knew that Booth had to be somewhere in the area, and they were determined to track him down as quickly as they could. The Sixteenth were also keenly aware that they were in enemy territory. No matter what politicians might say about the war being over, if the 26 cavalrymen of the Sixteenth ran into a Confederate unit of sufficient strength, they would be in great danger.

It was close to 11:00 p.m. when the Sixteenth quietly rode into Bowling Green. They quickly found and surrounded the Star Hotel but were unable to get anyone to answer the door, so they broke into the building through the servant's quarters in back. After rousing some of the occupants from bed, they were told that Willie Jett was upstairs sleeping. They soon burst into his room and dragged him downstairs for questioning. Within minutes, he was telling them everything they wanted to know - Booth was at a farmhouse along the road to Port Royal, the same road the soldiers had just traveled along.

Jett even agreed to guide them to the Garrett farm. "I will go there with you, and show you where they are now, and you can get them," he told them.

Baker and Conger worried that Booth might have fled when the cavalry unit raced past the farmhouse that evening but they also knew this might be their chance to end the chase. The unit left the hotel at 12:30 a.m. with Jett leading the way. It took almost two hours to get to the farm. When they arrived, the men dismounted and then the soldiers and the two detectives, with guns at the ready, crept up the dirt lane from the main road to the farm.

After passing through a second gate, they climbed back on their horses and charging the house and the farm buildings. As the horses galloped across the open ground, the family's dogs began barking furiously. The Garretts were startled awake. The children began to scream with the adults fumbled for clothing and lamps.

Inside the tobacco barn, Booth, too, quickly sat up and listened in the darkness. He knew right away what was happening and he shook Herold awake. Herold jumped to his feet and ran to the barn door. He later testified, "We went right up to the barn door and tried to get out, but we found it was locked."

They were trapped.

As the federal soldiers surrounded the house, Booth and Herold did everything they could to try and break out of the barn. They used all their weight against the door, but it wouldn't budge. They even tried to kick loose boards from the old building's walls, but it was no use. The tobacco barn didn't look like much - the boards four-inch gaps between them - but it was solidly built.

Inside the house, the detectives were forcefully interrogating the Garretts. When Richard Garrett told them that the two men who had been staying with them had left, Conger threatened to hang him from a tree in the yard. When he told one of the soldiers to get a rope from his saddle, young John Garrett rushed to his father's defense. He cried out that he would tell them everything - just don't hang his father! Lieutenant Doherty grabbed the boy by his shirt, put a revolver to his head, and told him that he'd shoot him if he didn't tell where Booth was hiding.

"In the barn!" John screamed.

Terrified of what might happen to his family, the boy quickly marched to the front of the house and pointed out at the tobacco barn. "There!" he said.

The soldiers spread out and surrounded the barn. Inside, Booth and Herold could hear everything that was happening. There was enough light for them to see that they were both outgunned and outnumbered.

The detectives ordered John Garrett to go into the barn and inform Booth that he had to give up his weapons and come out. John balked at the order - it was a suicide mission. He had been the one who had locked Booth into the barn the night before. But he had no choice. He was told that if he didn't do it, the farm would be burned to the ground.

Expecting to be shot, John cautiously turned the lock and opened the door. Booth was standing in the shadows at the back of the barn, a pistol in each hand. John nervously informed him that the barn was surrounded, and the soldiers demanded that he give himself up.

"Damn you!" Booth hissed at the young man. "You have betrayed me! If you don't get out of here, I'll shoot you. Get out of this barn at once!" As the actor limped toward him, John turned and ran for his life.

Booth could have shot him in the back, but he didn't. The soldiers outside could have opened fire after the boy was out of the barn, but they didn't. Secretary Stanton probably wanted Booth alive. If he was questioned, he might reveal the name of the Confederate leaders who helped him. If he were placed on trial, it would be a public spectacle for those who wanted vengeance for the murder of the president.

The detectives decided to try a different approach. Baker yelled through the door that if Booth didn't surrender in the next 15 minutes, he would set fire to the barn.

Booth replied that he would think about the offer. He knew he had no chance, but he wanted to die fighting. He also knew that he should let Herold leave. At first, he had threatened to shoot Herold himself, calling him a "damned coward," but then he relented and told Baker that his companion "wanted to surrender awful bad."

What followed with a strange period of bickering about Herold's weapons. He was told to hand them over and come out, but Herold said he was unarmed. Nonsense, the detectives argued. The Garretts had given the detectives an itemized list of the weapons the men had with them. Herold and the men outside continued to argue over this until finally, Booth grew frustrated. He shouted that the weapons were his and he wasn't giving any of them to Herold, who he claimed was innocent.

"I own all the arms and intend to use them on you gentlemen," Booth called out.

More bickering followed until the detectives finally allowed Herold to leave the barn as long as he walked out with his hands in the air. The barn door opened slowly. Herold stuck out one empty hand and then another - and then was grabbed and dragged from the building.

There was some debate about whether the barn should really be set on fire. The detectives had been told to bring in Booth alive, if possible. Burning the barn might force him to come out, but it also might kill him. If they rushed the barn, some of the men were likely to be killed. Time ticked by and then the decision was made by Baker and Conger - they would set the barn on fire and burn Booth out. If he refused to leave, then he would perish in the flames.

The soldiers forced the Garrett boys to gather sticks, straw, and leaves from the yard and lay it along the sides of the old barn. At one point, as John Garrett was piling up straw against the barn wall, he heard Booth whisper to him from between the boards. "Young man, I advise you for your own good not to come here again. If you do not leave at once, I will shoot you."

Booth taunted the detectives outside, telling them he could have killed them easily through the slats in the boards but had spared them. He even challenged them to make the fight fair. "If you take your men 50 yards from the door, I'll come out and fight you. Give me a chance for my life," he shouted. The detectives declined the offer.

Using a wax candle that Baker had been idiotically holding in the darkness - making himself a target for Booth, who was growing desperate - Conger lit the straw and kindling around the barn. In moments, the fire began to spread and to climb the walls of the building. Through the slats in the boards, the soldiers could now see Booth inside. He was in the center of the barn, flinching away from the flames. He was standing there with a crutch under his arm, pistol in one hand and a Spencer carbine in the other.

An illustration of the soldiers setting fire the barn and dragging out Booth's body after he was shot.

(Below) Booth was taken to the front porch of the Garrett house, where he died

As he was fumbling with his weapons and his crutch, a soldier, Sergeant Thomas H. "Boston" Corbett, crept up the side of the barn. He could see every move that Booth made. Corbett was a strange man. Earlier, he had volunteered to go into the barn and fight Booth one-on-one, but Lieutenant Doherty had turned down the offer. Now, Corbett was aiming his pistol through an opening, pointing it directly at Booth. He held his fire, even when Booth came directly toward him.

The fire grew hotter. According to Corbett, Booth was preparing to fight his way out of the barn. He later testified that he saw Booth raise the rifle and take aim at one of the soldiers outside. Before he could, Corbett steadied his own weapon and pulled the trigger. A deafening shot rang out and Booth collapsed to his knees. The carbine and the pistol clattered to the floor. Moments later, the two detectives burst through the door and caught Booth before he fell forward onto his face. Corbett's bullet had passed through the assassin's neck, paralyzing him.

When the detectives reached Booth, they assumed that he had shot himself at first. It was later when they discovered that Corbett had taken matters into his own hands. Despite Stanton's wish to take Booth alive, no such orders had ever been given to the enlisted soldiers. Corbett insisted that he had shot Booth to save the lives of his fellow soldiers.

He also stated that he had acted on orders directly from God.

The tobacco barn was now an inferno. Baker, Conger, and a few of the soldiers lifted Booth up off the barn floor and carried him outside. He looked dead, but as President Lincoln had done, he fought to stay alive. His eyes flickered open when the detectives splashed water on his face and Booth struggled to speak.

Baker leaned down and put his ear close to the dying actor's mouth. "Tell mother, I die for my country," he whispered painfully.

But he wasn't dead yet.

Booth was picked up and carried away from the burning barn. They placed him on the front porch of the Garrett house. He was bleeding from his neck wound and some of the children went to get bedding and pillows to make him more comfortable. Herold was tied to a tree with a rope, just a few feet away from where his friend was taking his last breaths. He watched as Booth writhed in agony on the wooden porch. He couldn't swallow and could barely speak, but he begged Conger several times to kill him. Booth became delirious, passing in and out of consciousness.

The detectives searched through his pockets, looking for identification that would prove they had their man. They found a compass, his diary, and photographs of several women, including his fiancée, Lucy Hale. As the search continued, a woman who had been staying with the Garretts, Lucinda Holloway, knelt by Booth's head and tried to comfort him. She could see he was thirsty, so she used a handkerchief to soak up some water and wet his tongue. Again, he repeated what he wanted to be his last words - "Tell mother, I die for my country."

But, as it turned out, they were not his final words after all.

Paralyzed, Booth tried to move his hands, but he couldn't. "My hands!" he gasped. At this point, even the hardened detective Baker had some pity on the dying man. He grabbed Booth's hands in his own, wiped them off a little, and then raised them so that Booth could see them. But Booth's head shook back and forth just a little. "Useless," he said sorrowfully. "Useless."

Just as the sun was starting to rise in the eastern sky, Booth began to choke in air. Lucinda Holloway rubbed his temples, feeling his pulse grow weaker. Baker was standing over him, looking down at his face. Booth's body convulsed one last time - and he died.

Or did he? Or, the better question is - was the man who died on that porch actually John Wilkes Booth?

What happened to John Wilkes Booth after he fled Washington seems fairly straightforward - he hid, he ran, he was cornered in the Garretts' tobacco barn, was shot, and died on the family's porch. There were plenty of people who saw it happen and plenty of people who were quick to identity the man who died that night was John Wilkes Booth.

Or was he?

Strangely, the nine-day pursuit, capture, and death of John Wilkes Booth became one of the most controversial, contradictory, and, according to some, conspiracy-filled events in our history. For many decades after the Lincoln assassination, that event - along with what happen to Booth - became one of the most talked-about conspiracies in America. In fact, until the Kennedy assassination took place a century later, what happened in April 1865 was constantly discussed, detailed, and argued about events that our country had ever seen.

Even now, all these years later, there are still many researchers who are convinced that Booth was not captured and killed in Virginia at all. They insist that Booth escaped and that a Confederate soldier who looked like him was killed in his place.

Skeptical? You should be, but as you will soon find, the mystery of John Wilkes Booth is not as simple as you might imagine it to be.

Mummies, Mayhem, and Mischief

After his death on the morning of April 26, Booth's body was placed on Lieutenant Doherty's old service blanket. Soldiers borrowed a heavy needle and thread from Mrs. Garrett and sewed Booth up in it, leaving an opening for only his feet. Confiscating a rickety old cart, they loaded Booth onto it and headed back north to the ferry crossing

Harper's Weekly illustration of Booth's autopsy on the Montauk. Unfortunately, nagging doubts about the identity of the dead man lingered for many years

at Port Conway. It was said that Booth's corpse dripped blood most of the way there.

After crossing the Rappahannock River, the soldiers continued on to Belle Plain on the Potomac. Baker and some of the others loaded the body into a small boat and rowed out to a steamship, *John S. Ide*, that was just offshore. The ship sailed up the river to Washington and arrived there at 1:45 a.m. The steamer met *Montauk*, a ship that had played host to Abraham and Mary Lincoln just two weeks before. Stanton had decided to keep Booth's body - along with some of the imprisoned conspirators - on the ship to prevent attempted lynchings of the prisoners and ghoulish souvenir picking of the corpse.

Booth's body was laid out on a carpenter's bench aboard the ship, stripped naked, photographed, and examined by doctors. The photographs and the plates have never been found and are presumed to have been destroyed - which is like throwing fresh meat to conspiracy theorists, of course.

A short but gruesome autopsy was then performed and then Booth's body was identified by many people who knew him in life. They knew him by a scar on the back of his neck, as well as by the crude "JWB" tattoo that he had on his hand.

Or so it was claimed. There are some who say that not everyone was convinced of Booth's identity. They stated that the corpse wasn't Booth, it only looked like him.

It should be remembered, though, that the handsome actor's body was not in great condition by then. He had been on the run for nine days when he was killed. He'd eaten poorly, had been hiding in the woods, had not had time to bathe or shave, and had been suffering from a broken leg. He was also dead. He'd been shot in the neck, leaving him in agony. It's no surprise that he might be hard to recognize by people who didn't know him intimately.

That's logic speaking, however, which usually has nothing to do with a good conspiracy.

How did a conspiracy get started around Booth's death anyway? A lot of it likely had to do with the era. There were no fingerprints used to identify people, and, of course, forensic evidence didn't exist. Most people were identified only by photographs and as mentioned, Booth didn't look much like the publicity photographs of him that circulated in stage books and magazines. Anyone who might think they could recognize him from a performance would have also found a man who looked nothing like what they expected in real life, especially after his ordeal.

But if you want to know who it was that started it, I'd have to blame that on the federal government and probably Edwin Stanton in particular.

It was decided that an elaborate ruse would be carried out with Booth's body. It was decided that the military would pretend to bury Booth at sea. A rowboat from *Montauk* was even sent out to act out this story. Stanton feared that, in death, Booth might become a martyr to the Confederate cause and his grave might become some kind of shrine or rallying point for further rebellion.

Stanton wanted to create as much mystery around the disposal of Booth's corpse as he could and this had the unintended consequence of giving people even more to talk about - and started the rumors that perhaps Booth was not dead at all.

Late on April 27, Booth's body was placed back in the old blanket shroud and taken to the Washington Arsenal Penitentiary - now part of Fort McNair - which was located where the Potomac and Anacostia Rivers meet. Inside the building, soldiers dug up a section of the brick floor. A musket case was turned into a coffin and the corpse was placed inside. They sealed it tightly and scrawled Booth's name on the lid. The soldiers then buried the box in the ground and replaced the bricks so that the unmarked grave could only be found by those who knew exactly where it was located.

The door to the room was locked and the body stayed there, decaying in the darkness, for the next four years.

But was it really John Wilkes Booth in that grave?

This was a question that was widely asked from the moment that news reached the public that Lincoln's killer had been gunned down. Word had already spread rapidly that Booth had been the assassin and that a man had been shot to death in a Virginia barn - but was the dead man Booth? The government's handling of the body in question and statements from those who saw the body didn't add much credence to the official version of the story. The soldiers at the Garrett farm had certainly killed someone and the War Department and the newspapers told a breathless nation that someone had been John Wilkes Booth, but after four years of war, trust in the government was not exactly at an all-time high.

Rumors started, almost from the moment the dead man was brought back to Washington, that it wasn't Booth. The War Department refused to comment on the matter. They maintained that the corpse was that of Booth but refused to let the body be examined. Initially, they were still claiming that he had been buried at sea. Instead of a body, they offered items for examination that had been in Booth's possession when he was killed, including the left boot he'd abandoned when his broken leg was put into splints, and the revolver he'd been carrying when he was killed. They also had affidavits from the soldiers who brought the body back to Washington, swearing that the face of the corpse matched the photos of Booth they had been given. The investigators studied these, but they were never shown to the public. The government refused to even consider the idea that the body might not be that of Booth.

The conspiracy continued to thrive for years. More than 22 men would eventually claim to be John Wilkes Booth in books, anecdotes, and sworn testimony. It became a small cottage industry for a while. The newspapers got hold of each story and fanned the flames of doubt about the assassin's death. By June 1865, stories spread that witnesses had seen Booth on a steamer to Mexico, or on his way to South America. It was said that several people saw him out west and others recognized him in the Orient, England, India, Rome, Paris, and Vienna. In Ohio, a man claimed that Booth had stopped in his tavern on the way to Canada. In the Southwest, several people who claimed to know Booth said that he owed his escape to Union troopers because of his membership in a fraternal order. They had spirited him away rather than see him hanged. It was no wonder that many dark-haired, pallid men who walked with a limp began to be pointed out across the country and identified as John Wilkes Booth.

The story became so popular that in July 1867, Dr. John Frederick May, one of the men who initially identified the body as Booth, felt that it was now necessary to make an emphatic denial about the once positive identification he'd made. He now stated that he could have been wrong when he said the dead man had been John Wilkes Booth.

Two years before the assassination, May had removed a tumor from the back of Booth's neck. The surgery had left a jagged scar on his neck and this scar was how the doctor had identified the remains. He said that the body he saw did not exactly resemble Booth, but since he found a similar scar on the back of the neck, he assumed it must be him.

His new testimony also brought to light another, more damning bit of strange evidence -- his detailed examination of the dead man's broken right leg. Right leg?

According to government officials, and witnesses at Ford's Theater, Booth had broken his left leg when he jumped to the stage from the president's private box. The fact that the doctor noted the mysterious body had a broken right leg meant one of two things -- either the body did not belong to Booth, or Dr. May was too careless of an observer to be credited with any authority in the matter of an accurate identification.

That's a weird bit of history that has never really been explained, except to say that Dr. May had apparently been mistaken about which of the corpse's legs had been broken.

At least we assume that he was mistaken, right?

Finally, in 1869, President Andrew Johnson gave permission to the War Department to turn over Booth's remains to his family for reburial. This would certainly dispel all the rumors that had been lingering for the past four years. Unfortunately, it didn't quite work out that way.

In 1869, government workers exhumed the body that had been buried beneath the floor of the old prison dining hall. In an odd twist of fate during the moving process, Booth's body was temporarily housed in a shed behind Ford's Theater, right off the alley where he had left his horse on the night of the assassination. It was there were the family was allowed to positively identify the remains as Booth.

Many believed the mystery of the body would be settled once and for all by his brother, Edwin, but he simply added to the confusion by bungling the whole thing. First, he attempted to keep the exhumation a secret and then decided that he couldn't bear to look upon the face of his dead brother. He remained outside of the shed while friends went inside to examine the corpse. There was no way that they could identify the decomposed body with any authority.

The remains of the dead man - John Wilkes Booth or not - were buried by his family and friends in the Booth family plot in Baltimore's Green Mount Cemetery. In the decades after the war, the government's fears were realized as many Confederate veterans began leaving flowers at Booth's grave. Today, there is a plain, unmarked, white headstone that visitors believe marks Booth's burial site, but it may actually be the grave of his sister, Asia. On top

Booth was buried in an unmarked grave in the family plot in Baltimore's Green Mount Cemetery.

of the marker, visitors leave copper pennies with Lincoln's face looking upwards - it's a rebuke to the man who killed the president and an affirmation of Lincoln's final victory over death.

Edwin Booth

As for the rest of Booth's family, the assassination changed the course of their lives forever. It didn't destroy Edwin's acting career, but it certainly didn't help it. It wouldn't be for a number of years before he regained his fame and fortune.

Strangely, Edwin had actually saved the life of Abraham Lincoln's son, Robert, a few months before the assassination. Robert had fallen from a train platform onto the tracks when a stranger - who turned out to be Edwin - jumped down, snatched him off the tracks, and saved him from death.

It was only later when Edwin learned from eyewitnesses that he had saved the life of Lincoln's son - a heroic act that earned Edwin, and the rest of the Booth family, a little redemption in the eyes of the public.

Edwin later founded a famous club for actors and theater patrons, the Players, in New York City. Sadly, though, he only lived to be 59. He died from a stroke on June 7, 1893. His apartment at the Players club still remains today exactly how it was on the night he died.

The rest of Booth's family didn't fare so well. The shame of the Booth family name weighed heavily on all of them. Booth's mother, Mary Ann Holmes Booth, would live to bury six of her children and her husband. In 1878, she sold the family land and home in Baltimore, Tudor Hall, and spent the rest of her life living with her surviving children, Edwin, Junius, and Rosalie. In 1883, she slipped on an icy street and never really recovered from the fall. She died two years later at the age of 83.

Junius Brutus Booth, Jr., the oldest son, retired from his own acting career and settled in seclusion in Manchester-by-the-Sea, Massachusetts, where he built a luxury hotel. He died at the age of 61 in 1882.

Booth's beloved sister, Asia, became a poet and later wrote a secret memoir about her infamous brother, but she felt so ashamed about what he'd done, she moved to England with her husband and children. Her husband, John Sleeper Clarke, proved to be both opportunistic and disloyal. He joined her in England and became a famous comedian but treated Asia terribly. In her memoirs, she described him as living "a free going bachelor life and does what he likes." John Wilkes Booth had warned his sister about Clarke when she married him. Asia died in 1888. She was only 52-years-old.

Asia Booth

Booth's youngest brother, Joseph, became a respected doctor and lived until 1902. His only child died in infancy. Booth's sister Rosalie never married. She cared for their mother until her own death in 1889.

Most of the Booth children are buried in the family plot in Baltimore, near their parents and their infamous brother.

If John Wilkes Booth is actually buried there, of course.

This should have been the end of the Booth story, but it isn't. It stretches on into the twentieth century. As Booth's alleged skull was being displayed at fair carnivals across the country, there were still questions being asked about the assassin's eventual fate. If people were willing to pay a nickel to look at a skull that almost definitely wasn't really Booth's, then the conspiracy could not yet be put to bed.

Historians tried to resolve the ongoing issue in the early 1900s, since many of the people involved in the case were still living. Statements were taken from surviving soldiers who aided in Booth's capture and all information was thoroughly researched. They even checked out the claims of men still posing as Booth and found all of them transparently fraudulent.

The question remained - was it possible that Booth could have survived the manhunt after the assassination? Although logic seemed to say he'd been killed, there were still nagging questions about conflicting evidence and the fact that there was not a single eyewitness, sufficiently impartial to be above suspicion, which had seen the corpse in 1865 and could say, with absolute certainty, that it was John Wilkes Booth.

Even so, why would a story that should have been greeted with skepticism end up garnering so much support? It might have had something to do with the man who killed Booth at the Garrett farm and the odd details included in his story that did nothing to quiet the suspicions of a conspiracy.

You see, the man that killed Booth, Sergeant Thomas "Boston" Corbett, was certifiably insane.

Corbett is understandably considered to have been the Jack Ruby of his day -- he was the man who killed the killer of the President of the United States.

Jack Ruby's shooting of Lee Harvey Oswald on November 24, 1963, in the basement of the Dallas, Texas, jail was witnessed by reporters, police officers, and a shocked national television audience. But Boston Corbett's shooting of John Wilkes Booth on April 26, 1865, at a tobacco barn in Virginia was hardly witnessed by anyone -- and it attracted controversy from the beginning. While he was celebrated for a short time as Booth's killer, his real place in the Lincoln assassination remains in question after all these years.

Sergeant Corbett had been assigned to Lieutenant Edward Doherty, one of the Federal officers that had been given the task of tracking down Lincoln's assassin. After Booth was found hiding in the tobacco barn on the Garrett farm, it was Corbett - who wasn't acting on orders from his lieutenant -- who fired the fatal bullet that killed Booth.

Over the years, many conspiracy theorists have come to believe that Corbett was acting on secret orders to kill Booth by everyone from Vice President Andrew Johnson to Edwin Stanton. Everyone named in the conspiracy had been secretly working with Corbett so that they would not be implicated in the plot against the president. But how would a lowly soldier have been in contact with high-up government officials before leaving Washington?

Make no mistake, though, Corbett was acting on orders to kill Booth. They came from an authority that was much higher than the vice president or the Secretary of War.

Corbett killed Booth on direct orders from God.

Although he would later change his name to "Boston," he was born Thomas H.

Thomas "Boston" Corbett

Corbett in England in 1832. Seven years later, he emigrated to New York with his family. As a young man in the 1850s, he became a milliner at a time when the dire occupational hazards of the hat-making trade had yet to be discovered. As he worked, he was exposed to large quantities of mercury, which often caused insanity - hence the expression "mad as a hatter." The inescapable breathing in of the vapors from the mercury affected the brain and caused hallucinatory episodes, twitches and tics, and psychotic behavior.

Corbett worked as a milliner in Troy and Albany, New York, in Richmond, Virginia, and Boston. He was married for a short time, but both his wife and baby died during childbirth. The tragedy led to an alcohol problem and to his becoming homeless.

In 1857, while working in Boston, Corbett found religion at a revival meeting. He was "saved" and baptized and was so moved by this experience that he adopted the name of the city where he found his faith as his own. During the later 1850s, he became a street preacher and began wearing his hair long to look more like the popular image of Jesus Christ.

Corbett's religious fanaticism, loud but harmless, took a violent turn in the summer of 1858. After a revival meeting at a Boston church, he was propositioned on the street by two prostitutes. The experience so disturbed him that he returned to the boarding house where he lived and castrated himself with a pair of scissors. He was treated at Massachusetts General Hospital from the middle of July to the first week in August for his self-inflicted wound.

What happened to Boston Corbett over the course of the next two years is unknown, but at some point, he returned to New York and in April 1861, enlisted as a private in Company I, Twelfth New York Militia. Behavioral problems marred his record from the start. They began when he heard Colonel Butterfield, commander of the militia regiment, using profanity toward his new recruits. Corbett reprimanded the Colonel for using the Lord's name in vain and for this, was marched off to the guardhouse. A few days later, Butterfield offered to release him if he apologized, but Corbett refused.

Corbett later re-enlisted, this time in Company L, Sixteenth New York Cavalry, where he was promoted to corporal and later rose to the rank of sergeant. This was despite the numerous disciplinary problems that he had over his demand that officers not use profanity and his condemnation of fellow soldiers who drank. New York cavalrymen remembered their odd comrade for his periodic punishment tours where he carried a knapsack filled with bricks around the guardhouse, but his commanders saw him as a fierce and resolute fighting man. He fought bravely in battle, although his odd and erratic behavior often made his superiors wary of using him for some assignments.

In June 1864, Confederate raiders under John Singleton Mosby cornered a squad of Union troopers, including Corbett, at Culpepper Courthouse in Virginia. Corbett refused to surrender, found cover, and opened fire on Mosby and his 26 raiders. He only gave up after his ammunition ran out. Mosby was impressed.

Corbett and his comrades were sent to the notorious Andersonville prison in Georgia and endured five months of incarceration there, three of them in an outdoor compound. He was released during a prisoner exchange in November 1864 and was sent to an Army hospital in Maryland to recover from exposure, malnutrition, and scurvy.

By the early spring of 1865, Corbett had returned to his unit and in April was the first man to volunteer for service in the pursuit of President Lincoln's assassin, John Wilkes Booth.

Corbett was among the men who cornered Booth and David Herold at the tobacco barn, and he was stationed at a point on the building's perimeter when it was set on fire. Through a gap in the barn's siding, he saw a lone figure inside. He stated at the conspiracy trial one month later that he had never seen Booth before but the man in the barn had a broken leg and made "desperate replies" to the Federal officers who demanded his surrender. He gave a statement on May 1, 1865, that read:

I saw Booth in the act of stooping or springing, and concluded he was going to use his weapons. I immediately took steady aim upon him with my revolver and fired – shooting him through the neck and head. He was then carried out of the barn before the fire reached him; was taken to the Piazza of the house... Lt. Doherty, and the detective officers who were in front of the barn, did not seem to know that I had shot him, but supposed he had shot himself, until I informed Lt. Doherty of the fact – showing him my pistol which bore evidence of the truth of my statement, which also confirmed by the man placed at my right-hand who saw it.

Corbett's shot was an extraordinary one considering the distance, the weapon, the smoke and fire in the barn, and the confusion that was occurring outside of it. The bullet struck Booth in the neck, slightly to the back of the head and severed his spinal cord.

The assassin was dragged from the burning barn and eventually taken to the porch. He was scarcely recognizable as the handsome actor. The man was filthy, his hair in tangles, and a patchy beard covered part of his emaciated face. He died a few minutes after being taken from the barn.

After the shooting at the farm, Corbett was placed under arrest by Colonel Everton Conger, Doherty's superior officer in the search party. The charge against him was a breach of military discipline "in firing without Doherty's order and in defiance of Gen. Baker's order." Corbett was placed under guard, along with David Herold, and returned to Washington. When they arrived, Corbett was imprisoned, awaiting court martial. However, Secretary of War Edwin Stanton, upon hearing the story of the incident, ordered Corbett to be released. He announced theatrically, "The rebel is dead, the patriot lives - the patriot is released!"

One officer even said that God must have been directing Corbett's hand, playing right into his delusions. Keep in mind that Corbett also thought he was acting under God's direction when he cut off his testicles with a pair of scissors that night, too.

Corbett mustered out of the Army on August 17, 1865, and moved to Danbury, Connecticut. In the years that followed his very brief time as a national hero, he worked again making hats and supplemented his income with occasional lectures, accompanied by lantern slides, about his exploits as "Lincoln's Avenger" - even though he had a habit of turning every speech into a religious sermon that contained whoops, rambles, and yells of spiritual joy.

You might assume that he'd never need to work, thanks to the reward that he should have got for killing Booth, but it never worked out for him. There were many questions about whether Corbett actually fired the fatal shot - especially since rumors were running rampant that Booth had escaped, and the man killed in the barn was an imposter.

Colonel Conger, commander of the Sixteenth New York, received a suspiciously high $15,000 of the combined reward offered for Booth and Herold's capture, even though he had little to do with it. Lieutenant Doherty received $5,250 of the reward, which led many to believe that he may have done the actual shooting. Many never seriously considered Corbett's claim of the near-impossible shot. In 1903, an early Lincoln assassination researcher, David M. DeWitt, wrote that Corbett was at least 30 feet from the barn when the shot was fired that killed Booth.

In the end, though, Corbett did receive $1,653.85 as part of the reward for bringing Booth to justice. His petition for a federal pension for his service in the Army, specifically for his work as a volunteer in the search for Lincoln's assassin, came through in 1882. He was granted $7.50 a month in appreciation for his service to the United States.

Corbett eventually gave up making both speeches and hats and moved to Camden, New Jersey, where he became a preacher again. In the 1870s, he turned up in Kansas, lived as a recluse on an isolated farm and showing signs that his mental state had deteriorated even further. He was now convinced that John Wilkes Booth had belonged to a secret society that had vowed to avenge his death. In 1885, he was arrested after threatening some boys with a baseball bat and threatening to kill anyone who set foot on his property. When the authorities came to arrest him, he waved a revolver at them and shouted, "That's a lie, a lie, a lie... I'll shoot any man who says such things about me!" The case was dismissed by the county attorney.

A year after the incident, through the efforts of the Grand Army of the Republic and a state legislator from Cloud County, where Corbett lived, he was hired as an assistant doorkeeper at the Kansas House of Representatives in Topeka. He reported for duty in January 1887, but the job didn't last for long.

Corbett began to believe that the other doorkeepers and the politicians were laughing at him behind his back. This led to him threatening a janitor with a knife and then charging into the House gallery with a gun, threatening to kill the Speaker of the House. Lawmakers and their staff members fled for their lives. A quick verdict was pronounced, and he was sent to the Topeka Asylum for the Insane.

He failed on his first attempt to escape but then, on May 26, 1888, he succeeded. Walking around the grounds of the asylum with other inmates that day, Corbett saw a pony that belonged to the young son of the superintendent tied up in front of the hospital office. He hurried over, stole the horse, and rode away.

A week later, Corbett surfaced in Neodesha in the southeastern part of the state. There, he met a local schoolmaster named Richard Thatcher and Irwin Ford, the son of a soldier who had been imprisoned with Corbett at Andersonville. The two men supplied Corbett with a fresh horse, food, and money. They said that Corbett told them that he had been "shamefully treated" and intended to flee to Mexico.

He may have done that, but we'll never know for sure. He disappeared from history, although there are rumors that he may have died in a fire in Minnesota in 1894. There are also stories that say he sometimes surfaced in small towns across the west, working as a traveling preacher or a medicine salesman. Newspaper stories kept him alive - much like John Wilkes Booth - long after he probably died.

With Corbett's strange life and mysterious disappearance feeding into the conspiracies of Booth's alleged death, it was no surprise when a new claim emerged stating that Booth had not died in 1865, but many years later, in 1903. And if the man that died in 1903 in Enid, Oklahoma, was Booth, he was then living under the name of David E. George.

Finis Bates, later in life

In order to delve into the story of the man who might have been Booth, we introduce the man who would eventually bring the story to the public - a young lawyer from Granbury, Texas, named Finis L. Bates.

In the early 1870s, Bates was a struggling attorney and must have been happy when a new client who called himself John St. Helen walked into his office one day and asked for help in defending him against a charge of operating a saloon without a license in the nearby town of Glen Rose. St. Helen admitted that he was guilty of the offense but did not want to appear in federal court over it. John St. Helen was not his real name, he confessed, and feared that his true identity might be exposed in court.

Bates took the case and resolved the issue for him. St. Helen became a regular client and he got to know the man fairly well. He later recalled that St. Helen seemed to have more money than his status should have allowed and that he had an intimate knowledge of the theater and of the works of Shakespeare, most of which he could recite from memory.

Then, late one night in 1877, Bates was summoned to the sickbed of his client. St. Helen was seriously ill, and he told Bates that he did not expect to live much longer. He directed Bates to reach under his pillow and the attorney pulled out an old tintype that showed a much younger St. Helen. The sick man told the attorney that if he died, he was to send the photograph to a man named Edwin Booth in Baltimore with a note that said the subject of the tintype had passed away. In between coughing fits, St. Helen explained to the stunned attorney that his name was actually John Wilkes Booth and that he had assassinated former President Abraham Lincoln.

Bates was shocked and dismayed at the revelation, but he knew that he could not betray his client's confidence. He replied that he would send the photograph if needed and he sat next to St. Helen's bed throughout the rest of the night, waiting for the man to die. His mind whirled throughout the night, stunned by the secret that he learned. He wondered what he would have done about it had his client not been dying.

But John St. Helen didn't die.

He was sick for several weeks but then he began to recover. Once he was mobile again, he met with Bates and again confessed to being John Wilkes Booth. He begged for the attorney to keep the secret and Bates was bound by attorney-client privilege - he had to agree. He did demand some answers, though, knowing full well that John Wilkes Booth was reportedly dead.

Booth explained that Andrew Johnson, the vice president, was the principle conspirator behind the assassination. St. Helen said that he had met with Johnson just hours before Lincoln was killed and Johnson told him that with General Grant away from Washington, Booth would have an easy escape route into Maryland. St. Helen then went on to provide details of the assassination plot, the actual event, his escape from Ford's Theater, and flight into the countryside. His descriptions were detailed and to Bates, who initially believed none of the farfetched story, they seemed to have intricacies that only someone intimately involved with the assassination plot would have known. Most of all, they were different enough from the already published accounts of the events that Bates began to give some credibility to St. Helen's version of the story.

St. Helens told the attorney that he had escaped into Kentucky in late April and eventually made his way west of the Mississippi and into the Indian Territory. After spending some time there, he disguised himself as a priest and entered Mexico. In 1867, he traveled to California and met with his mother and older brother, Junius, in San Francisco. Later, he drifted to New Orleans, where he taught school, and then moved to Texas. Here, he assumed the name John St. Helen and opened a tavern.

Bates was never entirely convinced by the story - it was just too much to believe -- and the two eventually parted ways. Several months after he heard the confession, Bates moved to Memphis and established a law practice. He became very successful and as the years passed, he developed a deep interest in Abraham Lincoln, especially in the events surrounding his death. In his spare time, he read everything that he

The preserved body of David E. George in Enid, Oklahoma. Was he really John Wilkes Booth?

could get his hands on about Lincoln and Booth and the more he studied, the more convinced he became that his old client had been telling the truth. John St. Helen, he believed, really had been John Wilkes Booth.

The story of John Wilkes Booth and Finis Bates took another turn in 1903. On January 13, the corpse of a man named David E. George arrived at the undertaking parlor of W.B. Penniman in Enid, Oklahoma. George, who had been working in Enid as a handyman and house painter, had apparently committed suicide by ingesting a large dose of strychnine. He was known about town as a heavy drinker and was frequently depressed. No one was terribly surprised that he had ended his life.

As Penniman's assistant, W.H. Ryan, was embalming George's body, the Reverend E.C. Harper stopped in at the funeral parlor. Harper urgently needed to talk to the undertaker. He had a stunning story to tell - the dead man on the embalming table was none other than John Wilkes Booth! He had confessed his identity to the minister's wife in 1900. Mrs. Harper was summoned, and she identified the corpse of David E. George as the man who had told her that he was Booth. She later wrote out and signed a statement, swearing that the confession had taken place.

Over the course of the next few days, a number of newspapers carried the story that a man believed to be Booth had died in Oklahoma. One of the newspaper stories caught the attention of Finis Bates in Memphis and he wondered if the late David E. George might be the man that he had once known as John St. Helen. Curious, he decided to go to Enid and see.

Bates arrived in Oklahoma on January 23 and the next morning, went to the undertaker's parlor to compare the face of the dead man with the tintype photograph that he still possessed. He placed it next to the face of the corpse and compared them. It was, Bates stated without a doubt, the same man.

The body remained on display at Penniman's parlor and after it went unclaimed for some time, it was eventually moved into a back room and stored there for some time. Apparently, Penniman injected the corpse with a heavy dose of preservative because in every photograph that remains, the dead man looks more than embalmed - he appears to be mummified.

A few years later, Finis Bates made Penniman an offer and he purchased the body of David George, still convinced he was John Wilkes Booth.

In October 1931, the mummy was examined by a group of seven doctors at Chicago's Northwestern University. It was studied, x-rayed, and dissected and the team did find evidence of a healed broken leg, although the report did not state whether it was the right or the left. The most compelling discovery was that of a ring that had somehow become embedded in the flesh of the body cavity. Digestive juices had damaged it over time, but the researchers present believed that the initials "JWB" could be discerned on the surface of it. Dr. Otto L. Schmidt, president of the Chicago Historical Society at that time, subsequently wrote, "I can say safely that we believe Booth's body is here in my office."

The "John Wilkes Booth" mummy in 1931

The eventual fate of this intriguing mummy remains a mystery. Bates tried to sell the mummy several times but then in the 1920s and 1930s, leased the mummy to two carnival promoters - one of which was a former private detective named J.W. Wilkerson -- who charged 25-cents to view "The Assassin of President Abraham Lincoln" at fairs and exhibitions all over the country.

The mummy was still being displayed into the 1940s, but after the promoter went bankrupt and moved to Idaho, he placed the mummy in a chair on his front porch and charged visitors a dime to look at it. Eventually, the mummy disappeared and to this day, no one knows what became of it. It is rumored to be in a private collection somewhere, but no one knows for sure.

The final resting place of the mummy is just as mysterious as the questions that linger about John Wilkes Booth. Could the man that Bates knew as John St. Helen and David George also have been John Wilkes Booth?

Let's look at the possibilities: the two men certainly possessed many of the same characteristics, including heavy drinking, an intimate knowledge of Shakespeare, a penchant for the theater, the same style of dress, and an extensive education. In addition, studies of physical characteristics between George and Booth showed many striking similarities, including the shape of their heads, jaw lines, and the bridges of both men's noses. And while this does not offer positive proof, it is intriguing.

But there are also problems. According to the undertaker in Enid, George had blue-gray eyes, while government documents say Booth's eyes were black. On the other hand, Asia Booth, the actor's sister, wrote that they were hazel. Finis Bates wrote that George had a broken right leg, not the left leg that Booth broke jumping from the theater box. Of course, the government's own records stated that the body that was dug up from beneath the floor of the Old Penitentiary had a broken right leg, but that was just one notation. Everyone else agreed that Booth's left leg was broken.

Bates showed photographs of St. Helen and George to a number of people who had known Booth, including those who had seen him perform many times. All of them stated that the men in both photos were John Wilkes Booth.

Another mysterious piece of evidence involved the signet ring worn by Booth. The actor was seldom seen without the ring, which was inscribed with his initials, and he was photographed wearing it many times. The ring was not on the finger of the man who was killed in Virginia.

David E. George wore a similar ring, many recalled. Some weeks before his death, George told one of his neighbors that he was being followed. One afternoon, when he saw two sheriffs' deputies coming his way, George was so afraid that he would be identified that he removed the ring from his finger and swallowed it. This strange anecdote would provide startling evidence to researchers in 1931 that the body they were examining, with a ring inside of the body cavity, was that of John Wilkes Booth.

While I believe the chances that Booth escaped death in the Garrett barn, only to die almost 40 years later, are somewhere between slim and none, there are enough odd bits of evidence mixed into the events that the story has remained alive.

There have been bestselling books - like the 1977 book *The Lincoln Conspiracy* - as well as documentaries and articles that claim Booth didn't die in 1865. In the mid-1990s, distant relatives of Booth filed multiple court challenges to have Booth's and his brother Edwin's bodies exhumed to prove that an imposter lies in the assassin's grave, but the court challenges all failed.

And that's all a good conspiracy needs to thrive.

The Spirit of John Wilkes Booth

On March 5, 1866, less than a year after the assassination, a reporter from the *Chicago Tribune* attended a séance that - if you believe it was authentic - confirmed the fact that Booth had died in Virginia at the Garrett farm.

You see, the reporter was present when the spirit medium made contact with the ghost of John Wilkes Booth - and he assured everyone there that he was dead. In fact, he was making an appearance that night from Hell.

This was apparently not Booth's first visit to the medium's séance room. He'd been there several times before and he was always "very noisy and demonstrative." His communications came by pointing to letters and rapping on the table. On this night, he told the story of the night of the assassination, claiming that he did not break his leg in the fall from the presidential box, as was so often said, but after a fall from his horse later on.

Though Andrew Johnson had been one of the targets for the assassination plot, the spirit said that he was now glad that Johnson had not been killed.

The medium asked, "Do you like Johnson?"

Booth's spirit said that he did, although he did not want Johnson to be re-elected. He preferred a ticket that would include George McClellan and Robert E. Lee in 1868 since Booth believed they were men "destined to restore the powers of slavery and democracy."

The real culprit behind the Lincoln assassination was, of course, the Devil!

The medium asked the spirit if he was in Heaven. Booth replied that he was not. He was in Hell, and, yes, the Devil was down there with him.

"Does he treat you rough?" the medium wanted to know.

"Yes." The reply was so emphatic that the reporter claimed that it caused the séance table to rattle. The spirit added that he didn't think he deserved it.

One of the séance guests suggested that Booth should materialize or communicate in a way that was more dignified than just knocking on the table, and the spirit replied that he would do so in a dark room, as long as the Devil allowed it. The group moved into another room, darker than the parlor they were in, but Booth never appeared. Knocking on the walls continued, though, and through the knocks, he said he would communicate through writing. The medium, with a cloth over his eyes, allowed Booth to send messages through his hand. He scrawled replies to questions on a sheet of paper, which the reporter later copied. The paper read:

> Johnson is trump. He went back on his party and is a Southern man at heart. Bully for him. He's a good Democrat. Democracy will again be stronger than ever. Slavery will be established again... McClellan and General Lee will be next President and Vice President. Slavery and Democracy must flourish again.

By the way, the meaning of the word "trump" implied a deceptive form of victory involving cheating. It's not used much anymore but is still around in the term "trumped up," meaning something that's been falsely made up.

The spirit then went on to tell a rambling, painfully not funny joke about an Irishman whose wife gives birth to a black baby. When finished, the spirit said, "I can't stay any longer. I'm wanted. I'll see you another time. I must stand not upon the order of my going but go at once."

With that, the alleged spirit of John Wilkes Booth broke off communications, but it was the Tribune reporter who got in the last word, "It must be consoling to Johnson to know that he has supporters and friends in another world, even if they are no more reputable characters than those who swear by him here."

This was not the only time that Booth was said to have made contact from the next world. In 1870, a séance in Brooklyn made the newspapers, too. During that event, Booth's spirit was said to have been sorry for killing Lincoln. They had now reconciled, the spirit told the séance guests, and "are now good friends and walk out together."

Since the heyday of Spiritualism ended around the time of the Great Depression, Booth's ghost has been rather quiet for the last century or so. There is, however, one place to which he had been spiritually connected - Ford's Theater in Washington.

Ford's Theater, where Abraham Lincoln and John Wilkes Booth fatally collided one fateful night, was originally a house of worship. It was constructed in 1833 as the First Baptist Church of Washington. In

John T. Ford, owner of Ford's Theater

1861, after the congregation relocated to a new structure, John T. Ford bought the former church and renovated it into a theater. He first called it Ford's Athenaeum, but when it was destroyed by fire in 1862 and rebuilt, it opened the next year as Ford's New Theatre.

Just five days after General Lee's surrender at Appomattox Court House, Lincoln was killed during a performance at Ford's Theater. Following the assassination, the United States Government appropriated the theater, and an order was issued that forever prohibited its use as a place of public amusement. Ford was arrested and held as a prisoner, without charges, for nearly a month. When he was finally released, he had nothing left.

Facing massive debts, he set out to rebuild his fortune - and soon succeeded. Ford was able to lease the National Theater, along with several other buildings in Baltimore. And then was paid $100,000 for the loss of his theater in Washington. He became very wealthy, was the father of 11 children, and died in 1894 at the age of 64.

But the building that was once Ford Theater did not fare as well as its namesake. It was taken over by the military and used as a records storage facility until 1887. War Department records were housed on the first floor, the Library of the Surgeon General's Office was on the second floor, and the Army Medical Museum was on the third.

Then, on June 9, 1893, all three floors in the interior of the building collapsed, knocking out part of an outside wall and killed 22 clerks and injured another 68. This led some to believe that the former theater was cursed.

The building was repaired and used as a government warehouse until 1931. After that, it was abandoned until 1964, when it underwent an extensive reconstruction to restore it to the condition it was in when Lincoln was assassinated.

Today, the theater is a National Historic Site, run by the National Park Service and a private nonprofit group, which includes the restored theater and a museum dedicated to the assassination. The Petersen House across Tenth Street, where Lincoln died, was purchased by the government in 1896 and is now also a museum. The Star Saloon, located on the south side of Ford's Theater where Booth and many members of the theater company spent much of their time, was torn down in 1930. The site is now a parking lot.

The collapse inside of the former Ford's Theater killed 22 people and injured another 68

But Ford's Theater remains, looking just as it did in 1865, and according to many, it is haunted by the events of that April night.

Shortly after Ford's was closed in the wake of the assassination, the famous photographer Matthew Brady, took a picture of the interior of the building. It revealed what looked like a nearly transparent figure standing in Lincoln's box. It might be nothing more than a shadow or a mistake on the photograph's plate, but there were those who suggested the image was that of the spirit of John Wilkes Booth. There have been rumors suggesting that Booth haunts the theater ever since.

On April 14, 1975, the ninetieth anniversary of the Lincoln assassination, actor Billy Dee Williams was onstage at Ford's Theater playing the role of Martin Luther King, Jr. At one point in the first act, Williams - in character as Dr. King - was speaking about his love for Abraham Lincoln and his role in the civil rights movement when he was interrupted by the sound of someone running across the stage and out of the theater's back door.

The photograph taken by Matthew Brady inside of Ford's Theater after the assassination. Some who have closely studied the original believe that a figure can be seen in the presidential box. They claim that it's the spirit of John Wilkes Booth

It was the same route taken on that same night 90 years earlier when Booth had fled from the theater.

Everyone on stage and in the audience clearly heard the sound - but there had been no one there. It was later found that a live microphone was dragged across the stage and out the back door. It was later found in the alley. This was just as much of a mystery as the running footsteps. Frankie Hewitt, executive director of the theater, stated clearly, "No one working at Ford's did that."

Billie Dee Williams - who continues to declare that the ghostly event actually occurred - has not been the only actor to have unsettling encounters at the theater. In the 1980s, actor Hal Holbrook, who performed at Ford's in his one-man Mark Twain show, once stumbled in the middle of a speech because he "felt a presence - a nameless 'something' coming from the Lincoln box."

He also wasn't alone. Other actors have claimed to feel an icy cold presence at left center stages. Others have forgotten their lines or have trembled involuntarily around that same spot. It's rumored that this is caused by a presence that Booth left behind there on the night of the assassination.

Mysterious lights began to be reported in the presidential box in the 1970s. One actress in a gospel musical even walked offstage at intermission and complained of being distracted by a light that kept flashing on and off in Lincoln's box. However, that box is permanently closed to the public, so no one could have been in there.

One night, soon after the theater had been reopened, there was a night when all the lights in the box went out, though none of the other lights in the theater did. They came back on, and then went off again, before they finally remained on. Staff members suspected someone was playing a practical joke, but no one ever admitted to it.

Paul Tucker, a speaker who gave lectures about the theater's history in the 1970s, once claimed to see a ghost in the presidential box. In 1976, he told a newspaper reporter, "I saw him sitting there. He was in color. I saw about three quarters of his face. It struck me that what I saw was a little bit different than pictures I have seen - a human being."

But not all the activity in the building may be linked to the assassination and the presence of John Wilkes Booth. The deadly accident that occurred in 1893 claimed 22 lives and may also have left a lingering spirit or two in the theater.

There have been many reports of mysterious footsteps, disembodied voices, laughing, and the sound of someone weeping in the darkness. Lights in the theater have a habit of turning on and off on their own.

There are also reports of ghosts at the boarding house across the street, where Lincoln died, although those hauntings don't involve John Wilkes Booth. These stories got their start in the 1890s and are among the early claims of Abraham Lincoln lingering after death.

Strange sounds were reported there not long after the president was killed. One of the tenants was apparently so frightened while changing his clothes one day that he ran outside in his underpants.

A newspaper article from 1894 claimed that a man who bought the house was surprised to find that he was unable to keep servants working there. Each would quit after only a day or two on the job. The article noted, "It is one of the traditions of Washington that the ghost of Mr. Lincoln returns four times a week to the house in which his spirit breathed its last day after his shooting by Wilkes Booth in the theatre across the street."

In the Aftermath

The assassination of Abraham Lincoln was a defining event in the history of the United States - and one of the greatest disasters to ever occur in our country. Just as the nation had reached the end of a bloody war that claimed more than 600,000 lives, Booth's insane act threw the government into confusion and the nation into a state of terror.

And it had repercussions that went far beyond the murder at Ford's Theater and the death of a president.

Lincoln's plans for a broad amnesty and mercy toward the conquered people of the south were quickly tossed away by Radical Republicans and by the Democrats alike. In a gesture of national reconciliation, Lincoln had tapped a Southern Democrat, Andrew Johnson, to serve as his vice president. Now that Lincoln was dead and he had assumed the presidency, Johnson immediately reversed Lincoln's lenient policies toward the south. He also did his best to sabotage Lincoln's plans for the emancipation and advancement of former slaves. It would take more than a half century - and longer when it came to civil rights - before reconstruction and reconciliation ended and the country had truly become one nation again.

All because of a single bullet.

When John Wilkes Booth jumped from the Lincolns' theater box that night, he left behind not only a dead president, but dozens of shattered lives, many of which would meet tragic ends.

The assassination had a sobering effect on the lives of the eyewitnesses and workers in the immediate areas. While the government was initially restrained in its attempts to impose legal justice, its investigative methods were much less so. The country was still at war. The leader of the government had just been killed. It was possible that it had been an attack by Confederate terrorists. As a result, the police and the military simply rounded up anyone who might possibly have information that might help the investigation - and held them for days, weeks, and even months without charges.

This included employees of Ford's Theater, including actors, stagehands, staff members, and even owner John Ford. He ended up being held for a month, along with his two younger brothers.

Even those not arrested had their lives disrupted. Secretary of State Seward, of course, suffered near-fatal wounds at the hands of Lewis Powell that left him permanently disfigured. He recovered completely but was rarely ever photographed again.

Dr. Charles Leale, the doctor who attended to Lincoln right after the shooting, had a long and illustrious career as a physician in New York. His written account of Lincoln's final hours, long thought lost, were discovered in the National Archives in 2012.

Lucy Lambert Hale, John Wilkes Booth's alleged secret fiancée, was able to keep her involvement with the assassin a secret for some time. Government investigators knew who she was - her photograph had been with Booth when he died - but since her father was a former U.S. Senator and then Minister to Spain, she was never arrested and never called to testify. Eventually, though, her story went public and by the 1870s, was shamed into hiding.

Laura Keene, the star and producer of *Our American Cousin*, who held Lincoln's head in her lap on the floor of the presidential box, was somehow not arrested with everyone else that night. However, with her name forever linked with Lincoln's death, her health and career suffered terribly in the years after the assassination. Audiences stopped coming to see her shows, her manager and second husband died, and she contracted tuberculosis. At age 47, she suffered a stroke and died in November 1873.

Major Henry Reed Rathbone and his fiancée, Clara Harris, had been in the presidential box with the Lincolns on the night of the assassination. Rathbone was stabbed and slashed by Booth as he tried to apprehend him after the shooting. After Booth had escaped, Henry and Clara tried to care for the First Lady while her husband was being examined but then, quite unexpectedly, Henry fainted from a loss of blood. When he awakened, he was taken to his fiancée's home so that his wound could be treated. He didn't respond well to the doctor's efforts. Henry became delirious, talking about the shooting and his failure to apprehend Booth.

He would be haunted by the assassination for the rest of his life.

Meanwhile., Clara accompanied Mary across the street to the Petersen house. They sat together in the parlor while the dying president was placed in bed. Clara was still in her formal gown, which was soaked with Henry's blood.

Mary Lincoln was hysterical and every time she looked at Clara's dress, she would shriek, "My husband's blood! My husband's blood!" There was no way to explain to her that the blood was actually from Major Rathbone's wounds.

Unlike President Lincoln, Henry recovered from his wounds - his physical ones, at least. He and Clara both had a very difficult time dealing with the memories of the tragedy in the years to come.

Henry Rathbone and Clara Harris became two of the most tragic figures of the Lincoln assassination

For instance, Clara made the peculiar decision to pose for photographer Matthew Brady while wearing the dress that she had on the night of the assassination. It was still crusted with Henry's dried blood. She could never throw the dress away, or even bear to have it cleaned. Later, she took the dress to her parents' home in Albany, New York - Loudon Cottage -- placed it in the back of her closet, and never planned to look at it again.

And then came the dream -- that likely wasn't a dream.

On April 14, 1866 - the anniversary of the assassination - Clara was staying at the house in Albany and woke to see the ghost of Abraham Lincoln, sitting in a chair, facing the closet. He was laughing to himself, as though watching a humorous play. He vanished when the clock struck midnight and Clara ran screaming to tell her family what she had seen. Of course, they told her it had just been a dream, but she was so terrified that she had the door to the closet bricked over so that it could never be used again. The dress linked to that tragic night, she believed, would stay entombed forever.

In 1867, Henry and Clara were married, and he retired from the Army a few years later. The marriage turned out to be a volatile one -- largely due to the post-traumatic stress that Henry suffered from. As the years passed, he became increasingly unstable, plagued by health problems, including chronic heart palpitations.

Loudon Cottage in Albany, where Clara's bloodstained dress was hidden behind the wall – and where Clara believed she saw Lincoln's ghost

After Henry's retirement, he moved his family to Germany. If they were hoping that a fresh start would help their marriage -- or Henry's precarious mental health -- they were tragically mistaken.

Two days before Christmas, in 1883, Henry went into a rage and, gripping a revolver and knife in his hands, made his way to the bedroom of his children. He had become convinced that they needed to die. Clara tried to stop him, but he shot her, and then stabbed her to death. When he saw what he had done, Henry stabbed himself in the chest five times. The wounds did not prove fatal.

The broken man never stood trial for his wife's murder. He was declared insane and was sent to the Provincial Insane Asylum, where he died in 1911, at age 74.

But that was not quite the end of the story.

In 1910, the year before his father's death, Henry Riggs Rathbone, the oldest of Henry and Clara's children, reportedly broke down the brick wall at his grandparent's cottage that his mother had built decades before to shut out the past. He recovered the blood-stained dress that she had left there and burned it in the yard.

It was an end, he hoped, to the Rathbone family curse.

The Conspirators

In the wake of the assassination, the government enacted its vengeance - with the exception of Mary Surratt - on those who actually aided Booth during the assassination, including Lewis Powell, David Herold, and George Atzerodt. The government also wanted to arrest Mary's son, John Surratt, Jr., who was part of the original kidnapping plot but backed out when things turned to murder. He may have been in Washington on April 14 but likely was not. Either way, he escaped to Montreal.

By the time Booth was killed at the Garrett farm, the main conspirators were in custody. The government ultimately decided to seek lesser charges for those involved in the kidnapping plot - men such as Booth's friends Michael O'Laughlen and Samuel Arnold. Dr. Mudd was a special case and he came very close to being hanged. His obvious lies and evasions hurt his case and, although unknown to him, the majority of the military tribunal that tried the cases voted in favor of his death.

The government was also convinced that the hapless theater carpenter Ned Spangler - a Confederate sympathizer who wasn't fond of Lincoln - was involved in the plot. Witnesses had overheard Booth say to him that night, "You'll help me all you can, won't you, Ned?" It was only a courageous stand by John Ford, who stood up to military prosecutors and insisted that Spangler was innocent, that saved the carpenter's life and kept his prison sentence a short one.

The federal government had no intention of allowing civilian courts to block its will by following the letter of the Constitution. Stanton insisted that the conspirators be tried by military tribunal, not in civilian courts. After all, the murder of the commander in chief was an act of war and at least some of the accused were either former Confederate soldiers or, in the case of John Surratt, Jr., agents of the Confederate government.

Everything moved swiftly. On April 29, eight of the people charged with Lincoln's murder were brought to cells in the Washington Arsenal Penitentiary - the same building where Booth had been secretly buried two days before. They were Ned Spangler, Samuel Arnold, Michael

The Washington Arsenal Penitentiary

O'Laughlen, Lewis Powell, Mary Surratt, George Atzerodt, Dr. Samuel Mudd, and David Herold. John Surratt, Jr. was still at large.

On May 1, President Johnson issued an executive order that the prisoners be tried before a military tribunal. The charge was conspiracy. Even though some of the accused had been involved only in the kidnapping plot, that did not absolve them of complicity in the murder, as far as the law was concerned. The government only needed to prove that those on trial had knowledge of, and participated in, a conspiracy to carry out an illegal act.

The trial was held on the third floor of the arsenal building in a large area that had been converted into a courtroom. It lasted for 50 days, from May 10 to June 29, 1865. Seven combat generals and two colonels presided over the trial, although none of them had judicial or legal experience. They had been selected by Judge Advocate General Joseph Holt and his assistant, John Bingham. During the trial, 366 witnesses testified, and the prisoners were all well-represented by capable attorneys. However, the proceedings were initially conducted in secret, without any members of the press allowed in. Even worse, at the time the tribunal's judgments were final - there were no appeals to a higher court. The only appeal permitted was to the president.

On June 30, the tribunal announced its decision - all eight defendants had been found guilty. The sentences varied. Samuel Arnold,

Mary Surratt – was her execution a miscarriage of justice?

Michael O'Laughlen, and Dr. Samuel Mudd were sentenced to life in prison. Ned Spangler was sentenced to six years in prison. The four considered to be most involved in the assassination - Lewis Powell, David Herold, George Atzerodt, and Mary Surratt - were sentenced to die by hanging.

But no one expected Mary Surrat would be executed. The devout Catholic mother in her forties had been protesting her innocence since the beginning. Lewis Powell spoke on her behalf, stating that she knew nothing of Booth's plans. Even most of the tribunal had sympathy for her - five of the nine had signed a recommendation for clemency for Mary. A furious campaign was launched on her behalf, pleading that she be spared the rope.

Her trial had been a travesty. It's true that Mary had been the proprietor of the boarding house where Booth and the others had stayed when planning the kidnapping, then assassination, of President Lincoln, but there was no evidence that she knew anything of the plan. Mary had been arrested on the same night that Lincoln had been shot, accused of being a Booth conspirator, and was taken to the prison at the Old Brick Capitol. She constantly insisted that she was innocent and that she barely knew Booth, but no one listened.

The testimonies of two people became instrumental in Mary's conviction. One of them was a notorious drunk and the other was a known liar, a former policeman to whom Mary had leased her tavern in Maryland. At the trial's conclusion, she and three other defendants were found guilty and sentenced to death by hanging.

Mary Surratt would become the first woman to be executed by the United States government.

It has often been said that a person who dies violently under the shadow of unresolved circumstances becomes trapped in this world -- a disturbed spirit in the realm of the living, waiting for a time when the truth behind his or her death can be revealed. If this is true, then Mary Surratt qualifies as one of the most prominent ghosts of the Lincoln assassination.

The true facts of her guilt or innocence in the Lincoln assassination may still be unknown, but there is little question that her spirit is restless.

Mary Surratt lived a hard life, as photographs of her from the 1860s make obvious. Sent as an orphan to be educated by the Sisters of Charity in Alexandria, Virginia, she became a convert and strict Roman Catholic. She also had a love for the south that would endure throughout her entire life and which may have sent her to the gallows.

At age 17, she married John Harrison Surratt, an ardent secessionist and debt-ridden drunk. They purchased land in Prince George's County, Maryland and built a home that was also used as a tavern, hotel, post office, and a polling place for a town that became known as Surrattville. Located in a county that had deep Southern loyalties -- Lincoln received just one vote there in the 1860 election -- and with Surratt's vocal opposition to Union policies, the establishment became a meeting place for those of similar opinions. There is ample evidence that the tavern, just 12 miles from the nation's capital, became a safe house for members of the Confederate underground.

When John Surratt died in 1862, his wife was left with the burdens of the farm, as well as the many debts of her shiftless husband. With her oldest son, Isaac, serving in the Confederate Army, and with John Surratt, Jr. working as a Confederate courier, it became nearly impossible for Mary to keep the tavern operating. She decided to rent the property to a former Washington City policeman, John Lloyd, and move to a boarding house that she and her husband had purchased in Washington a few years earlier.

John Wilkes Booth became a frequent visitor to the boarding house. The impassioned actor had allied himself with John Surratt, Jr. and the two men began forming a plot to kidnap President Lincoln. The boarding house became a meeting place for those recruited to carry out the plan, which was intended to create a better settlement for the

Andrew Johnson, the first American President to be impeached – and the man who sent Mary Surratt to the gallows

south near the end of the war. The kidnapping plan, a rather inept effort, failed miserably and Booth's intentions turned to murder. The plan was finally carried out, of course, with Booth himself pulling the trigger, on April 14, 1865.

The nation, which was struggling to reunify with the south, was stunned by the assassination and Stanton became obsessed with immediately restoring a semblance of stability in the country. He sought swift justice for the horrible crime. After Booth went on the run and then was killed in a Virginia tobacco barn, the government began seeking out his fellow conspirators.

By some accounts, Mary Surratt was a minor character in the plot, swept up in the frenzy that followed the assassination. Others claimed, though, that she was one of the masterminds behind the conspiracy. Lincoln's successor, Andrew Johnson, declared that she had "kept the nest that hatched the egg" of the murderous conspiracy and the military tribunal that he ordered to try Mary Surratt and seven others ensured that his opinion would prevail.

The trial opened on May 8, 1865, less than a month after Lincoln had been killed. A quick, decisive resolution appeared to be its primary concern because a fair trial for the defendants certainly wasn't. Four of the defendants, including Mary, were sentenced to die.

Two days before the scheduled execution date, on July 5, the judge advocate general, Joseph Holt, carried the tribunal's recommendation for the death sentences and for clemency for Mary to Andrew Johnson. He signed the execution documents but did not sign the recommendation for clemency. Johnson would later claim that he never saw it - a claim that Holt strenuously denied.

Mary's daughter, Anna, begged to see Johnson so that she could plead for her mother's life. She knew Mary was innocent and that her trial had been unfair. Even if she did have some knowledge of the conspiracy, most historians doubt that she was directly involved in the murder plot. To say that the evidence against her was circumstantial is a gross understatement and considering that, and other factors, the punishment did not fit the supposed crime.

But Johnson refused to see Anna. He then went a step further by issuing an executive order that suspended a writ of habeas corpus in Mary's case - in other words, directly countermanding an order of the Supreme Court of the District of Columbia that Mary be brought before the court.

Mary Surratt died at the hands of Andrew Johnson.

On July 6, two generals in charge of the Washington Arsenal Penitentiary visited the condemned prisoners and informed them all, including Mary, that they were to be hanged the next day. Work had already begun on the gallows in the courtyard of the Arsenal - work that continued all through the night and which was clearly heard by the prisoners. Next to the gallows, four shallow graves were dug. Next to each hole was a musket box, just like the one in which John Wilkes Booth had been buried.

Major General Winfield Scott Hancock, the general in charge of the execution, was so sure that a last-minute reprieve would arrive for Mary on the day of the execution that he stationed messengers on horseback along the shortest route from the White House to the prison. He even delayed the hanging as long as he could. Until the time the hood was placed over Mary's head, officials were sure that Mary would be spared. But Johnson had no intention of sparing her life.

The four prisoners were brought out from their cells into the hot midday sun and were made to climb the steps to the high gallows' platform. It was over 100-degrees in the shade that day. Four, large black umbrellas were used to shield Mary and the others from the sun. Mary, dressed all in black with a black veil, was accompanied by two Catholic priests. A clergyman also accompanied Lewis Powell.

A line of soldiers, witnesses to the execution, stood atop the brick wall that surrounded the courtyard. Nearby, on the ground, was a group of reporters and other witnesses.

The Lincoln conspirators on the gallows

The prisoners were allowed to sit in chairs while one of the generals reads aloud the orders of execution. The prisoners were then told to stand, and their arms and legs were bound with white cloth. Thick rope nooses were placed over their heads and white hoods were placed on their heads, covering their faces. They were then carefully positioned on two large trapdoors that had been cut into the gallows' platform.

Mary, weeping inconsolably, could barely stand. She asked those next to her, "Please don't let me fall." The officials and the clergy stepped back away from the trapdoors.

Only George Atzerodt had any last words. "Goodbye, gentlemen, may we all meet in the other world."

At 1:25 p.m., an Army captain clapped his hands four times, signaling the soldiers below to swing large hammers and knock down the wooden beams that held the trapdoors closed. The four prisoners fell six feet to their doom, the sound of their necks breaking echoing off the stone walls of the courtyard.

The Lincoln conspirators were dead - and so was Mary Surratt, who likely had nothing to do with the assassination. Why she was

The Lincoln conspirators after the trapdoors were open and they plunged to their deaths. The bodies were hastily buried just a few feet away in shallow graves

sentenced to die, and what stopped President Johnson from signing the order for clemency, remains unknown. Many today believe that Mary is innocent of the crimes she was executed for - which may be the reason her spirit still lingers behind.

She and the three men were buried in those shallow graves next to the gallows. After being reinterred twice, Mary's body was returned to her family in 1869, and she was buried at Mt. Olivet Cemetery in Washington.

In 1878, rumors began to spread about the "martyred Mrs. Surrat" and the curse that had led her "murderers" to die "violent and miserable deaths." A newspaper story in the *Cleveland Plain Dealer* focused closely on the men who had stopped Mary's daughter, Anna, from asking President Johnson for clemency - Edwin Stanton and Senators Lane and King.

Senator King had committed suicide in November 1865 by tying a bag of bullets around his neck and jumping from a boat in New York Harbor. Senator Lane had killed himself the following year, shooting himself in the head while jumping from a carriage. Edwin Stanton had only lived until 1869, when, four days after being appointed to the Supreme Court, he allegedly slashed his own wrists with a razor - or so the story claimed. The "suicide" was denied by the surgeon general and most historians believe that he died of an asthmatic ailment. But dead is dead and four days after such an important appointment made his death more tragic.

Andrew Johnson, who could have stopped the execution but didn't, was not immune from the "curse," if there was one. He was impeached by Congress and is remembered today more for his drunkenness and his hostility toward freed slaves than for anything worthwhile that he did while in office.

Another person who played a role in the trial - and who was allegedly touched by the "curse" - was Judge Advocate General Joseph Holt. He had presided over the trial and had been in favor of seeing Mary go to the gallows. In the years that followed, some believe that the judge grew to regret what many felt was a heartless decision. According to those who knew him, his personality changed dramatically after the trial.

Holt had apparently never been a popular man in Washington, even before the assassination. It was said that he was "taciturn, vindictive and ill-mannered" and this led to him being universally disliked. Attitudes toward Holt didn't change much after the trial and he began to lead the life of a recluse. Newspaper articles from the period reported that he withdrew into his home and rarely saw, or spoke with, anyone. To further establish the fact that he was withdrawing from society, they also described his home as "decaying," with bars on the windows and heavy shades that did not permit outside light, nor the gaze of passersby, to venture inside. It was also said that the gardens of the house became tangled and overgrown and that people who walked along the street would often cross to the other side to avoid passing directly in front of the dilapidated mansion.

Holt spent his remaining years in almost total isolation, coming out only on occasion to buy food or to wander the few blocks to the Old Brick Capitol prison, where Mary Surratt had been imprisoned before her death. There, he would stare at the barred windows for some time before returning to his house. Rumors began to spread that Holt lived in deep regret over his harsh punishment of Mary Surratt. It was also somehow learned, at least according to the local stories, that he spent hours reading and re-reading the transcripts of the conspiracy trial.

After Holt died, the new owners attempted to renovate his house and to remove some of the austere atmosphere of the place, but it was to no avail. Soon after they took up residence, they told people in the neighborhood about the strange chill that pervaded various rooms of the house and the phantom sounds of a man's boots pacing in the upstairs library. It was believed the ghost of Judge Holt had remained within the house, still wracked with guilt over the terrible decision that he had been forced to make.

Judge Advocate General Joseph Holt – a victim of the Surratt curse?

Years later, after the house had been torn down, another tale began making the rounds. In this version, people reported seeing the ghost of the judge, walking a relentless path between his former home and the Old Brick Capitol. When he reached his destination, he always vanished.

The Washington Arsenal Prison, where Mary was incarcerated and executed, eventually became Fort Leslie McNair. The courthouse in which Mary was tried, and found guilty, was turned into an officer's quarters for the Army base, while the courtroom itself became a five-room apartment. For years, it was reported that occupants of the apartment would hear chains rattling throughout the rooms. According to records, the defendants in the conspiracy trial were shackled together with chains and sat on a bench where the apartment is now located. Tradition holds that the reported sounds are these same chains, still echoing over the decades.

And sounds are not the only things reported. Several residents of this apartment, and others which are located close to it, have claimed to see the apparition of a stout, middle-aged woman, dressed in black walking down the hallways of the officer's quarters. They have also heard the unexplainable sound of a woman's voice and have reported the sensation of being touched by an unseen hand. Could this be the ghost of Mary Surratt?

Within a year of Mary's death, rumors began circulating that something strange was taking place at her former boarding house on H Street in Washington. Her daughter, Anna, had sold the house for less than half its value not long after her mother was executed, which is not really surprising considering the notoriety of the case.

But that may not have been the entire story. In the years which followed, the house was plagued with a rapid succession of new owners. People would move in and out very quickly, sometimes in a matter of months. Someone who worked for a newspaper heard about the story and soon local journalists began to interview the former owners.

A story in a Boston newspaper in 1866 noted, "Mrs. Surratt's house is haunted. There can be no reasonable doubt on the subject. She herself persists in treading its halls in the dead of night, clad in those self-same robes of serge in which she suffered the penalty of the law."

Most of the accounts reported "strange sounds" and "whispers" in the building, voices that seemed to come from nowhere, and sounds heard inside of rooms where no living person was present. Children who lived nearby, it was said, stayed indoors at night rather than go near the old house after dark.

Like many old newspaper stories, it's often hard to know what to take seriously about haunted house reports, but there was no question that the haunting became a part of local lore. Years later, the accounts of phantom footsteps, whispers, and Mary's ghost pacing back and forth on the second floor continued to be told.

Mary's ghost was also said to frequent her home in Clinton, Maryland, located off Brandywine Road. It was at this tavern, which she leased out, where Booth stopped after making his escape from Washington and asked for items that had been left for him by Mary - or so the tenant claimed when he informed on Mary to the authorities.

Stories of odd events at the tavern began in the 1940s when a widow lived in one half of the house and rented out the other side. People spoke of seeing Mary's ghost on the stairway between the first and second floors, while others spoke of hearing men's voices, engaged in conversation, in the back of the house when no one was there.

In 1965, the site was taken over by the state and turned into a historical landmark. People who have worked and have visited there since claim to have seen apparitions of people in period clothing, have heard the phantom cries of children, and footsteps pacing through the upper floor of the house when no one else was present.

If Mary's spirit is still around, it seems she is not alone.

After the hanging, most seemed to feel that justice appeared to have been done. The fate of the other convicted conspirators almost seemed an afterthought. The remaining men -- O'Laughlen, Arnold, Spangler, and Dr. Mudd - were shipped off to a military penitentiary at Fort Jefferson in the Dry Tortugas, about 75 miles from Key West, Florida.

Four years later, Dr. Mudd's life sentence would come to an end - not by his death, but by his heroic efforts during an epidemic that struck the prison. There had also been an outcry after his conviction about the responsibilities that faced an ordinary doctor. What choice did Mudd have but to care for an injured man? Was he simply an innocent physician or had he assisted Booth in his escape from Washington?

Those questions are still being asked, all these years later, and many believe this may be the reason why the restless ghost of the often-maligned doctor still walks.

Samuel Mudd was born in Charles County, Maryland, the fourth of 10 children of Henry Lowe Mudd and his wife, Sarah Ann Reeves. His father owned a large plantation called Oak Hill, grew tobacco, and owned about 90 slaves. Samuel was raised in a well-to-do environment that valued education. After several years of home schooling, he was sent to a boarding school in Frederick, Maryland. He later attended Georgetown College in Washington and then studied medicine at the University of Maryland in Baltimore. He graduated in 1856 and returned to his Charles County home to work as a physician. The following year, he marked his childhood sweetheart, Sarah Frances Dyer, and they eventually had nine children together.

As a wedding present, Mudd's father presented him with 218 acres of prime farmland and built a new house for his son on the property. To supplement his income as a young doctor, he grew tobacco and held slaves, just as his father had, but on a smaller scale.

When the Civil War began in 1861, slavery in southern Maryland began to collapse. Slaves began to run away to freedom in Washington and other northern cities and in 1864, Maryland, which was exempt from Lincoln's Emancipation Proclamation, abolished slavery on its own. With the end of slavery in Maryland, farmers like Mudd could not find field hands to plant and harvest their crops. He pondered the idea of selling the plantation and moving his medical practice to Benedict, Maryland. A short time later, he was introduced to someone who said that he might be interested in buying his property -- a young actor named John Wilkes Booth.

Most historians agree that Booth visited Bryantown, Maryland, in November and December 1864, allegedly to look for real estate investments. Bryantown is about five miles from Dr. Mudd's farm. The real estate story was just a cover. Booth's real purpose was to see if the area would work as an escape route in his plot to kidnap President Lincoln.

Booth was introduced to Dr. Mudd at St. Mary's Catholic Church in Bryantown during one of those visits and then visited the Mudd farm the next day and stayed there overnight. The following day, Booth purchased a horse from Dr. Mudd's neighbor and returned to Washington. Some believe that Booth used his visit to Bryantown to recruit Mudd to his kidnapping conspiracy, although no evidence exists to say that this was the case.

A short time later, on December 23, 1864, Mudd went to Washington where he met Booth a second time. There is no evidence to state as to whether this was an arranged meeting or an accidental one, further adding to the mystery. The two men, along with John Surratt, Jr., and Louis J. Weichmann, had a conversation and drinks together. They met first at Booth's hotel and then later went to Mudd's hotel to end the night.

Mudd would not see Booth again until he arrived at the Mudd farm looking for medical assistance after the assassination. Booth and Herold arrived in the early morning hours of April 15. Mudd set, splinted, and bandaged Booth's broken leg, and arranged for a carpenter, John Best, to make a pair of crutches for Booth. They remained at Mudd's house for close to 15 hours and slept in a bedroom on the second floor.

By noon, the news of Lincoln's assassination --- and of Booth's involvement in it -- had reached Bryantown. Dr. Mudd went to Bryantown during the day on April 15 to run errands and if he did not already know about the assassination from Booth, he certainly learned of it during this trip. He returned home that evening, and accounts differ as to whether he came home shortly after Booth and Herold had left, or he met them as they were leaving. Whichever version of the story is true; he did not immediately contact the authorities. When questioned about this later, he stated that he had not wanted to leave his family alone in the house in case the assassins returned and found his family unprotected. He waited until the following day, when he asked his second cousin, Dr. George Mudd, to notify the Thirteenth New York Cavalry in Bryantown under the command of Lieutenant David Dana that Booth had passed through. Mudd's delay in contacting the authorities caused suspicion and likely led to him being accused of involvement in the conspiracy.

When he was being questioned, Mudd initially stated that he had never met the two men who came to his house before, but later admitted that he had met Booth in Bryantown. He deliberately hid his meeting with Booth in Washington in December 1864 and when Louis Weichmann later told the authorities of this meeting, they realized that Mudd had misled them. When questioned, he claimed it was a chance meeting during a Christmas shopping trip. Several days later, Dr. Mudd was arrested for his alleged role in the Lincoln assassination.

Mudd was tried and convicted by the military tribunal and was sentenced to life in prison at Fort Jefferson. He was pardoned in 1869, not because of new evidence that proved him to be innocent but because of a request that had been signed by the warden, officials, and all the inmates at the prison. They believed they owed the doctor their lives after his aid during a Yellow Fever epidemic that swept through the penitentiary. One of the other conspirators, Michael O'Laughlen, died from the outbreak on September 24, 1867.

Mudd was released on March 8, 1869 and returned home to Maryland. Friends, well-wishers, and newspaper reporters besieged

The Dr. Samuel Mudd house in Maryland

him. He avoided the press as much as possible. He was simply happy to enjoy the companionship of his friends and neighbors. Mudd resumed his medical practice, slowly brought the family farm back to productivity, and became active once again in his community. When Ned Spangler was released from prison, Mudd allowed him to come and stay with his family and even gave him a parcel of land on which to build a house.

Mudd had always had an interest in politics and seven years after being released from prison, he was elected Vice President of the local Democratic Tilden-Hendricks presidential election committee. Tilden lost that year to Republican Rutherford B. Hayes in a hotly disputed election. The next year Mudd ran as a Democratic candidate for the Maryland House of Delegates but was defeated by the popular Republican William Mitchell.

He was only 49 years old when he died of pneumonia on January 10, 1883. He was buried in the cemetery at St. Mary's Catholic Church in Bryantown, the same church where he was introduced to John Wilkes Booth.

There is still disagreement today over Mudd's role in the Lincoln assassination. It is known that he was a southern sympathizer, as were most of the residents of southern Maryland, but it is also widely realized that Federal officials rushed to judgment in the aftermath of Lincoln's death. They were anxious to punish anyone who might have been in any way involved in the murder and possibly innocent people like Dr.

Mudd, and perhaps Mary Surratt, may have been caught up in the frenzy.

However, it was said that before his death, Mudd confessed to many people that he had, in fact, known it was Booth all along when he set his broken leg - an admission that would likely have led to his execution if it had been known at trial, even though it still didn't make him guilty of assisting in the assassination plot.

In any case, Dr. Mudd's strongest supporters have been his descendants, who have fought to clear his name for many years. They have also restored the Mudd farmhouse and it is open today as a historic site.

Strangely, the restoration effort was said to have been prompted by the ghost of Dr. Mudd himself.

According to Louise Mudd Arehart, the doctor's granddaughter, she had always been interested in the family history and in preserving the house, but that interest was piqued when she began experiencing some rather strange events there. She began to hear knocking on the front door, but when she went to answer it, she found no one there. She also began to hear footsteps going up and down the stairs and back and forth in the hallways but, again, she would find the areas to be empty when she would go to check.

Soon, she began to catch glimpses of a man in the yard. This figure was always dressed in black trousers, a vest, and a white shirt with the sleeves rolled up to his elbows. After seeing him a few times, he also began appearing inside of the house, where she finally got a good look at him. She was convinced that the apparition was that of her grandfather, Dr. Samuel Mudd.

She felt that Dr. Mudd had returned to tell her and her family to restore the old farmhouse, which had fallen into a state of disrepair. Thanks to her efforts, the house was listed on the National Register of Historic Places in 1974 and was opened to the public in 1983. Since then, the spirit of Dr. Mudd has only returned when restoration of the house slows down, or when it seems as though it is not proceeding to his expectations.

Like Mary Surratt, Dr. Mudd may have returned for a reason. His family had no question about his guilt or innocence so it's easy for them to believe he lingers at his former home in hopes that they will preserve it for future generations - but the haunting may not be so simple.

Perhaps he, too, like Mary, remains as a silent protest to his mistreatment in the past. The two of them may not have been as innocent as so many believe, but again, it's likely that their small role in the conspiracy didn't justify the extent of their punishment. Dr. Mudd may have escaped the noose, but he never escaped the belief that the public had in his guilt.

John Surratt, Jr. in his Zouave uniform from the papal army

The last person charged in the conspiracy was John Surratt, Jr., the only one of them who escaped. He had been a Confederate experienced courier, who often traveled to Montreal, so he was better prepared than any of the others to make a getaway. As Surratt later admitted, he traveled directly to New York as soon as he heard about the assassination - an act he wanted no part of. From there, he went on to Montreal and found refuge in a small town where he was hidden by a Catholic priest. He stayed there throughout the trial and during his mother's subsequent execution.

From Quebec, he went to England then on to, of all places, Vatican City. At the Vatican, he enlisted in the small papal army known as the Zouaves, using the alias of John Watson. He soon became involved in fighting against Italian nationalist forces led by Giuseppe Garibaldi.

An old family acquaintance, also serving in the Zouaves, betrayed Surratt to the U.S. consul and received a $10,000 reward. Surratt was arrested by the Vatican police but managed to escape before he could be turned over to American authorities. He traveled to Egypt by ship, but U.S. diplomats were tipped off and he was met by Egyptian police when he arrived in Alexandria.

Surratt was returned to the United States and was subjected to a reply of the original conspiracy trial, with many of the same witnesses giving testimony. However, this time, the trial was held before a civilian judge with a jury - and it ended with the jury unable to reach a verdict. The government tried him again, this time charging him with treason.

Surratt's luck held out. The judge dismissed the case on a technicality because the statute of limitations for this type of treason was two years and it had been three years since the alleged offense. He walked out of the courtroom a free man.

Surratt went briefly on the lecture circuit, was married in 1872, and began a long career with an established steamship company, rising to the rank of top executive. He died in 1916 at the age of 72.

As for the others who aided Booth in his plans, virtually all escaped punishment - some because they were never caught and others because the government simply lost interest.

Detectives eventually tracked down and arrested the two Confederate agents who helped Booth and Herold after they left Dr. Mudd's house, Samuel Cox and Thomas Jones. They tried to get the two men to implicate each other, even threatening to hang them on the spot. But the two trained agents stuck to their stories and admitted nothing. The only witnesses to their crimes were Booth and Herold and they were both dead. Both men were eventually released and never charged. Two decades later, a journalist named George Townsend talked Jones into telling his story for $60. That was when the nation learned, for the first time, how Booth had managed to evade the manhunt for so long.

Other people who aided Booth and Herold - like Elizabeth Quesenberry, the Garretts, and those who fed them and hid them from the pursuing soldiers - simply faded into history without facing any charges.

It would be easy to say that the story was over once those last conspirators went to the grave, but the events of the Lincoln assassination, and its aftermath, continue to resonate in our nation today.

14. CARNIVAL OF DEATH

The Story of the Lincoln Funeral Train and the Twenty Days of Madness that Gripped America

Two days after the death of the president, the casket that had been built for him was ready to receive his body. Soldiers carried it to the second-floor guest room in the White House where Lincoln's corpse had been resting since Saturday afternoon, when it had been moved there from the boarding house where he had died. The soldiers approached the president and lifted him from the table where he lay to the coffin -- a coffin that now looked too small. He was deftly placed inside, but without his boots. Lincoln's lanky frame measured six feet, four inches, which was longer than most caskets of the day. As the soldiers lifted the coffin and carried it down the stairs, at least one of them must have considered the idea that the Lincoln funeral ritual was off to a rather inauspicious start.

Gaslight illuminated the silent, eerie journey to the famous East Room, where so many public receptions and events had been held. The coffin was taken to the center of the room and placed on the catafalque. It was a magnificent casket, more impressive than any Abraham Lincoln had likely ever seen. In life, Lincoln had dismissed his wife Mary's love of frills and finery. He never would have chosen such a stately and expensive coffin for himself. It had cost almost as much as he had paid for his house back in Illinois. He would have preferred a simple pine box, like the one he had helped build for his mother when he was a boy.

And then there were the decorations in the East Room. Lincoln had always laughed about Mary's obsession with decorating the White House. But no one who entered the East Room over the next two days mocked its lavish vestments of mourning. When the public and press saw it, they were so impressed that they named it the "Temple of Death." Ward Hill Lamon would always claim that Lincoln had foreseen this stark tableau in one of his prophetic dreams.

"Who is dead in the White House?" Lincoln had demanded of the shadowy faceless soldier standing guard in his dream.

"The President," was the reply. "He was killed by an assassin."

Lamon always recalled how Mary had recoiled from the account, telling her husband that it was a horrid story to tell.

But it was only a dream, Lincoln assured her. "Let us say no more about it and try to forget it."

And then days later, Lincoln's body was on display in the East Room, just as he had dreamed it.

The funeral display in the East Room had been hastily arranged, just like everything else that took place in the wake of the president's death. Washington was a scene of chaos in mid-April 1865. As the search continued for Lincoln's killer, there was also the matter of swearing a new president into office, while others labored over the funeral for President Lincoln. The initial details of the proceedings were decided on and arranged by Secretary of War Edwin Stanton, who was embroiled in just about everything that was going on in Washington at the time. Unfortunately, there was little choice in the matter. Mary Lincoln had locked herself in her room and young Robert Lincoln was still too stunned by his father's death to be of much assistance.

Stanton dealt with Lincoln's embalming and even supervised the dressing of the corpse. But once his corpse was ready for burial, it became unclear where that would occur. Mary had the right to choose the site, but given her mental state, she was in no condition to discuss the subject only hours after her husband's death. Stanton would confer with her and Robert Lincoln later. In the meantime, whatever the final destination of the president's remains, official funeral events would have to take place in the nation's capital within the next few days. Stanton did not have time to plan and supervise a major public funeral, the biggest, no doubt, that the District of Columbia had ever seen. He needed to delegate this responsibility and had to choose between several candidates, including Ward Hill Lamon, Lincoln's close friend and unofficial bodyguard. It had been Lamon who had organized Lincoln's trip to Gettysburg in November 1863, planning everything with less than one week's notice. There was also Benjamin Brown French, a Washington veteran with great experience with decades of historic events, including the deaths of other presidents. French was perfect but was needed for another role -- decorator in chief of public buildings. He was needed to drape the city in mourning. Stanton also considered Major General Montgomery Meigs, the quartermaster general of the U.S. Army, an expert planner with superb organizational skills. But the war was not yet over and Meigs was still needed in the field. He also considered another military man, Brigadier General Edward D. Townsend, the assistant adjutant general of the army, but Stanton had Townsend in mind for a special duty of utmost importance, one even more critical than planning the president's funeral in Washington --- and that was getting the president home to Illinois, if that was where Mary wanted him to go.

In the end, Stanton chose George Harrington, Assistant Secretary of the Treasury. Harrington was experienced in the ways of Washington, was well-known and liked by both Lincoln and Stanton, and Stanton believed him to have the keen, quick, and organizational mind that was essential for the assignment. He was soon in charge of all the Washington events to honor the late president. Harrington accepted the appointment and quickly went to work.

Stanton was now free to focus on what should be done with Lincoln's corpse after the Washington ceremonies. Would he be interred at the U.S. Capitol, in the vault beneath the great dome that had once been intended as the final resting place of George Washington? Or would Mary Lincoln take the body back to Illinois, for burial in Chicago, the state's most important city, or in Springfield, the state capital and the Lincolns' home for 24 years?

The clock was ticking.

On April 17, Stanton requested an interview with Mary and Robert to ascertain the family's wishes for the final disposition of Lincoln's remains. Some federal officials argued in favor of the tomb at the capitol building. From Kentucky came an urgent telegram imploring consideration of Lincoln's birthplace as a suitable final resting place. Chicago, where Lincoln had practiced law in the federal courts and earned the nomination for the presidency, put in a bid. But the city of Springfield lobbied the hardest.

Within an hour after news of the president's death reached Springfield, the shocked city council had met and began forming a plan to take to the citizens. A mass meeting was held at noon and it was decreed that Springfield was going to try and make sure that the assassinated president was laid to rest in the city that he had called home. Fortunately for Springfield's wishes, the newly elected Governor Oglesby and Richard Yates, the wartime governor and recent Senator, were both friends of Lincoln and were both in Washington. Through Robert Lincoln, they made an appeal to Mary, who was locked in her bedroom, asking that her late husband's body should be returned home to rest among his friends and neighbors.

Mary, however, was torn between the fact that she had quarreled with just about all her old friends and her family in Springfield and never wanted to set foot there again, and the sincere desire to choose a burial place that would have been what her husband wanted.

On April 17, she insisted that Chicago was her first choice and her second was the crypt under capitol building. Her husband had promised her that after he left the Presidency, they would make a tour of Europe and then retire in Chicago and so she favored a quiet burial place near Lake Michigan. It appealed to her that he would be buried close to the resting place of his old adversary, Stephen Douglas. Of course, Mary had not been to Chicago since Douglas' death and did not know that his grave was desolate and after four years, had no monument to mark it.

And then she changed her mind again.

When Mary looked back at her last days with Lincoln, she realized that he had a foreshadowing of his own death. "You will see Europe, but I never shall," he told her. She also remembered her husband's dream to live once more in Springfield. She also recalled his saying, just a few weeks before his death, that he wanted to be buried in "some quiet place."

She thought she knew what he'd had in mind. He had once told her, back in 1860, that the new Springfield cemetery, Oak Ridge, was one of the most beautiful spots that he had ever seen. The day of the cemetery's consecration was a grand event in the city and just about everyone in Springfield walked the two miles to Oak Ridge in an informal procession. The new cemetery -- carved from woods, hills, and unbroken forest -- was a beautiful place. It made the overcrowded graveyard in downtown Springfield look shabby and old. Lincoln spoke of its beauty many times.

Mary agonized and then finally announced that Oak Ridge was the "quiet place" that Lincoln would have wanted and directed that his coffin be placed in the public receiving tomb there until a proper site could be chosen for his monument. Her decision was telegraphed to Springfield and days and nights of frantic preparation were made. Mary wanted Lincoln to be buried at Oak Ridge --- but the city of Springfield had other plans.

As it happened, when the body of President Lincoln eventually arrived in Springfield, he actually had two different graves waiting for him. One of the graves was the temporary vault at remote and wooded Oak Ridge, which Springfield officials believed was no place to bury a fallen hero, regardless of what Mary wanted. The other site was a small hill located in the heart of the city. It was called Mather's Hill and it had been the site of the magnificent stone house that was owned by Thomas Mather. Builders were employed to work around the clock and convert the house into a tomb, complete with a handsome vault and stone urns on either side of the entrance. They were sure they could convince Mary this was a more fitting place for the president's remains.

When Mary learned of the downtown tomb through "troublemakers," she sent a telegram stating that her husband absolutely was to be buried at Oak Ridge. Springfield officials remembered the Mrs. Lincoln of old and recalled her erratic nerves and fits of temper, so they tried to be very diplomatic with the widow. They telegraphed Edwin Stanton and told him that her wishes would be respected --- but continued the work at the Mather tomb. They simply could not believe that Mary would want her husband buried out in the woods and even if she did, they were sure that they could change her mind when she arrived in Springfield. Even so, they did make the other preparations that she and Robert asked for -- namely moving Eddie Lincoln's body to the vault at Oak Ridge. The boy had died many years before and had been buried in the cemetery downtown.

Even after Lincoln arrived in Springfield, the plan concocted by Springfield officials continued. They placed Lincoln at Oak Ridge but still had no intention of leaving him there. They were so sure that he would be moved to the Mather Tomb that plans had already started to be made for a huge celebration. Mary once again refused to go along with it. In the summer of 1865, she moved to Chicago and a delegation from Springfield went to plead with her again. She refused to see them and at last, they surrendered to her wishes. A temporary tomb was built for Lincoln at Oak Ridge and in seven months, on December 21, he was finally placed inside.

But in April, Stanton simply needed to know where the body was supposed to go. If Lincoln's corpse had to travel to some distant place, it would be the task of the War Department and the U.S. Military Railroad to get him there. Such a journey would take time to plan and the Washington funeral was just two days away. Stanton did not want to be involved in Mary's dispute with Springfield, he only needed to know where to send the train. The Lincolns finally decided on Illinois. The president would return to Springfield.

Now the Secretary of War could plan the route and devise the timetables. The train could proceed directly to Illinois on the shortest and most direct route, stopping along the way only to replenish water for the steam engine and fuel for the fire.

This was the most efficient route, but it was not the most desirable one.

Lincoln had set a precedent four years earlier when he had traveled east as the president-elect. Instead of a hurried trip to Washington, he took a circuitous route through several of the major northern states that had elected him so that he could meet the American people. Lincoln hoped to reassure the country, sustain support for the Union and avoid a civil war. His train stopped many times. He offered impromptu, unscripted speeches, mingled with the people, accepted tributes and well wishes, and participated in public ceremonies. Lincoln presented himself to the people as a simple man who had been elevated temporarily to higher office. The inaugural train came to symbolize a living bond between Lincoln and the American people.

Now the beloved president was dead. In their grief, Americans had not forgotten the inaugural train of 1861. The nation now cried out to see the fallen president. Never had any nation so mourned a fallen leader. Lincoln's friends and admirers were heartbroken and even his numerous critics, who had mocked him in life, had ridiculed him as a baboon, and had damned him as an ignorant backwoodsman, now lamented his death and grieved for the country. It was the first time in the history of America that a president had been felled by an assassin's bullet and this was a tragic event in every corner of the Union.

Telegrams began to pour into the War Department from the cities and towns that had wished him goodwill on his journey four years before. Now they begged Stanton to send Lincoln back to them. Once the news spread that the president would make the long westward journey home to Illinois, a groundswell of public opinion clamored for his inaugural trip to be re-created in reverse. The assassination of the president was a national tragedy and yet the American people could not come from all over the country to see Lincoln's body and attend his funeral -- so why couldn't Abraham Lincoln come to them?

Stanton knew it was possible to do what they wanted. It would require a special train fitted out properly to transport the body, a military escort to guard Lincoln's corpse around the clock to make sure that the remains were treated with utmost dignity, coordination between the military railroad and the major commercial lines, cooperation between the War Department and state and local governments, and the resources and will to do it. Stanton believed it could be done. There was only one obstacle -- the president's grieving, tightly-wound, and unpredictable widow. The plan would be impossible without her explicit consent.

Stanton carefully broached the subject with the First Lady. He outlined the plan, asking her to try and assuage the people's profound sadness by allowing the president's body to take an extended route that would take him through Maryland, Pennsylvania, New Jersey, New York State, then turning west through Ohio, Indiana, Illinois, Chicago, and across the prairie to Springfield. The route would take many days to travel, longer than a quick run to Illinois. The exact duration of the extended trip would depend on the number of times the train stopped for water, fuel, and public ceremonies along the way. Stanton promised that if she agreed, he and his aides would handle all the details.

And there was one more thing. The people wanted to see their president, not just his closed coffin. They wanted to look on his face, which meant an open casket. Mary had consented to this at the Washington ceremonies, but an open casket all the way to Springfield, a trip of more than 1,600 miles? In warm weather, without refrigeration, it would test the limits of the embalmer's art. Mary thought the idea seemed morbid and ghoulish, but a grand, national funeral pageant that affirmed her husband's greatness appealed to her. She consented to the trip.

Plans for the epic journey -- unlike anything America had seen before -- began immediately.

Lincoln's funeral services were planned for Wednesday, April 19, but the president's adoring public was allowed to view the body the day before. Many waited outside all night to make sure that they were in line when the gates opened. Upstairs, Mary and Tad remained in seclusion in her room. Tad would have liked to see the people who came to honor his father. He would, perhaps, have found more comfort in the consoling company of strangers than in the dark, secluded bedchamber of his unstable mother, but Mary refused to allow him to leave her side.

The doors of the White House were opened on Tuesday morning and people crushed inside, inching past the body, weeping and speaking to the President, whose head lay on a white pillow with a faint smile frozen on his pale and distorted face. By the end of the day, an estimated 25,000 people had crowded past the mahogany coffin.

While the public viewing was taking place, George Harrington was becoming overwhelmed by the last-minute deluge of requests for funeral tickets, press passes to the White House, and permission to march in the procession. For every request that Harrington took care of, two more came in the door.

As final visitors filed past the coffin, carpenters restlessly loitered nearby, anxious to get started on their work. They impatiently watched the public file past, waiting for the last one to leave so that the doors could be closed and locked behind them. If the public had its way, the viewing would have continued through the night. Thousands of people were turned away so that crews could begin preparing the East Room

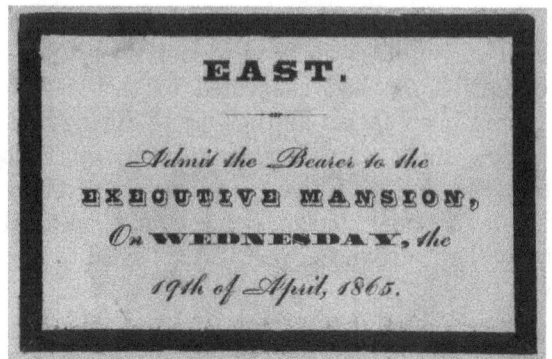

One of the black-bordered tickets that were printed for admittance to Lincoln's funeral

for the funeral. Disappointed mourners would have one more chance to view the remains, after they were transferred to the capitol.

Harrington had been faced with a seating dilemma for the funeral. There was no way to fit enough chairs into the room for everyone that had to attend -- so he would not seat the guests in chairs at all. He had calculated that, allowing for the space required for the catafalque and the aisles, it was impossible to squeeze 600 chairs into the room. He decided that only a few of the most important guests, including the Lincoln family, would have chairs. But if he built risers, or bleachers, for the rest, he could pack slightly more than 600 people into the East Room, the minimum number of important guests he needed to seat.

The White House thrummed with activity after the viewing as men carried stacks of lumber into the East Room, where carpenters sawed, hammered, and nailed them into bleachers.

On Wednesday, Lincoln's body rested in the East Room, which was now hushed and dim and draped in hundreds of yards of black crepe. Upstairs, Mary was locked in her room, too deranged from grief and hysterical weeping to attend the services. Tad tried to console her. Though stricken himself, Tad would throw his arms about his mother's neck and plead with her, "Don't cry so, Momma! Don't cry, or you will make me cry, too! You will break my heart!" But it was no use, Mary was simply too crazed to be able to pull herself together.

Services began around 11:00 a.m. To thwart gate-crashers, funeral guests were not allowed direct entry into the Executive Mansion. Instead, guards directed the bearers of the 600 coveted tickets, printed on heavy card stock, next door, to the Treasury Department. From there, they crossed a narrow, elevated wooden footbridge, built just for the occasion, which led into the White House.

As guests entered the building, none of them knew what to expect. The East Room overwhelmed them with its decorations, flowers, and the catafalque. It was an unprecedented scene. Two presidents had died in office -- William Henry Harrison in 1841 and Zachary Taylor in 1850 -- but their funerals were not as grand or elaborate as this. No president had been so honored in death, not even George Washington, who, after modest services, rested in a simple tomb in Virginia.

The scene lives on today only in the written accounts of those who were there and a few artist's sketches and newspaper illustrations. No one took a photograph, before or during the funeral. It could have been done. Alexander Gardner had photographed more complex scenes, including the second inaugural, where he took close-ups of the East Front platform and one of his operators had managed to take a long view of the Capitol dome while Lincoln was reading his address.

But Stanton had failed to invite Gardner, or his rival Matthew Brady, to preserve the history of Lincoln's funeral.

The guests crowded into the East Room. Robert Lincoln, his face ashen and grave, was wearing his military uniform and he stood at the foot of the coffin. He tightly held the hand of his little brother and Tad trembled, his face swollen with tears. General Ulysses S. Grant, a black mourning band on one arm, sat alone at the other end, staring at a cross of lilies. He began to cry, unable to believe what had happened. He would always maintain that this was the saddest day of his life.

By now, nearly all of Washington was there, including President Andrew Johnson and his Cabinet, Charles Sumner and his congressional colleagues, numerous military officials, Lincoln's personal cavalry escort, his secretaries and bodyguards, and mayors and government delegates from across the country.

Four different ministers spoke and prayed for Lincoln and after that, 12 reserve corps sergeants carried his casket out to the funeral car. As they stepped out into the bright, sunlit day, church bells all over the city began to toll. From the forts that still surrounded the city, cannons began to boom. Throngs of people lined Pennsylvania Avenue and thousands more peered from windows and roofs along the parade route. Many of these people had been there for hours, waiting for Lincoln's casket to appear.

Crowds lined the streets of Washington as the procession took the president's body to the rotunda of the Capitol building

Federal troops moved into formation to accompany the hearse, which now waited outside the White House. The coffin was placed on a high platform, surrounded by glass, and elevated so that everyone could see. Soon, the hearse moved forward, pulled by six white horses, all festooned with black cloth and decoration. The procession moved in a slow, measured cadence with a detachment of African-American troops in the lead. The hearse was followed by a riderless horse, befitting a fallen general, and all walked to the steady muffled beat of drums. The lines swelled with wounded soldiers, who left their hospital beds and marched along, ignoring their pain as they hobbled after their slain leader. There was a procession of black citizens, walking in lines that stretched from curb to curb, holding hands as they walked along.

Lincoln's body was carried to the Capitol building and placed in the rotunda. An honor guard took up position around it and remained in place until the next morning. Shortly after the sun appeared, wounded soldiers were allowed to file past the casket and pay their final respects. After this, the viewing was opened to the public once more. The crowds were so large that the soldiers outside had to remove wooden barricades around the building so that no one would be injured. It was said that more than 3,000 people per hour filed past the coffin before the doors were finally closed at midnight.

Noah Brooks, the reporter who had become friends with the Lincolns, described the scene: "Directly beneath me lay the casket in which the dead President lay at full length, far, far below; and like black atoms moving over a sheet of gray paper, the slow-moving mourners, seen from a perpendicular above them, crept silently in two dark lines across the pavement of the rotunda, forming an ellipse around the coffin and joining as they advanced toward the eastern portal and disappeared."

While Lincoln lay in state in the Capitol rotunda, Stanton received a telegram from Governor Andrew Curtin of Pennsylvania, asking if Mary Lincoln would accompany her husband's remains on their journey. He wanted to offer his home to her while the train was passing through his state.

But Governor Curtin did not know Mary Lincoln's condition. Overwrought, she still had not left her room, or viewed the President's remains and did not attend the funeral. She had refused almost all visitors, even close friends of the president from Illinois and high officials in her husband's administration. She had already started her first descent into instability, a journey she would make without the president to save her from drifting away.

Stanton promised to relay the governor's kindness to the first lady, but he suspected it would be met with silence and indifference. Mary did not accompany the President on the train. He would make the journey home without her.

On Friday, April 21, one week after the assassination, Edwin Stanton, Ulysses S. Grant, Gideon Welles, Attorney General James Speed, Postmaster General William Dennison, several senators, members of a delegation from Illinois, and various army officers arrived at the Capitol at 6:00 a.m. to escort Lincoln's coffin to the funeral train. Soldiers removed the coffin from the catafalque in the rotunda and carried it down the stairs of the East Front. Four companies of the Twelfth Veteran Reserve Corps stood by to escort the hearse to the train. This was not meant to be a grand procession. There were no drums, no band, and no cavalcade of thousands of marchers. It was a short trip from the Capitol to the Baltimore and Ohio Railroad station, just a few blocks away, but this did not deter the crowds. Several thousand onlookers lined the route and crowded the station's entrance. Although this last, short journey in Washington was not part of the official public funeral events, Stanton supervised it himself to be

The Lincoln Funeral Train

sure that the final movement of Lincoln's body in the nation's capital was conducted with simplicity, dignity, and honor.

Earlier that morning, another hearse had arrived at the station. It had come from Oak Hill Cemetery in Georgetown and carried the body of Willie Lincoln, the president's son. When the soldiers carried Abraham Lincoln aboard the private railroad car at 7:30, Willie was already there, waiting for him. Lincoln had planned to collect the boy himself and take his coffin home when his term in office ended, but now two coffins shared the presidential car.

The railroad car that would transport Lincoln's body across the country was never meant to be a funeral car. Constructed over a period of two years at the U.S. Military Railroad car shops in Alexandria, Virginia, the car was built to be a luxurious vehicle intended for the living president's use. However, even though it was completed in February prior to Lincoln's second inauguration in 1865, he never rode in it or even saw it. The elegant interior, finished with walnut and oak, and upholstered with crimson silk, contained three rooms -- a stateroom, a drawing room, and a parlor or dining room. A corridor ran the length of the car and offered access to each room. The exterior was painted a dark brown, hand-rubbed to a high sheen, and on both sides of the car hung identical oval paintings of an eagle and the coat of arms of the United States. As soon as Stanton knew that Lincoln's body would be carried home to Illinois by railroad, he authorized the military to modify the car, decorate it with symbols of mourning, and build two catafalques so that it could accommodate the coffins of the president and his son.

The special train car that had been redesigned to take the bodies of President Lincoln and his son, Willie, across the country

Before the train could leave the station, members of the honor guard took their places beside Lincoln's coffin. Under protocols established by Stanton and General Edward Townsend, the president was never to be left alone. Townsend later recalled, "There was never a moment throughout the whole journey when at least two of this guard were not by the side of the coffin."

The hearse and the horses that had carried Lincoln's body to the train were not boarded. Instead, in every city where the train was stopping for funeral services, local officials were required to provide a suitable hearse to transport the coffin from the train to the site of the ceremonies.

Robert Lincoln in 1865

At 7:50, Robert Lincoln boarded the train, but he planned to leave it after a short while and return to Washington and wrap up his father's affairs. Mary Lincoln did not come to the station to see her husband off -- nor did she permit Tad to go. He should have been allowed to come to the station and then ridden with his father and brother to Illinois. After Willie's death, Tad and his father had been inseparable. Sometimes, Tad would fall asleep in the president's office and Lincoln would carry the boy over his shoulder and take him to bed. Tad loved to go on trips with the president and relished their recent visit to Richmond after it had fallen to Union troops. He loved to see the soldiers and he enjoyed wearing a sort-of junior-sized army officer's uniform, complete with a short sword, that his father had given him. Tad would have marveled at the sights of the 1,600-mile journey to Illinois and he would have been proud of, and taken comfort in, the tributes paid to Lincoln.

But it was not meant to be. Mary refused to allow it.

A pilot engine departed the station 10 minutes ahead of the funeral train to inspect the tracks ahead and then, with five minutes to spare, Lincoln's secretaries, John Nicolay and John Hay, arrived from the White House and boarded the train to be sure that all was in order. In all, about 150 men were on the train that morning, including 29 men from the Veteran Reserve Corps who would serve as the guard of honor. Also on the train were many military officers, senators, congressmen, delegates from Illinois, four governors, seven newspaper reporters, and David Davis, an old friend of Lincoln's and a justice on the U.S. Supreme Court.

With so many dignitaries arriving at the station, two of the train's most important passengers went unnoticed. In the days to come, the success of the funeral train would depend on their work. To make sure that all ran smoothly, they had to have unfettered access to the president's corpse at any time day or night. Those two men were embalmer Dr. Charles Brown and undertaker Frank Sands. For the next 13 days, they had to try and control the decomposing flesh of Abraham Lincoln.

The train left the station in Washington at exactly 8:00 a.m. Over the course of the next two weeks, the train steamed north and then westward, passing through the greatest crowds ever assembled in America at that time. Reporters followed its passage, telegraphing details to their newspapers back home of the strange, circus-like atmosphere surrounding the funeral train. It is believed that seven million northerners looked upon Lincoln's hearse or coffin and that at least one million actually looked upon his silent face. Ninety different funeral songs were composed in his honor while thousands - or even millions -- cried, fainted, took to their beds, and even committed suicide in the frenzy of Lincoln's passing.

Lincoln's train would first stop in Baltimore and in the days ahead, it was scheduled to stop many times for official honors, processions, ceremonies, and viewings, but, for the most part, those plans were merely words and timetables printed on paper. The official documents said nothing about the things to come -- the spontaneous bonfires, torches, floral arches, hand-painted signs, banners, and masses of people who haunted the tracks at all hours of the day and night. No official in Washington had ordered these strange public manifestations. Edwin Stanton never expected the train to literally take on a life of its own and to become a venerated symbol in its own right.

The progress of the train was moved along not just on fire and water, but on human passion, which animated it and moved it along the tracks. At each stop, it took on the tone and temper of the town and its people. The train was almost like a battery, soaking up the energy of the place. The more time that it spent on the road, and the greater distance it traveled, the more it absorbed the emotions of the nation's pride and grief. It became more than the funeral train of just one man and evolved into a symbol of American sorrow -- about the death of a president and the cost of the great Civil War. It came to represent a mournful homecoming for all the men who never came home from the war. In the hearts of the grief-stricken American people, an army of the dead -- and not just its commander in chief - came home aboard that train.

In every city where the train stopped -- or even just passed through -- the people knew it was coming and had read newspaper accounts of the events that had occurred in other cities that preceded it up the line. This created a fever pitch of excitement and created a desire to outdo the honors already offered in other cities.

This would create a madness in America -- a "carnival of death" like nothing the country had ever seen before.

The train arrived first in Baltimore, where a hard rain had started to fall, four hours after leaving Washington. Baltimore was a strange but necessary destination. Maryland had remained in the Union during the war, but it was anti-Lincoln and pro-Confederate. Four years earlier, when president-elect Lincoln passed through the city, he had to do so secretly to avoid being killed. Baltimore was also the home of John Wilkes Booth and he had recruited some of his conspirators there. This alone made it seem to some that it was wrong to stop Lincoln's train in Baltimore. Who in the city would mourn the president when they had wished him ill and might be reveling in his assassination?

Lincoln's men feared the worst, but they could not have been more wrong. Lincoln was mourned in Baltimore. As the train arrived, guns boomed, and church and firehouse bells tolled. The schedule only allowed Lincoln to remain in the city for four hours, so thousands jammed the train tracks, hoping for a glimpse of the President's coffin. The casket was removed from the train and the pallbearers had to elbow their way through streets jammed with people, many of whom were selling funeral crepe and photographs of Lincoln. The coffin was placed in what Baltimore newspapers called "the most beautiful hearse ever constructed," made from genuine rosewood, gilded and fitted with a back and two sides of French plate glass. The procession of military and civic representatives was so large that it took three hours to get to the Merchant's Exchange, where the coffin was opened for viewing. The coffin was displayed next to flowers -- heaps of flowers, a mountain of striking and fragrant fresh-cut flowers -- which would set the standard for the journey. Soon, the lilac, above all other flowers, would come to represent the death carnival for Lincoln's corpse. It went on to become the "death flower" for generations of American funerals.

In Baltimore, there were no official ceremonies, sermons, or speeches; there was no time for anything. Instead, as soon as Lincoln's coffin was in position, and after military officers and dignitaries saw him first, they threw open the doors and allowed the public mourners inside. Over the next four hours, it was believed that nearly 10,000 people looked on Lincoln but thousands more were turned away, disappointed that the funeral train had to be on its way. There was no one to argue with and no one to intercede on behalf of those turned back or for the long lines of schoolchildren who stood patiently in the rain for a last look at the president.

Those few hours changed the way that officials looked at Baltimore. It was a city in grief. Lincoln's enemies could have masqueraded as mourners and come to gloat over his murder, but the crowd would have torn them to pieces.

While in Baltimore, General Townsend established two rules that became the standard for every stop during the 13-day journey to come. No bearers, except the veteran guard, were allowed to handle the president's coffin. Whenever Lincoln's body needed to be removed from the train, loaded, or unloaded from a hearse, or placed upon or removed from a ceremonial platform or catafalque, his personal military guard would handle the coffin.

Each city would furnish a local honor guard to accompany the hearse and to keep order while the public viewed the body, but these men did not lay hands upon the coffin.

Townsend also forbade mourners from getting too close to the coffin, touching the president's body, kissing him, or placing anything, including flowers, relics, or other tokens, in the coffin. Any person who violated these standards would be seized at once and removed.

But nothing untoward occurred in Baltimore. The viewing ended at 2:30 p.m. and Lincoln's bearers closed the coffin and carried it back to the hearse. The orderly scene in Baltimore was a good omen for the long journey ahead, or so they believed at the time.

As the train passed through Pennsylvania, people began to line the tracks and watch it pass. Little towns were filled with people waiting to honor the president and local bands played funeral dirges as the train went by. The old and sick were carried to the stations to see the train and babies were held up high to get a glimpse of it.

Only at the station in York did the train make a stop. The women of the city made an urgent request to lay a wreath of flowers on Lincoln's casket. General Townsend could not allow dozens of emotional mourners to wander around inside the train and hover around the coffin, so he offered a compromise: He would permit a delegation of six women to come aboard and bring the wreath. While a band played a dirge and bells tolled, they approached the funeral car with great ceremony, stepped inside, and laid their large wreath consisting of a circle of roses and, at the center, alternating parallel lines of red and white flowers. The women wept bitterly as they left the train. Soon, at the next stop, their wonderful flowers would be moved aside in favor of new ones.

In Harrisburg, thousands waited all night in the rain for a glimpse of Lincoln the following morning. Violent thunderstorms had descended on the city but despite the rain, the massive crowds still came. Jagged streaks of lightning crossed the sky as church bells rang and cannons thundered. The crowds followed the hearse and its military escort to the House of Representatives at the State Capitol, where a black-draped catafalque was waiting. The procession took so long that the casket was not opened for viewing until late that evening. Thousands passed

The Lincoln Funeral Train in Harrisburg, Pennsylvania

in a double line until the next morning when the funeral train once again prepared to leave.

Before the casket was closed, though, the undertaker was forced to re-chalk Lincoln's face to hide the growing discoloration. Lincoln had become America's first public embalming and it would be some time before the methods of preservation would be perfected. In addition, the body also had to be dusted. The coffin had been opened and closed so many times that the President's face and beard had started to attract dust particles from the air.

It was still raining the next morning, but more than 40,000 people still jammed the streets to watch the procession as the casket was returned to the funeral train. At a few minutes after eleven, the train steamed out of Harrisburg toward Philadelphia, passing through Middletown, Elizabethtown, Mount Joy, Landisville, and Dillersville. As it steamed through the countryside and moved slowly through Lancaster, the men on board saw a huge sign that had been erected by the crowd. It read, "Abraham Lincoln, the Illustrious Martyr of Liberty, The Nation Mourns His Loss. Though Dead, He Still Lives." More than 20,000 people, including Congressman Thaddeus Stevens and Lincoln's predecessor, former president James Buchanan, paid tribute.

The train pushed north through Penningtonville, Parkesburg, Coatesville, Gallagherville, Downington, Oakland, and West Chester. At every depot, and along the railroad tracks between them, people gathered to watch the train pass by.

In Philadelphia, more than 500,000 people were already waiting at Independence Hall when the train arrived on Saturday, April 22. It was

Lincoln's funeral procession made its way through the streets of Philadelphia, but the massive number of people that turned out caused the first crowd control problems of the journey

in Philadelphia that a new aspect was added to the viewing of Lincoln --- violence. For the first time, people were actually hurt in the frantic crush to get into Independence Hall and see the president's body.

The trip into the city had been orderly. Thousands had come out beside the tracks to stand in silence, or kneel, while the train passed. All the shops had closed, and farms stood silent and deserted in Lincoln's honor. For miles before the Philadelphia station, there were no gaps in the crowd, just solid lines. The train arrived at Broad Street station in late afternoon, more than two hours ahead of schedule, but then the careful organization of the city officials began to go to pieces.

It took nearly two hours to get the procession under way and afterward, the city would claim that it offered the most gigantic display of all. Eleven military divisions marched to the inevitable booming of cannons, tolling of bells, firing of guns, roll of muffled drums, and eerie funeral dirges. At the square, when the Old State House was passed, a large transparency was uncovered --- a picture of Lincoln with a background of a huge coffin, spectacularly lighted by gas jets that formed letters that spelled out "He Still Lives." The coffin was carried to the East Wing of Independence Hall, where the Declaration of Independence had been signed. The hall was filled with flowers, emitting what the newspapers called a "delicious perfume." Those accounts failed to describe the practical purpose of the sweet-smelling flowers, but they were there for a reason. Lincoln had been dead for a week and the embalmers were fighting against a ticking clock. They had slowed but they could not stop the decaying of his flesh. The fragrant flowers masked the odor.

The viewing that night was by invitation only and handpicked people had been given cards by the mayor. As these special guests departed during the early morning hours, they passed long lines of the public, who were already forming to be admitted hours later. The exhausted throngs waited all night and by Sunday morning, the entire city was on edge. When pickpockets began to terrorize a portion of the line, it surged into a mob, pressing against the guide ropes. Then the ropes were cut --- by "villains" the newspapers later said --- and bedlam ensued. People who had been almost to the doors were sent back by the police to the end of the nearly three-mile-long double lines to wait for another six or seven hours. The crowd surged out of control and the police fought to keep order. Bonnets were pulled from women's heads and their hair turned loose, dresses were torn away and ripped, all to a chorus of women's screams. As many of the young women fainted, they had to be extricated from the lines and passed over the people's heads. One woman had her arm broken and word got out that two little boys were dead but were finally revived. The closer people got to Lincoln, the more impassioned they became. The police refused to let people stop for even a second to view the body, insisting that they keep moving at all times. Even with these precautions, a number of women tried to climb over the wooden barricade to touch the president or to kiss his face.

It was all finally over early on Monday morning and the casket was returned to the train. It steamed on toward New York, where ceremonies had begun the day before. All of New York, it seemed, had been draped in black, and in the hours before the train's arrival, the streets of the city became impassable. The police and military fought to keep them open, but it was no use.

Thousands of people lined the tracks on the journey into the city. In the early morning darkness of Monday, April 24, the train stopped in Trenton, New Jersey for about half an hour. Trenton was wounded because it was the only state capital on the route where Lincoln was not taken from the train and funeral services held. The people stood and stared as the train pulled into the station and one observer noted that "it did not occur to the male part of the throng that a general lifting of the hat would have been a silent but becoming mark of respect to the dead." Far different, he noted, was the scene at Newark, where every man removed his hat and feelings were so deep that women also removed their bonnets out of respect.

The train arrived in Jersey City a few hours later. Crowds had been gathering there since early morning. Only ladies and their escorts were allowed into the gallery at the depot, where the large clock had been stopped at the precise moment of Lincoln's death. When the train arrived, a German singing group thundered forth with a funeral dirge.

The Lincoln Funeral Train arrived in New York and as the procession made its way along the streets, it was watched by a young boy named Theodore Roosevelt

New York had been building a magnificent hearse, but it would have been risky to ferry it across the Hudson, so the coffin was sensibly transferred to a small hearse and carried across the river. A second ferry took the train's funeral car, with Willie's casket in it, and a third took the big car that carried the official escort that journeyed through to Springfield. In New York, a new engine, a new pilot engine and seven cars would be supplied by the Hudson River Railroad.

New York would be the biggest test of the funeral procession since it had left Washington. The city had the biggest population, the greatest crowds, and the most volatile citizens in the north. New Yorkers had proven that they loved a good riot, most notably during the recent Civil War draft riots. Given the strong Copperhead presence in the city, still loyal to the Confederacy, many believed that Manhattan cried false tears for the fallen president. But mourning Unionists outnumbered Lincoln's enemies on the streets of the city in April 1865.

Lincoln's body was taken to City Hall and more than 600,000 spectators accompanied it while more than 150,000 stood in line for a

The New York City Hall, where Lincoln's body was placed on display for hundreds of thousands of people to view

glimpse of the president. The honor guard had a full-time job on their hands trying to keep people from touching Lincoln and trying to keep women from kissing his face and hands. Although no rioting broke out, as it did in Philadelphia, the police had their hands full with surging crowds, most of whom were beaten back with clubs, and with pickpockets, who freely roamed the area, stealing at will. Only one thing happened to break the boredom of the wait - someone threw a lighted cigar at the black festoon just under a huge banner proclaiming "The Nation Mourns." It burst into flames, but a brave officer climbed up and tore down the mass of burning material and others stamped out the fire on the stone steps.

During the viewing at City Hall, some people tried to do more than touch Lincoln. Some of them wanted to place mementoes in the coffin. Captain Parker Snow, a commander of polar expeditions, presented some relics to the honor guard from Sir John Franklin's ill-fated expedition. They consisted of a tattered leaf from a prayer book, on which the first legible word was "martyr," a piece of fringe, and some portions of a uniform. These relics were found in a boat lying under the head of a human skeleton.

What possible connection did these relics have to Abraham Lincoln? None. They did not belong in the coffin and the officials refused to place them there. Such practices, if tolerated, would have turned Lincoln's coffin into a traveling cabinet of curiosities that would have weighed more than the president's corpse.

That night, after the doors were closed, the embalmer brushed a heavy coating of dust from Lincoln's face, beard, and clothing. He also rearranged his facial features, which had become twisted from exposure.

The coffin was closed at 11:00 a.m. on Tuesday. The final procession back to the train became New York's moment of glory. Peter Relyea, the official undertaker for the city of New York, had been issued a special permit to accompany Lincoln's body to Springfield. For three days, he had been building an elaborate funeral car that would marvel the crowds on the city streets. He had been living and sleeping in the car, trying to get it finished before the procession. Now, just in the nick of time, he led the hearse into the park enclosure in front of City Hall. The hearse, pulled by 16 gray horses, was said to have nearly "paralyzed" all who saw it. Its platform was huge --- 14-feet-long and almost seven-feet-wide --- and on the roof of the canopy was a gold and white Temple of Liberty with a half-masted flag on its crown. Inside of the canopy was white fluted satin that matched the inside trimmings of the coffin and hanging down from it, so that it would hang directly above the casket, was a glittering gilt eagle with its wings spread. It was an amazing work of art and would remain the most elaborate creation on the funeral route.

An hour later, Lincoln was placed aboard the Relyea creation and the procession began to move. Led by a squad of mounted police, who made sure the route was clear, it started off with 100 dragoons with black and white plumes and red, yellow, and blue facings on their uniforms. They were followed by military officers and their staffs and then the magnificent hearse. Behind that were more than 1,100 soldiers, Irishmen in bright green with black rosettes in their lapels, Zouaves with baggy red trousers and black ribbons on their chests, military and government representatives from foreign countries, and eight divisions of civilians. One of them was made up from the trades --- cigar-makers, waiters, cooks, clerks, carpenters, and others --- and there were divisions of medical men, lawyers, members of the press, the Century Club, the Union League, Freemasons, Civic Societies, and finally, nearly 300 African-Americans.

The procession took nearly four hours to pass each point on its route. The streets were jammed with spectators and it was said that window seats could be rented for $50 from those who lived in the apartment buildings along the path. At Chamber Street, a shaggy St. Bernard dog trotted out from the crowd and walked alongside the hearse for a block or so. A whisper spread that the dog and his master had recently paid a visit to Lincoln at the White House and the president had kindly patted the dog on the head. A spurious legend -- or could the dog have known who he trotted next to in the amazing hearse?

All through the afternoon, church bells and fire bells tolled, bands wailed, guns boomed, and people wept for the great and fallen leader. Eventually, the train moved on to Albany, leaving thousands disappointed. Many who did not get a chance to see the president boarded trains and planned to try again in Chicago or in Springfield. The Springfield delegates, who were accompanying the train, realized in horror just how many people could be descending on the small city. One of the delegates hurried home to Springfield to prepare for the worst.

After leaving the city, the train steamed across the countryside toward Albany. It passed scores of small towns along the way, where people gathered to watch it pass. Each of the towns had gone to enormous trouble to build a display, an arch, or to inscribe a huge motto for the train as it passed. At towns where there was no station, there was often a minister and his parishioners, kneeling or singing a hymn. At Yonkers, the people lined up and the men all raised their hats. At Tarryton, a gathering of young women appeared, all dressed in white, save for black sashes, creating an effect both chaste and mournful. At Peekskill, the train stopped as a band played a dirge and guns fired. At Poughkeepsie, the train made another stop. The hilltop there was black with people, guns were fired, and church bells and fire bells clanged with a fury. The train also stopped at Garrison's Landing, opposite the U.S. Military Academy at West Point. The corps of cadets assembled to honor their fallen commander in chief. They passed through the funeral car and saluted. It was now growing dark and as the train continued toward Albany, torches and bonfires illuminated the tracks.

At Hudson, thousands of people gathered to see the train. General Townsend described the scenes as "one of the most weird ever witnessed." Along the Hudson River, people assembled with torches, illuminating the bizarre tableau they had created. Beneath an arch hung with black and white drapery and evergreen wreaths was a scene that represented a coffin resting on a dais. A female figure in white, mourning over the coffin, stood on one side while a soldier and a sailor stood at the other end. While a band of young women dressed in white sang a dirge, two others entered the funeral car, placed flowers on the president's coffin, knelt for a moment of silence, and then quietly withdrew. Townsend noted that the solemnity of the scene was "intensified by the somber lights of the torches, at that dead hour of night."

It was approaching midnight when the train entered Albany. The coffin was carried to the State House and all through the night, the residents of the capital and the neighboring countryside passed by it.

The next day, there was another procession but this time, the 300 people now accompanying the train, except for a portion of the military, went straight to two hotels where the city had arranged them to be lodged. They were worn out both physically and emotionally from the never-ending mourning ceremony and there were still six more funerals ahead of them. Albany had been there first chance to rest on the route so far.

At noon on Wednesday, April 26, Albany's grand parade got under way with a specially built catafalque, marchers, bands, tolling bells, and huge crowds of people. It was a grand event but was not the type of "circus" that Albany crowds had been expecting. Van Amburgh's traveling menagerie was in town and had been planning to offer a parade and celebratory show to entertain the crowds when the assassination occurred. The circus owner, Van Amburgh, quickly proclaimed, "There will be no exhibition given until the president's remains have left the city and the grand parade scheduled for this morning will be postponed until tomorrow." Albany was probably the only one of the funeral cities that had the chance to pick up its spirits so rapidly after being drenched in sorrow.

It was while the funeral train was in Albany that a disquieting incident that had occurred in New York reached the ears of Edwin Stanton. As was the usual, General Townsend had telegraphed Stanton when leaving the city to let him know that all was well. But his telegram did not mention what had taken place while Lincoln's remains were on view at New York's City Hall. When Stanton learned of the incident by reading newspapers later that night, he became enraged and dispatched an angry telegram that threatened to ruin the reputation and military career of the man he had personally chosen to command the funeral train.

Stanton wrote: "I see by the New York papers this evening that a photograph of the corpse of President Lincoln was allowed taken yesterday at New York. I cannot sufficiently express my surprise and disapproval of such an act while the body was in your charge. You will report what officers of the funeral escort were or ought to have been on duty at the time this was done, and immediately relieve them and order them to Washington. You will also direct the provost-marshal to go to the photographer, seize and destroy the plates and any pictures and engravings that may have been made, and consider yourself responsible if the offense is repeated." Stanton ordered Major Eckert at the War Department to make sure that it was sent and hand-delivered to Townsend that very night.

Stanton had assumed, no doubt, that close-up images had been made of Lincoln's face. That was not an unusual custom in the nineteenth century. It was common for mourners, especially the bereaved parents of deceased infants and children, to commission photographers to preserve for eternity the faces of the loved and lost. Many photographers would pose the children in the arms of their parents, as though sleeping and not dead.

But Stanton was likely thinking about the condition of Lincoln's body. By the time he was photographed in New York, he had been dead for nine days. Mortuary science of the era could not preserve his body indefinitely. The undertakers attended to the body aboard the train, but there were limits as to what they could do. Stanton undoubtedly feared that horrific images depicting Lincoln's face in a state of gruesome decay would be distributed to the public.

Stanton's telegram did not reach Townsend until the morning of April 26 and he was stunned by its contents. He knew Stanton well, including his propensity for angry tirades. If Stanton sounded this upset on paper, Townsend could only imagine how furiously he was raging back in Washington. And once Stanton knew the whole story, Townsend feared, the man that Lincoln referred to as his "god of war" would become apoplectic.

It was Townsend himself who had allowed Lincoln's corpse to be photographed. He decided, before others could report the details of what he had done, to confess and accept the consequences. He immediately

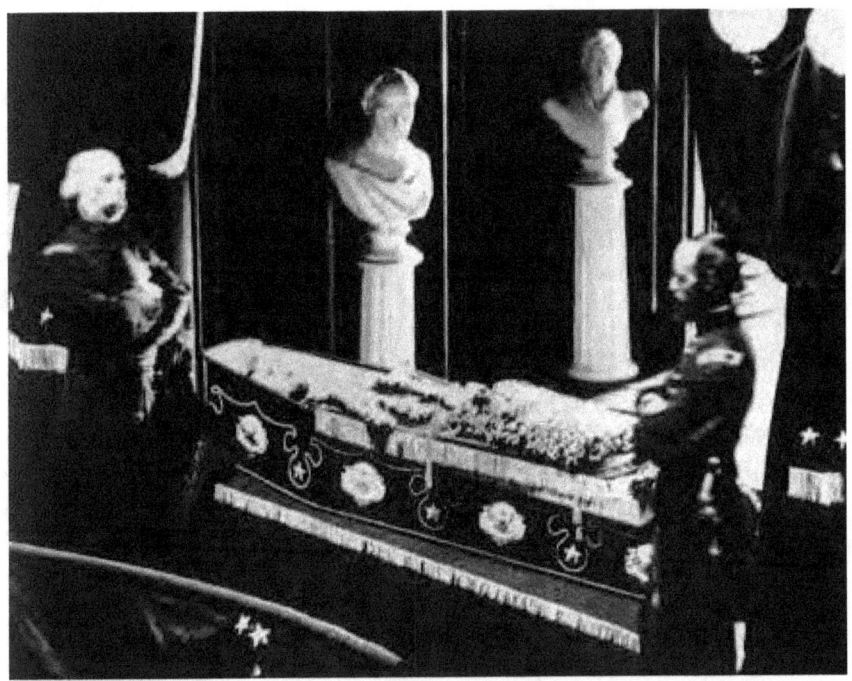

The controversial postmortem photograph that General Townsend allowed to be taken in New York. Edwin Stanton was enraged when he found out about its existence

telegraphed Stanton: "Your dispatch of this date is received. The photograph was taken while I was present, Admiral Davis being the officer immediately in charge, but it would have been my part to stop the proceedings. I regret your disapproval, but it did not strike me as objectionable under the circumstances as it was done. I have telegraphed General Dix your orders about seizing the plates. To whom shall I turn over the special charge given me in order to execute your instructions to relieve the officers responsible, and shall Admiral Davis be relieved? He was not accountable."

When Stanton learned that Townsend had permitted the photograph, he decided not to relieve him of command. The train was on the move, in the middle of a complicated cross-country journey, and no one on the train possessed greater organizational skills than Townsend. He sent him a tempered reply, excusing Admiral Davis from fault and laying the blame with Townsend. He told him that he could

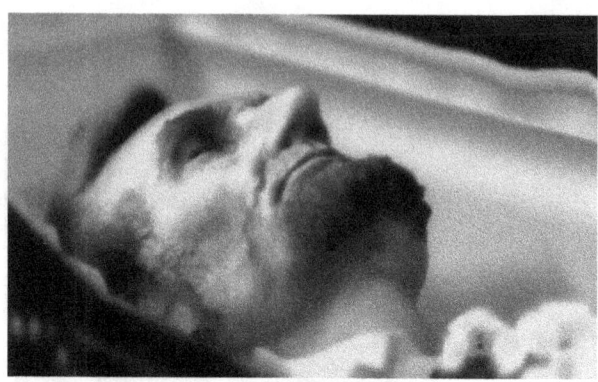

Modern technology allows us a closer look at Lincoln's face than would have been possible from the photo in the 1860s. This is the only known postmortem photograph of Lincoln that was ever taken

not relieve him of command because there was no one to take his place but filled the man with guilt by stating that the taking of photographs had been expressly forbidden by Mrs. Lincoln. Stanton added, "I am apprehensive that her feelings and the feelings of her family will be greatly wounded."

Townsend, offended by the suggestion that he had disobeyed an order from the martyred president's widow, tried to defend himself. He replied, "I was not aware of Mrs. Lincoln's wishes, or the picture would not have been taken with the knowledge of any officers of the escort. It seemed to me the picture would be gratifying, a gratifying view of what thousands saw and thousands could not see."

But Townsend had not admitted to everything. It was bad enough that he had allowed the photographs. It was even worse that he had posed in the pictures while standing next to President Lincoln's body. Stanton might have considered this perceived attempt at personal publicity unforgivable. But Townsend did not see it that way. The remains had been arranged at City Hall at the head of a stairway, where the people could ascend on one side and descend on the other. The body was in an alcove, draped in black, and just at the edge of a rotunda formed of American flags and mourning drapery. The photographer was in a gallery that was 20 feet higher than the body and 40 feet away from it. There was no equipment to make the camera seem closer than it was in those days. It offered a distant view. Townsend stood at one end of the coffin and Admiral Davis stood at the other. No one else was in view. The effect of the picture was that it was showing the scene as a whole, not offering the features of the corpse.

General Townsend was not the only one worried about the situation. The man who had photographed Lincoln, Thomas Gurney, proprietor of one of Manhattan's most prominent studios, T. Gurney & Son, was also concerned. He had taken unprecedented, newsworthy, and commercially viable photographs. No other American president had been photographed in death and no one -- not the famous Mathew Brady nor Alexander Gardner, not any of the photographers along the funeral train route -- had succeeded in photographing the president in his coffin.

Gurney hoped to gain publicity by distributing prints of the photograph to the press as newspaper woodcuts and to reproduce the photo for sale to the public. On April 26, Gurney sent an urgent telegram, not to Stanton, but to a man he thought might be more sympathetic -- Assistant Secretary of War, Charles A. Dana. Gurney also reached out to Henry Ward Beecher, the widely-known clergyman, abolitionist, and author, as well as Henry Raymond, the famous editor of the *New York Times*. He asked them to lobby Stanton and prevent the seizure and destruction of the glass-plate negatives. They agreed to try and Beecher and Raymond both telegraphed the War Department. It earned Gurney a temporary reprieve, of sorts. A telegram from the War Department arrived at Gurney's studio, saving the negatives from destruction for the time being, but only if Gurney surrendered all the glass plates and agreed to abide by Stanton's decision once he determined whether or not to smash them.

Gurney surrendered the glass-plate negatives, plus all the photographs that he had already printed from them. He had no choice. In the aftermath of Lincoln's assassination, emotions in the country were running high. More than 200 people had been shot, stabbed, lynched, or beaten to death for making anti-Lincoln statements or for defending his killer. Stanton had ordered the indiscriminate arrest of more than 100 people, including the owner of Ford's Theater, as suspects in the crime. In Baltimore, a mob stormed into a photography studio based on rumors that the proprietor was selling images of the infamous John Wilkes Booth.

During this turbulent time, Gurney had no legal avenue to pursue. If Gurney had attempted to sue to protect his photographs, no court would have recognized his First Amendment right to protect and publish the images. If he failed to surrender them voluntarily, the War Department would have raided his studio and seized them. He complied. The next day, an army general notified Stanton from New York that the offending images were in government custody.

Stanton's suppression of the photographs did not succeed entirely. He had wanted to prevent Gurney's images from surfacing in any form, but the photographer had already gotten the prints into the hands of a few artists. At least two newspapers printed front-page interpretations of the scene and Currier & Ives published a fine engraving based partly on Gurney's work. But Gurney's negatives were never seen again. Perhaps Edwin Stanton had them brought to his office in Washington and, after viewing them, smashed them into pieces. Perhaps he put them away in some secret place, where, to this day, they languish in some dusty and forgotten War Department file box, never to be seen again.

However, Stanton could not resist preserving one image of Lincoln's corpse for himself. Almost a century after the president's death and burial, a sole surviving photographic print made from one of Gurney's negatives was discovered by a student in an old archive. It was traced back to Stanton's personal files. Perhaps he saved it for history. Or perhaps he never intended for it to be seen and to remain his private memento -- a vivid reminder of the spring of 1865.

On Wednesday afternoon, the train left Albany and steamed east through Amsterdam, Fonda, Palatine Bridge, Rome, Green Corners, Verona, Oneida, and Kirksville. Late in the evening, the train made a short stop at Syracuse, where veteran soldiers paid honors, a choir sang hymns, and a little girl handed a small bouquet to a congressman on the train. A note attached to the flowers read: "The last tribute from Mary Virginia Raynor, a little girl of three years of age."

In Rochester, at 3:20 a.m. on Thursday, a collection of military units stood in a line on the north side of the station, and on the south side stood the mayor, 25 members of the common council of Rochester, and former president Millard Fillmore, who got on board and rode to the next stop, which was Buffalo.

The city of Buffalo holds an unusual place in the history of the funeral train. It was the only city on the list that was likely disappointed by the arrival of the president's body. A short time earlier, on the day of the Washington funeral, Buffalo's citizens, grieving at the news of the assassination, were not content to simply hold church services. Instead, the people put on their own mock funeral, just as though the coffin and body had been there. They had built a magnificent catafalque, had a huge procession, offered prayers and eulogies and had gone through the motions as if the real thing were taking place. Then when they got the news that their city had been chosen to hold a funeral on the procession route, there was, along with a feeling of pride, a bit of a letdown, as well. Buffalo had exhausted its first frenzied extravagance during the mock ceremony, although citizens assured themselves that having the real thing would be many times better. Somehow, though, when the time came, it wasn't.

Massive crowds filled the streets in Buffalo, but the arrival of the train was a bit of a letdown since the city had already held a "mock funeral" for Lincoln before his body ever arrived

They used the same magnificent hearse car with its six white horses, draped in black and the well-attended viewing was held in St. James Hall, with the coffin up-tilted and brilliantly lit. Thousands filed past the coffin, but between the dirges, the silence was oppressive and the "utter decorum" and "remarkable order" were somehow not as much of a tribute as the wild straining to get near the coffin or to touch the President's hand, as had occurred in other cities.

Under a simple canopy of drooping black crepe, the coffin was placed on a dais while the Buffalo St. Cecelia Society, a musical group, sang "Rest, Spirit, Rest." Women from the Unitarian Church placed an anchor of white camellias at the foot of the coffin. For more than 10 hours, thousands of people, including many from Canada who crossed the border for the occasion, viewed the remains.

At some point, while crowds were passing by the coffin, news reached Buffalo by telegraph that electrified General Townsend and the mourners in line: John Wilkes Booth had been killed in Virginia.

The coffin was closed that evening and Lincoln's body was returned to the train. It steamed on through New York and into the darkness of the night. Townsend knew that the train had begun to leave behind waves of emotion that swelled by the hour. He later wrote, "As the president's remains went farther westward, where the people more especially claimed him as their own, the intensity of feeling seemed, if possible, to grow deeper. The night journey of the 27th and 28th was all through torches, bonfires, mourning drapery, mottoes, and solemn music."

The train pushed on through North Hamburg, Lakeview, Angola, and Silver Creek. Just after midnight, the train passed through Dunkirk on Lake Erie. There, 36 young women, representing the states of the Union, appeared on the railway platform. They were dressed in white, and each wore a broad, black scarf on her shoulder and held an American flag in her right hand. The tableau was so irresistible that when officials in other cities read about it in the newspapers, they copied the idea for their local tributes.

The train later passed through Brocton and then stopped in Westfield, where, during Lincoln's inaugural journey, he had visited with Grace Bedell, a little girl who had written him a letter during the 1860 campaign that encouraged him to grow a beard. She told him that it would make him more appealing to women, who would then, Grace promised, make their husbands and brothers vote for him. Lincoln grew the beard and won the election. Now, four years later, a delegation of five women, led by a woman whose husband had been killed the previous year during Grant's futile assault at Cold Harbor, came aboard bearing a wreath of flowers and a cross. Sobbing, they approached Lincoln's closed casket and were allowed to touch it. They "considered it a rare privilege to kiss the coffin." They knelt and each in turn kissed the coffin. Kissing the coffin, with its solid barrier of wood and lead, was a desperately futile gesture but it never failed to move those who watched the action to tears.

The train crossed the Ohio state line and passed through Kingsville, Ashtabula, Geneva, Madison, Perry, Painesville, and Wickcliffe, where Governor John Brough received the funeral party.

General Joseph Hooker, now commanding the Northern Department of Ohio, also boarded the train there. Although Lincoln had once given command of the Army of the Potomac to the boastful general, Hooker failed him several times. After the disaster at Chancellorsville in May 1863, Lincoln fired him, but Hooker never lost his personal affection for the president. When the funeral train crossed the Ohio line into Indiana, Hooker did not disembark as he'd originally planned. He stayed with Lincoln all the way to Springfield.

Vast crowds stood on the hills outside of Cleveland as the train passed beneath prepared arches that bore sad inscriptions. Of all the funerals held, Cleveland's was the strangest so far. The funeral was both a solemn wake and a theatrical pageant of flowers, with the city showing its appreciation for the president by introducing an Oriental note to the proceedings. In the city park, a huge Chinese pagoda was erected for Lincoln's coffin to be displayed on for what turned out to be more than 100,000 mourners.

Thirty-six cannons fired a national salute to the president. At that moment, noted the reporters who looked out of the window of the car, a bizarre scene was taking place -- perhaps the strangest of the journey so far. A woman, identified in the press only as "Miss Fields of Wilson Street," had erected an arch of evergreens near the tracks. As the train passed, Miss Fields, wearing a costume, stood under the arch, and struck poses as the Goddess of Liberty in mourning.

The train arrived on the outskirts of Cleveland in the early hours of Friday, just one week after leaving Washington. As it moved slowly into the city, officials on board the train saw crowds of people on the hillsides and high up, a young girl draped in a flag under an archway that read "Abraham Lincoln." People had flocked to the city from all over northern Ohio, western Pennsylvania, and eastern Michigan and boatloads of them had arrived by water from Detroit. All the ladies in attendance had been warned to leave the hoops for their skirts at home --- the breakage of such attire by the throng, officials said, would be swift and total. With the thousands in attendance however, standing in the pouring rain, there was not a hint of disorder.

Legions of marchers and mourners descended on the city park, with its Chinese Pagoda that had been built for the president. The wooden structure was eccentric, to say the least. It was an amazing confection of wood, canvas, silk, cloth, festoons, rosettes, golden eagles bearing the national shield at each end, and "immense plumes of black crepe." As with all the other venues along the journey, the interior was stuffed with flowers. Evergreens covered the walls, and thick matting carpeted the floor to deaden into silence the sound of all footsteps. Over the roof, stretched between two flagpoles, was a motto from Horace: *Extinctus amabitur idem*, which mean "Dead he will be loved all the same."

The Lincoln Funeral in Cleveland

The embalmer opened the coffin and judged the body ready for viewing. The journey was taking its toll on the corpse. Lincoln's face turned darker by the day and the embalmer tried to conceal this with a flesh application of chalk-white potions.

All through the day and night, people came, thousands upon thousands of them, before the gates to the park were closed at 10:00 p.m. An hour later, the coffin was carried by hearse back to the train.

The rain continued to fall as the train traveled from Cleveland to the Ohio capital of Columbus. But the foul weather did not keep people from coming to watch the train pass along the route. Bonfires and torches were lit, buildings were draped in mourning, bells tolled, flags flew at half-mast, and the sorrowful inhabitants stood in groups, rain and tears mixing to stream down their faces, as the cortege moved slowly by.

The Lincoln Funeral Service in Columbus, Ohio

Columbus also offered a funeral of flowers. People had roses in their hands, which they tossed under the wheels of the hearse as it passed and invalid soldiers from the Soldier's Hospital had literally covered the street near the hospital for several hundred yards with lilac blossoms.

The Columbus hearse was a somber vehicle, drawn by six white horses, but it did have one aspect to it that would have amused Lincoln himself. On one side of the dais, in silver block letters, was the name "Lincoln." The President tried, whenever possible, to avoid the obvious. When, in the spring of 1864, he had been asked to sign a letter presenting a sword to General Dix, Lincoln signed his name and then was asked to add "President of the United States." His answer, putting down his pen, was, "Well, I don't think I'll say, 'this is a horse'." When the coffin was placed on a dais at the State Capitol building, the platform was noticed to have been also fitted with the same helpful identification. Lincoln would have gotten a chuckle out of this bit of tragic absurdity.

The Columbus procession moved through drapes and flowers and mottos from the city to the sounds of guns firing, bells ringing, and the muffled beat of drums. The hook and ladder car of the fire department carried 42 young ladies on it, all singing hymns. The coffin was placed on the dais, which had no canopy and no flags. However, instead of black velvet, the surface of it was a carpet of moss and tender green leaves, which let off a fragrant aroma as the casket sank into it. The people gathered in the rotunda watched in awe as the undertaker unscrewed the coffin lid, made a slight adjustment to the position of the body, and then made a motion that the viewing could begin. People began to stream by, and their passing was in complete silence. A carpet had been laid in the hall so that the shuffling of feet and the click of shoe leather would not be heard. For the eighth time, thousands of Americans said goodbye to their fallen president.

In the press accounts of the funeral train, little mention was made of Willie Lincoln. His coffin was never unloaded from the train. He did not ride in the hearse with his father in any of the funeral processions. His closed casket -- he had been dead for three years -- did not lie next to his father's casket at the public viewings.

But in Columbus, Willie was not forgotten. General Townsend was the recipient of the gesture: "While at Columbus, I received a note from a lady, wife of one of the principal citizens, accompanying a little cross made of wild violets. The note said that the writer's little girls had gone to the woods in the early morning and gathered the flowers with which they had wrought the cross. They desired that it might be laid on little Willie's coffin, 'they felt so sorry for him.'"

From Columbus, the train steamed on toward Indiana, crossing the state line in the middle of the night. More scenes appeared along the line while in Ohio. At Woodstock, there were 500 citizens waiting beside the tracks and a contingent of young women was allowed to board the train and lay flowers in the funeral car. At Urbana, more than 3,000 people surrounded a huge, floral cross as the train steamed on toward Indiana. At Richmond, Indiana, the first town across the border, the church bells of the town rang for an hour as the train arrived and over 15,000 people greeted the funeral with pantomimes, scenes, and stage effects that must have looked ghastly and somewhat horrifying to the party looking out from the railroad car windows. One such display featured a beautiful young woman who was illuminated by red, white, and blue lights over a mock coffin, creating one of the most eerie displays on the funeral train's journey.

The train reached Indianapolis near midnight, arriving during a torrential rainstorm. At first, it was hoped that if the rain stopped, the procession could go on during the afternoon. However, the rain continued to fall, increasing in power from minute to minute, until the black decorations on every house sagged desperately and black dye formed dark streaks on the front of stone buildings. Reluctantly, the huge Indianapolis procession had to be canceled and the time devoted to it was set aside for viewing instead.

All the way from the train depot to the State House, soldiers were lined up at attention, forming two long lines of blue uniforms and drawn swords. The hearse was pulled by eight white horses, six of which had pulled Lincoln as the president-elect a few years before. They took the coffin into State House square and under a large arch to which portraits of Lincoln, Indiana Governor Oliver Perry Morton, General Grant, General Sherman, and Admiral Farragut had been affixed. On the points of it were busts of George Washington, Daniel Webster, Henry Clay, and Lincoln. The busts were all crowned with laurel wreaths.

The first to view Lincoln were 500 Sunday School scholars and the last were the Colored Masons and hundreds of African-American citizens who each carried a copy of the Emancipation Proclamation. The casket lay under a black velvet canopy, which was sprinkled with golden stars. The mourners all saw a coffin that was heaped with flowered crosses and wreaths.

It had been during this epic cross-country journey that an American tradition was created. Prior to Lincoln's funeral, it was not customary to send flowers to funerals. With the death of a beloved president, many people searched their hearts about the best way to express their sympathy and thousands of them decided upon flowers. Although with the best of intentions, the sheer numbers of flowers sent to Lincoln were greatly overdone, emptying the contents of each city's hothouses. The colors ran heavily to red, white, and blue, which would have pleased a president who stated that he felt emotional each time he looked at the flag. In Springfield, there would be a tremendous red heart, covered with thousands of red roses, that would travel with the coffin all the way to the tomb.

When the viewing was completed, the coffin was escorted back to the train with Governor Morton and most of the population of Indianapolis following behind. The governor had greeted and entertained Lincoln when he was traveling to Washington as the president-elect and he watched his casket leave the state with great sorrow.

With Indianapolis behind, the train steamed on toward Illinois. There was a massive funeral planned in Chicago and then, it would go on to Lincoln's hometown in Springfield.

An impromptu service was held at Michigan City, Indiana, before the train continued to Chicago

But due to an unexpected delay, there was to be one more funeral, an impromptu service at the depot in Michigan City, Indiana. The funeral train was supposed to travel straight through and arrive in Chicago during the late morning hours of Monday, May 1. But it was forced to wait for one hour in Michigan City for a committee of more than 100 important Chicagoans to arrive. They were coming out to escort the train into the city. The residents of Michigan City made the most of the unexpected stop, especially since the rain of the past few days had cleared to brilliant sunshine. The occupants of the train were greeted by the depot arch of evergreens and roses, decorated with black ribbons and "tasteful" portraits of Lincoln.

The 300 weary mourners that traveled with the funeral were taken off the train for a large breakfast in the station. After that, the rule was broken about not opening the coffin except in the cities that were putting on funerals. The townspeople were allowed to pass through the car and view Lincoln and then a small funeral service was held with young women singing hymns.

Abraham Lincoln had always been among the first to alter procedures and break rules on the spur of the moment for something better. His office hours were always flexible, and he often received people at all hours of the day and night. He was the bane of all who

The Lincoln Funeral Car in Chicago

tried to protect his time from the people. The people wanted so little, he often said, and there was so little that he could give -- he must see them. Because of this, the Michigan City meeting with the people would have made Lincoln happy.

A short time later, Lincoln was almost home. As the train steamed into Chicago, he was finally entering the greatest city of his home state, which had been a prairie mudhole when he first settled in Illinois and now was a rich and crowded city of more than 300,000 souls. Although a few years away from the Great Fire that would change the city forever, Chicago was already claiming its place as one of the greatest cities in America. Lincoln had many ties with Chicago. He had spent a lot of time there pleading cases as a lawyer and it was in Chicago that his presidential nomination was gained. And it was in Chicago that, just before the famed Lincoln-Douglas debates began in 1858, Lincoln and Stephen Douglas spoke to large audiences on successive July nights, gaining the attention of newspapers and readers across the country.

It was to this magnificent city that Lincoln's body came on Monday, May 1, 1865. It had traveled more than 1,500 miles to reach this point and the hearts of the people who awaited him in Chicago were heavy.

The funeral train did not go the entire distance on the Illinois Central tracks to the Union Depot but stopped on a trestle that carried the line out in the lake some distance from the shore. The train arrived in silence, save for the ringing of its bell. A temporary platform had been built, with steps leading down to the ground, and from there, a Veteran Guard carried the coffin the short distance up the street to where a platform was waiting beneath a dramatic Gothic, three-section arch. The city had employed three distinguished architects and had spent more than $15,000 to create the arch, design the hearse, and build the decorations for the Court House.

Thirty-six young women walked beside the platform that carried the president and they showered flower petals in all directions. The streets were packed with over 100,000 people as excursion trains had been coming into the city for more than 24 hours, carrying curiosity-seekers from the east. Thousands lined up at the courthouse in the rain and mud to see Lincoln. Exhausted soldiers and police officers recalled that the lines moved less than one foot per hour on Monday and Tuesday. More trains arrived, bringing more people to add to the chaos as at least 125,000 lined up to view the casket. Ambulances came and went, carrying injured onlookers and women who fainted from grief and exhaustion. At one point, a section of wooden sidewalk gave away and plunged hundreds into the mud and water beneath it.

The route of the funeral procession ran through what was the most elegant section of town. It passed down Michigan Avenue first, then along Lake Street, then along Clark to Court House Square, avoiding the world's largest stockyards, the McCormick Reaper Works, and the flour mills. On each side of the hearse walked six pallbearers, each of them old friends of Lincoln. Marching second on the left-hand side was "Long John" Wentworth, the mayor of the city. Standing six feet, six inches in height, he had started off in Congress as a Democrat but later became a Republican and a staunch supporter of Lincoln. When Wentworth was elected the mayor of Chicago in 1857, he made cleaning out crime and corruption his top priority. The story went that the rough and tumble candidate once made a one-sentence campaign speech from the front steps of the Court House --- "You damn fools, you can either vote for me or go to hell."

The procession in Chicago was much as it had been in other cities. There was a legion of clergy with white crosses adorning their black armbands and a division of Zouaves in baggy red pants. There was also a group of captured Confederate soldiers who had taken the oath and now belonged to the Union Army. They were followed by a troop of more than 10,000 schoolchildren, walking with saddened faces and wearing black ribbons in their hair, along with sashes, armbands, and badges. In the procession were also immigrants from Germany, France, Ireland, and Eastern Europe. They were butchers, bricklayers, tailors, and carpenters, all carrying banners with clumsily worded but unmistakably heartfelt messages about the president. The parade was followed up with a humble, yet unwanted, procession of "colored citizens."

The President's funeral service in Chicago

When the hearse finally arrived at the city's Court House, the great bell in the tower began to ring so loudly that it could be heard in the farthest reaches of Chicago. It was not until early evening that the doors were opened to the public and the viewing went on all night long and all through the following day. It was believed that more than 7,000 people per hour passed by the coffin for a quick viewing of the president.

The light in the Court House was kept purposely dim but there was a general feeling that the discoloration that had been present under Lincoln's eye from the bullet wound was starting to spread over his entire face. The continual application of white chalk was no longer able to hide the dark stains. It had been in New York that the blackness had really started to distress the mourners, but now, the body was starting to look even worse. Lincoln had started to shrivel, making it appear as though his coffin -- once considered too small -- was several sizes too big for him. To many, his cheeks seemed hollow and his face much more gaunt than it had been in life. The reporters had been positive that after New York, there would be no more open casket viewings, but constant care and powdering had managed to keep the body in a decent condition. Even so, the undertaker was glad that Chicago was nearly the last stop on the route.

Late Tuesday evening, the great procession re-formed and by the light of 10,000 torches, the eight black horses drew the hearse with Lincoln's coffin on it back to the railroad depot. The train finally began the last leg of its journey on that night, leaving Chicago and passing under arches which were illuminated with bonfires and decorated with sentiments like "Coming Home," "Bear Him Home Tenderly," and "Home is the Martyr."

As the train passed out of Chicago, the excitement on board increased. This was the last night of travel. In the morning, the funeral train would reach its destination and the journey would come to an end. Lincoln was in his home state now and the grief of the people huddled around fires along the tracks reached a fever pitch. The passengers on the train saw more signs that they passed in the darkness. "Illinois clasps to her bosom her slain but glorified son, Come home," read a sign posted on a house in Lockport. "Go to thy rest," said a sign atop a large arch in Bloomington.

The sun came up on the funeral train as it reached Atlanta, Illinois, and then steamed on towards the south. Emotions ran high aboard the train as it steamed into Lincoln, a town that had been named for the president when he was still a young lawyer. In 1853, Lincoln had been called upon to draft the town's incorporation papers and the founders decided to name the place in his honor. Lincoln responded to the suggestion with his usual humility. "I think you are making a mistake," he said. "I never knew of anything named Lincoln that ever amounted to much." Lincoln then presided over the town's dedication and on April 27, the official story has it that he poured out juice from a watermelon to christen the ground, but other stories say that he spit out a mouthful of seeds as a christening instead. Knowing Lincoln's sense of humor, the latter is probably correct.

During the night of May 2 and during the early morning hours of May 3, the residents of Springfield were restless. They had anticipated Lincoln's homecoming since they had heard the news of his death. After the initial battles with Mary Lincoln about her husband's burial site, it was not clear that Lincoln would return to Springfield at all. But once the citizens knew that Springfield would be his final resting place, they began frenzied preparations.

They had finished hanging the decorations and painting the signs. Crepe and bunting blackened the town. The townspeople had waited 20 days since Lincoln's death and 13 days since the train had left Washington. Beginning on May 3, Springfield would show the nation that no town loved Abraham Lincoln as much as they did.

Springfield would be the final stop in the "carnival of death."

The train steamed into Springfield at mid-morning and was greeted by a mass of people at the station and on the surrounding rooftops. They met the train in silence. Only the sound of weeping could be heard. It seemed the entire city of Springfield had been draped in black but two of the most important buildings to be decorated with mourning weeds were the old State House in the center of the town square, where the body would be placed for public viewing, and the home that Lincoln had owned and lived in for nearly 16 years.

The Lincoln Home draped in black

The Tilton family now lived in the house. Lucien A. Tilton was the president of the Great Western Railway and over the four years of their occupancy, had been kept busy by an estimated 65,000 people who had visited the home and had asked to tour it. Mrs. Tilton was rather apprehensive about what might happen during the Lincoln funeral, but she was a kind-hearted person and had already resolved herself to the fact that she was going to allow people to take grass from the yard, flowers from her garden, or leaves from the trees. She had no idea what was coming --- by the end of the funeral services, her lawn and gardens had been stripped, paint had been scraped from her house, and bricks had been carried away from her retaining wall as souvenirs. She had to request federal soldiers to guard the house against further damage.

The Illinois State Capitol Building, where Lincoln's body lay in state before the final funeral services

The rotunda of the State House had been draped in black cloth and the second floor House of Representatives, where Lincoln was to lie in state, had been renovated with the speaker's podium being removed to allow more people to pass through it. The columns inside had been draped with black cloth and banners and signs decorated the interior. At the center of the room, a catafalque had been built to hold Lincoln's coffin. The catafalque was one of the most amazing of the entire funeral route. Its canopy was "Egyptian" in design with columns and "half-Egyptian" suns depicted between the columns. It was 24-feet-high and more than 10-feet-long. The top was made from black broadcloth and at the tops of the columns were black plumes with white centers, hiding large eagles. The inside roof of the canopy was blue, spangled with silver stars.

It was at the State House where Lincoln had served as a legislator, given his famous "House Divided" speech and, in another part of the building, set up an office after his election as president. Springfield was not a great American city and its officials knew that they could not hope to rival the pageantry displayed in Washington, Philadelphia, New York, or Chicago. Springfield couldn't match the impressive crowds or financial resources marshaled by the major cities. Indeed, the president's hometown had to borrow a hearse from St. Louis. However, what the Illinois state capital could not offer in splendor, it vowed to outdo every other city in the nation when it came to their emotion over the loss of their native son.

Few in Springfield were disappointed that Mary Lincoln was not on the train, even if it meant none of the living Lincolns had made the trip from Washington. This morning, for the first time since the funeral train left Washington, the honor guard also removed Willie's coffin from the presidential car.

On the morning of May 3, the public viewing was scheduled to begin, and thousands of people began to gather outside of the State House. Long before the imposing procession arrived from the station, huge, motionless lines began to form at the north gate. Time ticked by and soon, people began to grow restless --- but there was an unavoidable delay inside.

When the undertakers had opened the coffin upstairs, even these hardened professionals were shocked. Thomas Lynch was a courtesy undertaker for the occasion, and he had been invited to assist Dr. Charles D. Brown, Lincoln's embalmer. The doors of the room were locked and Dr. Brown, in great distress, informed the other man that he had no idea how to remedy the condition of Lincoln's face - it had turned totally black.

Lynch later wrote, "I asked to have the body turned over to me and the other undertaker readily consented. Making my way with difficulty through the crowds which thronged the corridors of the State House, I called at a neighboring drugstore and procured a rouge chalk and amber, with such brushes as I needed, and returned to the room. I at once set about coloring the President's features, placing the materials on very thick so as to completely hide the discoloration of his skin. In half an hour, I had finished my task and the doors were thrown open to the public."

The crowds were admitted, and they walked upstairs to the House of Representatives, where they were sorted out by guards and were sent in groups past Lincoln's casket. Everyone was afforded a few moments to look inside and then they were ushered out through the exit and down the stairs. Before they left, they were asked to make a donation to the Lincoln Monument fund. Very few of those who filed past the coffin shed any tears. They were too shocked by what they saw. But outside on the street, they broke down and wept.

Over the next 24 hours, thousands streamed past the coffin, but these were not the hysterical crowds of New York and Chicago, these were the folks that Lincoln had known and loved in life. They were the people he talked to in the street, laughed with, ate with, and the people he had missed while living in Washington. They were now the people who wept in the streets of the city that he had called home.

On the morning of May 4, the last service was held in Springfield. Robert Lincoln had arrived. His mother and Tad remained behind in Washington. She was still refusing to leave her room -- and the White House. Andrew Johnson, Lincoln's successor, was unable to take up residence there.

General Hooker led Lincoln's riderless horse, "Old Bob" in the final funeral procession

Shortly before the service, Dr. Charles Brown worked to make Lincoln presentable for one last occasion, dressing him in a clean collar and shirt and applying more powder to his face. He finished just before the procession formed outside. The procession included Robert Lincoln, who rode in a buggy with members of the Todd family; John Hanks, one of Lincoln's only remaining blood relatives; elderly Sarah Lincoln; Thomas Pendel, Lincoln's door man from the White House, and a representative of the household servants; and Billy, Lincoln's barber and friend.

The final parade was presided over by General Joseph Hooker and he led "Old Bob," the tired and rider-less old horse that Lincoln had ridden the law circuit on. The parade, like the others before it, was long and marked with music, banners, and signs. The journey was to end two miles away at quiet Oak Ridge Cemetery, traveling over what were then rough, country roads.

The scene at Oak Ridge Cemetery when the last service was held and Lincoln was temporarily laid to rest next to his two sons in the receiving vault

From time to time, bands broke out in dirges, including four newly composed "Lincoln Funeral Marches." When the music was silent, all that could be heard was the unbroken and ominous roll of drums. Finally, the procession wound under the evergreen arch at the cemetery's entrance, down through the little valley between two ridges, along the small stream and to the receiving tomb that was half-embedded in the hillside. It stood with its iron gates and heavy new vault doors open to receive the president. With no delay, the coffin was carried from the hearse and placed on the marble slab inside of the vault. As soon as the hearse and horses moved away and let the people come close, it could be seen that there were two coffins on the slab. The small casket of Willie Lincoln had been brought to the vault first and was waiting for his father's casket to arrive.

People were standing and sitting behind the tomb on the hillside and along the valley in front of it, with the brook, swollen by the spring rains, dividing the audience. Robert Lincoln stood grimly on one side of the tomb and Ward Hill Lamon, stood nearby. Lamon had stayed close to the president's body all the way west, skipping meals and acting as if he were still protecting his old friend from danger. He alternated between helpless weeping and helpless rage over the fact that he had not been present that night at Ford's Theater. On this day in May 1865, Lamon cried unashamedly at the fate of Abraham Lincoln.

As the service began, Reverend A.C. Hubbard began to read Lincoln's words from his second inaugural address. As it drew to a close, Bishop Matthew Simpson of the Methodist Church rose to give his funeral oration. The Bishop's voice was shrill and harsh, and people found it unpleasant, but the sound was forgotten when they listened to the words that he spoke of their friend and fallen leader. He spoke so eloquently that people applauded parts of the sermon. When he was finished, a hymn was sung and then Dr. Gurley, who had officiated at the funeral in Washington, delivered the benediction. A final hymn was sung, the words printed on black-edged cards that were distributed throughout the audience, and then the gates to the tomb were closed and locked. The key to the tomb was handed to Robert Lincoln, who passed it to his cousin, John Todd Stuart, who would become the guardian of the president's body for many years to come.

When the lock turned in the door of the president's tomb, the seemingly endless days of travel and the grand spectacles were finally over. Lincoln was laid to rest in Oak Ridge Cemetery in the holding crypt while his tomb and monument were constructed.

Carl Sandburg wrote about those last moments at the crypt better than any witness who was present that day. He wrote:

> Evergreen carpeted the stone floor of the vault. On the coffin set in a receptacle of black walnut they arranged flowers carefully and precisely, they poured flowers as symbols, the lavished heaps of fresh flowers as though there could never be enough to tell either their hearts or his.
>
> And the night came with great quiet.
> And there was rest.
> The prairie years, the war years, were over.

The 20-day "carnival of death" transformed Abraham Lincoln from a man to a legend. On the day he was assassinated, he was not universally loved -- even in the north. His traveling corpse became a touchstone that offered relief from the pain that the American people had been suffering from during the four bloody years of the war. They mourned for the president and yet, the outpouring of sorrow was greater than for just one man. They mourned for every husband, father, son, and brother who died during the war. The frenzied death carnival for Abraham Lincoln was a glorious farewell to the president and to the hundreds of thousands of men of the Union who, like Lincoln, had perished for cause and country.

But Abraham Lincoln would not rest in peace for many years to come. No one knew it at the time, but the trip across the country from Washington to Springfield was just the beginning of travel for President Lincoln's remains.

The Phantom Funeral Train

The Lincoln Funeral Train, which traveled across the country in the spring of 1865, was an unprecedented event in American history. Millions had seen the fallen president's face, had attended services, or had simply stood and watched as the train passed by. It is no wonder that the Lincoln Funeral Train has become a great American legend --- or that many eerie tales have been attached to its passing.

For well over a century-and-a-half now, the phantom of the Funeral Train has been reported making its eerie run along the tracks from Washington to Springfield. Countless people have reported seeing the eerie train as it rolls along the tracks and sometimes, hearing its keening whistle as it echoes in the night.

The first sightings of the train were in New York but soon spread westward into Ohio, Indiana, and Illinois. One of the earlier reports of the ghost train appeared in New York's *Albany Evening Times* on March 23, 1872. The title of the article was "Waiting for the Train: Interviews with the Night Watchman - Story of Phantom Cars." The first part of the article talks about the mundane work of the night watchman - and then things take a bit of a macabre turn:

There is a supernatural side to this kind of work, which is as wild as its excitement to the superstitious is intense. Said the leader," I believe in spirits and ghosts. I know such things exist, and if you will come up in April I will convince you."

He then told of a phantom train that every year comes up the road, with the body of Abraham Lincoln. Regularly in the month of April, about midnight, the air on the tracks becomes very keen and cutting. On either side of the tracks it is warm and still. Every watchman when he feels the air, slips off the track and sits down to watch.

Soon after, the pilot engine with long black streams, and a band with black instruments playing dirges, and grinning skeletons sitting all about, will pass noiselessly, and the air grows very black. If it is moonlight, clouds always come over the moon, and the music seems to linger as if frozen with horror.

A few moments after the phantom train glides by. Flags and streamers hang about. The track ahead seems covered with a black carpet, and the wheels are draped with the same. The coffin of the murdered Lincoln is seen lying on the center of a car, and all about it, and on the train behind are vast numbers of blue coated men, some with coffins on their backs, others leaning upon them. It seems that all the vast armies of men who died during the war are escorting the phantom train of the president.

The wind, if blowing, dies away at once, and over all the air a solemn hush, almost stifling, prevails. If a train were passing, its noise would be drowned in this silence, and the phantom train would rise over it.

Clocks and watches always stop, and when look at are found to be from five to eight minutes behind. Everywhere on this road about the 20th of April the time of watches and trains is found suddenly behind. This, said the leading watchman, was from the passage of the phantom train.

The story of the Phantom Train passed into local and regional lore in many locations along the route of the original Lincoln Funeral route. Many of the stories are still told, even in areas where the railroads have since faded into oblivion, disuse, and abandonment. Legends still tell of

a phantom train that appears in late April or early Mary, steaming along tracks that no longer exist.

Another newspaper story appeared on September 6, 1879. It was printed in Kansas in the *Wichita Herald*, but it was an interview with a former nightwatchman who had worked for the Hudson River Railroad in New York.

This is his eyewitness account:

"I have seen the Phantom Train," the old man said, in a tone such as he might have used had someone denied the fact; "I have seen the Phantom Train more than once."

Impressed by the earnest manner of the old man, and influenced no doubt by natural curiosity to hear a ghost story in which a train played the leading part, the writer requested the old man to recite his ghost-like experiences. He complied without delay and began:

"I'm out of service now, but ten years ago, and for many a year before that, I was a switchman on the Hudson River Railroad. I'm retired now but through no fault of my own. It was in April 1865, that President Lincoln's body was brought over our road. I did not see the train, and as I was no great reader of newspapers, I saw no description of it. I want you to remember this. Just one year after the funeral train passed over the road, I saw its ghost. I was at my post waiting for the midnight express, which was due about 12:30 in the morning. I had read the assassination and knew that President Lincoln's body was sent West, but I was sick a-bed when the train passed my station and didn't see it.

"It was the night of April 24, 1866, as far as I can remember, that I first saw it. It was a phantom train. I was at my switch station and had a good while to wait before the next regular train was due I was about to retire into my little house when I heard a sullen, rumbling sound that gave me warning of the approach of a train. We expected a freight train that night, which was to leave half a dozen cars on the side track, and the noise I heard seemed to me to come from that train. Knowing that there were no regular trains on the road at that hour, except freights (the midnight express had passed before I heard the Phantom Train), I fixed the track accordingly. The switch was so set that the train could run upon it and detach such cars as was designed to leave.

"While I arranged the first switch the rumbling in the distance became louder and louder, and I knew that the train was not far away. I had posted myself at the upper end of the siding in order to make no more delay than was absolutely necessary. Just as I had completed my arrangements, I heard a sullen roar made up of a thousand different noises blended together. Looking down the road I saw a headlight whose power and intensity I had never seen equaled in my experience of thirty years. There was a chill about the air that I couldn't understand.

"I saw rushing along the main track with reckless speed a locomotive draped from one end to the other in crape, and carrying at least a dozen little flags, also shrouded in crape, on her side rails. I could read her name as she passed by me – it was the Constitution – and I could see three men as plainly as I see you. One had his hand on the lever, and was peering out into the night as if in search of something on the track; another was shoveling coal into the furnace and making a deal of noise about it, and a third, dressed in black, with crape dangling from his arm and encircling his stiff high hat, sat upon a stool doing nothing.

"You ask me how I saw so much in so short a time? I can't explain it. All I know is that I saw what I'm telling you. There was something ghastly in the faces of the men, but that might have been caused by the terrific rate at which they were speeding along. As soon as the Constitution had passed, I ran to the lower end of the siding to fix the switch, which I feared somebody had been tampering with. It was just as I had left it.

"While I was puzzling my head over the mysterious engine a second headlight threw its reflection upon me and I saw another black-draped locomotive. It was not going as fast as the first but making what we used to call express time – say thirty-five or forty miles an hour. I could scarcely see any of the iron and steelwork of the engine, so thoroughly was it covered with crape, ribbons, and black cloth. The handrail was hidden from sight by masses of crepe, as was also the steam chest, and in front of the boiler was a heavy fold of black cloth. Even the smokestack had streamers of fleecy crape and ten little national flags that ornamented the handrail were shrouded in the same material. Just below the window of the cab, I saw a portrait framed in wood as black as ebony. It was that of the martyred President!

"I could see the faces of the engineer and brakeman and several passengers who were seated near windows, whose black curtains were raised. They all looked pale and ghostly, but those who moved at all moved naturally and transacted their business in just about the same way that any other train hands would have done. I expected to see her turn off upon the siding. But she didn't turn off. Instead of that, she kept right along on the main track as though there were no such as switches in the world. The cars followed her as easily as though the going was clear, and in a few seconds all that I could see of the train was the lamp of the flagman on the rear car."

"Have you ever seen the Phantom Train since?" stated the reporter.

"Yes, twice, and both times on the anniversary of that night. Nothing was changed, not even the wreath of flowers, which were still fresh," replied the night switchman.

In other places, where the tracks are still in use but have long since been taken over by companies that did not even exist in 1865, the stories also tell of a phantom train.

One such place is Chicago, where one of the most impressive funerals was held for the fallen president. Many still believe the train makes an appearance each year on May 1, the anniversary of the Funeral Train's arrival in the Windy City.

The old Illinois Central tracks are now used by the Metra Line, which brings commuters back and forth to the city from Indiana, along Lake Michigan, and it's not unusual to find history buffs, Civil War enthusiasts, and ghost hunters literally camped out around the tracks in the early days of May. It's been a long-standing tradition that, if the train does pass by, clocks and watches along the tracks always stop and never work again.

One of my favorite stories of the Lincoln Funeral Train dates back to the 1940s. It tells of a woman in Indiana who was driving home one night and was about to cross over the local railroad tracks when a signal light began to flash, warning of an oncoming train. She stopped her car to wait and then, a few moments later, the quiet night was split by the sound of a train whistle.

As she watched, she saw a bright headlight coming along the tracks and then the train itself came into view. It was an old-fashioned steam train, like nothing she had seen on the tracks in years. It was pulling a long line of cars behind - fancy sleeping cars that the railroads had stopped using a long time before. But the cars weren't ordinary antiques. Each of them was decorated with black drapes of cloth that were hung beneath each of the windows. Flags decorated the cars, flapping in the wind as it traveled.

It was a strange sight, but then she realized what was wrong with the scene in front her -- it was completely silent, except for the sound of the lonesome train whistle. There should have been a hiss of steam, a clatter of steel, and the shrieking sound of brakes as the train started to slow down in front of her.

But there was inexplicably no sound.

The train slowed, then stopped at the small train depot that was located just across the tracks from where she was sitting in her automobile. It paused there, still silent. Then, after what seemed like forever, the whistle sounded again, and the train began to lurch forward on the tracks. It slowly crept away from the small town and eventually, it vanished into the darkness down the tracks.

The entire experience had only lasted for a few minutes, but it had left the woman understandably unnerved. Glancing out her window, she saw that a pair of railroad employees were standing outside the depot. The two men looked as shocked as she felt - they had seen the train, too.

She drove over the train tracks and stopped next to the depot, where she got out of the car. She walked over to the two men, hoping they would have some answers, but she was disappointed - what they told her only added to the mystery. They did tell her that they, too, had witnessed the mysterious train but they insisted that no train had been scheduled to pass by the depot at that time.

All three of them had seen the train and all three of them were also able to agree on something that each of them had gotten a glimpse of through the windows of one of the cars that had been draped with black cloth.

It had been a coffin - a coffin that was covered with an American flag. The coffin had been surrounded by soldiers who were dressed in what appeared to be blue uniforms from the Civil War era.

The woman returned to her car, still upset, unsteady, and with rattled nerves. She knew the other men had also seen the train, so she hadn't imagined it, but she wondered if they had also seen the part of the incident that unsettled her the most.

As the train passed, one of the soldiers in the car had turned and looked out at her. His face, she later claimed, wasn't a face at all - it was the sharp, white image of a human skull.

15. THE HAUNTED LIFE OF MARY LINCOLN
From the White House to the Grave

For the American people, Lincoln's "Carnival of Death" had been a necessary, cathartic event that allowed them to grieve for the fall president, as well as for the nation, which had been ripped apart by the four long years of war. But for Mary Lincoln, it had been a tortuous event that only prolonged the tragedy.

Lincoln's entire remaining family had been devastated by the assassination. Mary never really recovered, sending her down a path of erratic, perhaps even insane behavior, that would eventually land her in a private asylum. The mysterious death of Tad Lincoln had been the tragedy that had sent her over the edge.

Mary was committed at the hands of her oldest son, Robert, and it would cause the two of them to remain estranged until Mary's death. But Robert had difficulties of his own in the wake of his father's murder, which his grief-stricken mother was never able to address.

Robert eventually became the only one of the Lincoln sons to survive into adulthood. He had been born in Springfield and had graduated from the Phillips Exeter Academy in 1860. He then studied at Harvard University, graduating and starting law school and then deciding that he wanted to join the Union cause. Much to Robert's embarrassment, though, Mary prevented him from joining the Army until 1865. He held the rank of captain, serving in the last weeks of the war as part of General Grant's personal staff, a position that prevented him from seeing combat. He was present at Appomattox when Robert E. Lee surrendered the Confederate Army.

Robert Lincoln

Although he loved him intensely, and had great respect for him, Robert had a rather distant relationship with his father. This was caused in part by Lincoln's many months on the law circuit while his oldest son was growing up. Robert would later recall that his most vivid image of his father as a child was Lincoln packing his saddlebags for his travels across Illinois.

Lincoln was always proud of Robert and had a great respect for his kindness and intelligence. While the two lacked the strong bond that Lincoln had with his younger sons, Willie and Tad, Robert wept openly at his father's deathbed and funeral and was a fierce advocate in protecting his final resting place in the years after the assassination.

After the assassination, Robert moved with his mother and his brother Tad to Chicago, where Robert completed his law studies. He was admitted to the bar in February 1867 and became a very successful Chicago attorney.

On September 24, 1868, he married the Mary Eunice Harlan, daughter of Senator James Harlan of Iowa. They had three children together - two daughters and a son. Their daughter was named Mary and their sons were Jess and Abraham. He went by the name "Jack" since Robert told him that he needed to earn his given name, but he never used it. Abraham died when he was only 17.

In 1875, Robert had a falling out with his mother after he committed her to an asylum. He'd had the best of intentions - believing she was a danger to herself - but she never forgave him.

A few years later, Robert became involved in politics. He turned down an offer from President Rutherford B. Hayes to serve as Assistant Secretary of State, but later accepted an appointment as President James Garfield's Secretary of War. He served from 1881 to 1885 under Garfield and President Chester A. Arthur.

Following his service as Secretary of War, Lincoln helped Oscar Dudley in establishing the Illinois Industrial Training School for Boys in Norwood Park in 1887, after Dudley discovered "more neglected and abandoned children on the streets than stray animals." The school relocated to Glenwood, Illinois, in 1899 and still operates today.

From 1889 to 1893, he served as the United States ambassador to Great Britain under President Benjamin Harrison and after that, returned to the private sector as the attorney for George Pullman, the often-despised owner of the Pullman Palace Car Company. Robert became the company's president after Pullman's death in 1897. In 1911, he became chairman of the board, a position he held until his death in 1926.

After going to work for Pullman, Robert never again delved into the world of politics. In fact, he stayed as far away from it as possible because by that time, he was a very haunted man.

He believed wholeheartedly that a curse hung over his life.

This strange belief was rooted in the events of April 1865, when Robert was with his father at the moment of his death. This was, understandably, something that Robert would never forget, but he had no reason to believe that it was anything more than a tragic, but isolated, incident in his life. No other American president had ever been assassinated before and there was no reason to believe that something so horrible would ever happen again, especially in the presence of Robert Lincoln.

Sixteen years later, though, in 1881, Robert was in the company of another American president whose life was ended by an assassin. President James Garfield, who had only been in office about four months, was walking through the railroad station in Washington, accompanied by Robert Lincoln. Suddenly, a crazed killer named Charles Guiteau appeared from nowhere and gunned down the president.

In 1901, President William McKinley invited Robert to tour the Pan-American Exposition with him in Buffalo, New York. While the two men were together, an anarchist named Leon Czolgosg approached them with a pistol. Moments later, President McKinley was dead.

For the third time, Robert had been present at the death of an American president.

After this, he became convinced that he was "cursed" and that somehow, he had contributed to the deaths of these men - including his father. From that time on, he refused to ever meet, or even be near, another American president. Although invitations arrived from the White House, and from other Washington social gatherings, he declined them all.

Mary Lincoln found it impossible to move on after her beloved husband's death. She had still been grieving Willie's death three years later when Lincoln was assassinated. She struggled with family problems and more heartbreak, even being locked in an asylum for a time. She believed that she had been cursed - cursed by being forced to live another 17 years after the murder of Abraham.

Mary remained in mourning, dressing only in black, for the rest of her life. The deaths of her husband – and eventually three sons – left her unable to stop grieving.

There is little question that today, we might see Mary's longtime erratic behavior as evidence of bipolar disorder or as a sign of the trauma and loneliness that she experienced following Willie and Abraham's deaths. But at that time, Mary's behavior was evidence that she was an improper woman.

Mary had always had a hard time meeting the severe expectations for women of her era. Women, even the wives of famous men, were expected to focus on the home and not seek attention or appear in public, but Mary loved spending money, loved the spotlight, and had a knack for publicity. This often created problems for her husband and after his death, it would prove disastrous for the former First Lady.

Trouble began as rumors spread about Mary's reaction to Lincoln's assassination. Even though the era was already starting to become known for its lavish displays of mourning, social customs dictated that upper class women needed to suppress their emotions in public. But Mary, who had also lost two of her sons and who is thought to have been possibly bipolar, showed no restraint with her grief.

Soon after Lincoln's death, Washington gossip swirled around about the terrible scenes that Mary was making in the White House. She terrified onlookers with her expressions of grief.

Later, in a book she wrote about her time in the White House, Mary's servant, dressmaker, and confidante, Lizzie Keckley recalled "the wails of a broken heart, the unearthly shrieks, the terrible convulsions" of the widow. Though these reactions might seem appropriate for a woman who witnessed her husband being shot in the head just inches away from her, they were seen as an "unladylike craving for attention" in 1865.

Mary did not attend Lincoln's funeral. She stayed in her bedroom for 40 forty days after the assassination and would wear nothing but black mourning clothing for the rest of her life. When the new president, Andrew Johnson, didn't visit her or even write her a note of sympathy, Mary was infuriated and took her time moving out of the White House. She talked incessantly about Lincoln's death until her friends began to drift away, their sympathy at a breaking point. She began to accuse her husband's friends and his Cabinet members of complicity in his murder, from his bodyguards to Andrew Johnson.

As Mary dragged her feet leaving the White House - pausing occasionally to spar with the group of prominent Springfield men about Lincoln's dramatic resting place - she became the object of mockery in Washington. In an effort to get far away from the city, she settled in a hotel in Chicago.

Mary knew she had never been well-loved in Washington. As First Lady, she had raised many eyebrows with her sharp opinions and spending habits. She had been raised in a wealthy family and she shopped for herself, her family, and her new home with abandon. She was given a generous budget for redecorating the White House, but spent far above it and fell under official scrutiny for her extravagant wardrobe. People widely mocked her for her spending, especially as the nation was enduring the privations of the war.

Now that Mary was a widow, shopkeepers who had been eager to extend her credit before came knocking, hoping to be paid. She hadn't been given much money by Congress - only the balance of Lincoln's annual $25,000 salary. And Mary knew that if anyone learned the truth about her debt, which she thought could be as high as $38,000, it would mean the destruction of her already shaky reputation.

Mary had a great fear of poverty. She often begged her friends to help her with money. Unlike the widows of generals and governors, for whom money was easily raised, Mary's handful of supporters found it impossible to raise funds on her behalf because she was just too unpopular. In fact, she was despised across America. Newspapers wrote unflattering stories about her and she was ridiculed by members of Washington society.

Desperate, she moved to a cheaper hotel as her expenses mounted. She began to petition Congress for a widow's pension, but lawmakers were skeptical -- they hadn't given William Henry Harrison's wife a pension after he died in office in 1841 from pneumonia - and Mary's spending habits were notorious. Lincoln friend Charles Sumner kept up the fight for her in Washington, while Mary turned her attention to New York.

She had an idea for how to solve her debt problem and it involved the clothing that she had invested in for so long. As a widow, it wasn't proper for Mary to wear the extravagant ball gowns and other clothing that she had worn in the past. Custom - as well as her mental state - would keep her in black mourning clothing for the foreseeable future, so why not sell the old clothing?

Mary, along with Lizzie Keckley, traveled to New York under assumed names and took along trunks filled with clothing and jewelry. But the trip was a disaster from the start. Lizzie, a former slave, could not dine or stay with Mary in the segregated hotel that she had booked, and Mary's identity was soon pieced together by jewelers and others who recognized the name on her trunks and markings on her jewelry and clothing.

With her identity out in the open, she fell victim to a man named W.H. Brady, a merchant who convinced Mary that wealthy New Yorkers would donate money to her cause if she consented to sell her clothing at public auction. Brady later claimed that he convinced her to hand over private letters –- some of which suggested that members of New York society had engaged in government impropriety –- to "authenticate" her clothing. But there had been no letters. They had been fabricated by Brady to generate publicity for the sale, which he stood to gain a large percentage from. When news of Mrs. Lincoln's "fire sale" hit the newspapers, though, she became a laughingstock. The press attacks were more brutal than her bleakest days in the White House.

Humiliated, Mary retreated to Chicago, poorer than she had been before she left for New York. It was not until 1870 that Congress grudgingly gave her a $3,000-a-year- pension and that was not enough for her to pay off her debts or live in her own home. The pension was later raised to $5,000 but Mary suffered from financial problems for years. It wasn't until she received an inheritance from Lincoln's estate that her finances were stable again.

But worse things than humiliation were coming.

By now, Tad had become Mary's sole source of comfort from her grief. Tad - or Thomas, as he'd been born - was named after his paternal grandfather. It had been a hard birth, and Tad was born with a cleft palate and its resulting speech impediment. Lincoln's staff would often say they had trouble understanding anything the boy said, but his father had no difficulties.

Tad's early years were happy. His brother, Robert, was older by 10 years and his brother, Eddie, had died six years before Tad was born but Willie was his best friend and constant companion.

Abraham and Mary were loving parents and wildly permissive for the era in which they lived. Tad was only seven when he came to the White House. The Lincolns were keenly aware of Tad's trouble with speaking, as well as difficulties that caused him to learn at a slower pace, so they encouraged him to "remain a boy" as long as possible. He and Willie took advantage of this by turning the White House into their playground. There were Union soldiers camped nearby, which was a constant attraction for the boys, and they visited them often. They made many friends among the soldiers, the staff, Cabinet members, and politicians. Men who normally would have been shocked to see children running wild through offices of state were won over by Tad and Willie.

But in 1862, Willie died. The Lincolns were devastated. Tad was eight and he had lost his brother, best friend, and playmate. He could barely deal with his own loss or grief. His distraught parents, distracted by their own problems, had little time to comfort him.

Three years later, when his new best friend - his father - was assassinated, Tad, only 12, immature and still unable to read, had to grow up quickly.

Barely able to cope. Mary refused to return to Springfield and its memories. Instead, she took her two remaining sons to Chicago. Despite her own cares, she realized Tad's education had been woefully neglected, and it became a priority. He was soon enrolled in school, but he was so far behind the other boys his age that a private tutor became essential. Tad did the best he could, fighting his speech impediment, his inability to read, and his often smothering mother.

In 1868, Robert, now 25, was married to the daughter of a prominent senator. Mary and Tad went to Washington for the wedding -- and then sailed to Europe. Pathologically worried about her finances and fresh from her shame in New York, Mary believed that it would be cheaper to live abroad than in America. Since Germany offered some of the best educational opportunities in the world, she decided it was where she wanted to go. They remained there for most of the time over the next three years. Tad was kept busy with either schoolwork or as a companion for his mother.

In 1871, however, an event occurred that made Tad want to go home - he became an uncle. Robert's wife had given birth to a daughter, another Mary Lincoln, and Tad was delighted. He had always idolized his older brother but the years between them had always gotten in the way of them being close. Tad wanted to change that, so Mary booked passage home in mid-May 1871.

Mary's arrival in New York was of modest interest so one of the newspapers sent a reporter to cover it. The reporter was none other than John Hay, one of President Lincoln's private secretaries and a friend of the family. John was particularly interested in seeing Tad and was delighted with his improved speech, even though he now had a slight German accent. Before he filed his story, John dashed off a letter

Thomas "Tad" Lincoln was the third of the Lincolns' sons to die at a young age

to Robert that was filled with glowing praise for "young Mr. Thomas Lincoln."

Robert was excited by his brother's arrival in Chicago. Married and a father with a growing law practice, he wanted to be there to help guide Tad with his future plans.

But that would have to wait. Tad had caught a serious cold during the return journey to America and by the time he reached Chicago, it had worsened.

To make matters worse, Mary and Robert's wife, also named Mary, clashed immediately. Their once-cordial relationship deteriorated so quickly that Robert's wife packed up the baby and went to stay with her mother during her mother-in-law's visit. So, of course, Mary packed up and left, too. She and Tad went to stay at the Clifton House hotel on Wabash Avenue.

Tad's illness had become serious. Robert summoned Dr. C.G. Smith to examined him. Tad was feverish and having trouble breathing. Most likely, it was more than cold - suggestions for what was ailing him have ranged from dropsy, or pleurisy, to tuberculosis. Whatever it was, it was extremely serious without the benefit of modern antibiotics. He suffered horribly in his final days and had to be confined to a chair with an iron bar across it to prevent him from falling forward or lying down, a position that made breathing impossible.

Mary remained by his side. Robert came each day, as did the doctors. They were joined by a few old Lincoln friends who could offer words of sympathy, but not much else.

Tad died on July 15, 1871.

A private funeral was held at Robert's home. Not surprisingly, Mary was too distraught to attend. Some of Lincoln's old friends were in attendance, as were some of Tad's former Sunday School classmates.

Tad had never spent enough time away from his mother to make many friends of his own.

When it was over, Robert accompanied the coffin to Springfield, along with his father-in-law Senator James Harlan of Iowa, Judge David Davis, and other family friends. Another private service was held at the home of his aunt and uncle, Elizabeth and Ninian Edwards, Jr. before final interment in the Lincoln Tomb at Oak Ridge Cemetery, where his father and two older brothers had been laid to rest.

A few obituaries appeared in the newspapers to mark Tad's passing, but for the most part, the boy who was never allowed to become a man was largely forgotten.

Tad's death - on top of the grief that Mary was still dealing with from the assassination and Willie's death before that - further aggravated Mary's mental state. She was now inconsolable and perhaps this was the reason that she turned back to the only thing she believed she had left - Spiritualism.

Like so many millions of others who had lost loved ones during the war, Mary embraced Spiritualism to cope with her pain. Before the war, the movement had started to fade in popularity, but after the devastation felt by untold wives, mothers, children, and loved ones, the hope of communication with the dead was greater than it had been before.

Mary needed that now. Just as she had been desperate to hear from Willie after he had died, she now also ached for a message from Tad or from her husband. After Tad's death, Mary had bitterly written, "Ill luck presided over my birth and has been a faithful attendant ever since." She was urgently looking for hope from the spirit world.

For a time, she moved into a Spiritualist commune, where she began to develop her psychic "gifts." Now a medium herself, Mary believed that she could "communicate beyond the veil" and see "spirit faces" among the living. She began claiming that she was having daily conversations with her dead husband.

It was to enhance her psychic gifts that Mary traveled to Boston in 1872. She had been reading about a famous medium there that might allow her to obtain proof that her communications with Lincoln were real.

That medium - who really wasn't a medium at all - was named William Mumler and he had recently become one of the most famous men in America.

Mumler, a Boston engraver and amateur photographer, first found publicity in October 1861 when, after he developed some experimental self-portraits, he was startled to find that the image of a ghostly young woman appeared in one of the photos with him. It was a cousin, he said, who had passed away 12 years earlier.

The photograph attracted great attention and it was examined by not only Spiritualists but by some of the leading photographers of the day. They all came to accept the fact that, as Mumler stated: "This photograph was taken by myself, of myself, and there was not a living soul in the room besides myself." Mumler was soon overwhelmed by public demand for his photographs and he gave up his regular job as an engraver to devote himself entirely to spirit photography.

William Black, a leading Boston photographer and the inventor of the acid nitrate bath for photographic plates, was one of the professionals who investigated Mumler and his methods. After sitting for Mumler in his studio, Black examined his camera, plate, and bath and kept his eye on the plate from the moment its preparations began until it was locked into the camera. After his portrait was taken, Black removed it from the camera and took it into the darkroom himself, where, as it developed, he was stunned to see the image of a man, leaning over his shoulder. Black was convinced that Mumler was the genuine article and could somehow entice the spirits to appear on film.

Others were, of course, not so sure.

Mumler had never been interested in the spirits or Spiritualism prior to his first alleged spirit photograph and his steep charge of $5 per photograph began to arouse suspicions that he was just in it for the money. He became the object of great controversy and eventually moved to New York, where he then began charging $10 for photographs. His critics howled once more. Mumler had many supporters, though. One of them was U.S. Court of Appeals Judge John Edmonds, who had originally come to Mumler's studio with intentions to expose him as a fraud but left convinced that he could actually conjure up genuine psychic photos.

In 1863, Dr. Child of Philadelphia reported that Mumler was willing to allow him to thoroughly investigate the methods of his spirit photos and, as he said, find a rational explanation for the mystery. He permitted Child to watch all his operations in and out of the darkroom and allowed him to examine his apparatus. Dr. Child displayed the pictures made at the time, while he and several friends watched the entire process, from the plate cleaning to the fixing. He took the precaution to mark each plate with a diamond before it was used and yet on each one of them was a spirit image. Child had failed completely to discover any human agent that was responsible for the formation of the spirit picture. Each of them differed considerably from one another and Child could not come up with a way to duplicate them.

However, the "extras," as they came to be called, in Mumler's photographs did not amaze everyone. After much controversy, pressure from city officials led to him being arrested and charged with fraud. But the testimony of several leading New York residents helped to exonerate him. Famed Broadway producer Jeremiah Gurney, who was also a professional photographer, stated that he had never seen anything like the images that were produced.

Mumler was still a sensation when Mary went to see him. The photograph that he took shows Mary with her mourning veil lifted and two "spirits" behind her. On the right is an image that resembles her late husband and on the left is a fainter image that is supposed to be her son, Tad.

Her sitting with Mumler made news at once. In February and March 1872, several newspapers reported that Mrs. Lincoln had been in Boston - "incognito and closely veiled" - consulting with Spiritualists. According to reports, she visited a "well-known lady medium on Washington Street" and during the séance that followed, "the spirit of her lamented husband appeared, and by unmistakable manifestations revealed to all present the identity of Mrs. Lincoln, which she had attempted to keep secret."

The *Boston Herald* confirmed the story - or at least the part of it that stated Mary had come to Boston and had checked in at the Parks House under the name of "Mrs. Lindall." She stayed 10 days and visited several mediums.

They also confirmed that she had been to see William Mumler. The photographer had sent a letter to the editor, along with a copy of the

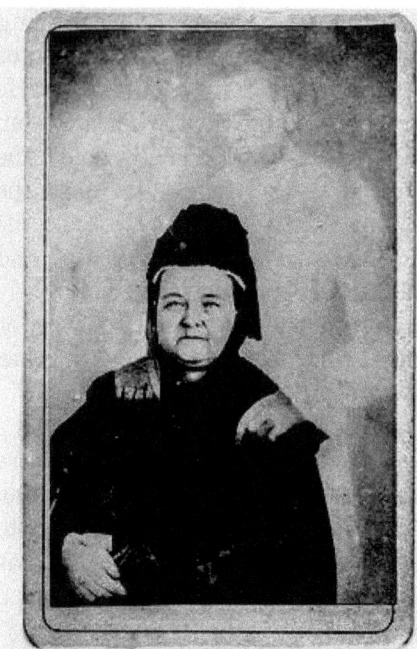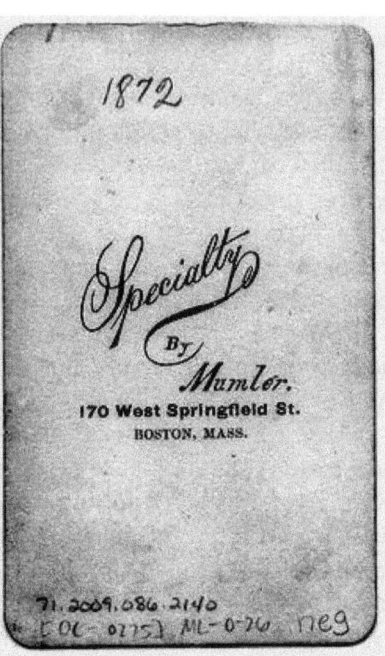

The spirit photograph taken by William Mumler that allegedly shows the ghost of Abraham Lincoln standing behind Mary and the blurry shape that some claim is Tad's spirit on the left. Mumler always maintained that he was unaware of Mary's identity when she came into the studio.

photograph that had been taken while she was there. Though printing technology of the time kept the newspaper from reproducing the photograph, the editor assured readers, "The resemblance of the principal shadowy image upon the plate to the martyred president is certainly unmistakable. The other developed figure is less distinct, but that of a tall, handsome boy who might be Tad."

Obviously, we have to treat these reports with skepticism but Mary certainly could have contradicted Mumler's story, but she never chose to do so, even after he published a memoir in 1875 and spoke about her visit at length. In fact, she never publicly claimed that anything about Mumler's account was wrong.

The photograph is certainly not anything that would convince a skeptic of the spirit world - Tad is too blurry to make out and Lincoln's hand appear smaller than Mary's - but Mumler's story of how the photo came to be is pretty convincing.

According to his story, Mary was traveling under the name "Mrs. Lindall" and she arrived at his studio wearing a mourning veil that hid her identity. After speaking to Mumler, she decided to sit for a photograph. While she waited in a chair, her face still covered, Mumler went into his darkroom and prepared a plate.

When he returned, he asked her if she intended to remove the veil and she replied that she would remove it when he was ready. Mary was still greatly concerned about her anonymity.

She lifted the veil just before the photo was taken but apparently, Mumler did not recognize her. It's not surprising. Time had been terribly kind to Mary. The developed photograph showed a woman in widow's black, her hands folded, her round face older, more tired, and heavier than only a few years before.

Mumler marked the negative "Mrs. Lindall" and it was placed aside to be developed.

Mary returned to the studio a few days later and according to Mumler, his wife, who was also a medium, was with him at the studio that day. He wrote that when she gave Mary the photograph, Mrs. Mumler instantly became "entranced" by a spirit, turning a simple exchange into an impromptu séance.

When she handed the image to Mary, Mrs. Mumler had asked her if she recognized the likeness. Mary hesitatingly replied that she did. And with that, Mrs. Mumler slipped into an eerie trance.

"Mother, if you cannot recognize father, show the picture to Robert, he will recognize it," said a voice that came spilling out of the medium's mouth.

Startled, Mary said, "Yes, yes, dear. I do recognize it, but who is speaking now?"

"Thaddeus," the voice answered, who would turn out to be Mrs. Mumler's "spirit control" - the otherworldly being who helped her make contact with the other side.

A long conversation began that eventually involved Lincoln himself. When Mrs. Mumler regained her senses, she found Mary weeping tears of joy. She had found her loved ones, she said, and was anxious to learn, if possible, how long before she would join them in their spirit home.

"But," Mumler wrote, "this information of course could not be given."

Mary was certain that Mumler did not recognize her when she came to see him the first time and was also certain that the photograph was genuine. This photograph became Mumler's most famous image. Was it genuine? There is no clear answer to that question - but it should be noted that Mary found great happiness from the photo and from the séance that occurred.

She truly believed that Mumler's photograph showed her with the spirits of her husband and son. But if she was waiting to die so that she could join them in the spirit world, she would have to wait for another 10 years to pass.

Mary's troubles were far from over.

Robert Lincoln had watched his mother become more erratic since the death of his brother, Tad. He was becoming alarmed by her behavior.

In March 1875, during a visit to Jacksonville, Florida, Mary became absolutely convinced that Robert was deathly ill. She traveled to Chicago to find him in fine health. On her arrival, she told her son that someone had tried to poison her on the train and that a "wandering Jew" had taken her pocketbook but would return it later.

While in Chicago, Mary spent money lavishly on useless items, such as draperies that she never hung and elaborate dresses that she never wore because she refused to wear anything but black. She often walked around the city with $56,000 in government bonds sewn into her petticoats. She was afraid of banks and still feared losing all her money.

After Mary had an 'episode' during which it was feared she would jump out of the window to escape a non-existent fire, Robert decided that his mother might be safer locked away in an asylum. He filed a petition with the courts stating that she was incapable of managing her estate and submitted a certificate from the family physician, saying that he believed Mary was insane.

Mary was "escorted" from her room at the Grand Pacific Hotel and was taken to the courthouse, where Robert was waiting, along with a judge, jury, and counsel. As news had spread of what was happening, curious onlookers rushed to the courthouse. Mary must have been mortified when she saw the crowd.

Robert's motives are still debated but he seems to have had her best interests at heart. Mary always believed that he was trying to get her money, but he had plenty of his own. Regardless, there is little doubt that this was not a fair hearing even by those who really think she was insane. The proceedings were a farce. The judge was a known opponent of Abraham Lincoln and the jury was mostly made up of Robert's friends. Many believe that the 17 witnesses were coached ahead of time about what to say.

Mary was given no time to prepare a defense or summon her own witnesses. She was railroaded into an asylum using Spiritualism as evidence of insanity - even though, based on that, more than half of America could likely have been judged insane at the time.

Even so, newspaper accounts noted that Mary's Spiritualist beliefs were often referred to in the testimony. As one article put it, "The evidence showed that for several years she had been a confirmed Spiritualist, and she believed her husband's spirit was constantly hovering over her and directing her." Several witnesses also mentioned a story that she'd told about Lincoln's ghost telling her that she would die on September 6, 1874, and all she'd done to prepare for the date.

The most damning testimony was offered by Dr. Willis Danforth, who said that he had treated Mary professionally for several weeks in November 1873 for "fever and nervous derangement of the head."

He said that Mrs. Lincoln had, "Strange imaginings... thought that someone was at work at her head, and that an Indian was removing the bones from her face and pulling wires out of her eyes."

He had also treated her in September 1874 for "debility of the nervous system." During this time, she told him that "someone was taking steel springs from her head and would let her rest; that she was going to die within a few days, and that she had been admonished to that effect by her husband."

Danforth went on to claim that Mary imagined that she heard raps on a table predicting her time of death and would sit and ask questions and repeated the alleged answer that the table had given. In order to test the reliability of the answers she got from the rapping table; she had a system of "putting the question in a goblet she found on the table. If the goblet was found to be cracked, she regarded it as a corroboration of the raps."

Robert testified that Mary was being preyed on by phony Spiritualists. He said that she had given valuable silverware to a "clairvoyant" who was one of his neighbors. He had written a letter to David Davis complaining, "She hardly thinks of anyone else. Her only companions are Spiritualists." The letter was entered into testimony at the trial.

Spiritualism was not the only thing used against Mary, though. There were other, more concerning things, Robert claimed, that led him to seek help for his mother.

Samuel M. Turner, the manager of the hotel where she'd been staying, said that she had recently come into the office complaining of hearing strange noises, which had left her afraid to be alone. She also said that she'd seen a strange man appearing and disappearing in her room, though the female staff member who'd been asked to stay with her saw no one.

A hotel housekeeper said that Mrs. Lincoln had been disturbed by one of the windows in her room - a window that "boded ill." Another employee said that Mary had complained about voices that were speaking to her from the walls and floors.

Mary was locked away at Bellevue Place – a private, upscale sanitarium located in Batavia, Illinois.

One by one, people from the hotel and various doctors who knew her took the stand and testified to Mary saying she believed she'd been poisoned by former Confederates, that Robert was dying, or seeing her mix up her medicines in an attempt to poison herself.

Others spoke of her reckless spending, which she'd been doing for years. All of them said that they didn't think Mary was safe on her own. They may have been coached, or even paid off, to come into court and testify against her, but if even half the stories they told seemed believable, then no jury would have decided in Mary's favor.

If the ghost of Abraham Lincoln really was communicating with her, then he wasn't doing her any favors.

Less than five hours after Mary had been brought to the courthouse, she was found insane and ordered to be confined at a private asylum in Batavia, Illinois. After the court proceedings had ended, Mary was so enraged that she attempted suicide. She went to the hotel pharmacist and ordered enough laudanum to kill herself.

However, the pharmacist caught on to her plans and substituted the drug with a harmless liquid.

On May 20, 1875, she arrived at Bellevue Place, a private, upscale sanitarium in the Fox River Valley. With his mother in the hospital, Robert Lincoln was left with control of Mary Lincoln's finances. Robert insisted that committing his mother wasn't as bad as it looked, but not everyone believed him. Lincoln friend Colonel Simon Kase - the man who had allegedly been on a floating piano with the startled president during a séance - wrote a letter to Robert about his mother's Spiritualistic beliefs and stated that "if he left her in the asylum he would be responsible for any harm that happened to her."

Three months after being locked away at Bellevue Place, Mary engineered her escape. She smuggled letters to her lawyer and his wife, who was not only her friend but also a feminist lawyer and fellow Spiritualist. She also wrote to the editor of the *Chicago Times*, known for its sensational journalism. Soon, the public embarrassment Robert had hoped to avoid was looming, and his character and motives were being publicly called into question. The director of Bellevue -- who at Mary's trial had assured the jury she would benefit from treatment at his facility - changed his story in the face of potentially damaging publicity. He declared that she was suddenly well enough to go to Springfield to live with her sister.

Mary was released into the custody of her sister, Elizabeth Edwards, and in 1876, was once again declared competent to manage her own affairs. The committal proceedings led to Mary severing all ties with Robert. She called him a "wicked monster" and despised him for the rest of her life. Before she died, she wrote spiteful letters to him, cursing him and telling him that his father had never really loved him.

Mary went to live with her sister in Springfield, but it was not a good situation. The two of them had been distant for several years. It seems that Elizabeth's husband, Ninian, had been involved in some questionable business deals during the war and the president had declined to run interference for him.

The bright spot in Springfield, however, was Edward Lewis Baker, Elizabeth's grandson. Lewis' father was a diplomat, and his parents were both living overseas. The young man - who had just turned 17 and, in a way, resembled Mary's beloved son Tad - had decided to live in Springfield with his grandparents. He had ambitions to become a journalist and found particular delight in the company of his "crazy" great-aunt Mary.

Mary could not have been happier to have him around. Lewis had a great interest in her Washington stories, and she found his complete disregard for the innuendoes and gossip about her madness to be endearing. He had given her back a little of the happiness she had lost and, more importantly, she had someone to love.

After a few months of living with her sister, though, Mary had reached her limit. She decided to return to Europe, believing it could provide her with the solitude and privacy that she needed and claimed to want. This was not like her three-year exile with Tad, however. Mary was going to Europe alone as a frail, friendless woman in her late fifties.

Edward Lewis Baker

Lewis traveled with Mary from Illinois to New York, although they did take a slight southern detour to Lexington, Kentucky, where Mary and Elizabeth had been raised. She found that the town had changed dramatically after 40 years. None of the Todds still lived there. Their old family home was a decaying ruin. But Lewis was the perfect companion for the journey. He knew little about his grandmother's early life and Aunt Mary was the perfect guide to go back in time with. They created a bond on that journey that would last for the rest of Mary's life.

Mary Lincoln wrote few letters during the last years of her life and even fewer of them were personal letters. Most of those that she did write were to Lewis Baker - affectionate letters filled with motherly advice about his future and education. Mary feared that the young man was the last person on earth who cared about her.

Mary spent the next three years living in a small hotel in France. Her health was failing, she was losing her eyesight - probably from cataracts that were complicated by undiagnosed diabetes. She refused to come back to the United States until she was injured during a fall in her room that may have broken some bones in her back. She was now barely able to walk and was usually wracked with pain. It was time to return to Springfield, this time for good.

Lewis met Aunt Mary in New York and escorted her back to Illinois to live with her sister once again. She saw little of Lewis after that. He was now a man with his own life and responsibilities. While he had a deep affection for Mary, he was living his life while Mary, now a recluse, would finish her days living in the past.

Mary lived her last days in her room, keeping her fortune with her always in a money belt. She kept the shades in her room drawn and spent most of her time packing and unpacking the many crates of clothing that she had been traveling with for years.

She died in July 1882 at the age of only 63 - a faded shell of the happy young woman that she had once been.

16. STEALING LINCOLN'S BONES

Mayhem and Mystery at Lincoln's Tomb

After President Abraham Lincoln was assassinated in April 1865, his body traveled west from Washington, spending several weeks visiting towns and cities along a circuitous route. His funeral service in Springfield did not take place until May 4, and it followed a parade route from the former Lincoln home to Oak Ridge Cemetery, on the far edge of the city.

But Lincoln would not rest in peace for decades.

Even after he was entombed in the magnificent monument that was built in his honor, he was unable to escape from the mystery, intrigue, speculation, and bizarre history that surrounds the stone edifice.

There are some who say that Abraham Lincoln's spirit walks at the tomb in Oak Ridge Cemetery but if the tomb is really haunted, then it is because of a crime that occurred here in 1876 that set in motion a series of strange events that went on for decades.

And perhaps left a haunting behind.

The city of Springfield had gotten news of the assassination of Abraham Lincoln by telegraph less than an hour after the event had occurred. Ned Baker, newspaper editor and a friend of Lincoln's, ran

The receiving vault at Oak Ridge Cemetery, where Lincoln and his sons were first placed in May 1865

from his office on North Sixth Street to the home of James Conkling, another of Lincoln's old friends. He pounded urgently on the door. Conkling came down from bed, heard the tragic news, and then weeping, went upstairs to tell his family.

The news was in every home in the city before dawn and soon, groups of people began to gather in the square near the newspaper offices. There was a low murmur of talk, of grief, anger, and vows of revenge, but when the final notice came that Lincoln had died, silence fell over the crowd. No one whispered, or even moved --- they simply began to cry.

It had not been an easy task to get Lincoln's remains back home to Springfield. There had been the long train journey, the funerals in various cities, the outpouring of public grief, and, of course, the battles with Mary Lincoln over where her husband would be laid to rest.

She had insisted on Oak Ridge Cemetery, but city officials had balked, wanting a much more extravagant tomb for the fallen hero in the downtown part of the city. They knew that having Lincoln's grave in a central location was key to bringing business and tourism into the city - no one wanted to go out to a country graveyard like Oak Ridge.

The city had played along. They appeared to follow Mary's wishes, while continuing their own plans downtown - until Mary Lincoln found out what they were doing, of course. Once again, Springfield gave in to Mary's wishes and Lincoln and his two sons were locked away in the temporary receiving vault at Oak Ridge.

But officials still had no intention of leaving the president there. A huge celebration was planned to mark the opening of the tomb downtown but when Mary heard about this, she was apoplectic. She dashed off a telegram that threatened to remove Lincoln's remains from Springfield altogether. Even a delegation of city officials that visited her in Chicago were unable to change her mind - Lincoln would remain at Oak Ridge.

The first tomb for Abraham Lincoln in Oak Ridge Cemetery took seven months to build. On December 21, the bodies of he and his sons were moved from the hillside vault where they had been resting to the new, temporary building.

Six of Lincoln's friends who presided over the move wanted to make sure that the body was safe so they enlisted a plumber's assistant named Leon P. Hopkins to make an opening in the lead box that held the president's remains. All of them peered inside at Lincoln's pale, preserved face and the box was sealed. All was well and Lincoln, Willie, and Eddie were allowed a five-year rest.

The first tomb for Lincoln at Oak Ridge was built in seven months while construction was taking place for the elaborate monument for the fallen president

In a newspaper story that was written about the move, Leon P. Hopkins was quoted saying, "I was the last person to look upon the face of Abraham Lincoln."

Of course, he had no idea at the time just how many others would look upon the president's face in years to come - or how many times that he would do it himself.

As work began on Lincoln's permanent tomb, stories began to circulate about a ghostly presence wandering around the site. Some claimed it was the ghost of Lincoln himself

Construction began on Lincoln's permanent tomb in the spring of 1866. The site was a short distance away from the temporary tomb and it was during this time that locals began to tell stories about a spectral figure that had been seen in the cemetery. Legend had it that it was the spirit of Abraham Lincoln, walking back and forth between the tomb and the new construction site, as if inspecting the work that was being done. The rumor of the president's ghost appeared in newspapers and became the talk of Springfield.

Even after Lincoln was moved to the new tomb, the eerie stories continued. Inside of the monument, strange sobbing noises and footsteps were heard, unnerving many visitors. Were the stories simply tall tales and overactive imaginations? Maybe, but regardless, they were the first ghost stories about Abraham Lincoln that were ever told.

They certainly wouldn't be the last.

Work was completed on the tomb five years later. On September 19, 1871, the caskets of Lincoln and his sons were removed from the temporary vault to the catacomb of the new tomb. Plumber Leon P. Hopkins opened the coffin once more and the same six friends peered again at the president's face. There were several crypts waiting for Lincoln and his sons, although one of them had already been filled. Tad Lincoln had recently died in Chicago and his brother, Robert, had escorted his body to Springfield and oversaw his arrival at what was then the nearly finished tomb.

Lincoln's casket being moved into the new monument in 1871. He was moved again in 1874 and placed inside of a marble sarcophagus in a viewing area in the back of the tomb

During the move, it was noticed that Lincoln's mahogany coffin was beginning to deteriorate, so a new iron coffin was brought in and the inner coffin of lead, containing Lincoln's body, was transferred into it. The President was laid to rest again, for another three years, while the workmen toiled away outside.

Three years later, on October 9, 1874, Lincoln was moved again. This time, his body was placed inside a marble sarcophagus, which was located in the center of a semi-circular viewing area at the rear of the public portion of the tomb. A few days later, the monument was officially dedicated.

The long journey taken by Lincoln's remains from Washington to Springfield was finally over and the martyred president could finally spend eternity in peace.

Or he could have if not for what happened next. It was an event that still stands unique in the annals of American crime and just may be the source of the many ghostly and mysterious stories that have become connected to Lincoln's tomb.

The events began with the arrest of Benjamin Boyd, a petty criminal who had, by 1875, established himself as one of the most skilled engravers of counterfeit currency plates in the country. Boyd had been doggedly pursued by Captain Patrick D. Tyrell of the Chicago office of the U.S. Secret Service for eight months before he was finally captured in Fulton, Illinois, on October 20. Following his trial, Boyd was sentenced to a term of 10 years at the Joliet Penitentiary.

The arrest of Benjamin Boyd had repercussions on a group of men who based themselves in - ironically - the town of Lincoln, Illinois. They used the town as a staging point for their successful gang of counterfeiters. The boss was a man named James "Big Jim" Kneally. They used Lincoln as an ideal refuge for Kneally's "shovers," pleasant-looking fellows who traveled around the country and passed, or "shoved," bogus money to merchants. It's been said that, around this time, at least half of the currency being used in Logan County was counterfeit. Almost all of that could be traced back to Kneally's gang.

Following Boyd's arrest in the spring of 1876, business took a downturn for the Kneally Gang. With their master engraver in prison, the gang's supply of money was dwindling fast. Things were looking desperate when Kneally came up with a plan. He would have his men kidnap a famous person and as the ransom, they would negotiate for the release of Benjamin Boyd from Joliet prison.

Kneally knew the perfect candidate for his kidnapping victim: Abraham Lincoln, or at least his famous corpse.

Kneally placed Thomas J. Sharp in charge of assembling the gang and leading the operation. Sharp was the editor of the local *Sharp's Daily Statesman* newspaper and a valued member of the counterfeiting gang. Meanwhile, Kneally returned to St. Louis, where he owned a legitimate livery business, so that he could be far away from suspicion as events unfolded and have an airtight alibi. In June, the plan was hammered together at Robert Splain's saloon in Lincoln. Five of the gang members were sent to Springfield to open a tavern that could be used as a base of operations.

It was soon established as a tavern and dance hall on Jefferson Street, the site of Springfield's infamous Levee District, a lawless section of town where all manner of vice flourished. Splain served as the bartender while the rest of the gang loitered there as customers. They made frequent visits to the Lincoln Tomb at Oak Ridge, where they found the custodian, John C. Power, more than happy to answer questions about the building. On one occasion, he innocently let slip that there was no guard at the tomb during the night. This clinched the last details of the plan, which involved stealing the body and spiriting it away out of town. It would be buried about two miles north of the city, under a Sangamon River bridge, and then the men would scatter and wait for Kneally to negotiate the ransom. They chose the night of July 3, 1876 to carry out their plan.

The Springfield saloon was up and running by the middle of June, leaving the men with several weeks to do nothing but sit around the tavern, drink, and wait. One night, one of the men got very drunk and spilled the details of the plan to a prostitute, who worked at a nearby parlor house. He told her to look for a little extra excitement in the city on Independence Day. He and his companions planned to be stealing Lincoln's body while the rest of the city was celebrating the holiday. The story was too good to keep and the woman passed it along to several other people, including the city's Chief of Police, Abner Wilkinson, although no record exists how these two knew one another. The story spread rapidly and Kneally's men disappeared.

Kneally didn't give up on the plan, however. He simply went looking for more competent help. He moved his base of operations to a tavern called the Hub at 294 West Madison in Chicago. Kneally's man there was Terence Mullen, and he operated a secret headquarters for the gang in the back room of the tavern. One of Kneally's operatives, Jack Hughes, came into the Hub in August and learned that a big job was in the works. Kneally wanted to steal Lincoln's corpse as soon as possible. Hughes and Mullen had no desire to do this by themselves, so they brought another man into the mix. His name was Jim Morrissey and he had a reputation for being one of the most skilled grave robbers in Chicago. They decided he would be perfect for the job.

Unknown to the gang, "Morrissey" was an undercover Secret Service operative named Lewis Swegles. He had a minor criminal background and had served time for horse stealing. When released, he went to work as an agent for Captain Patrick Tyrell. When he heard what was happening with the counterfeit gang, he posed as a grave robber.

In 1876, grave robbery was still a national horror and would remain that way for some years to come. Illinois, like most other states,

Captain Patrick Tyrell of the Chicago office of the U.S. Secret Service

had no laws against the stealing of bodies. It did, however, have a law that prevented selling the bodies that were taken. This put medical schools into dire need. They often had to depend on grave robbers, to provide fresh corpses for their anatomy classes. These men became the terror of communities, and friends and relatives of bereaved families sometimes patrolled graveyards for several nights after a funeral, with shotguns in hand.

Swegles, pretending to be "Jim Morrissey," came into the Hub and discussed the methods of grave robbery with the other two men. The three of them quickly devised a plan. They would approach the Lincoln monument under the cover of night and pry open the marble sarcophagus. They would then place the casket in a wagon and drive northward to the Indiana sand dunes. This area was remote enough to provide a suitable hiding place for however long it was needed.

Swegles, posing as the most experienced of the group, agreed to everything about the plan except for the number of men needed. He believed the actual theft would be harder than they thought and wanted to bring in a criminal friend of his to help them. The man's name was Billy Brown and he could handle the wagon while the others pillaged the tomb. The other two men readily agreed.

On November 5, Mullens and Hughes met with Swegles in his Chicago home for a final conference. They agreed the perfect night for the robbery would be the night of the upcoming presidential election. The city would be packed with people and they would be in downtown Springfield very late, waiting near the telegraph and political offices for news. Oak Ridge Cemetery, over two miles away and out in the woods, would be deserted and the men could work for hours and not be disturbed. It would also be a perfect night to carry the body away, as

Jack Hughes and Terence Mullen – the would-be grave robbers of Abraham Lincoln

the roads would be crowded with wagons and people returning home from election celebrations. One more wagon would not be noticed.

The men decided to leave for Springfield on the next evening's train. Swegles promised to have Billy Brown meet them at the train, but felt it was best if he didn't sit with them. He thought that four men might attract too much attention. Hughes and Mullen conceded that this was a good idea but wanted to at least get a look at Brown. Swegles instructed them to stay in their seats and he would have Brown walk past them to the rear car.

As the train was pulling away from the station, a man passed by the two of them and casually nodded his head at them. This was the mysterious fourth man. Brown, after examination, disappeared into the back coach. Hughes and Mullen agreed that he looked fit for the job.

While they were discussing his merits, Billy Brown was hanging onto the back steps of the train and waiting for it to slow down at a crossing on the outskirts of Chicago. At that point, he slipped off the train and headed back into the city. "Billy Brown" was actually Agent Nealy of the United States Secret Service.

As Nealy was slipping off the train, more agents were taking his place. At the same time the conspirators were steaming toward Springfield, Captain Tyrell and half a dozen operatives were riding in a coach just one car ahead of them. They were also joined on the train by a contingent of Pinkerton detectives, who had been hired by Robert Lincoln after he got word of the plot to steal his father's body. The detectives were led by Elmer Washburne, one of Robert Lincoln's law partners.

A plan was formed between Washburne and Tyrell. Swegles would accompany the grave robbers to Springfield and while assisting in the robbery, would signal the detectives, who would be hiding in another part of the monument. They would then capture Mullen and Hughes in the act.

When they arrived in Springfield, Tyrell contacted John Todd Stuart, Robert's cousin, and the head of the new Lincoln National Monument Association, which cared for the tomb. He advised Stuart of the plan and together, they contacted the custodian of the site. The detectives would hide in the museum side of the monument with the custodian. This area was called Memorial Hall and it was located on the opposite side of the structure from the catacomb where Lincoln's marble sarcophagus rested. They would wait there for the signal from Swegles and then they would rush in and capture the robbers.

The first Pinkerton agent arrived just after nightfall. He carried with him a note for John Power, the custodian, which instructed him to put out the lights and wait for the others to arrive. The two men crouched in the darkness until the other men came inside. Tyrell and his men explored the place with their flashlights. Behind the Memorial Hall was a damp, dark labyrinth that wound through the foundations of the monument to a rear wall of the catacomb, where Lincoln was entombed. Against this wall, in the blackness, Tyrell stationed a detective to wait and listen for sounds from the grave robbers. Tyrell then returned to the Museum Room to wait with the others. Their wait was over not long after darkness fell.

A lantern flashed outside the door and sounds could be heard as the grave robbers worked at the lock. Almost immediately, Mullen broke the saw blade that he was using on the lock and so they settled in while he resorted to the long and tedious task of filing the lock away. After some time, Mullen finally removed the lock and opened the door to the burial chamber. Before them, in the dim light, they saw the marble sarcophagus of President Lincoln.

Now, all they had to do was to remove the lid and carry away the coffin, which turned out to be much harder than they had anticipated. The stone was too heavy to move, so using an ax, they broke open the top, then moved the lid aside and looked inside.

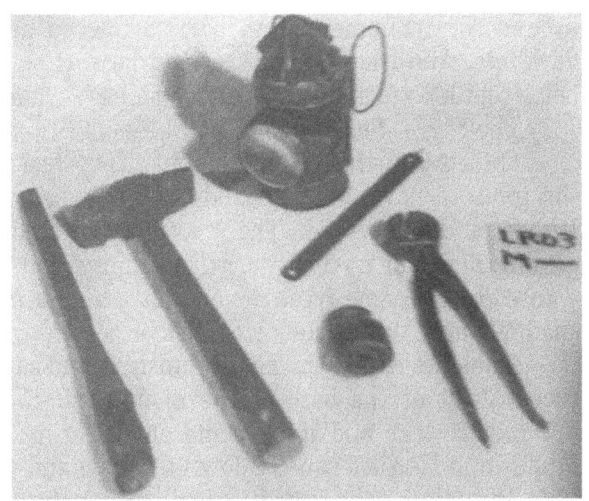

The tools used by the grave robbers on the night they attempted to steal Lincoln's body

Swegles was given the lantern and was stationed nearby to illuminate the work area. He had no other option. He was supposed to be at the door, lighting a match to alert the Secret Service agents that it was time to act, but he was stuck.

Meanwhile, Mullen and Hughes lifted out the heavy casket. Struggling and straining under the weight of it, they paused long enough to tell Swegles to go and have the wagon moved around. He had assured Mullen and Hughes that Billy Brown had it waiting in a ravine below the hill.

Swegles raced around to the Memorial Hall, gave the signal to the detectives, and then ran outside. Tyrell whispered to his men and, with drawn revolvers, they rushed out and around the monument to the catacomb. When they arrived, they found the lid to the sarcophagus was moved aside and Lincoln's casket was on the floor --- but the grave robbers were gone.

The detectives scattered to search the area. Tyrell ran outside and around the base of the monument, where he saw two men near one of the statues. He whipped up his pistol and fired at them. A shot was fired back, and the opponents fought it out in a hail of gunfire, dodging around the monument. Gun barrels flashed and shots echoed in the darkness. And then one of the men he was shooting at called out for help from his accomplices - but the name he called was Captain Tyrell's.

The Secret Service chief had been shooting at his own men.

Mullen and Hughes were gone. They had casually walked out of the tomb to have a smoke and wait for the return of Swegles, Billy Brown, and the wagon. The grave robbers didn't know they weren't coming and had no idea the whole things had been a trap. They just wanted to get some fresh air and have a cigarette so they went into a shadowy area where they wouldn't be seen.

Moments later, they heard gunshots and saw movement as figures raced about at the base of the monument. It definitely wasn't their missing partner and if by some chance it was, he was on his own. Mullen and Hughes ran off down a ravine and vanished into the night.

Assuming that Swegles had been captured, they fled back to Chicago, only to be elated when they found him waiting for them at the Hub tavern. He had returned with the horses, he told them, but found the gang gone. He had come back to Chicago, not knowing what else to do, to await word of what had happened. Thrilled with their good fortune, the would-be grave robbers spent the night in drunken celebration.

The story of the attempted grave robbery appeared in the newspaper following the presidential election, but it was greeted with stunned disbelief. In fact, only one paper, the *Chicago Tribune*, would even print the story because every other newspaper in the state was sure that it was not true. To the public, the story had to be false and most believed that it had been hoaxed for some bizarre political agenda. Most people would not believe that the Secret Service and Pinkerton agents would be stupid enough to have gathered all in one room where they could see and hear nothing, and then wait for the criminals to act. The Democrats in Congress charged that the Republicans had hoaxed the whole thing so that it would look like the Democrats had violated the grave of a Republican hero and in this way, sway the results of the election. In short, no one believed that Lincoln's grave had been, or ever could be, robbed.

But doubters became believers on November 18, when Mullen and Hughes were arrested. The newspapers printed the news the following day and America realized the story that had appeared a short time before had actually been true. Disbelief turned into horror. Letters poured into the papers, laying the guilt at the feet of everyone from the Democrats, to southern sympathizers, to the mysterious John Wilkes Booth Fund.

The people of Illinois were especially outraged and punishment for the two men would have been severe -- if the law had allowed it.

After their arrest, the conspirators were placed under heavy guard in the Springfield jail, and on November 20, a special grand jury was convened in Springfield and returned a bill against Mullen and Hughes for attempted larceny and conspiring to commit an unlawful act.

There was nothing else they could be charged with.

Grave robbery was not a crime in Illinois and the prosecution, bolstered by Chicago lawyers dispatched by Robert Lincoln, could find no grounds to charge them with anything other than the minor crimes of larceny and conspiracy. Ironically, the conspiracy charge was not even for conspiring to steal President Lincoln's body. It was for planning to steal his coffin, which was the property of the Lincoln National Monument Association.

The public was aghast at the idea that these men would get off so lightly, even though the grand jury had returned a quick indictment. Continuances and changes of venue dragged the case along to May 1877, when it finally came to trial. The jury was asked by the prosecution to sentence the men to the maximum term allowed, which was five years in prison. On the first ballot, two jurors wanted the maximum; two of them wanted a two-year sentence; four others asked for varying sentences; and four others even voted for acquittal. After a few more ballots, Mullen and Hughes were incarcerated for a one-year stay in Joliet.

And Abraham Lincoln was once more left to rest peacefully in his grave - but not for long.

It wasn't long before the story of the Lincoln grave robbery became a constant bother to the staff at the Lincoln monument. The custodians simply decided that it was something they did not wish to talk about. They grudgingly admitted that someone had tried to steal Lincoln's remains, but they had not succeeded. That was the end of the story.

John C. Power

But the public wouldn't let it go. It was a gruesome tale and one that appealed to the morbid curious of the nineteenth century.

Thousands of people came to see the Lincoln burial site and many of them were not afraid to ask about the stories they'd heard about the tomb. From 1876 to 1878, custodian John C. Power gave rather evasive answers to anyone who prodded him for details about the grave robbery. He was terrified of one question in particular and it seemed to be the one most often asked -- was he sure that Lincoln's body had been returned safely to the sarcophagus after the grave robbers took it out? Of course, he replied, but that answer was a lie.

At that time, Lincoln's resting place was completely empty.

When John Todd Stuart of the Lincoln National Monument Association learned about what had happened on Election Day, he rushed to the tomb. The would-be grave robbers were not captured for days and he was unable to sleep at night, fearing they would return to finish the job. So, he came up with a plan. He contacted John Power and told him that they needed to take the President's casket from the sarcophagus and hide it somewhere else in the monument. Together, they decided that it would be best to hide it in the passageway that was between Memorial Hall and the catacomb.

First, the broken sarcophagus had to be repaired. It wouldn't do to have visitors to the tomb to be able to look inside and see that it was empty. He contacted a Springfield marble-worker named Adam Johnson and he and his men repaired the damage that had been done. Johnson returned in secret that night to cement the lid back into place. He became one of the few people outside of the Memorial Association who knew the secret of the tomb.

That night, after the repairs, Johnson helped Power, Stuart, and several members of the association carry the 500-pound casket around

In 1877, when the naval and infantry statuary was added to the tomb, Power and the new Lincoln Guard of Honor had to hide the coffin of the president again

the base of the obelisk, through Memorial Hall, and into the dark labyrinth. They placed the coffin near some boards that had been left behind in the construction. The following day, Johnson built a new outer coffin while Power set to work digging a grave below the dirt floor. It was slow work, because it had to be done between visitors to the site, and he also had a problem with water seeping into the hole. Finally, he gave up and simply covered the coffin with the leftover boards and wood.

For the next two years, Lincoln lay beneath a pile of debris in the labyrinth, while visitors from all over the world wept and mourned over the sarcophagus at the other end of the monument. Many of them asked about the stories they'd heard, and each was assured there was no truth to it - President Lincoln's body was exactly where it was supposed to be.

In the summer of 1877, workmen arrived at the monument to erect the naval and infantry groups of statuary on the corners of the upper deck. Their work would take them into the labyrinth, where Power feared they would discover Lincoln's coffin. The scandal would be incredible, so Power made a quick decision. He called the workmen together and swearing them to secrecy, showed them the coffin. They promised to keep the secret, but within days everyone in Springfield seemed to know that Lincoln's body was not where it was supposed to be. Soon, the story was spreading all over the country.

Power was now in a panic. The body had to be more securely hidden and to do that, he needed more help. Power contacted two of his friends, Major Gustavas Dana and General Jasper Reece, and explained the situation. These men brought three others -- Edward Johnson, Joseph Lindley, and James McNeill -- to meet with Power.

On the night of November 18, the six men began digging a grave for Lincoln at the far end of the labyrinth. Cramped and cold, and stifled by stale air, they gave up around midnight with the coffin just barely covered and traces of their activity very evident. Power promised to finish the work the next day.

These six men, sobered by the responsibility that faced them, decided to form a brotherhood to guard the secret of the tomb. They brought in three younger men -- Noble Wiggins, Horace Chapin, and Clinton Conkling -- to help in the task. They called themselves the Lincoln Guard of Honor and had badges made for their lapels.

After the funeral of Mary Lincoln, John Todd Stuart told the Guard of Honor that Robert Lincoln wanted to have his mother's body hidden away with his father's. So, late on the night of July 21, the men slipped into the monument and moved Mary's double-leaded casket, burying it in the labyrinth next to where the President lay.

Visitors to the tomb increased as the years went by, all of them paying their respects to the two empty crypts. Years later, Power would complain that questions about Lincoln's empty grave were asked of him nearly every day. Finally, in 1886, the Lincoln National Monument Association decided that it was time to provide a new tomb for Lincoln in the catacomb. The sarcophagus had already proven that it was not strong enough. Lincoln's remains would be placed under the floor in a crypt of brick and mortar so that they would be much harder to reach.

Work was completed and the new vault was opened. The only thing missing was President Lincoln, but the move would have to be carried out in secret.

The press was kept outside the monument as the Guard of Honor - as well as a few others who shared the secret of the tomb -- brought the Lincoln caskets out of the labyrinth. Once again, the hole in the top of the lead casket was opened by Leon P. Hopkins. Eighteen people, who had known Lincoln in life, filed past the casket, looking into the

In 1899, the Illinois Legislature decided to rebuild Lincoln's monument and tomb, which required the removal of all the bodies of the Lincoln family to be removed – and hidden again

square hole. Strangely, Lincoln had changed very little. His face was darker after 22 years, but he still had the same sad features that all of them had known. The last man to look upon the corpse was Leon P. Hopkins, the same man who had closed the casket years before. He soldered the square back over the hole, thinking once again that he would be the last person to ever look upon the face of Abraham Lincoln.

The Guard of Honor lifted Lincoln's casket and placed it next to Mary's smaller one. The two of them were taken into the catacomb and lowered into the new brick and mortar vault.

There, they would sleep for all time.

"All time" lasted for about 13 more years. In 1899, Illinois legislators decided the monument was to be torn down and a new one built from the foundations. It seemed that the present structure was settling unevenly, cracking around the vault of the president.

There was once again the question of what to do with the bodies of the Lincoln family. The Guard of Honor came up with a clever plan. During the 15 months needed for construction, the Lincolns would be secretly buried in a multiple grave a few feet away from the foundations of the tomb. As the old structure was torn down, tons of stone and dirt would be heaped onto the gravesite both to disguise and protect it. When the new monument was finished, the grave would be uncovered.

When the new building was completed, the bodies were exhumed once more. In the top section of the grave were the coffins belonging to the Lincoln sons and Robert's son, Jack, who was also named Abraham. The former president and Mary had been placed the deepest and were so safely hidden that one side of the temporary vault had to be battered away to reach them.

Lincoln's coffin was the last to be moved and it was close to sunset when a steam engine finally hoisted it up out of the ground. The protective outer box was removed, and six construction workers lifted the coffin onto their shoulders and took it into the catacomb. The other members of the family had been placed in their crypts and Lincoln's casket was placed into a white marble sarcophagus.

The group dispersed after switching on the new electric burglar alarm. This device connected the monument to the caretaker's house, which was a few hundred feet away. As up-to-date as this device was, it still did not satisfy the fears of Robert Lincoln, who was sure that his father's body would be snatched again if care were not taken. He stayed in constant contact with the Guard of Honor, who were still working to ensure the safety of the Lincoln remains, and made a trip to Springfield every month or so after the new monument was completed. Something just wasn't right. Even though the alarm worked perfectly, he could not give up the idea that the robbery might be repeated.

Robert returned to Springfield and brought with him his own set of security plans. He met with officials and gave them explicit directions on what he wanted done. The construction company was to break a hole in the tile floor of the monument and place his father's casket at a depth of 10 feet. The coffin would then be encased in a cage of steel bars and the hole would be filled with concrete, making the president's final resting place into a solid block of stone.

The bodies of the Lincoln family were exhumed and moved into the new tomb in 1901

On September 26, 1901, a group assembled to make the final arrangements for Lincoln's last burial. A discussion quickly turned into a heated debate. The question that concerned them was whether Lincoln's coffin should be opened, and the body viewed one last time. Most felt this would be a wise precaution, especially considering the continuing stories about Lincoln not being in the tomb. The men of the Guard of Honor were all for laying the tales to rest at last, but Robert was decidedly against opening the casket again, feeling that there was no need to further invade his father's privacy. In the end, practicality won out and Leon P. Hopkins was sent for to chisel out an opening in the lead coffin. The casket was placed on two sawhorses in the still-unfinished Memorial Hall. The room was described as hot and poorly lighted, as newspapers had been pasted over the windows to keep out the stares of the curious.

The square piece of the coffin was cut out and lifted away. According to diaries, a "strong and reeking odor" filled the room, but the group pressed close to the opening anyway. The face of the president was covered with a fine powder made from white chalk. It

After the final identification of Lincoln's body, the 16 witnesses who were allowed into the tomb posed on the steps for a photograph

had been applied in 1865 before the last burial service. It seemed that Lincoln's face had turned inexplicably black in Pennsylvania and after that, a constant covering of chalk was kept on his face. Lincoln's features were said to be completely recognizable, though. The casket's headrest had fallen away, and his head was thrown back slightly, revealing his still perfectly trimmed beard. His small black tie and dark hair were still as they were in life, although his eyebrows had vanished. The broadcloth suit that he had worn to his second inauguration was covered with small patches of yellow mold and the American flag that was clutched in his lifeless hands was now in tatters.

There was no question, according to those present, that this was Abraham Lincoln and that he was placed in the underground vault. The casket was sealed back up again by Leon Hopkins, making his claim of years ago true.

Hopkins was the last person to look upon the face of Lincoln.

The casket was then lowered down into the cage of steel and two tons of cement was poured over it, forever encasing the president's body in stone.

That should have been the end of it, but as with all lingering mysteries, a few questions remain. The strangest are perhaps these: does the body of Abraham Lincoln really lie beneath the concrete in the catacomb? Or was the last visit from Robert Lincoln part of some elaborate ruse to throw off any further attempts to steal the president's body? And did, as some rumors have suggested, Robert arrange with the Guard of Honor to have his father's body hidden in a different location entirely?

Most historians would agree that Lincoln's body is safely encased in the concrete of the crypt, but let's look at this with a conspiratorial eye for a moment. Whose word do we have for the fact that Lincoln's body is where it is said to be? We only have the statement of Lincoln's son, Robert, his friends, and of course, the Guard of Honor. But weren't these the same individuals who allowed visitors to the monument to grieve before an empty sarcophagus, while the president's body was actually hidden in the labyrinth, beneath a few inches of dirt? It's interesting to consider, but it's likely that we will never know, one way or another.

Abraham Lincoln's Tomb today

And what of the stories that claim that Lincoln's ghost still walks the tomb?

Many have reported that he -- or some other spirit here -- does not rest in peace. Many tourists, staff members, and historians have had some unsettling experiences here that aren't easily laughed away. Usually these encounters have been reported as the sound of ceaseless pacing, tapping footsteps on the tile floors, whispers, voices, and the sounds of someone crying or weeping in the corridors.

Are these events merely caused by the acoustics of the tomb?

Or is it a ghost? And if so, is it Abraham Lincoln?

Even if you do believe the tomb is haunted, it's likely not haunted by Lincoln. In fact, it's unlikely that the tomb is even "haunted" in the traditional sense of what we think of when we consider a place to be haunted by ghosts. If there are strange things occurring here --and based on the hundreds of mysterious reports and encounters, there seems to be -- it's most likely that the things that people hear are "echoes" of events from the past that are still making themselves known today.

The weeping that is heard may be simply a residual memory that is left over from the millions of grief-stricken people who have visited the site over the last century-and-a-half. The voices may be the same. The banging sounds and the restless tapping may just be a residue left from the events that occurred on Election Night in 1876.

The Lincoln monument may act as a recording, soaking up energy from the past and replaying it again. Think of our everyday existence as a recording on an old cassette tape - if you remember those. You could record yourself, your friends, music, anything you wanted to on them and you could use them over and over again. But if you used it too much - and things were recorded too many times - some of the old recordings would bleed through into the new ones.

That's a simple way of describing what may be happening in Lincoln's tomb. The old stone building is the record and everyone who comes leaves a fresh track on the tape. This happens over and over, every single day until, eventually, some of what occurred there in the past is heard again.

There have been literally millions of people who have passed through this monument between 1871 and the present. They left a piece of themselves behind.

There was also the drama of the opening and re-opening of the grave and the wide range of emotion that went along with it.

Traumatic events may leave a stronger recording on the tape, which is the reason why the fear and excitement of the emotionally charged grave robbery left a stronger recording behind than other things have. It was etched on the atmosphere of the place in the same way that Leon Hopkins' chisel carved its way into the lead of Lincoln's casket.

17. HAUNTINGS

Abraham Lincoln Doesn't Sleep Here

I have often maintained that Abraham Lincoln is one of the most well-traveled ghosts in American history. I suppose, though, given the journey that his corpse took after he died, we should probably cut his spirit a little slack.

Needless to say, I don't really think that Lincoln haunts all of the places where his ghost has been allegedly seen - from Ford's Theater to the Petersen House, Gettysburg, Antietam, and the home of Clara Harris, where she stored her bloodstained dress. There are also stories of Lincoln spending his afterlife in private homes, theaters, schools, and assorted other locations that are even more far-fetched.

No one - not even a ghost - has that much free time to travel.

But don't misunderstand, there are still many locations that are connected to Lincoln that are infested by a spirit or two. And while I don't think that Lincoln himself is as busy in death as other people do, I am not convinced that he rests in peace.

Lincoln at the Seance Table

Given the popularity of Spiritualism in 1865, it's likely that mediums were claiming to be receiving messages from President Lincoln before his body was even cold.

The earliest account of a Lincoln séance comes from June 1865, when one of Lincoln's old friends found himself in a spirit circle and decided to ask - with great skepticism - if Lincoln had anything to say. He turned out to be impressed with the results.

That man was Carl Schurz - the Wisconsin politician who had come to Washington to help Lincoln recruit German immigrants and soldiers and who heard from Lincoln about the "phantom cannon" he'd heard in the city. Schurz had gone on to fight at Gettysburg and had been Lincoln's ambassador to Spain.

Schurz returned to Washington in 1865, summoned there by the new president, Andrew Johnson. On June 7, he was visiting friends and learned that a séance had been planned that night. They had been consulting mediums in hopes of receiving messages from two of their sons who had been killed in the war. A surviving teenage daughter had started to show talent as a "writing medium" and they were eager to see if she could make contact.

Schurz later wrote about the incident in his memoirs:

When the circle was formed around the table, hands touching, a shiver seemed to pass over her, her fingers began to twitch, she grasped a pencil held out to her, and as if obeying an irresistible impulse, she wrote in a jerky way upon a piece of paper placed before her the 'messages' given to her by the 'spirits.' The names of various deceased persons known to the family were announced, but they had nothing to say except they 'lived in a high sphere,' and were 'happy,' and were 'often with us,' etc.

Schurz was offered the chance to ask for any spirit he might want to speak with and he initially asked for the ghost of Friedrich Schiller, a poet from his native Germany, and then was stunned when the girl began to recite a few of the poet's verses in German. They were obscure pieces and Schurz had trouble believing that the young woman could have memorized them.

Intrigued, Schurz decided to ask her if she could contact Lincoln, who had only been dead about two months at the time. There was a brief pause and then the girl announced that Lincoln had arrived and was ready to write through her.

Schurz asked if the spirit knew why President Johnson has asked him to come to Washington and the girl wrote, "He wants you to make an important journey for him... he will tell you tomorrow." Asked if he should accept the task, the girl wrote, "Yes, do not fail." After that, the spirit predicted that Schurz would one day become a senator from Missouri. At that, he laughed. He had no intention of moving there.

When he met with President Johnson the following day, he was asked to visit the southern states to see how conditions were there and advise him about plans for Reconstruction. His accounts about the conditions being imposed on African Americans in the region would turn out to be one of the country's first reports on human rights.

Two years later, a business opportunity took Schurz to St. Louis and in 1869, he became a Senator for the state - just as the spirit of Lincoln had predicted at the séance.

Schurz was never entirely convinced that he actually spoke to his deceased friend, but he wrote, "We must conclude that there are forces active in and upon the human mind the nature of which we do not know."

Regardless, this may still be the earliest reported séance to contact Lincoln and was perhaps the most convincing, having given what turned out to be accurate predictions and having been reported by a source who knew Lincoln personally.

But there would be others. The *Banner of Light*, a Spiritualist newspaper, often reported messages from Lincoln, speaking through mediums in séance rooms across the country. In 1867, Lincoln's spirit stated that he had investigated Spiritualism during his life but was never really convinced of the truth of it. "I bore about the same relation to a belief in or acceptance of Spiritualism that I bear at present toward the reconstruction of the government," he said, taking a political swipe at Andrew Johnson and the officials who took over after his death. But he added, "I hope that certain causes will produce certain results, but I do not know."

Lincoln did add that he was a Spiritualist now, though. "I am indebted to your medium," he said, "for the reception of certain private warnings with regard to my assassination, purporting to have come from my son, Willie - and I now know they did come from him."

He had received one such warning from Willie, he explained, only a week or so before the assassination, which matched up with some of his accounts of his own prophetic dreams, which were not widely publicized in 1867.

Lincoln allegedly dropped in at seances all the time after his death, and appeared in spirit photographs, too. However, this one – staged by magician Harry Houdini – made no claims of being genuine

Not every séance that claimed to contact Lincoln was quite as convincing. Most of the others on record seem to have been conjured up by fraudulent mediums, of which the Spiritualist movement had many. Some of them received little attention because the spirit that had been contacted - which claimed to be Lincoln - didn't really fit with the public image of the "heroic, martyred president" that most people had. For instance, an article appeared in a Rhode Island newspaper in 1875 that stated Lincoln - calling himself "Uncle Abe" - had taken possession of a medium at a Spiritualist camp on Lake Pleasant and used the medium to shock the audience with swear words and racial slurs that the reporter called "simply disgusting." That, everyone insisted, could not have actually been Abraham Lincoln.

Dr. Henry T. Child was a medium who traveled on the lecture circuit telling stories about a spirit named Katie King, who had long been part of American lore. She was also making regular appearances in England at this same time in conjunction with another spirit medium named Florence Cook. But, you know, she's a ghost, so I guess she could travel, right?

At Child's performances, Katie and other phantoms would appear inside of his spirit cabinet and put on a show. They really didn't have any messages to pass on, it was really supposed to be a spectacle for audiences to watch. This is what much of Spiritualism had become in the 1870s. After audiences grew bored with rapping on tables, automatic writing, and ghostly voices, mediums upped their game by providing more and more excitement for their sitters to make sure they kept coming back.

During his lectures, Child spoke of contacting Abraham Lincoln in 1874. He said that at the séance in question, Katie had appeared in a white robe and after another ghost named "Black Hawk" threw blankets in everyone's faces, Lincoln himself appeared. According to Child, "He stood just within the cabinet, being twice seen distinctly as the door opened. He was clad in white from his head to his feet. He endeavored to speak but did not succeed. It is one of the most difficult things for a spirit to materialize vocal organs. Mr. Lincoln made a friendly gesture to a colored man who stood near him and disappeared."

In another account of the same séance, a member of the audience asked if it was really Lincoln, and the spirit nodded his head. When he appeared a third time, he was very indistinct, but he was seen holding an American flag.

By the way, the title of the article that described Child's lecture was "Spiritual Clap Trap," which gives you an idea of how seriously the reporter took what he heard that night.

I think he was right to be so skeptical when it came to the spiritual shenanigans of Dr. Henry T. Child.

Lincoln in the Wild

But Lincoln's ghosts did not always appear in séance rooms and lecture halls. In addition to the Harris House, where the bloodstained dress was stored, he has also been known for showing up at other places he never visited in life.

In 1869, two young women in Mount Pleasant, Iowa, claimed to see the ghost of Abraham Lincoln while going for a walk one evening after a thunderstorm. As they passed a street crossing, they turned to the left and saw Lincoln standing there. Rather than running away screaming, as many would have done, the girls decided to ask the ghost some questions. He answered each of them to their satisfaction but they refused to ever reveal what the conversation was about.

An article written about the incident said, "Very few citizens were disposed to believe it but the young ladies declare upon their honor it was so, and being willing to testify to it, and the assertion of other parties, to the effect that they saw the girls standing at that particular place, gazing intently at something, has convinced many that there is something to it."

There is really only a small connection between Lincoln and Mount Pleasant and it's a bit of a stretch. In 1868, Robert Lincoln had married Mary Harlan, a girl from Mount Pleasant, and Robert often visited the city over the years. She gave birth to Lincoln's first grandchild only a few months after this encounter but whether that would lure the president's spirit there is anyone's guess.

Some of the most active sightings of Lincoln's ghost have taken place at Fort Monroe over the years. The former military installation is in Hampton, Virginia, and if Lincoln's spirit does walk here on occasion, he does not do so alone.

There is at least one tortured soul connected to Fort Monroe who is a more famous spirit than Lincoln - his Confederate counterpart, Jefferson Davis.

Davis had fled Richmond, the rebel nation's capital on April 12, 1865, when it became apparent that the city would fall. In the hours that followed the Union invasion of the city, chaos reigned in Richmond. Citizens ran through the streets, trying to get to the railroad depots. Two regiments of southern militia were supposed to be maintaining order in the city, but the panic was beyond their control. A wave of destruction, looting, and terror washed over the streets. Homes and businesses were destroyed, and four tobacco warehouses were set on fire. The flames from those blazes spread to nearby buildings, burning out of control through the night.

During the chaos, Davis and his family had escaped. After Lee surrendered his army, Davis and his wife, Varina, managed to avoid the soldiers that were hunting them and planned to head for Texas. There, Davis planned to gather his still-loyal soldiers, establish a new capital for the Confederacy, and continue the war.

But before Davis could get far, the news spread that Abraham Lincoln had been assassinated. The search for the Confederate president now took on a new urgency because most federal officials believed that Davis and his government had been involved in Lincoln's death. The noose had started to tighten around Davis' neck, and he knew it was more important than ever to get away from Virginia.

He only made it as far as Georgia, though. On May 10, 1865, a contingent of federal cavalry soldiers surrounded a group of tents near the town of Irwinville. Davis was trapped and was quickly arrested. When the commanding officer stated that he had been implicated in the Lincoln assassination, Davis immediately denied it. "I would rather have dealt with President Lincoln than Andrew Johnson," he reportedly said.

Davis and his wife - who, incidentally, was the daughter of former U.S. President Zachary Taylor -- were taken into custody and transported by ship to Fort Monroe. It was America's first "escape-proof" prison and was

Jefferson Davis

known for being so impregnable that it was one of the few federal forts in the south not captured by the Confederacy during the war. For this reason, President Lincoln did not hesitate to visit the fort in May 1862 to help plan the attack on Norfolk, nor did General Grant in April 1864 when he stayed at the fort while designing his battle plans to bring about the end of the war.

Jefferson and Varina Davis are the most commonly reported spirits that linger at Fort Monroe. Varian usually appears late in the evening and has been spotted in the second-floor window of the quarters she was given, which were directly across from where her husband was once imprisoned. It's believed her ghost still keeps watch, hoping for a glimpse of her husband in the opposite window.

But it is Jefferson Davis who is trapped here for eternity.

Fort Monroe in Virginia, where the ghosts of both Abraham Lincoln and Jefferson Davis are still rumored to walk

Davis arrived with his wife on May 19. He was taken ashore and roughly hustled into a casemate cell that was about one step above a dungeon. He was left there for several days, until sunset of May 23. When the cell door opened, he was greeted by Captain Jerome Titlow, a blacksmith, and his assistant. They brought with them a set of leg irons and chains.

More men crowded into the cell - two privates from the Third Pennsylvania Heavy Artillery - with fixed bayonets. Two more soldiers were stationed outside. Another pair guarded the casemate door. More sentries were posted on the ramparts overlooking the courtyard and with the other armed guards at the prison, Davis had 70 men watching over him all the time. They were taking no chances that he might escape - with or without assistance from Confederate soldiers or spies.

When Captain Titlow entered the cell, he explained to Davis that he was following orders from Edwin Stanton to have him placed in chains. At this point, it was still believed that Davis was involved in Lincoln's assassination.

But Davis did not accept his fate easily. He fought the blacksmith, and it took four men to hold him down as the chains were shackled to his legs.

Captain Titlow was the last men to leave Davis' cell. As he walked out the door, he turned and looked back at the Confederate leader. He later remarked that Jefferson Davis was seated on the edge of his prison cot, his head in his hands, and tears streaming down his face. Even though Captain Titlow held no sympathies for the Confederate cause, he believed that the utter destruction of Jefferson Davis was one of the saddest things he had ever seen.

The days which followed were filled with humiliation for Davis. The fort's chief medical officer, Lieutenant General John Craven, recommended that Davis' chains be removed. The Confederate president's health was fragile and being chained like an animal was simply cruel. Not surprisingly, his recommendation was ignored. Soon however, word of the shackling leaked out and reached the newspapers. Public disapproval of the punishment, in the south and the north, created so many problems that the War Department finally ordered Davis to be unchained.

After more than four months in solitary confinement, Davis was moved to better quarters, although he remained a prisoner. Soon, the public would also begin to clamor for Davis' release. There was no proof that he had, in any way, been involved in the Lincoln assassination. Even men like Horace Greeley and Senator Thaddeus Stevens got behind the effort and created a stir that was simply too big to ignore.

At last, on May 13, 1867, after two years of confinement, Jefferson Davis was released. He lived on for 24 years after the end of the Civil War, traveling extensively and writing about the "Lost Cause" and its consequences. When he died in 1889, he was buried in Metairie Cemetery in New Orleans, where he had been living. His body was moved twice more before ending up in Hollywood Cemetery in Richmond.

His ghost has been nearly as restless, although he seems stuck at one place - Fort Monroe. Numerous witnesses have encountered him here over the years, usually in the casemate cell, where he was first help captive and then placed in shackles. Some claim to have seen his apparition, sitting on the edge of a cot, his face in his hands. Others have heard the slow pace of footsteps from the cell - a sound that is accompanied by the unmistakable sound of a rattling chain.

There have been other ghosts encountered here, too -- soldiers in the morning mist, the thump of phantom boots, laughter, loud voices, and that of Abraham Lincoln.

Lincoln appears in a guest room at the fort that has been dubbed the "Lincoln Room" over the years. It was where he stayed when he traveled to the fort to oversee the plans to attack Norfolk. Something about this event left a lingering impression of Lincoln behind. He has

always been seen wearing a dressing gown and standing near the fireplace in the room, deep in thought.

Lincoln's Springfield Home

One of the most famous allegedly haunted places connected to Abraham Lincoln is undoubtedly the home that he once owned at the corner of Eighth and Jackson Streets in Springfield, Illinois.

The Lincoln Home is an unusual place when it comes to haunted history and lore. Officially, it is not haunted. The property is managed by the National Park Service and they have a pretty strict policy when it comes to ghosts - there aren't any. And yet, many of the best witnesses to eerie events at the house are former staff members and park rangers who have either retired or moved on to other properties.

And another unusual thing about the Lincoln Home being haunted is that while it may truly be haunted, I don't believe that it's haunted by Abraham Lincoln.

In 1844, Lincoln bought the only home that he would ever own - a one-and-a-half story cottage in Springfield. It was a good purchase. It wasn't far from Lincoln's law office and the family knew it would need more room if they planned to have more children after Robert, who had been born a short time before Lincoln bought the house.

It had been built just five years before by a minister named Dresser. It was still a small cottage when Lincoln bought it with pine exterior boards, walnut interiors, and oak flooring. Wooden pegs and hand-made nails held everything together. In 1850, Lincoln improved the exterior of the property by having a brick wall constructed, and by adding a fence along Jackson Street, but nothing major was done to the house until 1856. At this time, the house was enlarged to a full two stories, adding new rooms and space that was desperately needed for a bunch of rambunctious boys.

Lucian Tilton

The house has seen its share of both happiness and tragedy. Three of the Lincoln children were born there and one, Eddie, died there.

After Lincoln won the presidency, the family left for Washington in 1861 and never returned. The first tenants were Lucian Tilton and his wife, who endured the thousands of people who came to the house for tours while Lincoln was in the White House and had to ask for military protection for the home during the funeral services in Springfield. When they had moved into the house, the Tiltons had bought most of the Lincolns' furniture and kept it with the property. Unfortunately, they took it with them when they left and most of the furniture was destroyed in the Great Chicago Fire in 1871.

After the Tiltons, the house was leased by George Harlow, a lawyer, former newspaperman, and two-term Illinois Secretary of State. He had wanted to buy the home from Robert Lincoln, but when Robert declined to sell it, the Harlows moved out.

In 1877, the house was rented by a bricklayer, butcher, and sewing machine salesman named Jacob Akard. During his brief time in the home, he used it as a boarding house and generally allowed it to fall into a state of disrepair.

Osborn Oldroyd's collection inside of the Lincoln Home

The decline continued over the next few years, while Robert was busy in his role as Secretary of War to Presidents James Garfield and Chester A. Arthur. The house was leased through Clinton Conkling, Robert's agent in Springfield, to German-born physician Dr. Gustav Wendlandt. He was apparently the first to start actually offering tours to the public and charging for them. A small newspaper article in 1883 made reference to the fact that he had put an old chair in the attic and had been telling people it belonged to Lincoln.

The next tenant in the house, Osborn Oldroyd, a collector of Lincoln memorabilia, a con artist, and, allegedly, a thief. He may not have been the most reputable person associated with the house but his lifetime obsession with Lincoln may have ended up preserving some of the history that may have otherwise been lost.

Oldroyd - his full name was Osborn Hamline Ingham Oldroyd so that his initial spelled out "Ohio," where he was born - began his collection when Lincoln ran for president in 1860. He moved to Springfield in the 1870s with his wife Lida's family and began a woodworking business. After going bankrupt, he decided to try bookkeeping - which seems an odd choice - and candy-making. He remained fascinated by Lincoln, though.

Around 1880, he got the idea to build a "memorial hall" that would showcase his growing Lincoln collection. To finance it, he put together a book in 1883 called *The Lincoln Memorial Album - Immortelles*. It was a collection of writings from more than 200 eminent people, including Ulysses S. Grant, Frederick Douglass, and P.T. Barnum, that was interspersed with Lincoln's own words. It was successful, but not successful enough to build a museum to show off his collection.

But he ended up with a better deal anyway --- the chance to rent the Lincoln Home. It was still owned by Robert at this time, although Oldroyd almost immediately began lobbying for the state of Illinois to purchase the house.

In the meantime, Oldroyd put his collection - an estimated 2,000 pieces by now - on display in the home. Some of the exhibits were historically important but many of them, all claiming a connection to Lincoln, were far-fetched at best. It was basically a "dime museum" of curiosities that were all allegedly connected to the president that included a batch of sermons preached around the country after Lincoln's death; accounts of the funeral train and maps of its route;

Osborn Oldroyd (Right) with Congressman Henry Riggs Rathbone, the son of the Lincolns' guests on the night of the assassination

pieces of the ropes used to hang the assassination conspirators; a bill of sale for a slave, framed next to a copy of the Emancipation Proclamation; cannonballs, swords, bayonets, canteens, and Civil War uniforms; a feather from the tail of "Old Abe," a bald eagle that was the mascot of Wisconsin's Eighth Volunteer Infantry regiment during the war; a wooden settee used by the Lincolns on their front porch; a rail said to have been split by Lincoln and Dennis Hanks; and more.

One interesting item was a cradle that was used by all the Lincoln boys who were born after Robert. I say this piece is interesting because it's still in the possession of the National Park Service today. They keep it locked in a warehouse on the site and they don't keep it on display. I was lucky enough to see it a few years ago, which allowed me to mark something off my list of Lincoln-related pieces that I most wanted to see.

Why? Because that cradle has a reputation of sorts. It's been dubbed the "Cradle of Doom." All the Lincoln sons slept in it - except for Robert, who was the only child to live to adulthood. Eddie, Willie, and Tad all slept in that cradle and all died young. Coincidence? Cursed? You can decide on that for yourself.

Oldroyd stopped paying Robert Lincoln the $25 a month rent for the house early in his tenancy, even though he continued to charge admission to see his collection and sold photographs and a 75-cent package of Lincoln "relics" that guests could take home with them. The "relics' were a small bag of joist, lath, plaster, and brick that had supposedly been removed during renovations, as well as bits of wood from trees in the yard.

Robert, hoping to avoid publicity, never pursued Oldroyd for the back rent but in 1887, he turned the house over to the state of Illinois. The only conditions that he had were that the state maintain the property and that it "be free of access to the public." Oldroyd had to stop charging admission, but the state turned around and hired him as the building's custodian, for a salary of $1,000 a year.

That job lasted until the inauguration of Governor John Peter Altgeld in 1893. Altgeld abruptly fired Oldroyd and replaced him with a loyal Democrat.

Oldroyd packed up and moved his collection to the Petersen House in Washington, the boarding house across the street from Ford's Theater where Lincoln had died. He was only there for three years before the federal government bought the house. Oldroyd was allowed to stay on - probably because no one looked very closely at the new additions to his collection. They were mostly pilfered items that he had stolen from the Lincoln house when he left like the "Cradle of Doom" and a number of items that had belonged to Mary Lincoln.

Eventually, those items were returned to the Lincoln Home, along with many things that Oldroyd had legitimately purchased. Everything in his collection was in wonderful condition and Oldroyd obviously felt that he had been doing a public service by stealing items from the house. They were not really valued at that time and if he had not taken them, they likely would have been thrown out.

The Petersen House in Washington at the time when Oldroyd's collection was on display there

The Democrat that Governor Altgeld had appointed to take Oldroyd's place as caretaker was Herman Hofferkamp, who had recently lost his bid for re-election as Sangamon County coroner. In the process, the governor disregarded Robert Lincoln's wishes. Robert had wanted Albert S. Edwards, his cousin as the new custodian.

He remained at the house for four years and at the end of his tenure, he unbelievably held an auction at which were sold "a lot of genuine relics of the lamented Abraham Lincoln, among them the desk he used in the legislature when it met in Vandalia in 1834-5," according to an advertisement in the *Illinois State Register*.

Hofferkamp later landed another political appointment as the keeper of the city prison and operated a hardware store. In poor health, he committed suicide in October 1922, shooting himself in the basement of his store.

Josephine Edwards

After Republican Governor John Tanner was elected, bookkeeper Albert Edwards was finally given the chance to oversee the former residence of his aunt, Mary Lincoln. Through his successors - his wife, Josephine and their daughter, Mary - the Edwards family were custodians of the Lincoln Home for 27 years.

It was during their tenure at the house that William Howard Taft became the first U.S. president to visit the home in 1911.

Albert Edwards died in the Lincoln Home in 1915, as did Josephine three years later. Until her death, she personally conducted most of the groups of visitors who came to tour the home. Her obituary was filled with praise about her knowledge of the life and times of President Lincoln and about her work keeping the home neat and well-maintained.

Mary Edwards Brown resigned as custodian of the house in 1924, saying that the flood of visitors to the home had become too great for her to keep up with after the deaths of her parents. When she left, she took most of the Lincoln relics and furniture in the house with her since they were heirlooms of the Edwards family.

More than 300 people applied to replace Mary Brown, but state officials chose a Chicagoan with Springfield roots as the new caretaker. Virginia Stuart Brown was no relation to Mary, but she was the great-granddaughter of John Stuart, Springfield pioneer and early law partner of Lincoln. One of the major factors in her selection was that, like the Edwards family, she owned a significant collection of Lincoln items that could be displayed in the home.

She retired in 1953 and this ended more than 90 years during which Lincoln Home custodians lived in the house itself. This change meant that the entire home, not just the first floor, could be opened to tourists.

The house continued as a state historic site until August 1971, when operations were taken over by the National Park Service, which continues to maintain and preserve the site today.

In its nearly two centuries in existence, the Lincoln Home has seen happiness, trauma, new life, and death. It is a place that has made an impact on the national stage and yet remains an integral part of experiencing Abraham Lincoln in the city that he called home.

Is it any wonder that it's linked to the supernatural?

Rumors about the Lincoln Home being haunted date back to the days when it was a state of Illinois property, before the National Park Service began overseeing it. Stories circulated then about the apparition of a woman that was encountered at the house. Not surprisingly, some believed it was Mary Lincoln. I don't believe it is, but whoever she was, she was seen by multiple people at different times of day, none of whom knew one another or were connected in any way.

There were other odd happenings, too. Toys, household items, and lamps moved around the house. Furniture would sometimes be rearranged, unlit candles would light on their own, and a rocking chair rocked by itself - often in front of several startled witnesses.

One staff member claimed to be tapped on the shoulder while moving furniture one afternoon. Another incident involved a key to a wooden box that disappeared one day and remained gone for more than a week. Then, suddenly, it was found inserted in its lock with an antique pink ribbon tied around it. No explanation was ever discovered for where the key had been or for who had tied the piece of ribbon around it.

One former guide said that she was on duty at the front door one afternoon when she heard the sound of music being played on the piano that used to be in the parlor. She turned to stop whoever had touched it and found that no one was in the room.

Another ranger who worked in the house recalled several occasions when strange feelings, and the touch of invisible hands, caused her to close up the house quickly on some evenings.

She didn't want to be in there alone.

And she wasn't the only one to feel that way. One ranger told me of one late afternoon when she was in the front parlor by herself. There is a display there of some of the items that could commonly be found

in households of the period, including some children's toys. As she was standing in the room, she caught a movement out of the corner of her eye. When she looked, she saw a small toy roll across the floor on its own.

Staff members are not the only ones to have odd encounters. A number of tourists have also noticed things that are a bit out of the ordinary, like hearing voices in otherwise empty rooms, hearing the rustle of what sounds like a period dress passing by them in the hallway, experiencing unexplainable cold spots, and most common, seeing that rocking chair as it gently moves back and forth.

Years ago, a former staff member told a newspaper reporter that he had rigged the chair to make it rock by itself as a prank on his co-workers. To skeptics, that might make them think that everything ever reported in the house was a hoax but that was a prank that's now more than 40 years old.

The chair still reportedly rocks - and without strings.

Visitors have also seen the apparition of the woman who has been seen around the house. She is often in an agitated state or is seen cleaning and straightening before she vanishes. A tourist, an attorney from Virginia, even wrote the staff after he returned home to tell them of his own strange sighting. He claimed to see a woman standing in the parlor of the house who abruptly vanished. He assumed it was Mary Lincoln, but as I have said, I don't believe it was.

One possible identity for this restless spirit is Mrs. Lucian Tilton. She and her husband had rented the house after Lincoln left for the White House. They were constantly bothered by people wanting to tour the house at all hours of the day and night and had watched as people scraped paint from the building, removed bricks, and pulled grass from the yard during the frenzy of Lincoln's funeral in 1865.

The Tiltons moved out of the house in 1869, but some believe that Mrs. Tilton's ghost has never left it. Many of the reports of a female spirit claim that she has been seen cleaning and straightening the house. Could it be Mrs. Tilton, still worried about the disruptions that continually marked her brief tenancy in this famous house?

Or could it be someone else?

I believe the other contender for resident ghost is Josephine Edwards. She and her husband, Albert, were highly praised when they served as caretakers for the house. Josephine personally conducted almost every tour that was given at the house and when she died there in 1918, tributes were written about her knowledge of Lincoln's life and her extraordinary care of the house in which he had lived.

She is just as likely as the spirit of Mrs. Tilton to have remained behind, working to make sure that the Lincoln Home stayed in perfect condition for generations to come.

The Haunted White House

I sit in this old house, all the while listening to the ghosts walk up and down the hallway. At four o'clock, I was awakened by three distinct knocks on my bedroom door. No one was there. Damned place is haunted, sure as shootin'!
President Harry S. Truman

There is no doubt that few presidents left the sort of mark on the White House that Abraham Lincoln did. His impact on the history of America has been immeasurable, and in 1864, when he sought re-

election, he did so with the idea that his plans were unfinished. When he was assassinated, his plans for reconciliation between the north and south were interrupted, and his work was left incomplete.

And I believe this is the reason that his spirit lingers there. It was at the White House where he saw the most turbulent years of his life. He agonized over a country that had torn itself apart by war and it was here that Willie died - an event that he called the worst thing that ever happened to him in life.

Unfinished work, tragedy, death, despair - is it any wonder that Lincoln has remained here after death?

Although there are few reports of Lincoln's ghost haunting the White House in the nineteenth century, there is nothing to suggest that his ghost wasn't around. In the years after his death - during the times when Andrew Johnson and Ulysses S. Grant were in the White House - residents sometimes reported eerie footsteps in one of the hallways. There are also some reports about Willie's ghost being seen during the Grant administration, but there aren't many details.

The first witness to Lincoln's ghost in the White House is said to have been Theodore Roosevelt, but I don't think that he meant his ghost sighting to be taken literally. Roosevelt had a lifelong appreciation for Lincoln and as a boy, had watched the Lincoln funeral procession as it made its way through New York City. Roosevelt's mention of Lincoln's ghost was in a letter to Dr. Henry S. Pritchett that he wrote in 1904. In it, he said, "I think of Lincoln, shambling, homely, with his strong, sad, deeply furrowed face, all the time. I see him in the different rooms and in the halls. For some reason or other, he is to me infinitely the most real of the dead presidents. So far as one who is not a great man can model himself on one who was. I try to follow the general lines of policy which Lincoln laid down."

I don't believe that Roosevelt actually saw Lincoln's ghost in the White House, but he did feel his presence, figuratively speaking. But there would be others who would encounter the former president face-to-face.

Grace and Calvin Coolidge on the White House lawn

By the time that President Calvin Coolidge took office, Lincoln's ghost had become a staple of the folklore of the White House. Every newcomer to the White House in Coolidge's day was told that whenever the light over the front door was dimmed for the evening, the ghost of Abraham Lincoln would walk silently back and forth on the North Porch.

It was First Lady Grace Coolidge who saw Lincoln's ghost. She said she passed by the Yellow Oval Room one day, she was startled to see Lincoln staring out the window in the direction of the Potomac, his hands behind his back. He was dressed in black with a shawl over his shoulders. Lincoln turned and looked momentarily in her direction and then vanished.

When he had been in the White House, the room had been Lincoln's library and he often stood at the same window, looking out over the city. Others have also seen and felt Lincoln in this room, including poet and Lincoln biographer Carl Sandburg. He also stated that he had felt Lincoln's presence in this room many times. Eleanor Roosevelt would

Franklin and Eleanor Roosevelt – Lincoln's ghost was especially active during the years that FDR was in office

later say that a number of White House employees also saw Lincoln in this room during her husband's years in office.

President Herbert Hoover also admitted to hearing mysterious sounds in the White House. Although he never acknowledged that it was Lincoln's ghost, Hoover left no doubt that he had heard something in the darkened corridors that he could not explain.

By the time that Franklin Delano Roosevelt began his long series of terms as President, Lincoln had been dead for nearly 70 years. However, his ghost remained, unwilling or unable to leave the White House. During Roosevelt's administration, Lincoln was at his most active, perhaps because of the concerns about the perilous state of the nation during the time of the Great Depression and World War II.

Years later, in 1954, Eleanor Roosevelt was asked about ghosts in the White House by a reporter. They probably expected the former First Lady to decline to talk about ghosts, but she turned out to be happy to share what she knew.

"Ghost scare?" she replied. "Yes, you might say we had one shortly after we moved into the White House."

In 1934, one of her staff members, Mary Eben, went up the second floor one day. Mrs. Roosevelt said that she could not have been up there three minutes before she came running back downstairs, visibly upset.

She had been walking down a hallway and noticed a man sitting on the edge of the bed, pulling on his boots. When she took a second look, she realized the man was Abraham Lincoln - and ran screaming down the stairs.

Mrs. Roosevelt admitted that she had never seen Lincoln but admitted that she often felt his presence late at night when she used the Lincoln bedroom as a study. She said she often sensed someone "standing behind her, peering over her shoulder." She also confessed to sometimes hearing "footsteps in the second-floor hallways" and noted that several employees reported seeing Lincoln's ghost looking out from the White House windows.

One of Mrs. Roosevelt's staff members, Mary Eben, saw Lincoln in one of the bedrooms, pulling on a pair of boots

John Mays, a doorman at the White House for several decades, often told a story about President Roosevelt's valet who "ran out of here into the arms of a guard, shouting that he had just seen Lincoln."

In addition to the residents and the staff, there were notable visitors who also encountered Lincoln's ghosts during the Roosevelt presidency.

Perhaps the most famous was Queen Wilhelmina of the Netherlands, who spent the night at the White House with her daughter, Princess Juliana, in 1942. The Queen was in exile from her own country after the German invasion and was in Washington to speak before a joint session of Congress.

The following evening, during a cocktail reception, the Queen surprised President Roosevelt and a group of guests by telling them that she had fainted the night before. The president was shocked and asked her what had happened. She said that she had been sleeping in the Rose Room and "someone knocked on my door in the middle of the night. I got up and opened it and - I know this sound ridiculous - but I saw Abraham Lincoln standing there. Then everything went black and I came to on the floor."

By the time she woke up, the ghost was gone.

Lillian Rogers Park, a maid and seamstress at the White House during the Roosevelt era, wrote freely about ghosts in her book *Backstairs at the White House*. She had many spooky encounters of her own. One day, while preparing a bed for the visiting Queen Elizabeth, she felt that someone was looking at her. She said she felt "something coldish" behind her, but she wasn't brave enough to turn and look.

Queen Wilhelmina of the Netherlands and Princess Juliana

She also spoke of another staff members who heard loud laughter coming from the Rose Room one night but when they checked to see who it was, the room was empty. This was not the first time that this sound had been heard, nor would it be the last. In Lincoln's day, the room had been an office for presidential secretaries.

On another occasion, Lillian was readying a room that was adjacent to the one that contained Lincoln's own bed and heard footsteps in the larger room, which held the bed. The sound crossed the floor coming toward the room where she was working. She looked up, but no one was there. After some time, she asked a male staff member if he had walked across the Lincoln bedroom.

"I just came on duty," he told her. "That was Abe you heard."

"He was," Lillian wrote, "perfectly serious."

Another famous guest who encountered Lincoln's ghost was Winston Churchill, who spent a few weeks at the White House around Christmas 1941. Churchill initially stayed in the Lincoln bedroom during his visit, which was common for all visiting male heads of state, but after several mornings of the staff finding him sleeping in a room across the hall, he asked to be moved somewhere else.

Winston Churchill allegedly had an encounter with Lincoln's ghost. And if the story isn't true – it should be!

It may - or may not - have been the ghost that chased Churchill out of the room, but he never talked about it. He only refused to spend another night there. The best story to come out of Churchill's stay at the White House doesn't have a definitive source but it's too good not to mention.

It seems that Churchill was taking a bath one evening in the Lincoln bedroom and got out of the water, naked and dripping, to find Lincoln standing in the room, smiling at him.

"Mr. President!" Churchill allegedly said, "You seem to have me at a disadvantage."

And with that, Lincoln disappeared.

By the time Harry Truman moved into the White House with his family in 1945, the haunting of the building had been well-established - and Truman would continue the tradition with his own stories in the years to come.

When the Trumans moved in, usher J.B. West was trying to figure out what to do with each of the rooms, including the Lincoln bedroom He later recalled that President Truman asked him, "Would we dare move Mr. Lincoln out of here, or would we be tampering with history too much?"

President Harry S. Truman never denied that he believed the White House was haunted

West told him that he was sure that Lincoln had probably slept in most rooms of the house in his day. West added, "Actually, the room that Mrs. Truman had chosen for her sitting room was probably where Lincoln slept. The Coolidges kept the Lincoln furniture there, and President and Mrs. Coolidge slept in the room together. The Hoovers slept in the same room, but they moved the Lincoln furniture across the hall to where it is now. You could just as easily move it down the hall over to the East Room, because that was the Lincoln Cabinet Room, where he signed the Emancipation Proclamation."

Truman listened to this and then grinned at West. "Now I know why they say Lincoln's ghost walks around up here at night," he said. "He's just looking for his bed."

President Truman had a wicked sense of humor but he was the first to admit that he believed the White House was haunted. It was, he also admitted, pretty rundown when they moved in. The old house had fallen into such a state of disrepair that the tub in his bathroom was starting to sink into the floor. He warned his wife that some day while she was hosting a Daughters of the American Revolution tea party downstairs, the tub might come crashing through the ceiling - with him inside. Bess didn't think it was as funny as he did.

Eventually, the Trumans moved out of the main residence so that repairs and renovations could be made. When the work was nearly completed in 1952, the president took reporters on a tour of the building, telling them that he was anxious to get back into the place, not least because he was anxious to get back to looking for Lincoln's ghost.

Truman would freely talk about his experiences in the White House, before and after leaving office. He recalled an incident that took place in the early morning hours, about one year after he took office. He was awakened that night by "unusually sad and melancholy" tapping on his bedroom door. He got out of bed, went to the door, and opened it, but found that no one was in the hallway. Suddenly, the air around him felt icy cold but the chill quickly faded as Truman heard footsteps moving away from him down the corridor.

Truman once described mysterious footsteps that he heard in the White House corridors from time to time. He said, "I think it's the ghost of Abraham Lincoln walking around, perhaps there to warn me about something."

In a letter to his wife, Bess, who often stayed at their family home in Missouri because she didn't like Washington, he stated, "I sit in this old house, all the while listening to the ghosts walk up and down the hallway. At four o'clock, I was awakened by three distinct knocks on my bedroom door. No one was there. Damned place is haunted, sure as shootin'!"

During his time in office, President Dwight D. Eisenhower made no effort to deny the experiences that he'd had with Lincoln's ghost. He told his press secretary, James Haggerty, that he frequently sensed Lincoln's ghost in the White House. One day, he explained that he was walking down a hallway and the ghost of Abraham Lincoln approached him from the opposite direction. Eisenhower took the encounter in stride. After all he had seen during World War II, Lincoln's ghost was probably a welcome sight.

Jacqueline Kennedy, who occupied the White House with her family and husband, John F. Kennedy, admitted that she sensed Lincoln's presence in the mansion. Although there is no record of President Kennedy ever encountering the ghost, Jackie told reporters in 1961 that she found the White House to be

Jackie Kennedy transformed the "cold and drab" White House, stirring up Lincoln's ghost in the process

"cold and drab" and decided to oversee a major renovation. When the widely-publicized refurbishment was completed, the White House was freshly painted and redecorated, and this was when Lincoln's ghost started to stir again. Perhaps unsettled by the massive alterations to the house, Lincoln's spirit was seen by several staff members and by Jackie herself.

Or maybe it was the expense that Lincoln didn't like. When he occupied the White House, he paid little attention to the furniture but sometimes became upset over the money that Mary spent "decorating this damned old house."

Liz Carpenter, press secretary to Lyndon B. Johnson, said that she believed the First Lady had seen Lincoln's ghost, or at least felt his presence in 1965. One night she was watching a television show about the anniversary of Lincoln's assassination and suddenly "she was aware, conscious of the fact, that the room she was in was special. Someone was compelling her eyes toward the mantel."

When she looked above the fireplace, she saw a plaque that had been placed that explained what Lincoln had used the room for. Lady Bird had never noticed it before but when she read it, Carpenter said that she "felt a chill. A draft."

In 1971, Julie Nixon, the daughter of then President Richard Nixon, was taking a group of blind children on a tour of the White House. She took them into the Lincoln bedroom and after finding out how many of them could fit into the bed at once - thirteen - she told them the story about Queen Wilhelmina and her encounter with Lincoln's ghost.

A reporter that was along on the tour asked her if she'd seen the ghost herself, but Julie said that while she had heard some "thumpings," that was all. "I've never seen a ghost, I've never heard a ghost," she said.

President Gerald Ford's daughter, Susan, didn't see the ghost either but admitted that it was because she was too scared to look. She acknowledged her belief in the spirit world and made it clear that she would never sleep in the Lincoln bedroom - or "that room," as she called it. In *Seventeen* magazine, Susan added that many people had seen the ghost and she didn't want to be the next one.

Lincoln's ghost was quiet through most of the 1960s and 1970s. Amy Carter, daughter of President Jimmy Carter, apparently once tried to contact Lincoln with a Ouija board during a White House sleepover with friends. They didn't have any luck.

Lincoln seemed to make a comeback in the 1980s, during the Reagan administration. In the early 1980s, White House operations foreman Tony Savoy was working on the second floor, flipped a light switch in a room in the residence, and saw Lincoln's ghost sitting in a chair with his hands folded and his legs crossed. Savoy said that he blinked his eyes several times and the image disappeared.

Though President Reagan claimed he never saw the ghost, he often joked

Ronald and Nancy Reagan and their dog, Rex, who the president believed sensed the ghost of Lincoln in the White House

about it and a few of his family members actually said they had seen it, along with his dog, Rex. At a 1987 press conference, he told reporters that he was never frightened by the spirit. "I haven't seen him myself," Reagan said, "but every once in a while, our little dog Rex will start down that long hall, just glaring as though he's seeing something." He also added that the dog would bark repeatedly as he stopped in front of the Lincoln bedroom. Reagan said that if he opened the door to the bedroom and tried to get the dog to come inside, Rex would growl fiercely but refused to step over the threshold.

Nancy Reagan also denied seeing ghosts. In one interview, she said, "If Ronnie is away for the night or something, I can be here alone," she said. "I'm not afraid. I don't hear Abe Lincoln knocking on my door."

But her daughter, Maureen, said that she had seen Lincoln's ghost. "I'm not kidding," she added," we've really seen it." She and her husband, Dennis Revell, slept in Lincoln's old bed when they visited. It wasn't comfortable but since Dennis was six-foot-seven, it was the only bed he would fit in. Maureen said that she would often see "an aura" around the bed late at night - sometimes red, sometimes orange - and believed this to be the spirit of Lincoln.

"When I told my parents what I saw, they looked at me a little weirdly," she said.

In her memoir, Nancy Reagan wrote a little about Maureen's experience, noting that it had actually been Dennis who had seen the ghost first, although as a shadowy figure by the fireplace. Maureen hadn't believed him until she saw it for herself. The figure was looking out the window but turned and stared at her for a moment before vanishing.

There were no reports of Lincoln's ghost during the Bush administration and both the President and Mrs. Bush denied seeing Lincoln or any other ghost in the White House. Early in her stay at the White House, Barbara Bush said that she was sure that if there was a ghost, she and President Bush's dog, Millie, would know.

However, during the Clinton years, Lincoln was back. President Clinton's brother, Roger, admitted that he sensed Lincoln's presence in the White House and staff members confessed to their own strange encounters in an interview on Halloween 1997.

Capricia Marshall, the social secretary, said, "A high percentage of people who work here won't go in the Lincoln bedroom." She knew of an usher who had gone into the room to turn out the lights and when he walked away, they turned themselves back on again. Another staffer claimed that he had seen Lincoln walking down a hallway one day.

When Hillary Clinton was asked about the ghosts that same year in an interview, her comments were similar to those from Eleanor Roosevelt decades before. "There's something about the White House at night," she said. "You just feel like you're summoning up the spirits of all the people who've lived there and worked there and walked through the halls there. It can be a little creepy. You know, they think there's a ghost."

She said that she didn't believe in the ghost herself but confessed that one of her friends refused to sleep in the Lincoln bedroom when she had come to the White House to stay.

Jenna Bush Hager, daughter of President George W. Bush, believes she encountered something ghostly while living in the White House. She and her twin sister, Barbara, were sharing a room and were awakened by eerie music from the fireplace. She insists they were not asleep.

During President Obama's time in the White House, the tabloid *Weekly World News* ran a front-page story about how Lincoln's ghost was advising the president on how to capture Osama Bin Ladin.

I'm afraid that I'm not going to put too much stock in that one.

As of this writing, no sightings of Lincoln's ghost have been reported since the early 2000s. Perhaps Lincoln has finally found some peace or perhaps he came to the same conclusion that Harry Truman did about the White House: "No man in his right mind would want to come here of his own accord."

BIBLIOGRAPHY

Alexander, John - *Washington Ghosts*, Washington Books, 1975

Alford, Terry - "The Spiritualist Who Warned Lincoln Was Also Booth's Drinking Buddy." *Smithsonian Magazine*, March 2015

Angle, Paul - *Here I Have Lived: Here I Have Lived: A History of Lincoln's Springfield*, Abraham Lincoln Association, 1935

Arnold, Isaac Newton - *Life of Abraham Lincoln*, McClurg & Co., Chicago, 1884

Baker, Jean H. - *Mary Todd Lincoln*. W.W. Norton, New York, 1987

Berry, Stephen - *House of Abraham*, Houghton Mifflin, New York, 2007

Birnes, William J. and Joel Martin - *The Haunting of America*, Forge Books, New York, 2009

Bishop, Jim - *The Day Lincoln was Shot*, Harper & Brothers, New York, NY, 1955

Bogar, Thomas A. - Backstage at the Lincoln Assassination, Regnery History, Washington, D.C., 2013

Books, Noah - *Washington, D.C. in Lincoln's Time*, Quadrangle Books, Chicago, 1971

Braude, Ann - *Radical Spirits: Spiritualism and Women's Rights in Nineteenth-Century America*, Indiana University Press, Bloomington, 2001

Canavan, Kathryn - *Lincoln's Final Hours*, University of Kentucky Press, Lexington, 2015

Carlson, Brady - *Dead Presidents*, W.W. Norton, New York, 2016

Carpenter, F.B. - *The Inner Life of Abraham Lincoln*, University of Nebraska Press, Lincoln, 1995

Carpenter, Francis B. - *Six Months at the White House*, Hurd and Houghton, New York, 1866

Chadwick, Bruce - *Lincoln for President*, Sourcebooks, Naperville, Illinois, 2009

Clinton, Catherine - *Mrs. Lincoln: A Life*, Harper, New York, 2009

Coleman, Christopher Keirnan - *The Paranormal Presidency of Abraham Lincoln*, Schiffer, Altglen, Pennsylvania, 2012

Cox, Robert S. - *Body and Soul: A Sympathetic History of Spiritualism*, University of Virginia Press, Charlottesville, 2003

Cook, Colonel William - *Through Five Administrations*, Harper and Brothers, New York, 1909

Donald, David Herbert - *Lincoln*, Simon and Schuster, New York, 1995

Emerson, Jason - *The Madness of Mary Lincoln*, Southern Illinois University Press, Carbondale, 2007

Epstein, Daniel Mark - *The Lincolns: Portrait of a Marriage*, Ballantine, New York, 2008

Evans, C. Wyatt - *The Legend of John Wilkes Booth*, University Press of Kansas, 2004

Farqhar, Michael - *A Treasury of Foolishly Forgotten Americans*, Penguin, New York, 2008

Faust, Drew Gilpin - *This Republic of Suffering*, Knopf, New York, 2008

Fleischner, Jennifer - *Mrs. Lincoln and Mrs. Keckley*, Broadway Books, New York, 2003

Foster, Feather Schwarz - Presidential History Blog, 2017

Gallagher, Trish - *Ghosts & Haunted Houses of Maryland*, Tidewater Publishers, 1988

Garrison, Webb - *The Lincoln No One Knows*, Rutledge Hill Press, 1993

Good, Timothy - *We Saw Lincoln Shot: One Hundred Eyewitness Accounts*, University Press of Mississippi, Jackson, 1995

Guttridge, Leonard F. & Ray A. Neff - *Dark Union*, Wiley and Sons, New York, 2003

Hamilton, Michelle L. - *"I Would Still be Drowned in Tears,"* Vanderberblumen Publications, La Mesa, California, 2013

Hanchett, William - The Lincoln Murder Conspiracies, University of Illinois Press, 1983

Herndon, William - *Herndon's Lincoln: The True Story of a Great Life*, Herndon's Lincoln Publishing Company, Springfield, Illinois, 1888

Hickey, James T. - "Own the house till it ruins me: Robert Todd Lincoln and His Parents' Home in Springfield," *Journal of the Illinois State Historical Society,* Winter 1981

Higham, Charles - *Murdering Mr. Lincoln*, New Millennium Press, Beverly Hills, California, 2004

Hodes, Martha - *Mourning Lincoln*, Yale University Press, New Haven, 2015

Holzer, Harold - *The Civil War in 50 Objects*, Viking, New York, 2013
------------------ - *President Lincoln Assassinated!* Library of America, New York, 2014

Horowitz, Mitch - *Occult America*, Bantam Books, New York, 2009

Hutchinson, Robert J. - *The Lincoln Assassination*, Regnery History, Washington, D.C., 2020

Ishbell, Ross - *Grace Coolidge and her Era*, Dodd Mead, New York, 1962

Jameson, W.C. - *John Wilkes Booth: Beyond the Grave*, Rowan and Littlefield, Lanham, Maryland, 2013
----------------- - *Unsolved Mysteries of the Old West*, Republic of Texas Press, Plano, Texas, 1999

Jauchius, Dean and James Rhodes - *The Trial of Mary Todd Lincoln*, Bobbs-Merrill, New York, 1959

Johnson, Clint - *Pursuit*, Citadel Press, New York, 2008

Kase, Simon P. - *The Emancipation Proclamation: How, and by Whom It was Given to Abraham Lincoln in 1861*, S.P. Kase, Philadelphia

Keckley, Elizabeth - *Behind the Scenes: Formerly a Slave, But More Recently Modiste, and Friend to Mrs. Lincoln Or, Thirty Years a Slave and Four Years in the White House*, Lakeside Press, Chicago, 1868 / 1998

Keneally, Thomas - *American Scoundrel*, Doubleday, New York, 2002

Kunhardt, Dorothy Meserve & Phillip Kunhardt Jr. - *Twenty Days*, Castle Books, New York, 1965

Kunhardt, Phillip B. Jr, Phillip Kunhardt III & Peter Kunhardt - *Lincoln*, Knopf, New York, 1992
-- - *Looking for Lincoln*, Knopf, New York, 2008

Lachman, Charles - *The Last Lincolns*, Sterling, New York, 2008

Lamon, Ward Hill - *The Life of Abraham Lincoln from his Birth to His Inauguration as President*, James R. Osgood and Company, Boston, 1872

Leonard, Elizabeth D. - *Lincoln's Avengers*, W.W. Norton, New York, 2004

Lewis, Loyd - *Myths After Lincoln*, Harcourt, Brace and Company, New York, 1929

Martin, Joel & William J. Birnes - *The Haunting of the Presidents*, Tor Books, New York, 2003

Martinez, Susan B., PhD - *The Psychic Life of Abraham Lincoln*, Weiser Books, Newburyport, Massachusetts, 2009

Maynard, Nettie Colburn - *Was Abraham Lincoln a Spiritualist?*, The Progressive Thinker Publishing House, Chicago, 1917

Mogelever, Jacob - *Death to Traitors*, Doubleday & Co., New York, 1960

Neely, Mark E., Jr and R. Gerald McNulty - *The Insanity File*, Southern Illinois University Press, Carbondale, 1986

Oates, Stephen B. - *With Malice Toward None*, Harper and Row, New York, 1977

Painter, Ruth - *Lincoln's Sons*, Little, Brown & Co., New York, 1955

Park, Lillian Rogers - *My Thirty Years Backstairs at the White House*, Fleet, New York, 1961

Pistor, Nicholas J.C. - *Shooting Lincoln*, De Capo, New York, 2017

Pitch, Anthony S. - *"They Have Killed Papa Dead!"* Steerforth Press, Hanover, New Hampshire, 2008

Rainey, Richard - *Haunted History*, Warner Books, New York, 1992

Reagan, Nancy - *My Turn*, Random House, New York, 1989

Roscoe, Theodore - *The Web of Conspiracy*, Prentice-Hall, Inc, Englewood Cliffs, New Jersey, 1959

Schurz, Carl - *The Reminisces of Carl Schurz*, John Murray, London, 1909

Selzer, Adam - *Ghosts of Lincoln*, Llewellyn Worldwide, Woodbury, Minnesota, 2015

Slaughter, April and Troy Taylor - *Disconnected from Death*, American Hauntings Ink, Jacksonville, Illinois, 2018

Soniak, Matt - "By the Light of the Moon: Abraham Lincoln's Adventure in Forensic Meteorology," *Mental Floss*, September 2011

Speer, Bonnie Stahlman - *Great Abraham Lincoln Hijack*, Reliance Press, Norman, Oklahoma, 1990

Stashower, Daniel - *The Hour of Peril*, Minotaur Books, New York, 2013

Steers, Edward, Jr. - *Blood on the Moon*, University of Kentucky Press, Lexington, 2001
---------------------- - *The Lincoln Assassination Encyclopedia*, Harper, New York, 2010

Stern, Phillip Van Doren - The Man Who Killed Lincoln, Literary Guild of America, New York, 1939

Swanson, James - *Bloody Crimes*, William Morrow, New York, 2010
---------------------- - *Manhunt*, Harper, New York, 2006

Taylor, Troy - *American Hauntings*, American Hauntings Ink, Jacksonville, Illinois, 2017
---------------- - *Haunted President*, Whitechapel Press, Decatur, Illinois, 2009

Temple, Wayne - *By Square and Compass: Saga of the Lincoln Home*, Illinois Lodge of Research/Masonic Book Club, Bloomington, Illinois, 1984

Thomsen, Brian M. - *Oval Office Occult*, Andrews McNeel, Kansas City, 2008

Titone, Nora - *My Thoughts Be Bloody*, Free Press, New York, 2010

Trostel, Scott D. - *The Lincoln Funeral Train*, Cam-Tech Publishing, Fletcher, Ohio, 2002

Walker, Dale - *Legends & Lies: Great Mysteries of the American West*, Forge Books, New York, 1997

Walsh, John Evangelist - *Moonlight*, St. Martin's Press, New York, 2000

Weichmann, Louis J. - *The True History of the Assassination of Abraham Lincoln and the Conspiracy of 1865*, Knopf, New York, 1975

West, J.B. - *Upstairs at the White House*, Coward, McGann, and Georghegan, New York, 1973

Wheeler, Daniel - *Abraham Lincoln*, McMillan, New York, 1921

Winer, Richard & Nancy Osborn Ishmael - *More Haunted Houses*, Bantam Books, New York, 1981

Winkle, Kenneth J. - *Abraham and Mary Lincoln*, Southern Illinois University Press, Carbondale, 2011
------------------------ - *Lincoln's Citadel*, W.W. Norton, New York, 2013

Winkler, H. Donald - *Lincoln and Booth*, Cumberland House, Tennessee, 2003

Winterbauer, John - "Ghosts of Route 66: New Salem," *Ghosts of the Prairie* magazine, 2004
-------------------- - "Stealing Abraham Lincoln," *Ghosts of the Prairie* magazine, 2003

Newspaper Sources

Aberdeen Daily News
Albany Daily Evening Times
Albany Evening Journal
Augusta Chronicle
Banner of Light
Biloxi Daily Herald
Boise Idaho Statesman
Boston Herald
Boston Saturday Evening Gazette
Buffalo Courier
Charleston Mercury
Chicago Daily Inter Ocean
Chicago Times
Chicago Tribune
Cleveland Plain Dealer
Daily Illinois State Journal
Daily Iowa State Register
Denver Post
Fort Worth Star-Telegram
Harrisburg Patriot
Illinois State Register
Indianapolis Journal
Indianapolis Sun

Kansas City Star
Macon Weekly Telegraph
Milwaukee Journal
Milwaukee Sentinel
New Haven Morning Star
New Orleans Times Picayune
New York Commercial Advertiser
New York Herald
New York Herald
New York Independent
Oregonian
Palm Beach Post
Philadelphia Daily Evening Telegraph
Philadelphia Inquirer
Pottstown Mercury
Providence Evening Press
Quincy Whig
Richmond Times-Dispatch
Rockford Register Star
Sacramento Union
Savannah Daily Advertiser
Schenectady Gazette
Spokane Spokesman-Review
Springfield Republican
Wichita Herald

Special Thanks to

April Slaughter: Cover Design and Artwork
Lois Taylor: Editing and Proofreading
Lisa Taylor Horton and Lux
Orrin Taylor
Rene Kruse
Rachael Horath
Elyse and Thomas Reihner
Bethany Horath
John Winterbauer
Kaylan Schardan

Maggie Walsh
Cody Beck
Becky Ray
Tom and Michelle Bonadurer
Susan Kelly and Amy Bouyear
And the entire crew of American Hauntings

ABOUT THE AUTHOR

Troy Taylor is the author of books on ghosts, hauntings, true crime, the unexplained, and the supernatural in America. He is also the founder of American Hauntings Ink, which offers books, ghost tours, events, and weekend excursions. He was born and raised in the Midwest and currently divides his time between Illinois and the far-flung reaches of America.

SURRAT.   BOOTH.   HAROLD.

War Department, Washington, April 20, 1865.

 # $100,000 REWARD!

THE MURDERER

Of our late beloved President, Abraham Lincoln,

IS STILL AT LARGE.

$50,000 REWARD

Will be paid by this Department for his apprehension, in addition to any reward offered by Municipal Authorities or State Executives.

$25,000 REWARD

Will be paid for the apprehension of JOHN H. SURRAT, one of Booth's Accomplices.

$25,000 REWARD

Will be paid for the apprehension of David C. Harold, another of Booth's accomplices.

LIBERAL REWARDS will be paid for any information that shall conduce to the arrest of either of the above-named criminals, or their accomplices.

All persons harboring or secreting the said persons, or either of them, or aiding or assisting their concealment or escape, will be treated as accomplices in the murder of the President and the attempted assassination of the Secretary of State, and shall be subject to trial before a Military Commission and the punishment of DEATH.

Let the stain of innocent blood be removed from the land by the arrest and punishment of the murderers.

All good citizens are exhorted to aid public justice on this occasion. Every man should consider his own conscience charged with this solemn duty, and rest neither night nor day until it be accomplished.

EDWIN M. STANTON, Secretary of War.

DESCRIPTIONS.—BOOTH is Five Feet 7 or 8 inches high, slender build, high forehead, black hair, black eyes, and wore a heavy black moustache, which there is some reason to believe has been shaved off.

JOHN H. SURRAT is about 5 feet 9 inches. Hair rather thin and dark; eyes rather light; no beard. Would weigh 145 or 150 pounds. Complexion rather pale and clear, with color in his cheeks. Wore light clothes of fine quality. Shoulder square; cheek bones rather prominent; chin narrow; ears projecting at the top; forehead rather low and square, but broad. Parts his hair on the right side; neck rather long. His lips are firmly set. A slim man.

DAVID C. HAROLD is five feet six inches high; hair dark, eyes dark; eyebrows rather heavy, full face, nose short, hand short and fleshy, feet small, instep high, round bodied, naturally quick and active, slightly closes his eyes when looking at a person.

NOTICE.—In addition to the above, State and other authorities have offered rewards amounting to almost one hundred thousand dollars, making an aggregate of about TWO HUNDRED THOUSAND DOLLARS.

www.ingramcontent.com/pod-product-compliance
Lightning Source LLC
Chambersburg PA
CBHW070957160426
43193CB00012B/1820